O STRANGE

NEW WORLD

HOWARD MUMFORD JONES

O STRANGE
NEW WORLD

American Culture:
The Formative Years

NEW YORK : THE VIKING PRESS

PREFACE

The essential matter of history, says Maitland, is not what happened but what people thought or said about it. These chapters concerning certain elements in the national culture as they shaped themselves from the discovery of the New World through the more flexible and formative years of the republic are attempts to find out what people thought or said or imagined about the New World and about the young republic of the West. I have omitted certain familiar components of the story. The political history of the colonies and of the United States has been sufficiently written about and so, I think, has its religious history, at least in these earlier epochs, nor do we lack histories of American literature. I have therefore touched upon those great themes but incidentally and have preferred to take what I hope is an imaginative look at other great trends or components in the transit of civilization across the Atlantic.

The only claim I can make to originality is, I fear, the originality of synthesis. We have accumulated in American studies a frightening number of monographs and other special studies, but despite the activities of the American Studies Association we do not seem able to set these studies in the context of general Western culture nor to make of them an understandable whole. Some scholars have tried to solve the problem of multitudinousness by the adoption of the mythic method, if it be one, so that we have a number of books, excellent but limited, concerning the American Adam or the quest for Paradise or the loss of innocence. "Myth," whatever is meant by that nebulous term, can on occasion be useful and revealing, as Henry Nash Smith demonstrates in *Virgin Land,* but in the hands of less competent investigators myth can become naïve as doctrine and simplicistic as scholarship.

My chapters rest on the labors of others, and I have tried to acknowledge these labors in my reference notes. The handling of thousands of scholarly items is, however, a difficult matter; and if I have failed to acknowledge my indebtedness in a particular case, it is inadvertently, and I ask indulgence.

There is a legend concerning the dean of a medical school that seems relevant here. The dean is said to have welcomed an entering class heartily enough, but he concluded his speech by saying: "Gentlemen, half of what we are about to teach you is wrong. The trouble is, we don't know which half." I shall not be taken aback if specialists find particular chapters of mine unsatisfactory, for I don't know which is the wrong half. I shall be content if these pages bring us back to the profound and central truth that American culture arises from the interplay of two great sets of forces—the Old World and the New. The Old World projected into the New a rich, complex, and contradictory set of habits, forces, practices, values, and presuppositions; and the New World accepted, modified, or rejected these or fused them with inventions of its own. That is why I have begun with the vague, vast image of the New World as seen through the European imagination, gradually narrowed my view to North America, and eventually confined myself to the United States. I have tapered off this volume with the 1840s, which seemed a conventional stopping point for a major statement, but I have in most of the chapters carried my findings beyond this decade because it seemed to me important to understand the influence of certain ideas and values for the rest of the nineteenth century and for the twentieth.

Some of the material in the chapter on "The Colonial Idea in England" originally appeared in the *Proceedings of the American Philosophical Society;* some part of the chapter entitled "Republican Culture" was first presented in a Horace M. Kallen lecture on "Republican Humanism" at the New School for Social Research; and some of that in "American Landscape" I have taken over from an article of mine in the *Tulane Studies in English.*

I am indebted to so many persons over so long a period of time for help that I despair of acknowledging all I owe to others. Part of the material I collected at the Henry E. Huntington Library long years ago when I was a Guggenheim Fellow. I have been aided by research grants from Harvard University and from the American Council of Learned Societies. I am indebted for help to the staff of the library of the University of Wisconsin and the Wisconsin Historical Society and to the present director of the American Antiquarian Society. I am so deeply indebted to the patient assistance and understanding of members of the staff of the Harvard College Library I scarcely know how to praise them. I owe special thanks for the research and secretarial help of Ann B. Hopkins, Anne Murtha, and Edith Gray. I am also deeply in the debt of Professor Richard M. Ludwig of Princeton for critical suggestions. Professor Walter B. Rideout of the University of Wisconsin has likewise been helpful. Nor can I omit mentioning the skill and thoughtfulness that Catharine Carver and others of The Viking Press brought to the preparation of the manuscript. And I pay tribute to the patient forbearance of my wife during the long period of the gestation and birth of this book.

HOWARD MUMFORD JONES

Harvard University
December 27, 1963

CONTENTS

modified Renaissance individualism. III. The doctrine of
leadership in Commines and Machiavelli. IV. Leadership
in the New World: anarchy, treachery, mutiny, Machiavellianism. V. Piracy and buccaneering as facets of leadership. VI. Machiavellianism in later American history.

PLATES

Plates II and III are reproduced from Justin Winsor, *Narrative and Critical History of America*, Vol. I; Plate VIII is from *Newport: Pleasures and Palaces* by Nancy Sirkis (New York: The Viking Press, 1963); the source of each of the other plates appears with the plate.

O STRANGE

NEW WORLD

O strange New World, thet yit wast never young,
Whose youth from thee by gripin' need was wrung,
Brown foundlin' o' the woods, whose baby-bed
Was prowled roun' by the Injun's cracklin' tread,
An' who grew'st strong thru shifts an' wants an' pains,
Nussed by stern men with empires in their brains.
                    —JAMES RUSSELL LOWELL,
                        The Biglow Papers

The Image of the New World

I

CONCERNING the actual existence of the New World the first reliable report available in the fifteenth century to Europeans who could read was a letter written by Christopher Columbus in a brief spell of pleasant winter weather in February 1493 during his homeward voyage in the *Niña*. This manuscript no longer exists, but only printed variants of a lost original. The letter was apparently addressed to Luis de Santangel and may have been endorsed over to Gabriel Sánchez (or a duplicate sent him). This was printed in Barcelona in the late spring or early summer of 1493 as a four-page pamphlet. But most Europeans read the letter in one of the nine editions of a Latin translation by Leandro de Cosco (see Pl. I) that were printed in Rome, Paris, Basle, and Antwerp in 1493 or 1494, or read other versions in Spanish or an Italian version in rather indifferent verse, sung, according to legend, in the streets of Italian cities.[1] * Some of the editions were illustrated by woodcuts, sometimes from other books or pamphlets. Englishmen, if they wanted to learn of the discovery, probably turned to one of the Latin versions, inasmuch as the first English translation of this famous document did not appear until December 1816 in the *Edinburgh*

---

* Numbered reference notes begin on page 397.

Review at the end of a muddy article on Columbus. The translation is not good. It is true that, fearing he might perish during a terrific storm at sea, Columbus wrote another account, which he wrapped in waxed cloth, put into a watertight barrel, and dropped into the sea in February 1493, but the cask has never been found, though there are various barefaced forgeries of the missing document. The actual surviving letter was sent from Lisbon, where Columbus was detained some ten days by the caution or the courtesy of the Portuguese king. He seems to have sent an official report to the Spanish monarchs. With this letter the modern cultural history of the New World begins.[2]

Before one turns to an analysis of Columbus's reports and associated documents it is well to understand the context in which the letter was read. Learned men in various European cultural centers—scholars, scientists, cartographers, statesmen, theologians—were aware of recent Portuguese discoveries, but the literate public had to be content with general books, especially since cartographical lore was the trade secret of pilots, monarchs, the fraternity of map-makers, and explorers jealous of one another. What the unlearned majority really thought about the vague and misty West we do not know. It is safe to assume a general belief that there was something "there." The bodies of men of unknown races, pieces of carved wood, branches of unfamiliar trees, and the like strange objects occasionally washed ashore on the Canaries or the Azores or even on the beaches of islands north of Scotland. And there were mariners who claimed to have discovered new lands in the West—for example, Niccolò and Antonio Zeno, who, if we are to believe an account compiled by a later Niccolò Zeno, published in 1558, sailed north and west about 1390 and found remarkable things. It is convenient to consult the translation in *Purchas His Pilgrimes* of 1625–1626, for it is thus that the contemporaries of Bacon read about them. The brothers went to "Groenland," where "There is a Fountaine of hot water, with which they heate the Church of the Monasterie, and the Friers chambers. It commeth also into the Kitchin so boyling hote, that they use no other fire to dresse their meate; and putting their Bread into brasse Pots without any water, it doth bake as it were in an hot Oven." The hot spring also heated the equivalent of a greenhouse, so that though "Their Winter lasteth nine moneths," there was always plenty. Niccolò returned to Friesland, where he died, but "Zichmui" employed the surviving brother on an expedition to "Estotiland," where he picked up a wonderful tale:

> Sixe and twentie yeeres before, foure Fisher-Boates were apprehended at Sea by a mightie and tedious storme; wherewith after many dayes, they were brought to Estotiland, above a thousand miles West from Friesland: upon which, one of the Boates was cast away, and sixe men that were in it, were taken and brought to a populous Citie; where, one that spake Latine, and had been caste by chance upon that Iland, in the name of the King asked them what Countrymen they were; and understanding their case, hee acquainted the King therewith. They dwelt there five yeeres, and found it to bee an Iland very rich, being little less than Iseland, but farre more fruitful. One of them said hee saw Latine books in the Kings Librarie, which they at this present doe not understand. They have a peculiar Language, and Letters or Characters to themselves. They have mines of Gold and other Mettals, and have Trade with Engroneland. They sow Corne, and make Beere and Ale. They build Barkes (but know not the use of the Compasse) and have many Cities and Castles.

The king sent them southward in twelve "Barkes" to a country called "Drogio," where they encountered cannibals who devoured many of the expedition. The account also speaks of a thirteen-year war among twenty-five chieftains and declares it "was a great Countrey, and (as it were) a New World." The Purchas translation omits much of the original. The authenticity of the voyages of the Zeni has been furiously disputed, but the point is, surely, not whether somebody got to Greenland and the North American continent or learned vaguely about the glories of pre-Columbian Mexico, the point is the splendor, the wonder, the haunting riches on the edge of the world.[3]

The belief in riches and perfection beyond the sunset is very old in Europe, a natural development, so to speak, among the cultures of the landlocked Mediterranean, whence the only sea route that leads at once everywhere and nowhere is through the Straits of Gibraltar. The sunset marks the end of day and, symbolically, the end of life; wherefore Homer's Elysian Fields lie vaguely in that direction, and Hesiod's Hesperides more decisively so. The Greek dramatists occasionally hint at a western paradise of some sort either for men or for their ghosts, and in Plutarch's life of Sertorius we read of Spanish sailors who had been to the Islands of the Blest. Seneca in a famous passage prophesied that mankind would one day discover a distant Western World. Moreover, Avalon was sometimes located westward, and so, for that matter, was Lyonesse—names that connote eternal spring, eternal peace, or eternal plenty. Indeed, as late as World War I the dying soldier "went west" as the heroes of Homer had done. These places are not on the maps, though there were some who identified the Fortunate Isles with the Canaries when the latter were discovered in the twelfth century and rediscovered in the fourteenth.

But there were other legends long before Columbus. Notably in the sixteenth century, when the expansion of empires westward made the assertion of precedent claims, however shadowy, a useful legal fiction, men remembered the belief that the New World had been populated, or discovered, or settled, by a second Adam and Eve and their descendants (the problem of the origin of the American Indians is still troublesome), or by the Egyptians, the Tartars, the Canaanites, the Chinese, the Celts, the Norse, the Arabs, the Venetians, the Portuguese, or the Danes (under the leadership of a Polish pilot).[4] Aside from that of the brothers Zeno, who came from Venice, the most substantial claim is clearly that of the Norse, since there is good evidence that Leif, son of Eric the Red, sailed to the New World in the year 1000, thus inaugurating a small succession of voyages of discovery that reached as far south as Cape Cod or Martha's Vineyard. An important element in the Norse accounts, as in that of the Zeno brothers, is the principle of plenitude.[5] Thus in 1007 Karlsefne came to Markland, where he found plenty of wood and wild animals, and to Vinland, where the low ground was covered with wild wheat and the rising ground with grapes. Let us add the more improbable tale of Madoc, Prince of Wales, with whose voyage Hakluyt opens the "American" section of his great collection. Madoc reached a fertile and beautiful land in 1170 —"Whereupon it is manifest that that countrey was by Britaines discovered, long before Columbus led any Spanyards thither." [6]

The Atlantic hid in its misty vastness many wonderful islands, and these island images, compounded of wonder, terror, wealth, religious perfection, communism, utopianism, or political power, conditioned the European image of America. They floated on the maps of the Ocean Sea like quicksilver globules, now here, now there, now nowhere at all, some of them remaining on British Admiralty charts into the nineteenth century. Beyond them westward was Asia or Eden or the Earthly Paradise, unless *they* were Asia or Paradise. The most famous of these islands is undoubtedly Atlantis, the legend of which we owe to Plato,[7] and the locus of which has challenged the imagination of American writers as different as Ignatius Donnelly, the author of *Caesar's Column,* and Edwin Björkman, the translator of Strindberg.[8]

We are told that Solon visited Saïs on the Nile, that Egyptian priests informed him the Hellenes were in comparison with the Egyptians only children, and that nine thousand years before Solon (who died about 558 B.C.) a rich kingdom under mighty rulers existed on the vast island of Atlantis beyond the Pillars of Hercules. The Atlanteans conquered other islands, parts of Libya as far as Egypt, and parts of Europe up to the Tyrrhenian Sea. But Athens even in those distant times was "first in courage and military skill" and beat off the invaders. Afterward "there occurred violent earthquakes and floods; and in a single day and night of rain all your warlike men in a body sank into the earth, and the island of Atlantis in like manner disappeared, and was sunk beneath the sea." The *Timaeus* also informs us that the sea became so shallow as to imperil navigation—possibly a reminiscence of the Sargasso Sea, that terror to primitive seamen.[9]

More specific islands, though none so impressive, were discovered by Celtic travelers. Thus Maeldune, an Irish prince of the eighth century, visited a succession of wonderful places. His voyage occasioned a musical poem by Tennyson describing the Isle of Silence ("a silent ocean always broke on a silent shore"), an Isle of Shouting, an Isle of Flowers, an Isle of Fruits, an Isle of Fire, and others, including an Isle of Witches and an island whereon lived a holy man three hundred years old. The Irish Saint Brandon likewise sailed to a series of islands, one of which was inhabited by fallen angels, another by a white-haired hermit, a third by demons, a fourth by a being covered with bright feathers like those of a bird, and an island that proved to be the back of a sleeping sea monster which awoke and dived when a fire was made on him.

Another type of island, somewhat more credible, is represented by Antillia (or Antilla), sometimes appearing as an archipelago, whither Christians had fled from the Iberian peninsula before the invading Moors. There they built seven fair cities, each ruled by a bishop and each a perfect community. Ferdinand Columbus did not see this island, but he saw some Portuguese map-makers who had seen people who had seen it, and he was assured that it lay about two hundred leagues west of the Canaries. The Portuguese had found it, but unluckily they could not find it again, a misfortune the more regrettable inasmuch as the sand they had gathered from its beaches for ballast proved on inspection to be one-third pure gold. It was conjectured that Antillia lay about halfway between Lisbon and Cipango (Japan). Sometimes the bishops were Portuguese, sometimes Spanish. Antillia eventually came to rest in a quite un-Utopian condition as the Greater and Lesser Antilles of the West Indies. Nor should we forget another fleeting island named Mayda, or Asmeida; and another one called O Brazil, or Brasil, existing long before the Latin American republic and vaguely appearing on maps as late as 1873. There was also the island (if it was an island) of Estotiland. And what was one to make of another sunken island, called Buss, somewhere about 57 degrees and 30 minutes north latitude, originally discovered by a fishing vessel ("buss") which coasted along it for three days, finding it fruitful, well wooded, and yet with broad, open fields? Unfortunately a second vessel reported it could find only ice and snow in that area—no fields, no woods, no well-watered plains.[10]

Mingled with this shadowy geography were other charming dreams. One, much debated by a growing minority of learned men, was that the shortest way to the fabulous East was to sail westward and be plunged into riches. The other important ideas implicit in some of these island stories are that life is prolonged, or men are happier, or one is nearer God somewhere in the Ocean Sea or on its distant borders. The cardinal Pierre d'Ailly, whose book Columbus took as his master text in geography, quoted with approval the opinion of the ancients that toward the south, where the days and nights are each six months long, people live who are so happy they never die except when, bored with life, they end it by throwing themselves from some high cliff into the sea—a notion he twice presents.[11] The excellent cardinal also seriously inclines to an Earthly Paradise on or near the Fortunate Isles by reason of the fertility of the soil, the excellence of the sun, and the benevolent influence of the stars—an idea so attractive that Columbus seriously presented it to "the most exalted monarchs in Christendom" when he wrote them from the island of Hispaniola during his third voyage. He informed Ferdinand and Isabella that the earth is shaped like a pear with a bump on top resembling a nipple; that, though he

doubts the Earthly Paradise is in the form of a rugged mountain, it is certainly high up; and that, granted no one can go
there except by the permission of God, yet a gradual ascent
up the waters flowing from it seemed to some degree possible.
He had been off the mouth of the Orinoco, though he did not
know it, and he wrote: "I have never read or heard of so great
a quantity of fresh water so coming into and near the salt. And
the very mild climate also supports this view, and if it does
not come from there, from paradise, it seems to be still a
greater marvel, for I do not believe that there is known in the
world a river so great and so deep." Thither, then, "where I
believe in my soul that the earthly paradise is situated," he
intends that three ships "well stocked with provisions" shall
go to make "further investigation." [12] In the Earthly Paradise
is the Tree of Life, and from it issues a fountain, and from
the fountain flow four of the chief rivers of this world—and
the Orinoco was obviously one of them.[13]

II

Columbus was born, so far as we can tell, some time in 1451.
It is difficult to prove any historical generalization, but the
mood of Europe in the mid-century and later was probably
one of weariness. The medieval order was dissolving, but no
one knew the shape of things to come. Specialists now point
to the half-century as that of the Renaissance in Italy, the cen-
tralization of monarchy in England, France, and Spain, the
beginnings of nationalisms, the foundation of efficient methods of commerce, banking, bookkeeping, and credit, the dawn
of modern scholarship and modern science. But this was not
evident to tired, thoughtful, and sensitive contemporary observers—unless we choose to dismiss their writing as mere
conventionalism, which some of it undoubtedly was. Yet in
their world anarchy was more common than order.

In the north of Europe, for example, the Hanseatic League
had declined. Its allies, the Teutonic Knights (defeated at

Tannenberg in 1410 by the Poles), were compelled in 1466 to declare themselves vassals of the Polish king, but that monarch ruled over an uncertain and disorderly realm. The condition of the Holy Roman Empire of the German People had been such that the population had taken the law into its own hands, creating a terrorist organization known as the Vehm or Veme, which, as was inevitable, degenerated into the anarchy it had been invented to suppress. In the east the Tartars had long since overrun most of what we know today as Russia; not until 1480 did Ivan III, Prince of Moscow, dare to announce he was an independent sovereign. Byzantium fell to the Turks in 1453. That un-Christian people, pushing steadily westward, were close to Vienna by 1529. The Hundred Years' War, the barbarities of which still shock us when we read Froissart, drained the population and the prosperity of France from 1337 to 1453. England had scarcely emerged from it when she plunged into the dynastic Wars of the Roses, which ended only with the accession of Henry VII in 1485. In France, to be sure, the crafty and superstitious Louis XI was laying the foundations for the state of Louis XIV and Colbert; yet the mid-century Paris of François Villon, dead some time after 1463, impresses nobody as a desirable city, and after the demise of Louis in 1483 there were bloody uprisings in the royal domains.

Italy was of course the home of the Renaissance, but from a political point of view it was also the home of treason, assassination, crime, disease, un-Christian savagery, and evident weakness—so much so that French armies invaded the peninsula in 1494 and again in 1499. If Italy produced the humanists, it also perfected the *condottieri,* professional soldiers to whom no human life was sacred except perhaps their own. It was, moreover, evident that the Church Universal was cracking up. The Great Schism continued from 1378 to 1417, when it was supposed to end, but not until 1449 did the last anti-pope give up his empty title. John Hus had been successfully burned in 1415, Joan of Arc in 1431, and the statute *De heretico comburendo* was passed as early as 1401. Nevertheless secular learning increased rather than diminished, Lollardry refused to be stamped out, and vast movements of discontent were eventually to give birth to Luther and Calvin. Most of the Renaissance popes—Pius II, Paul II, Sixtus IV, Alexander VI, and, eventually, Julius II—were more distinguished for secularity than for saintliness, and some of them took to the foughten field. Was this what the world had come to after fifteen centuries of Christianity? Was there nowhere any hope for mankind?

It is not without meaning that the greatest vogue of the Dance of Death as a theme in poetry and art is during the fifteenth century, that two of the leading lyric poets of the century, Villon and Jorge Manrique, are obsessed by death and misery, that the most notable work of German literature in the period, *Reineke Voss* aside (and what sardonic skepticism *that* expresses!), is Sebastian Brant's *Narrenschiff*, that one of the great themes of the age is the fall of princes (consider, says Huizinga, the life of King René of Jerusalem), and that fifteenth-century literature is obsessed with melancholy. As Huizinga says,

> A general feeling of impending calamity hangs over all. Perpetual danger prevails everywhere. To realize the continuous insecurity in which the lives of great and small alike were passed, it suffices to read the details which Monsieur Pierre Champion has collected regarding the persons mentioned by Villon in his *Testament,* or the notes of Monsieur A. Tuetey to the diary of a Burgher of Paris.
>
> At the close of the Middle Ages, a sombre melancholy weighs on people's souls. Whether we read a chronicle, a poem, a sermon, a legal document even, the same impression of immense sadness is produced by them all. It would sometimes seem as if this period had been particularly unhappy, as if it had left behind only the memory of violence, of covetousness and mortal hatred, as if it had known no other enjoyment but that of intemperance, of pride and cruelty.[14]

In so doubtful a universe one turned for relief, for imaginative escape, into dream-worlds of other cultures. Hence, on the one hand, the obsession of the age with allegorical and classical pageantry, whether in the Netherlands or in Italy; hence the vogue of what today we would call historical romance, exemplified in Caxton's *Recuyell of the Histories of Troy* (1475?) and Malory's *Morte d'Arthur* (written by 1469, printed in 1485), of Pulci's *Morgante* (1483) and Boiardo's *Orlando Innamorato* (left unfinished in 1494), and of the romances that constitute the "Iliada sin Homero" of Spain. The Spaniards, indeed, tried to transform romance into reality, as we shall see, but for most of the world chivalry lay in pageantry or vision. When the Italian humanist Politian was required to celebrate in verse a tournament held in 1475 by Giuliano di Piero de' Medici in Florence, he translated the whole thing into a dream of classical mythology, into Cyprus—that Cyprus where Venus is queen, little cupids sharpen their arrows on whetstones, Zephyr distills a thousand wandering odors on the meadow, and a whole population of Greek gods and goddesses, demi-gods and demi-goddesses replaces the population of Florence. In the Italian city-states the humanists were unhappy, as Trinkaus has shown, and the vogue of Platonism after 1450 is due as much to the attraction of a dream as it is to philosophical conviction.[15] Doubtless the Golden Age agreeable to Ficino and Politian was in some degree a philosophical concept, but what strikes the modern reader of Politian's *Stanze* is the number of times the word for gold appears in a quite physical denotation, just as the glitter of chivalry, the glitter of mythology, the glitter of pageants meant the physical possession of gold, silver, precious stones, costly garments, and the habiliments of wealth, even if the characters appear nude.[16]

The Cyprus of Politian (and Venus) includes the inevitable walled garden; and Sir Kenneth Clark is not alone in pointing out how often primitive landscape, whether in painting or poetry, juxtaposes the walled garden with the dark forest and the distant mountain, the one all beauty, regularity, harmony, springtime, and splendor, the other dark, mysterious, and threatening. The garden may be the home of the Virgin

and Child, or of a Chaste Maiden luring a unicorn, or of
Honor, Love, Fortitude, the Graces, the Christian virtues,
or any other dream concept. It does not snow in the garden,
it is never cold there, the flowers bloom eternally, the birds
sing, there are no weeds, no wild animals, no disease, and no
death. To emphasize innocence people take off their clothes,
as in a fifteenth-century picture of the Fountain of Youth, to
which I shall recur. This is all very charming, especially when
projected against the *selva oscura* of Dante as a symbol of
worldly wickedness, but a difficulty develops. When it is always May, when the trees are perpetually green, the brooks
perpetually clear and fresh, the sun perpetually bright, and
love, or marriage, or honor, or the church, or human nature,
or salvation perpetually young and timeless, it is all a little
monotonous, challenging neither invention, imagination, nor
style.

Here, for example, is part of a landscape poem concerning
such a garden, from the first quarter of the fifteenth century:

> *Hie quillt der gnaden brunne,*
> *der fröiden morgenrot,*
> *da glenzt der ewige summer,*
> *da alles leit zergot.*
>
> *Da hört man süsz erklingen,*
> *der vögeli getön,*
> *und auch die engel singen*
> *ir melodie gar schön.*[17]

This is so general, it might have been written four hundred
years later by Heinrich Heine. A hundred other fifteenth-
century poets were content with the same description of the
same garden in the same general terms—Lydgate, for example, in "The Churl and the Bird":

> Amyd the gardyn stode a fressh laurere
> Thereon a birde synging day and nyght
> With sonnysh feders brighter then gold were
> Whiche with hir song made hevy hertes light
> That to be holde it was an heuenly sight;

Lorenzo de' Medici:

> Cerchi chi vuol le pompe, e gli alti onori,
> Le piazze, i tempi, e gli edifizi magni,
> Le delizie, il tesor, quale accompagni
> Mille duri pensier, mille dolori.
> Chè verde praticel pien di bei fiori,
> Un rivolo, che l'erba intorno bagni,
> Un augelletto, che d'Amor si lagni,
> Acqueta molto meglio i nostri ardori;
> L'ombrose selve, i sassi, e gli alti monti,
> Gli antri oscuri, e le fere fuggitive,
> Qualche leggiadra Ninfa paurosa,
> Quivi vegg' io con pensier vaghi e pronti
> Le belle luci, come fosser vive;
> Qui me le toglie or una, or altra cosa;

and Charles d'Orléans:

> Le dieu d'Amours est coustumier,
> A ce jour de feste tenir
> Pour amoureux cueurs festier,
> Qui desirent de le servir.
> Pour ce, fait les arbres couvrir
> De fleurs et les champs de vert-gay
> Pour la feste plus embellir,
> Ce premier jour du mois de may.[18]

The resulting paradox is that while the imagination sought for something fresh and fair, some gleam of hope for humanity, some proof of Utopia or the Earthly Paradise or the Golden Age,[19] the artistic idiom, whether words, pencil, or paint, became so worn, so conventional, that exact rendering of landscape was virtually unknown. Even Petrarch, whose ascent of Mount Ventoux in the second quarter of the preceding century is supposed to substantiate his claim to be the first modern man, tells us nothing except that the way was steep, the journey unusual, and the view fine. Then, bethinking himself to read the Confessions of Saint Augustine, he descended as quickly as he could, without uttering a syllable: "How earnestly should we strive, not to stand on mountain-tops, but to trample beneath us those appetites which spring from earthly impulses." [20] However anxious explorers might be to attain Asia or Eden or America, it is not thus that they can be trained to describe what they have seen. Yet to describe what he had seen was, precisely, the technical problem before Columbus, who was neither artist nor writer, and what he had seen or inferred he had seen gave him hope for the miseries of the time.

III

Although for so great a genius as Alexander von Humboldt, Columbus was distinguished by a profound feeling for nature and for the specificity of his descriptions, this opinion has not been shared by modern scholarship,[21] and when we examine the text of his famous letter, which runs to about four thousand words, we find it vague. Possibly he did not want to reveal too much lest other navigators poach on his territory, but it seems more probable that the genius of the discoverer was not reportorial. Even if it had been, to what literary tradition could he turn? Neither in the letter nor in his journal (preserved in Las Casas's abridgment) do we find much beyond the repetition of a few simple formulas. It is perpetual spring, the nightingale sings, the flowers bloom, the trees are green, the rivers wind, the mountains are high, and the inhabitants are innocent and happy. The nightingale, by the by, which does not exist in the New World, haunted Columbus: twice on his outward voyage, when the weather was especially fine, he noted in the journal that nothing was wanting for perfection but the song of the nightingale.

Here are characteristic extracts from the letter:

This island [Hispaniola, the modern Haiti] and all others are very fertile to a limitless degree, and this island is extremely so. In it there are many harbours on the coast of the sea, beyond comparison with others which I know in Christendom, and many rivers, good and large, which is marvellous. Its lands are high, and there are in it very many sierras and very lofty mountains, beyond comparison with the island of Teneriffe. All are most beautiful, of a thousand shapes, and all are accessible and filled with trees of a thousand kinds and tall, and they seem to touch the sky. And I am told that they never lose their foliage, as I can understand, for I saw them as green and lovely as they are in Spain in May, and some of them were flowering, some bearing fruit, and some in another stage, according to their nature. And the nightingale was singing, and other birds of a thousand kinds in the month of November there where I went. There are six or eight kinds of palm, which are a wonder to behold on account of their beautiful variety, but so are the other trees and fruits and plants. In it are marvellous pine groves, and there are very large tracts of cultivatable lands, and there is honey, and there are birds of many kinds, and fruits in great diversity. In the interior are mines of metals, and the population is without number.

In short the New World is "a land to be desired, and, once seen, never to be left." But the only genera specified are nightingales, palms, and pines; and to differentiate between palm trees and pine trees requires no great knowledge of nature. The mode of the description is curiously compounded out of the poetical garden emblematic of the Golden Age and of memories of landscapes in altar pieces and other holy paintings presumably seen by the devout discoverer in Catholic churches.

What about the inhabitants? In Paradise before the fall, life was simple, naked, and without fear. So it was in the West Indies:

The people of this island, and of all the other islands which I have found and of which I have information, all go naked, men and women, as their mothers bore them, although some women cover a single place with the leaf of a plant or with a net of cotton which they make for the purpose. They have no iron or steel or weapons, nor are they fitted to use them, not because they are not well built men and of handsome stature, but because they are very marvellously timorous. They have no other arms than weapons made of canes, cut in seeding time, to the ends of which they fix a small sharpened stick . . . they are so guileless and so generous with all they possess, that no one would believe it who has not seen it. They never refuse anything which they possess, if it be asked of them; on the contrary, they invite anyone to share it, and display so much love as if they would give their hearts. . . . And they do not know any creed and are not idolators; only they all believe that power and good are in the heavens . . . not . . . because they are ignorant; on the contrary, they are of a very acute intelligence and are men who navigate all those seas.[22]

It has been remarked that because Europeans in the fifteenth and sixteenth centuries were heavily clothed and made much of the ritual of costuming, nakedness struck them the more forcibly. It is also true that nakedness is part of the iconography of innocence in medieval and Renaissance art.*

We, who cannot put a man into space without alerting the radio, television, newspapers, and the illustrated magazines, may find it incredible that only the first letter of Columbus had any general circulation.[23] Europeans, particularly in the Mediterranean countries, learned about the New World from the *Decades* of Peter Martyr D'Anghera, which were originally manuscript news-letters sent to prominent churchmen, including the pope, and to humanists from 1494 to 1526.[24] The first three *Decades* (there were never more than eight) were printed in Latin at Alcalá in 1516. Martyr was a humanist appointed by Queen Isabella to train aristocratic youth in all good learning, and his house was a meeting place for statesmen, nobles, ambassadors, churchmen, navigators, explorers, cosmographers, and colonial officials—in MacNutt's phrase, the empire-builders of Spain. He translated the reports of Columbus, Vespucci, and others into Renaissance terms, which means that, never having been in the West Indies, he saw the New World, though often with shrewdness, through a haze of Latinity. For example, he compares a captive Indian

---

* It is likewise part of the iconography of damnation as in paintings of the Last Judgment. But as the saved are also nude, one remarks that nudity is a mode of representing the soul.

woman who escaped with her female companions from Columbus's ship, to Clelia, a Roman virgin in Book II of Livy, who, fleeing from the Etruscan camp at the head of a band of female hostages, swam the Tiber under a shower of darts and got them all safe back in Rome. The state of Hispaniola he likens to Latium before the arrival of Aeneas, and the culture of the Indians is that of the Golden Age: "The islanders of Hispaniola, in my opinion, may be esteemed more fortunate than were the Latins, above all should they become converted to the true religion. They go naked, they know neither weights nor measures, nor that source of all misfortunes, money; living in a golden age, without laws, without lying judges, without books, satisfied with their life, and in no wise solicitous for the future." Cuba was like unto it: "It is indeed a golden age, neither ditches, nor hedges, nor walls to enclose their domains; they live in gardens open to all, without laws and without judges; their conduct is naturally equitable, and whoever injures his neighbor is considered a criminal and an outlaw." One almost feels that the learned Martyr had an Ovid open before him as he wrote.

> The first millennium was the age of gold:
> Then living creatures trusted one another;
> People did well without the thought of ill:
> Nothing forbidden in a book of laws.
>
> .   .   .   .
>
> No cities climbed behind high walls and bridges;
> No brass-lipped trumpets call, nor clanging swords.
>
> .   .   .   .
>
> The innocent earth
> Learned neither spade nor plough; she gave her
> Riches as fruit hangs from the tree. . . .
> Springtide the single
> Season of the year, and through that hour
> The soft breath of the south in flowering leaf.[25]

In Martyr, when Bartholomew Columbus set out on an expedition into the interior, the following was his reception at Xaragua.

When the company approached, some thirty women, all wives of the cacique, marched out to meet them, dancing, singing, and shouting; they were naked, save for a loin-girdle, which, though it consisted but of a cotton belt, which dropped over their hips, satisfied these women devoid of any sense of shame. As for the young girls, they covered no part of their bodies, but wore their hair loose upon their shoulders and a narrow ribbon tied around the forehead. Their face, breast, and hands, and the entire body was quite naked, and of a somewhat brunette tint. All were beautiful, so that one might think he beheld those splendid naiads or nymphs of the fountains, so much celebrated by the ancients. Holding branches of palms in their hands, they offered them to the Adelantado [Bartholomew Columbus]. Entering the chieftain's house, the Spaniards refreshed themselves at a banquet prepared with all the magnificence of native usage.[26]

The next day there were armed games between two groups of Indians. These Peter Martyr compares to the Trojan games. Four men were killed and many wounded, and only at the instance of the Spaniards did the cacique signal them to stop.

A like idyllic picture appears in the letter (1504) by Vespucci to René, king of Jerusalem. The Indians "have neither king nor lord, nor do they obey anyone, but live in freedom. . . . They do not bring men to justice, nor punish a criminal . . . nor . . . chastise their children," they eat whenever they feel like it, and they "speak little, and in a low voice." "We did not find," he writes, "that these people had any laws," [27] their habitations are in common, they are cleanly, shameless, care nothing for riches, neither buy nor sell, and are content with what nature has given them. He adds, as do most of the others, some horrifying details, to the significance of which we shall come by and by.

These simplicities, classical, pastoral, or biblical, are confined neither to the tropics nor to the first few decades of discovery. Eighty years after Vespucci's letter the English captains Amadas and Barlow came to the coastal waters of North Carolina, "where we smelt so sweet, and so strong a smel, as

if we had bene in the midst of some delicate garden abound-
ing with all kinde of odoriferous flowers. . . ." By and by
they landed on a beach "very sandie and low towards the
waters side, but so full of grapes, as the very beating and surge
of the Sea overflowed them." The reception a little later of
the weary, way-worn wanderers on Roanoke Island by the
sister-in-law of the Indian "king" has all the large simplicity
of the elder world:

> When wee came towardes it, standing neere unto the waters
> side, the wife of Granganimo the kings brother came running
> out to meete us very cheerefully and friendly, her husband was
> not then in the village; some of her people shee commanded to
> drawe our boate on shore for the beating of the billoe: others
> she appointed to cary us on their backes to the dry ground, and
> others to bring our oares into the house for feare of stealing.
> When we were come into the utter roome, having five roomes in
> her house, she caused us to sit downe by a great fire, and after
> tooke off our clothes and washed them, and dryed them againe:
> some of the women plucked off our stockings and washed them,
> some washed our feete in warme water, and shee her selfe tooke
> great paines to see all things ordered in the best maner shee
> could, making great haste to dresse some meate for us to eate.
> After we had thus dryed our selves, she brought us into the
> inner roome, where shee set on the boord standing along the
> house, some wheate like furmentie, sodden Venison, and
> roasted, fish sodden, boyled, and roasted, Melons rawe, and
> sodden, rootes of divers kindes, and divers fruites: their drinke
> is commonly water, but while the grape lasteth, they drinke
> wine, and for want of caskes to keepe it, all the yere after they
> drink water, but it is sodden with Ginger in it, and blacke
> Sinamon, and sometimes Sassaphras, and divers other whole-
> some, and medicinable hearbes and trees. We were entertained
> with all love and kindnesse, and with as much bountie (after
> their maner) as they could possibly devise. We found the
> people most gentle, loving, and faithfull, voide of all guile and
> treason, and such as live after the maner of the golden age.[28]

It is useless for the anthropologist to protest against the total
misreading of an alien culture, since it is thus that Nausicaa

in the land of the godlike Phaeacians welcomed Odysseus in
a still older travel account. Thus Europe of the early Renaissance saw the New World.

IV

Other examples of the components of this image of the
Golden Age can be found in books about the New World by
Oviedo, Acosta, Thevet, Garcilaso de la Vega, Hakluyt,
Purchas, and others. Some projects then undertaken read so
like fairy tales we wonder how sensible men could seriously
propose to carry them out. Such, for instance, was the search
by Ponce de León in Florida (or "Bimini" or both) for the
Fountain of Youth. But Leonardo Olschki hunts out pictures
of such a fountain in late medieval art and reproduces an
Italian miniature of the fifteenth century depicting the fountain (inevitably in a *hortus inclusus*), and Peter Martyr devotes a lengthy digression to the possibility of its existence.
Among the ancients, Martyr quotes Aristotle, Pliny, Homer,
and the legend of Medea and Aeson, just as he appeals to the
way of the eagle, the snake, the deer, the raven, and the crow
to support so fascinating an idea: "If, therefore, all these
things are true; if Nature, that astonishing creatrix, graciously
shows herself so munificent and powerful towards the dumb
animals . . . how should it be astonishing for her to create
and nourish in her bounteous breast similar phenomena in a
superior order?" [29] In the tradition of other enchanted lands,
Ponce de León thought Florida an island, naming it, as all
the world knows, for the Easter of the Flowers. Herrera tells
us there was not a river, brook, lake, or puddle in which the
Spaniards did not hopefully bathe. Half a century later
Fontaneda was still looking for the waters of rejuvenescence.[30]
The fairy-tale aspect of Ponce de León's search suggests
what is true: that, particularly in the Iberian peninsula (but
also in Italy and elsewhere), where the New World was concerned, men's imagination was conditioned by the elements

of chivalric romance. As I have already indicated, the late
fifteenth and early sixteenth centuries were the heyday in
Spain of the "romances" that, by and by, were to turn the
head of Don Quixote. In Italy meanwhile Pulci, Boiardo, and
Ariosto were contemporary poets, who, if they laughed at tales
of Charlemagne and his peers and of Arthur and his knights,
nevertheless retold them with the power of great poetry. Even
as late as 1590, in England, the association of the New World
with fairyland is in the living tissue of Spenser's verse:

> . . . none that breatheth living aire, does know
> Where is that happy land of Faery,
> Which I so much doe vaunt, yet no where show.
>
> .   .   .   .
>
> But let that man with better sence advize
> That of the world least part to us is red:
> And daily how through hardy enterprize
> Many great Regions are discovered,
> Which to late age were never mentioned.
> Who ever heard of th' Indian Peru?
> Or who in venturous vessell measured
> The Amazons huge river, now found trew?
> Or fruitfullest Virginia who did ever vew?
>
> Yet all these were when no man did them know,
> Yet have from wisest ages hidden beene:
>
> .   .   .   .
>
> Of Faery Lond yet if he more inquyre,
> By certein signes, here sett in sondrie place,
> He may it fynd.[31]

It should not be hard for us, who accustom our eyes to space-
men and the odd beings we imagine we shall find on the moon
or Mars, to understand the age of Ferdinand and Isabella and
that of Charles V in this respect. If Astolfo, Rinaldo, and
others in the Italian chivalric romances vanquish thousands,
defeat Satan, and deal chivalrously with a paynim prince, the
conquistadors did precisely the same thing. It was impossible
to number the Indian warriors; Christian knights are there-

fore described as vanquishing multitudes in the West Indies, in Mexico, or in Peru, and Satan flees from them.

Scholarship tells us that at the end of the fifteenth century in Spain the age of chivalry was resuscitated. One historian says:

> No other European country of the fifteenth century could have filled with its peculiar, perhaps limited, but intensely vital culture the vast spaces discovered and conquered. . . . Detached from life, Spaniards possessed a spirit of sacrifice and an endurance of which bands of adventurers inspired only by the lust of gold would never have been capable; the flight from reality in Europe not only induced people to buy romances of chivalry . . . but also to take ship and revive the life of fantastic freedom of knight-errantry.

Another calls the reign of the Emperor Charles V the last great age of the Spanish military hero of the old traditional type, the dauntless warrior whose feats of individual prowess became legendary, and cites two such warriors, Juan de Urbina and Diego García de Paredes, as representative successors to El Cid Campeador.[32] Indeed, if we examine Titian's portrait of the emperor at the battle of Mühlberg, fought in 1547, the year of Cervantes' birth, the monarch has been turned into a questing knight: the battle has disappeared, and the knight, like an invention by Tennyson, clad in body armor and with a long lance at half charge, spurs his steed through an empty landscape, intent upon some distant quest. Mühlberg was fought half a century after the defeat of the Moors, that chivalric tragedy which was to excite the romantic imagination of Irving in *The Alhambra* and *The Conquest of Granada*.

Images associated with the New World from its discovery to 1547 and beyond were frequently chivalrous. Thus the title page of a German translation of Vespucci published at Nuremberg in 1505 shows us a woodcut of the king of Portugal in complete mail, a crown on his head, the Portuguese coat of arms upright beside him, a scepter extended in his right hand, and a huge sword buckled to his waist. He looks

like a fairy monarch set down in an enchanted desert. A portrait of Balboa, more or less contemporary, reproduced in
Herrera's *Historia general de los hechos de los Castellanos*
(1728), gives us a man in body armor, his sword raised, his
eyes bewitched by a distant dream, a vague landscape over his
right shoulder, and a plume on his helmet. A "picture" of the
city of Mexico before the conquest, published in a Nuremberg edition of the letters of Cortés, shows an enchanted
island; little figures in boats toil against the streaming waters
that go round and round, and the waters in turn are guarded
by walls, towers, and turrets. One tower is labeled: *Domus
ad voluptatem*. Even a map of Iceland attributed to Olaus
Magnus and dated 1539 partakes of the chivalric concept:
three horsemen with lifted lances spur inland from the coast,
a figure, nude, playing the equivalent of a violin, lures two
swans (?) to shore, and the island is dotted with military tents,
flames emerging from the ground, a mysterious bear in a
cave, and a rider on a giant steed apparently running away
from a gigantic falcon. Why not? In the vastness of the New
World one might find anything chimerical—a mountain of
crystal like that described by Ralegh in *The Discoverie of
Guiana,* a king rolling in gold dust as in the same fabulous
narrative, a human-faced animal as large as a small elephant,
the "Haüt," which lives only on air as in Thevet, or a beautiful princess—for example, Marina of Mexico, who, daughter
of a chief, was enslaved, rescued from death through the substitution of a specially killed corpse in her stead, and became
the mistress of Cortés and a principal agent in conquering
Tenochtitlán.*

---

* The tales are endless. Lucas Vásquez de Ayllón, raiding the coast near
the Cape Fear River in 1521, captured a native who, taken to Spain, developed the tall tale this early. The natives had, he said, domesticated deer
in their houses, giving them milk and cheese, and were ruled by a giant
king whose size was produced by softening and stretching his bones in childhood; and there was another race having rigid tails who, when they sat
down, had to dig a deep hole to hold these curious appendages. (Peter
Martyr, *De Orbe Novo; The Eight Decades of Peter Martyr d'Anghera,*
translated from the Latin with notes and introduction by Francis Augustus
MacNutt, 2 vols., New York, 1912, Vol. II; pp. 258–59.) Juan de Oñate,

Confused and unified, a compound of dream and treachery, suffering and triumph, blood and gold, wonder and hardship, the image of the New World came to contain also the element of high emprise. The mood of knightly valor and impossible accomplishment lingered long in literature concerning discovery, exploration, and conquest. There appeared in Venice in 1534 an edition of Martyr and Oviedo, which was next collected into the third volume of Ramusio's *Navigazioni* (1556), and Ramusio, or part of him, reappears in Hakluyt at the end of the century, where we read of Sebastian Cabot's gallant failures: "But it seemeth that God doeth yet still reserve this great enterprise for some great prince to discover this voyage of Cathaia by this way [northwest]."

Such is the governing sentiment. Let us, out of a hundred possible instances, select one for analysis—the story of De Soto and Juan Ortiz as set forth in *La Florida del Ynca* (1605). The author, the Inca Garcilaso de la Vega, proud of his descent from the royal house of Peru and the lordly Spanish lines of Sierrabrava and Paria, and related to many important poets among the aristocracy, actively expresses the *personalismo* proper to a hidalgo, confesses his interest in chivalry, an interest tinged with theological regret, and says of Hernando de Soto that he was in no way inferior to Cortés, Pizarro, and Almagro but that because "it was not in his nature to serve as an inferior," "he forsook those noble exploits . . . and set out upon others which for him proved to be of even more serious consequence, for in them he lost his life, not to speak of his previously earned fortune." De Soto is one of the men Spain "reared to conquer the New World

---

exploring lower California, learned of a land where people slept under water and wore golden bracelets and of another tribe with ears that trailed on the ground, not to speak of a third that lived on smells. The Indian known as the Turk told Alvarado of the Coronado expedition that in a country called Quivira a huge river sported great canoes with twenty rowers to a side, high, curved prows of gold, and white sails. The chief of that land took his siesta under a tall spreading tree decorated with little golden bells, on which the zephyrs played a lullaby, and the common people ate and drank out of dishes, pitchers, and bowls of gold. (Herbert E. Bolton, *The Spanish Borderlands* [*Chronicles of America Series*, Vol. 23], New Haven, 1921, pp. 95–96.)

and at the same time . . . make themselves feared by the Old." In Book II of his chronicle, which especially shows the influence of chivalry, the Inca tells a tale that has all the accouterments of chivalric romance. An interesting light on the Inca's attitude is shed by an incidental remark: "It seems inappropriate to employ the term cavalier, or *caballero,* in referring to Indians because they possessed no horses, or *caballos,* from which word the name is deduced; but since in Spain this term implies a nobleman and since there is a nobility among the Indians, it may be used likewise in speaking of them."

The cacique Hirrihigua, though an ally of the Spaniards, had by treachery lured four of Narváez' soldiers into his power in revenge for a slight, tortured and killed three of them, and intermitted the torture of Juan Ortiz, who was scarcely eighteen, only at the instance of the cacique's wife and daughters, the wife saying that he was "deserving of forgiveness because of his tender age." But the cacique, like an ogre in a fairy tale, gave Juan Ortiz a set of disagreeable tasks that included being sentry over the bodies of dead Indians, and "should any corpse or any part of one be borne away," Juan Ortiz was to be baked alive. He was given "four darts to throw at the lions [*sic*] or any other wild beasts." A "lion" appeared and made off with the body of a child laid there two days previously. Juan Ortiz incredibly slew the lion with the cast of a single dart, and should therefore have been held in great veneration.

But the wicked cacique, recalling "that Spaniards had cast his mother to the dogs and permitted them to feed upon her body," was again seized by the devil and resolved to shoot Juan Ortiz full of arrows. The eldest daughter of the house, in the best manner of romance, secretly warned Juan Ortiz, and "added some words of quite another character": "Lest you lose faith in me and despair of your life or doubt that I will do everything in my power to save you . . . I will assist you to escape and find refuge if you are a man and have the courage to flee. For tonight, if you will come at a certain hour to a certain place, you will find an Indian in whom I shall entrust both your welfare and mine." The Indian was to guide Juan Ortiz to a "bridge," six leagues beyond it was a town, and the "lord" of the town was Mucozo, "a man," said the Indian maid, "who loves me exceedingly and desires my hand in marriage," and who "being the person he is . . . will do everything he can for you, as you shall see."

Juan Ortiz threw himself at the feet of the maiden in gratitude, and all went according to plan. The good Mucozo received the Christian affably, listened with compassion to his story, embraced Juan Ortiz, and kissed him on the face as a sign of peace. "In order to serve the one who sent you as well as yourself who have come to me and my house for protection . . . I will do all that I can, as you shall see by my actions; and you may be certain that so long as I live, no one will take the occasion to molest you." Juan Ortiz lived for ten years with Mucozo. That chief protected him against the threats of Hirrihigua and of Mucozo's brother-in-law, Urribarracuxi, held him in high esteem, and "regaled" him until the arrival of Hernando de Soto. The Inca pauses to preach a lesson to Christian princes who violate the laws of chivalry, praises the "magnanimity of an infidel," and declares that "God and human nature many times produce such souls in sterile and uncultivated deserts to the greater confusion and shame of people who are born and reared in lands that are fertile and abundant in all good doctrines and sciences, as well as the Christian religion."

The rest of the tale is on the same high plane. The governor asks for Juan Ortiz, the wicked Hirrihigua sends a deceitful guide to De Soto, there is a fight due to misunderstanding, Juan Ortiz stops it by shouting, "Xivilla, Xivilla" and making the sign of the cross, the governor gives him a suit of black velvet, and "Mucozo made him his Captain General on both land and sea." Nor is this all. Speeches full of chivalric rhetoric are exchanged between the Indians and the Spaniards, the mother of Mucozo, thinking her son a captive, arrives in the Spanish camp, offering to die in place of the brave Mucozo, "incidents of laughter and gaiety" occur for eight days before Mucozo returns home, and Mucozo behaves like a *caballero* during his entire stay in the Spanish camp.

> During that time he visited in their quarters the Lieutenant General, the Campmaster, the captains of the army and the officers of the Royal Exchequer, and in addition many individual cavaliers, since they too were of the nobility; and with all these men, he spoke so familiarly, cheerfully and courteously that he seemed to have been reared among them. He asked specific questions about the Court of Castile as well as the Emperor, and the lords, ladies and cavaliers who formed it; and he said that he would be most pleased to see that court if it were possible for him to go there. . . . This Cacique, who was twenty-six or twenty-seven years of age, was very handsome in both body and face.[34]

It is useless for the cultural anthropologist to protest that this is absurd or for the social historian to smile. History is a fable agreed on. The chivalric dream was too potent to be overthrown by reality. Europeans read what they wanted to read, and the New World belonged to Roland, El Cid, and King Arthur.

V

I have touched but incidentally upon the representation of New World scenes in the graphic arts. These are of course in this period principally "illustrations" to the accounts of voyages; and since at the end of the fifteenth century publishing was still in an elementary state, it was possible to use any likely woodcut for two or more likely purposes. Thus in the great Kroberger *Liber Chronicarum* of 1493 the same cut does duty for a number of cities in various parts of the world. Nevertheless he who turns over the pages of the earliest "histories" of the New World comes by and by to feel that the illustrations more often reflect the Mediterranean Renais-

sance than they do the North. When, for example, the printer
wants to illustrate cannibalism or some other horror he does
not in these books characteristically employ the skeleton
motifs that appear in Geisberg's *Geschichte der Deutschen
Graphik vor Dürer* (Berlin, 1939), nor does one find in illustrations of New World battles echoes of tournament scenes
drawn by Dutch and Flemish artists of the fifteenth century.[35]
What intervenes is the Italian Renaissance. The Earthly
Paradise as pictorially interpreted was more after the manner
of Giotto, and the problem of the nude was solved after the
manner of Pollaiuolo rather than after the manner of the
North before Dürer. This is of course not universally true—
the simple line drawings that sufficed for Benzoni's widely influential *Historia del Mondo Nuovo,* first printed at Venice
in 1565, illustrated in 1572, and often translated and reprinted, show no particular provenience, and of course tracing
woodcuts of the fifteenth and sixteenth centuries to their
origins is a problem for experts. It is also true that what pur-
ports to be the first pictorial representation of Indians, produced in Augsburg between 1497 and 1504 (Pl. III), gives us
a "cannibal" scene with figures more like cigar-store Indians
than like human beings.* Nevertheless the general rule
holds.[36]

The New World offered the illustrator unique problems.
In the first place there was no Christian symbolism in New
World landscape, especially since all the reporters denied
that the Indians knew anything about Christ. In the second

---

* The legend accompanying the excellent reproduction of this scene in
Justin Winsor, ed., *The Narrative and Critical History of America* (8 vols.,
Boston, 1884–1889), Vol. II, p. 19, runs: "This figure [i.e., illustration] represents to us the people and island which have been discovered by the Christian
King of Portugal, or his subjects. The people are thus naked, handsome,
brown, well-shaped in body; their hands, necks, arms, private parts, feet of
men and women, are a little covered with feathers. The men also have many
precious stones on their faces and breasts. No one else has anything, but all
things are in common. And the men have as wives those who please them,
be they mothers, sisters, or friends; therein they make no distinction. They
also fight with each other; they also eat each other, even those who are slain,
and hang the flesh of them in the smoke. They become a hundred and fifty
years of age, and have no government" (Winsor's translation).

place the artist had somehow to suggest a lush and tropical landscape, at least as long as he confined himself to the early reports. In the third place he had to employ an accepted iconology, yet set forth the unknown. And in the fourth place, and above all, there was the problem of the nude, now necessary to render actual human beings, not theological abstractions or classical figures. Prior to the Italian Renaissance the nude seldom went beyond the dead Christ, souls at the Last Judgment, Adam and Eve, and an occasional drunken Lot or Noah, or, more rarely, an allegorical figure. The results of attempts to depict naked Indians *before* the spread of Renaissance influence can be seen in the four awkward "Indian" figures on the title page of a German translation of Vespucci, issued at Strasbourg in 1505. They are so vilely drawn, they belong to no known school of art.

When, however, we turn to the famous woodcut of the landing of Columbus (Pl. II), printed in one of the Italian editions of Columbus's first letter (Florence, 1493), and often reproduced, we are in another universe of artistic discourse. The perspective, it is true, is still medieval: King Ferdinand, to show his greatness, occupies as much space as the New World and sits stiffly on a throne in Spain in the lower left-hand part of the picture, pointing at Columbus as he lands an inch away on a New World inhabited by gigantic Indians almost as tall as the solitary palm tree on the seashore. Two of the little ships have nobody aboard, and the third is uncomfortably crowded by four badly drawn figures. But if we study the border of the cut, we find it is of Florentine design; the arrangement of water and island, sky and cloud, and the general black and white pattern have a lightness, an ease, a harmony not discoverable in characteristic commercial work from the North in the same period. Above all, the more we examine the Indians, crude though the representation may be, the more we are impressed by the anatomical knowledge of the artist. There is even a kind of Attic rhythm in the disposition of their arms and legs. When we read Sir Kenneth Clark's magisterial treatment, *The Nude*, we know where this rhythm originates, especially after we read his chapter entitled "Energy." However feeble, this is Renaissance drawing.

When one studies the rich and elaborate title page of the edition of Vespucci published by Jehan Lambert in Paris, probably in 1505, one notes that the marvels of the New World have induced an outburst of griffins in the margin, but they have also brought into being two monkeys under an elaborate tree that bears on a sort of heraldic placard the word *felix*. The Renaissance elements predominate. It is not surprising to find the title page of the book of the discoveries of the Zeno brothers adorned with three flying nudes involved with a floating ribbon on which one reads: *Veritas figlia temporis*. The illustrations of New World humanity in the second volume of Thevet's influential *Cosmographie Universelle* of 1575, whoever drew them, are nudes in the full tide of Renaissance craftsmanship.

Thus a plate showing how the wives of the savages brew their drink exhibits four women kneeling before, or bending over, a huge tub or vat. They are all graceful, and the kneeling figures have their musculature carefully worked out. Behind them two Indians stand in poses suggesting Apollo, and other figures, we somehow feel, recall the Renaissance treatment of Bacchus. The tangle of nudes in the cut showing an Indian burial service has the circularity one associates with Michelangelo's "Battle of Cascina." Another picture of a savage banquet and dance is vaguely like a receding Renaissance *trionfo,* and a woodcut of savages curing a sick man conveys the most extraordinary sense of muscular torsion, energy, and balance among five nude figures, one of them (a female) in the attitude of Eve being expelled from the garden. An extraordinary complex of nudes appears in a picture of savage warfare, the center of which is the unclassical subject of one man biting off the fingers of another. This horror aside, however, the treatment of the bodies is that found in analogous drawings by Raphael. None of the work is more than journeyman work, and, of course, not all the illustrations in

Thevet are of this order. Yet a cut of savages kindling a fire is like a drawing made to illustrate the labors of Hercules.

The first full landscape of the New World, now in the Frans Halsmuseum in Haarlem, painted sometime before 1555 or 1556 by Jan Mostaert (if he painted it) and sometimes referred to as "Landscape in the West Indies" and sometimes as "An Episode of the Conquest of America" (Pl. IV), shows how Mediterranean influence has spread. This fantastic landscape has the usual rocky crag, apparently about to topple over, that one associates with mountains in religious pictures of the fifteenth and sixteenth centuries, but to the spectator's left the landscape is more like one from the school of Leonardo. A dark forest wanders halfway across the middle plane of the picture. Below it a row of naked Indians moves like a living frieze across the landscape. They are joined by other random figures, usually in pairs, running as nymphs run in a Renaissance pastoral. Various animals, mostly European, dot the landscape after the manner of "The Peaceable Kingdom" of Hicks. To the spectator's right the oncoming Spaniards, a dark mass, contrast with the naked cave-dweller figures casting rocks down upon them. The conflict, however it disturbs the Spaniards, does not trouble the animals. One somewhat inexplicable element is two or three dead trees—except as these suggest worldly tumult invading Arcadia and killing innocent life there. There are rudimentary attempts at fences and a quite formal set of paths—all in all, a strange potpourri of images. Yet the picture is definitely a product of an imagination influenced by the Renaissance of the South, an influence nowhere more evident than in the stance given some of the Indians. Two or three are bending the bow of Ulysses, and the three men hurling stones from a rocky cliff studied Hercules or Polyphemus before they allowed themselves to be painted.

The artistic development I have hinted at leads us eventually to the Indian pictures of Jacques le Moyne and John White, first engraved and published by De Bry in 1590 and

1591, though the Le Moyne pictures seem to have been painted in Florida in 1564–1565 and the White pictures in North Carolina in 1587. Both sets are of extraordinary anthropological interest; yet in both the Indians are more like Roman senators than like the red men we know. The musculature of the Le Moyne drawings suggests Rubens; and a number of Indian war scenes are obvious parallels to characteristic battle pictures by Renaissance painters. In one picture mourning widows crouch before a chief, all in the attitude of Niobe; in another wherein they cut off their long hair, they are posed like nymphs and graces; an engraving showing Indian women bringing fruits, animals, and fish in wicker baskets across a treeless landscape is, so far as the figures are concerned, derived from some "Triumph of Bacchus"; the sacrifice of firstborn children gives us a circle of dancing maenads; and when, in still another engraving after Le Moyne, the Indian king and queen take a walk he is posed like a Van Dyck gentleman, she has adopted a pose somewhere between that of Leonardo's Leda and Marcantonio's Eve, and behind her the three graces move leisurely along.

As for the John White paintings as engraved by De Bry (the original water colors are, apparently, more "anthropological"), his old man in winter clothes suggests Marius repudiating Rome; a sorcerer takes exactly the stand of the herald Mercury; three women in a circle of posts and dancing men assume the attitudes of the graces; and a noblewoman of Pomeiock has quietly stepped out of a Rubens canvas, changed her costume, picked up a huge gourd, and is speculatively estimating the performance of a somewhat overgrown Cupid at her left. The legs in White are all too thick, and the engravings emphasize physiological features as the original water colors do not—in itself an important point—but Europe looked at the engravings, not the water colors, and was presumably persuaded that Indians were noble animals and might rival antiquity in the proportions of their bodies and the simplicity of their lives.[37]

Such, then, are some of the principal elements in the image of the New World formed by Europe at the end of the fifteenth century as enriched by the sixteenth. First, the component of wonder, incarnated, as it were, in the concept of islands where men do not die unless they want to, where it is always summer, where food is plentiful, and where nobody works. Then to a weary Europe came news that seemed to say the Earthly Paradise, Arcadia, or the Golden Age was practicable and could actually be found. These idyllic promises were crossed by tales of derring-do, and the New World image absorbed as well the enchanted fairyland of chivalric romance. Finally, precisely as the chivalric imagination of the South had possessed itself of the new image, so the pictorial imagination of the Mediterranean Renaissance turned naked Indians into gods and goddesses, warriors and nymphs, and what had risen out of a dream of antiquity became a mode of picturing actuality.

In the doctrine of Bishop Berkeley that the course of empire must move westward, in that of Whitman defining America as an athletic democracy which proclaims

> I see not America only, not only Liberty's nation but other nations preparing,

in Lowell's exclamation about the brave new world that never yet was young, in the doctrine of progressive democracy and, for that matter, of an economy of abundance, in the dream of millions of emigrants that life is "better" in the New World,* we find continuing echoes of these Arcadian

---

* One passage will serve for a thousand. In the lower Shenandoah valley Andrew Burnaby (*Travels through the Middle Settlements in North America*, 3rd ed., 1798, reprinted New York, 1904) in the mid-eighteenth century saw some happy Germans: "I could not but reflect with pleasure on the situation of these people; and think if there is such a thing as happiness in this life, that they enjoy it. Far from the bustle of the world, they live in the most delightful climate, and richest soil imaginable; they are everywhere surrounded with beautiful prospects and sylvan scenes; lofty mountains, transparent streams, falls of water, rich valleys, and majestic woods; the whole interspersed with an infinite variety of flowering shrubs, constitute the landscape surrounding them: they are subject to few diseases; are generally robust;

preludes. Alas that the coin had baser metal in it! Alas that
the Golden Age turned almost immediately into the age of
gold! To the concept of Arcadia in reverse it is now necessary
to turn.

---

and live in perfect liberty: they are ignorant of want, and acquainted with
but few vices. Their inexperience of the elegancies of life precludes any regret that they possess not the means of enjoying them: but they possess what
many princes would give half their dominions for, health, content, and tranquillity of mind" (pp. 73–74). Burnaby made his observations about 1759.

———— ⟶ II ⟵ ————

The Anti-Image

I

THE concept that the New World is the peculiar abode of felicity lingered for centuries in the European imagination and, like the youth of America, is one of its oldest traditions. Virginia, wrote Michael Drayton in his famous poem of 1606, is earth's "onely paradise," and Goethe not long before his death declared: *"Amerika, du hast es besser/ Als unser Continent, das Alte."* As for France, the studies of Gilbert Chinard have shown the connection between America and an exotic dream of difference and perfection. The vitality of the idea runs so deep and long, the traditional image can be adapted to humor, so that William Byrd's satirical "Journey to the Land of Eden" in 1733 and Martin Chuzzlewit's unfortunate real-estate speculation in the fever-ridden Eden of Dickens' novel are proof of the vigor of a concept that has a thousand aspects, some of which I shall examine in other connections. But the coin, to change the figure, has another side. Before we study its obverse, however, it is relevant to examine three or four famous philosophic evocations of the New World as the home of social perfection.

For example, Sir Thomas More located Utopia in the New World five years before Cortés discovered the great Aztec capital of Tenochtitlán. More's imagined Paradise he learned about from one Ralph Hythloday, first seen "with a blake

35

sonne burned face, a longe bearde, and a cloke cast homely about his shoulders." He was a Portuguese learned in the tongues, a companion, it seems, of Amerigo Vespucci on his voyages. On the last of these Hythloday with twenty-two others, after much "intreataunce and . . . importune sute," was left behind in the country of "Gulike," which, I fear, does not appear on any map. From there with five companions he traversed the equatorial belt where there are only "greate and wyde desertes and wyldernesses," "intollerable heate," "wyld beastes and serpentes" and "people . . . no lesse sauage, wylde, and noysome then the verye beastes." But in the south temperate zone they came upon Utopia, the merits of which are now common knowledge. When at last they left that enchanting land, by "maruelous chaunce" they made their way to Taprobane (Ceylon) and Calicut (then a Portuguese station in India) and so to Europe. The two books that constitute the *Utopia* contrast the weakness and decay of Europe with the dream of a perfect society. Terror and cruelty, it will be observed, are confined to the torrid zone. Europe decays; America is promises.[1] Nor was all this idle dreaming. The vogue of Erasmus and of Sir Thomas More in Renaissance Spain was great; and when Vasco de Quiroga went to New Spain as a judge (*oidor*) in 1530 he drew up a scheme for governing the Indians after the manner of the *Utopia,* which was seriously considered by the Council of the Indies.[2]

But if More reported on the travels of Ralph Hythloday, Rabelais, in books iv and v of the chronicle of that hero's career, sent Pantagruel westward in order to consult the oracle of the bottle, a search that, as Chinard has shown, was strongly infiltrated with New World elements drawn from Peter Martyr and others; and the oracle of the bottle is not merely "Trinq," it is also, as the priestess announces, philosophical: "Down here, in these circumcentral regions, we place the supreme good, not in taking or receiving, but in giving and bestowing." [3] This appeared about 1565.

More influential was Bacon's *The New Atlantis,* published

posthumously in 1627, twenty years after Jamestown. This imaginary island lies in the South Seas somewhere west of Peru, a survivor from the catastrophe that overwhelmed Atlantis proper. *The New Atlantis* is a vision of a completely technological society, one in which wisdom and science are coterminous, an ideal to which many theorists would now like to push the United States. An interesting secondary element in Bacon's social paradise is his emphasis upon ceremony as essential to social harmony. Thus a formal family celebration in the book involves special robing, a throne, a canopy, a herald, emblematic grapes of gold, a scroll, and various other things. Nobody having stumbled upon Atlantean perfection in fact, Bacon is compelled to explain, through the Atlanteans, that America is younger a thousand years at least than the rest of the world. Imperfection has had at length to be reckoned with; and Bacon seems to regard the Indians as a race descending from some by-blow of Noah when he was repopulating the globe.

Utopianism *per se* is, indeed, not the whole of the story. A world coming fresh from the hand of the Creator must contain blessings for sick and weary mankind, and in 1569–1571 the Spanish physician Nicolas Monardes, born in Seville the year that Columbus's letter was first printed, a man much esteemed by his contemporaries, reported sufficient trial of plants, animals, medicinal stones, and other natural products in America to testify that a whole novel and miraculous pharmacopoeia was at last available to Europeans to heal them of their manifold diseases. This work [4] falling into the hands of John Frampton, merchant, he "Englished" it in 1577 as *Joyfull Newes out of the Newe Founde World,* a book "treatyng of the singuler and rare vertues of certaine Hearbes, Trees, Oyles, Plantes, Stones, and Drugges of the Weste Indias" which yield "wonderfull cures of sundrie greate deseases that otherwise then by these remedies, thei were incurable." As one turns over Frampton's astonishing pages, there seems to be no reason why mankind should ever be sick again. Anime and copall, a gum called tacamahaca, another known as caranna, the oil of the fig tree of hell, bitumen, liquid amber, balsamo, guaiacan, the China root, "sarcaparaillia," the bloodstone, pepper, mechoacan, tobacco, and other New World discoveries will obviously end the ills that flesh is heir to. One drug is as good as another. Take, for example, sassafras, which "comforteth the Liver and the Stomacke and doth disopilate," is good for headaches, "griefes of the breast" and of the stomach, casts out "gravell and stones," provokes urine, "taketh awaie merveilouslie" the toothache, is excellent for gout and the "evill of the Joyntes," "maketh a man go to the stoole," and "dooeth greate profite" in the evil of women. In short it is

> for all maner of deseases, without makyng exception of any. And beyng sicke of any maner of evill which commeth unto them [the Spaniards], sharpe, or large, hot, or colde, greevous or otherwise, they doe cure all with one maner of fashion, and they heale all with one maner of water, without makyng any difference, and the best is that all be healed, and of this they have so muche trust, that they feare not the evilles which are present, nor have any care of them that be to come, and so they have it for a universall remedy, for all maner of deseases.

Monardes, or Frampton for him, following the doctrine of correspondences, sometimes associates particular stones, plants, oils, or roots with particular diseases, but the general impression of *Joyfull Newes* is that most of the herbs and other flora tried by the Spaniards and reported by Monardes are good for anything.[5] Monardes also recognizes the existence of the pox, various fevers, and other new and mysterious ailments originating in America, but these are of course curable by his wonder drugs.* The American patent-medicine

---

* The theory of a special *vis naturae curatrix* in the New World lingered long. An amusing instance is John Josselyn's *New-Englands Rarities Discovered*, London, 1672 (reprinted in *Archaeologia Americana: Transactions and Collections of the American Antiquarian Society*, Boston, 1860, Vol. IV), in which Josselyn interpolates into his catalogue of birds, beasts, fishes, serpents, and plants such information as that a friend living in Virginia was cured of a bloody flux by drinking the fat-dripping of a goose, another man grown crooked, lame, and full of pain was cured by lying on new-flayed

man selling his Indian remedies has a more ancient heritage than he knows.[6]

By 1580, when the first edition of Montaigne's *Essays* appeared, which included the celebrated one "Of Cannibals," the problem of reconciling the unlovely aspects of New World life with the paradisiacal dream had become more acute. Like More but more credibly, Montaigne claims to have talked with a man who had been for ten or twelve years in the ill-fated French colony in Brazil founded by Villegaignon in 1557, but Montaigne has also read in Thevet, Jean de Léry, Benzoni, and other writers on discovery and settlement. Man, says Montaigne, should live according to nature, for nature's "purity" so shines forth as to put to shame our "vain and frivolous" performances. Among the Indians "the laws of nature still rule" uncorrupted by sophistication, and Montaigne admires the absence of laws, letters, labor, and the like burdens of humanity in that "very pleasant and temperate climate," where "the whole day is spent in dancing" and where even warfare is straightforward and simple.

But he must solve the problem of cannibalism, not to speak of that presented by polygamy, and it is amusing to watch the great Frenchman exercise his casuistry to get around these awkward practices. Of the two, polygamy is the more easily dealt with. "It is a remarkably beautiful thing about their marriages that the same jealousy our wives have to keep us from the affection and kindness of other women, theirs have to win this for them . . . they strive and scheme to have as many companions as they can, since that is a sign of their husbands' valor."

Cannibalism is a thornier question. In one sense Montaigne frankly faces facts:

After they have treated their prisoners well for a long time with all the hospitality they can think of, each man who has a

---

bears' skins, and a stone found in the belly of the codfish, being pulverized and drunk in white-wine posset or ale, is a "present remedy" for the stone. Perhaps the most astonishing remedy is the hard testicles of the beaver grated and drunk in wine as a remedy for wind in the stomach.

prisoner calls a great assembly of his acquaintances. He ties a
rope to one of the prisoner's arms, by the end of which he holds
him, a few steps away, for fear of being hurt, and gives his
dearest friend the other arm to hold in the same way; and these
two, in the presence of the whole assembly, kill him with their
swords. This done, they roast him and eat him in common and
send some pieces to their absent friends.

But this custom, he says, is not, as with the ancient Scythians,
a form of revenge, nor, as with the Portuguese, a form of
torture. Who are we to reproach the cannibals? "I am heartily
sorry that, judging their faults rightly, we should be so blind
to our own." Montaigne tacitly changes the basis of his discourse to one of admiration for bravery, whether among the
Indians, the Spartans, or the Hungarians. He abandons cannibalism to praise Indian poetry and the rationality of Indian comment on the French court.

In a subsequent essay, "Of Coaches," Montaigne recurs to
the New World, emphasizes the brutality of its European
conquerors, and argues: "I am much afraid that we shall have
greatly hastened the decline and ruin of this new world by
our contagion, and that we will have sold it our opinions and
our arts very dear. It was an infant world; yet we have not
whipped it and subjected it to our discipline by the advantage
of our natural valor and strength, nor won it over by our justice and goodness, nor subjugated it by our magnanimity." [7]
Montaigne was a powerful force in building up the general
concept of the delights of primitivism and the virtues of the
noble savage; yet, being an honest man, he admits that the
Earthly Paradise of the New World is somewhat less than perfection.[8] Montaigne prepares us to examine the other side of
the coin.

II

The association of the New World with unlimited riches
is a commonplace in the history of ideas, but until one realizes
how immediate, coarse, and brutal was the response of Euro-

pean greed to the prospect of boundless wealth, one cannot understand how quickly the radiant image became crossed with streaks of night. It may indeed be true that mere greed for gold will not suffice to explain the superhuman exploits of the conquerors, but it is also true that superhuman exploits would not have been undertaken without the dream of reward. The economic theory of the Renaissance could not think of wealth except in terms of a cash nexus binding man to man, a theory the more persuasive as rulers beheld the wealth of the Indies turning Charles V into the master of Europe and doing mysterious things to prices. Gold, pearls, and precious stones were tangible, were concrete evidence of success, were proof that the New World was, if not the kingdom of Prester John, the empire of the Great Khan, or Asia heavy with the wealth of Ormuz and of Ind, then next door to it, or a passage toward it, or, better still, a richer and more wonderful land. The lust for gold conquered morality, judgment, humanitarianism, and religion. To watch the banausic greed for it corrupt idealism is like watching the inevitable march of a Greek tragedy.

Columbus, his associates, his crew, and his rivals were convinced that gold was at hand, or concealed, or in the next island. They could not conceive that the indifference of the Indians to what the Europeans thought of as tangible wealth was anything less than cunning or treachery. In the interior, says the admiral in his first letter, there are mines of metals— though he never saw them. The evidence? In exchange for a European strap a sailor received gold to the weight of two and a half *castellanos* (46 decigrams). When Columbus returned on his second voyage, the Indians continued to barter casual gold for straps, beads, pins, fragments of dishes, and plates, and Indian kings who sought him out wore facial masks of beaten gold and gold ornaments in their ears and nostrils. The Indian chief Guacamari, suspected of responsibility for the murder of Columbus's original colony on Hispaniola, tried to placate the admiral with a gift of eight and a half marks of gold, five or six hundred stones of various colors, and a cap with a jewel that the Indian seemed to value highly. Then as later, alas! the real source of gold was somewhere else—in this case in an island called Cayre, where there is much gold and "they go there with nails and tools to build their canoes, and . . . bring away as much gold as they please." An expedition to "Cibao" "found gold in more than fifty streams and rivers," "so many rivers, so filled with gold, that all of those who saw it and collected it, merely with their hands as specimens, came back so very delighted . . . that I feel diffidence in repeating what they say."

By the third voyage the inevitable had happened: the thirst for gold had led to the enslavement of the Indians and to double-dealing among the whites, as, for example, Bobadilla, who stole all of Columbus's gold without measuring it or weighing it, once he had the Columbus family in chains. The Lord comforted the admiral, however, by sending him a vision of the Nativity during the night at Veragua on his fourth voyage, showing that gold is everywhere, and an Indian took him up to a hilltop and explained that gold was all around him so that he saw "greater evidence of gold on the first two days than in Española [Hispaniola] in four years." Perhaps uneasily conscious that gold and Christianity do not always mix, Columbus appealed to the great example of Solomon: "Gold is most excellent. Gold constitutes treasure, and he who possesses it may do what he will in the world, and may so attain as to bring souls to Paradise." [9]

The Indians, as Peter Martyr observed, "know no difference between *meum* and *tuum*," [10] but they learned to their sorrow that the white man's insatiable greed for property produced not happiness but treachery, enslavement, starvation, and death. The search for wealth became an obsession among the Europeans, sending Ponce de León, Hernando de Soto, Cabeça de Vaca, and scores of others on fruitless errands and often to miserable ends. Nothing is more characteristic than that Cabeça de Vaca, after his incredible sufferings in the New World, would neither affirm nor deny that there was gold in "Florida," an ambiguity that led many Spaniards to sell their possessions in order to join the ill-fated expedition of De Soto. Gold, it was thought, was everywhere. Fool's gold was solemnly loaded on Elizabethan ships and as solemnly assayed by London mineralogists—fool's gold or something like it. In the bleak Far North in 1577 Frobisher's historian, Dionysius Settle, could find no hurtful creeping beast "except some Spiders (which as many affirme, are signes of great store of gold)." As usual the natives made "signes of certaine people" living somewhere else "that weare bright plates of gold in their foreheads, and other places of their bodies." The mariners brought back some black stone. "And it fortuned a gentlewoman one of the adventurers wives to have a piece thereof, which by chance she threw and burned in the fire, so long, that at the length being taken forth, and quenched in a little vinegar, it glistered with a bright marquesset of golde. Whereupon the matter being called in some question, it was brought to certaine Goldfiners in London to make assay thereof, who gave out that it held golde, and that very richly for the quantity." Naturally the goldfiners "sought secretly to have a lease at her Majesties hands of those places, whereby to injoy the masse of so great a publike profit unto their owne private gaines." [11]

Sir Humphrey Gilbert was so certain he would discover a gold mine in Newfoundland that he promised to ask no man for a penny toward financing his next expedition; and Sir George Peckham's "True Report" lists as probable products of the same territory gold, silver, copper, lead, tin, turquoise, ruby, pearl, marble, jasper, and crystal.[12] Hariot in his *Briefe and True Report* on Ralegh's ill-fated colony tells of a man who gathered five thousand pearls from the Indians, "which for their likenesse and uniformity in roundnesse, orientnesse, and pidenesse of many excellent colors, with equality in greatnesse, were very faire and rare: and had therefore beene presented to her Majesty," but "through extremity of a storme," they were lost "in coming away from the countrey." [13]

Laudonnière reported "good quantitie of Gold and Silver" among the savages of Florida, who "say that in the Moun-

taines of Appalatcy there are Mines of Copper, which I thinke
to be Golde." [14] Perhaps more momentous than even this delusive idea is the effect of lust for wealth upon European conduct in Florida:

> Golde and silver they [the Indians] want not: for at the French-
> mens first comming thither they had the same offered them
> for little or nothing, for they received for a hatchet two pound
> weight of golde, because they knew not the estimation thereof:
> but the souldiers being greedy of the same, did take it from
> them, giving them nothing for it: the which they perceiving,
> that both the Frenchmen did greatly esteeme it, and also did
> rigorously deale with them, by taking the same away from them,
> at last would not be knowen they had any more, neither durst
> they weare the same for feare of being taken away.[15]

More commonly Indians were enslaved, tortured, or killed
if they would not reveal the existence of gold they knew nothing about in fact.

These instances, though they illustrate the fixed idea of
Renaissance man that gold, silver, precious stones, and pearls
were easily to be found anywhere from the Arctic Circle to
the Straits of Magellan, are not prerogative instances; for
these we must turn to the incredible history of the Spaniards
in Mexico and Peru. The pages of Prescott narrate a tale of
gold and greed, blood and bravery, treachery and daring
made so familiar by the literary skill of a great romantic historian, one need here merely recall a few familiar episodes.
On receiving the first embassy from Montezuma, which
brought, among other gifts, a wicker basket filled with gold
ornaments, Cortés sent back a gilt helmet, asking that it be
filled with gold, and told the ambassadors the Spaniards were
troubled with a disease of the heart, for which gold was a
specific remedy—one of the great ironical statements in the
history of the New World. A second embassy brought Aztec
"armor" embossed with gold, birds and animals in gold and
silver, two circular plates, one of silver, one of gold, as large
as carriage wheels, and much else. Far from placating the
Spaniards, these gifts inflamed their cupidity, and the fateful

invasion pushed forward. After they had entered Tenochtitlán the Spaniards broke into Montezuma's private treasury, a large hall filled with riches that included ingots of gold and silver and many precious jewels. Montezuma sought vainly to ransom himself and his empire by causing three great heaps of gold and golden objects to be piled before his conquerors, heaps so big that even after three days they were not turned into ingots. The predictable consequences followed: the common soldiers, charging their leaders with bad faith, came near mutiny over the division of the spoils, Montezuma was eventually killed, and his successor, Cuauhtémoc [Guatemozin], last of the Aztecs, refusing under torture to tell where there was more treasure except that it had been thrown into the water, was judicially murdered by the Spaniards. The reconquest of the city and the failure to uncover more treasure stirred up the soldiers once more.

> The first ebullition of triumph was succeeded in the army by very different feelings, as they beheld the scanty spoil gleaned from the conquered city, and as they brooded over the inadequate compensation they were to receive for all their toils and sufferings. . . . Some murmured audibly against the general, and others against Guatemozin, who, they said, could reveal, if he chose, the place where the treasures were secreted. The white walls of the barracks were covered with epigrams and pasquinades levelled at Cortés, whom they accused of taking "one fifth of the booty as commander-in-chief, and another fifth as king." [16]

Gómara reports a sentence worthy of an ancient Roman uttered by Cuauhtémoc while under torture, when a weaker victim complained: "And do you think I, then, am taking my pleasure in my bath?" Whatever the truth of the charges against Cortés, when he married upon his return to Spain, he gave his bride five invaluable emeralds cut by Aztec workmen, a gift that excited the greed and envy of the Queen of Spain. It is all like the curse of the Rhinegold.

The story of the conquest of Peru repeats in more lurid colors the story of the conquest of Mexico. The greed of Pi-

zarro and his men was excited by glimpses of wealth caught
on the coastal land, in Peru they seized the Inca Atahuallpa
by treachery and simultaneously massacred some thousands
of his attendants, the Inca, like Montezuma, sought to ransom
himself and his people by filling a hall with gold, roving bands
of Spaniards despoiled the Inca temples of their golden ornaments, the Inca was judicially murdered by the conqueror,
civil war and conspiracy became commonplace, cruelty grew
to be the daily experience of both Indian and Spaniard, and
Pizarro and his attendants were eventually assassinated by
Juan de Herrada and his followers. The epigraph from Lope
de Vega's *El Nuevo Munðo* affixed by Prescott to the title
page of the *History of the Conquest of Peru* could not be
more ironically appropriate:

> *So color de religión*
> *Van a buscar plata y oro*
> *Del encubierto tesoro.*

The massacre of Atahuallpa's attendants followed upon the
exclamation of a Christian priest to Pizarro: "Do you not see,
that, while we stand here wasting our breath in talking with
this dog, full of pride as he is, the fields are filling with Indians? Set on, at once; I absolve you." [17]
One final document, too important as literature to be
omitted, and we shall be done with this nightmare. This is
Ralegh's *Discovery of Guiana* (1595), which, better than anything else in Elizabethan literature, represents the shimmering mirage of gold and glory through which the sixteenth
century saw the New World. The fact that Ralegh is interested in making out the best possible case for himself increases our sense that gold was the obsession of the age. He
actually found none, nor did a subsequent expedition, but he
saw some of the "kind of white stone (wherin gold ingen-
dred)" in "divers hils and rocks in every part of Guiana,
wherein we traveled." He reported that "al the rocks, mountains, al stones in ye plaines, woods, & by the rivers side are
in effect throughshining, and seem marvelous rich" and were

probably "El madre del oro" or at least "the scum of gold."
He paraphrases from López de Gómara's *General History of
the Indies* this description of the magnificence of Guayna-
capa, ancestor of the supposed "emperor" of Guiana:

> All the vessels of his house, table and kitchin were of gold
> and silver, and the meanest of silver and copper for strength
> and hardnesse of metall. He had in his wardrobe hollow statues
> of gold which seemed giants, and the figures in proportion and
> bignesse of all the beasts, birds, trees, and hearbes, that the
> earth bringeth foorth: and of all the fishes that the sea or waters
> of his kingdome breedeth. He had also ropes, budgets, chestes
> and troughs of golde and silver, heapes of billets of gold, that
> seemed wood marked out to burne. Finally, there was nothing
> in his countrey, whereof he had not the counterfait in gold:
> Yea and they say The Ingas had a garden of pleasure in an
> yland neere Puna, where they went to recreat themselves, when
> they would take the aire of the Sea, which had all kinde of
> garden-hearbs, flowers and trees of golde and silver, an inven-
> tion, and magnificence till then never seene.

Ralegh struggled up the mighty Orinoco toward the golden
city of Manoa, but accident, ignorance, the season of the year,
and the weariness of his men prevented him from reaching
that fabulous capital. But Martínez, a solitary Spanish survivor of one of Ordas's wholesale executions, had seen it,
learned the language of that place, and departed from it blind-
folded. He christened the city El Dorado, and "As Berreo informed mee," *

> Those Guianians, and also the borderers, and all other in that
> tract which I have seene, are marvellous great drunkards; in
> which vice, I thinke no nation can compare with them: and at
> the times of their solemne feasts, when the emperour carowseth
> with his captaines, tributaries, and governours, the maner is
> thus: All that pledge him are first stripped naked, and their
> bodies are anointed all over with a kind of white balsamum
> (by them called curca) of which there is great plenty. . . .
> When they are anointed all over, certeine servants of the

---

* "Berreo" was Don Antonio de Berrio, who made at least three expeditions
into Guiana.

emperour, having prepared golde made into fine powder, blow it thorow hollow canes upon their naked bodies, untill they be all shining from the foot to the head: and in this sort they sit drinking by twenties, and hundreds, and continue in drunkennesse sometimes sixe or seven dayes together.

Ralegh never saw Manoa, but "whatsoever prince shall possesse it, that Prince shall be Lord of more golde, and of a more beautiful Empire, and of more Cities and people, then either the King of Spaine, or the great Turke." Guiana is the country of the future,

the most eyther rich in golde, or in other marchandizes. The common souldier shall here fight for golde, and pay himselfe in steede of pence, with plates of half a foote broad, whereas he breaketh his bones in other warres for provant and penury. Those commanders and chieftaines that shoot at honour and abundance, shall finde there more rich and beautifull cities, more temples adorned with golden images, more sepulchres filled with treasure, then either Cortez found in Mexico or Pizarro in Peru. . . . Guiana is a countrey that hath yet her maydenhead, never sackt, turned, nor wrought . . . the graves have not bene opened for golde, the mines not broken with sledges, nor their Images puld downe out of their temples.[18]

Alas! Ralegh had more influence upon literature than upon kings: within ten years he was a prisoner in the Tower, a final expedition proved a complete fiasco, and on October 29, 1618, he was beheaded. Fantastic as the dream of El Dorado may seem, let us not forget that in 1577 Sir Francis Drake, putting in at a Pacific coast port called Tarapaze, found on the seashore a sleeping Spaniard "who had lying by him 13. barres of silver, which weighed 4000. ducats Spanish; we tooke the silver, and left the man." [19]

The consequences of this *idée fixe* were of first importance in altering the picture of an Earthly Paradise. Though it was not the sole cause, the hunt for gold was one of the principal causes for the enslavement of the Indians. On Hispaniola, for example, by the end of the fifteenth century anarchy was more common than order. The Indians, when they rebelled against their conquerors, were condemned to pay tribute in gold, and when they were unable to find gold they were condemned to slavery—unless, indeed, slavery had been a prior punishment for rebellion. The *hidalgo* was supposed to fight and govern, not to labor; wherefore the Indians had to labor for him, and their women serve as his harem. As the Indian was himself unaccustomed to toil, notably toil in the mines, the population rapidly declined. European madness led to suicide,* to aborticide, to infanticide; and since, unfortunately for the subjugated race, the white man brought his own diseases with him, sickness took off thousands. The population of Hispaniola has been estimated at a million in 1492; even if the figure is far too high, it is appalling to learn that the number of Indians living on that unhappy island had dropped to 14,000 by 1509. The Spanish court did what it could at long range to alleviate the lot of the Indians, and the great propaganda campaign of Montesinos and Las Casas finally ended the concept that the Indian was a natural slave.[20] But the damage had been done.

Bloodshed, cruelty, and abuse could not last forever. The Anglo-Saxons remained alone in thinking that the only good Indian is a dead Indian, since the Spanish, the Portuguese, and the French, once the period of slaughter had waned, altered their philosophy and incorporated the Indians into their colonial cultures in greater or less degree. I have already said enough about the degrading effect of the lust for wealth upon the white conquerors. There is, apparently, something inherent in the extractive industries that awakens the baser emotions, as witness the California gold rush and that into the Yukon. But I suggest that the obsession with easy tangible wealth did more than cast a delusive mirage over the period of discovery and exploration. Its effects have never disappeared. The legendary Sicilian peasant who came to New

---

* Kidnaped Indians sometimes went on a hunger strike and starved to death and familial suicide among the Cuban Indians was notorious. (John Grier Varner and Jeannette Johnson Varner, editors and translators, *The Florida of the Inca*, Austin, Texas, 1951, pp. 10, 41–42.)

York City only to be disappointed that the streets were not
paved with gold is a symbolic cultural figure. Colonial promotion literature in France and England during the sixteenth
and seventeenth centuries continually sounds the note of
quick and rapid wealth, nor does this lure cease when, in the
eighteenth century, it intermingles with the attractive picture of a radical republic. Greedy shipping interests had
already begun to exploit the gullibility of simple men, as de-
luded immigrants swarmed aboard vessels that were sometimes no better than slave ships.[21] These immigrants arrived
in the New World in thousands of cases ill-equipped to survive—as ill-adapted to the New World as were the elder
Shimerdas in *My Ántonia* or the sodden proletariat pictured
in *How the Other Half Lives, The Jungle,* or *Twenty Years
at Hull House*. The tough-minded, of course, survived, and
became the "New Americans."

III

If the discoverers, in Peter Martyr's words, "ruined and
exhausted themselves by their own folly and civil strife, fail-
ing absolutely to rise to the greatness expected of men who ac-
complish such wonderful things"—a judgment at once understandable and premature—the natives of the New World
proved to be something less than pastoral inhabitants of an
Earthly Paradise. The contrast between the two sides of the
shield was sometimes merely puzzling and sometimes horrifying. When Verrazano made his voyage along the Atlantic
seaboard in 1524 he found the Indians of the Carolina coast
friendly and good-looking. They showed, he said, "the greatest delight on beholding us, wondering at our dress, countenances, and complexion"; they were "of good proportions,
of middle stature, a little above our own, broad across the
breast, strong in the arms and well formed in the legs and
other parts of the body." They lived in a plentiful and lovely
country where "the air is salubrious, pure and temperate, and

free from the extremes of both hot and cold" and the sea is "calm, not boisterous, and its waves are gentle." But when he got to Cape Cod or its vicinity all was changed. The vegetation was "indicative of a cold climate," and the people were "entirely different from the others we had seen . . . so rude and barbarous that we were unable by any signs we could make, to hold communication with them." Clad in skins, living by hunting and fishing, and raising no crops, the Indians were hostile. "No regard was paid to our courtesies; when we had nothing left to exchange with them, the men at our departure made the most brutal signs of disdain and contempt possible." And when the expedition tried to enter the interior, the Indians shot the white men with arrows and raised the most horrible cries.[22]

But this contrast was comparatively mild. The Europeans also discovered cannibals. In the West Indies Columbus's men came across "a great quantity of men's bones and skulls hung up about the houses like vessels to hold things" and reported bestial habits of the Caribs that were far, far different from the bookish theoric Montaigne was to build on the cannibals. The Caribs raid other islands and treat their captives

> with a cruelty which appears to be incredible, for they eat the male children whom they have from [captive women] and only rear those whom they have from their own women. As for the men whom they are able to take, they bring such as are alive to their houses to cut up for meat, and those who are dead they eat at once. They say that the flesh of a man is so good that there is nothing like it in the world, and it certainly seems to be so for, from the bones which we found in their houses, they had gnawed everything that could be gnawed, so that nothing was left on them except what was too tough to be eaten. In one house there was a neck of a man found cooking in a pot. They castrate the boys whom they capture and employ them as servants until they are fully grown, and then when they wish to make a feast, they kill and eat them, for they say that the flesh of boys and women is not good to eat.

The Spaniards captured three such *castrati*, who had fled from the cannibals; [23] four more *castrati* were captured by Vespucci.

Vespucci's men, if his letters are to be believed, were compelled to witness a practical demonstration in cannibalism. On his third voyage the mainland natives seemed to want to parley, and the voyagers in good faith set on shore a "very agile and valiant youth" to treat with them. Thereupon an Indian woman ran from the hill toward the shore, felled the young Christian with a club, and dragged his body up the hillside while the Indian warriors sent such a shower of arrows at the Europeans they could not rescue their shipmate. Other Indian women appeared, tore the young man to pieces, roasted him in the fire, and ate him before the eyes of his horrified companions.* Vespucci also dwells upon the libidinousness of the Indian females, Indian promiscuity, treachery, and cannibalism—qualities scarcely offset by his belief that they live for 150 years and are rarely sick.[24] All this was in South America. In the far north Dionysius Settle concluded that the inhabitants were "Anthropophagi, or devourers of mans flesh," "for that there is no flesh or fish which they find dead (smell it never so filthily) but they will eate it, as they finde it without any other dressing. A loathsome thing, either to the beholders or hearers." [25] † Loathsome, indeed, for as Peter Martyr is made to say in Richard Eden's colorful English, "There is no man able to behowlde them, but he shall feele his bowelles grate with a certen horroure, nature hath endewed them with soo terrible menacynge, and cruell aspecte." [26] Ritualistic cannibalism was imitated by the *cimar-*

---

* The English experienced something similar, as may be just made out by putting together the details in "The Voyage of the Barbara to Brazil, 1540," R. G. Maarsden, ed., *The Naval Miscellany*, II, London, *Publications of the Navy Records Society*, Vol. XL, 1912. See pp. 9, 29, 50, 57, 59.

† The expectation of being eaten if captured lingered until the end of the seventeenth century. Thus Jonathan Dickinson, with a group of fellow Quakers, shipwrecked on the Florida coast near Cape Canaveral, was roughly treated by the Indians, whom they feared as "'man-eaters," but the Indians murdered no one, looted only what they thought was their due, and eventually got the shipwrecked Europeans into the hands of friendly Spaniards. See Evangeline Walker Andrews and Charles McLean Andrews, eds., *Jonathan Dickinson's Journal or, God's Protecting Providence*, New Haven, 1945, p. 29.

róns, escaped Negro slaves, who, when they could, "to feede their insatiable revenges," were "accustomed to rost and eate the hearts of all those Spaniards, whom at any time they could lay hand upon," [27] and on occasion starving Spaniards also ate the flesh of the dead.[28]

Equally appalling was human sacrifice, for example, that practiced by the Aztecs. There are many accounts, one of the most graphic being that by Gómara in his *Historia General de las Indias* (1552), which, despite attempts to suppress it, was widely disseminated in Spanish, Italian, French, and English, especially Part II, the *Conquista de México,* translated into English by Thomas Nichols as *The Conquest of the VVeast India* (1578). The Nichols translation carries an even more authentic repulsion than does the Spanish original. Elizabethans read of the great temple in Tenochtitlán with its two great altars, its twin hideous idols, its gutters of blood; and of

> other darke houses full of idols, greate & small, wrought of sundry mettals, they are all bathed and washed with bloud, and do shewe very blacke through theyr dayly sprinklyng and anoynting them with the same, when any man is sacrificed: yea and the walles are an inche thicke with bloud, and the grounde is a foote thicke of bloud, so that there is a diuelish stench. The Priests or Ministers goe dayly into those Oratories, and suffer none others but great personages to enter in. Yea and when any such goeth in, they are bounde to offer some man to be sacrificed, that those bloudy hangmen and ministers of the Diuell may washe their handes in bloud of those so sacrificed, and to sprinkle their house therewith.

The priest bound the victim face upward on a large sacrificial stone with convenient runnels, opened his living breast with a flint knife, tore out the heart, and, offering it to the idol, smeared the god with fresh blood. "This done, they pluckt of the skinnes of a certeine number of them, the which skinnes so many auntient persons put incontinent upon their naked bodies, al fresh & bloudy, as they wer fleane from the deade carcasses. . . . In *Mexico* the king him selfe did put on one of these skinnes, being of a principall captiue, and daunced among the other disguised persons, to exalte and honor the feast." [29] I spare the reader other gory details but I must add that according to Gómara and Bernal Díaz del Castillo the victim was then cut up and eaten.

The torture of prisoners taken in Indian warfare was, Montaigne to the contrary notwithstanding, common practice before the Portuguese or any other Europeans taught torture to the aborigines. A single episode of such torture, drawn from the *Jesuit Relations,* ought to suffice:

> There is no cruelty comparable to that which they practice on their enemies. As soon as the captives are taken, they brutally tear off their nails with their teeth; I saw the fingers of these poor creatures, and was filled with pity, also I saw a large hole in the arm of one of them; I was told that it was a bite of the Savage who had captured him; the other had a part of a finger torn off, and I asked him if the fire had done that, as I thought it was a burn. He made a sign to show me that it had been taken off by the teeth. I noticed the same cruelty among the girls and women, when these poor prisoners were dancing; for, as they passed before the fire, the women blew and drove the flames over in their direction to burn them. When the hour comes to kill their captives, they are fastened to a stake; then the girls, as well as the men, apply hot and flaming brands to those portions of the body which are the most sensitive, to the ribs, thighs, chest, and several other places. They raise the scalp from the head, and then throw burning sand upon the skull, or uncovered place. They pierce the arms at the wrists with sharp sticks, and pull the nerves out through these holes. In short, they make them suffer all that cruelty and the Devil can suggest. At last, as a final horror, they eat and devour them almost raw.

This, says one of the Jesuits cheerfully, is what some of us may look forward to.

So much for a Catholic martyr. In May 1782, near Muddy Creek, Pennsylvania, the Reverend John Corbley started to church with his wife and five children, suspecting no danger and, apparently, walking ahead of his family while he meditated deeply on his sermon. He was suddenly aroused by frightful shrieks as the Indians leaped on his family.

My dear wife had a sucking child in her arms; this little infant they killed and scalped. They then struck my wife sundry times, but not getting her down, the Indian who had aimed to shoot me ran to her, shot her through the body, and scalped her. My little boy, an only son, about six years old, they sunk the hatchet into his brains, and thus dispatched him. A daughter, besides the infant, they also killed and scalped. My eldest daughter who is yet alive, was hid in a tree about twenty yards from the place where the rest were killed, and saw the whole proceedings. She, seeing the Indians all go off, as she thought, got up and deliberately crept out of the hollow trunk; but one of them espying her, ran hastily up, knocked her down and scalped her; also her only surviving sister, on whose head they did not leave more than one inch round, either of flesh or skin, besides taking a piece out of her skull. She and the before-mentioned one are still miraculously preserved.

The whole ghastly operation took, he says, about ten minutes.* The father fainted and was found and borne off by a friend who arrived after the massacre.[30]

Not inexpert in torture, Europeans nevertheless felt there was something hellish and obscene about these animals that looked like men. Anything wicked could be postulated of them—lying, treachery, filthiness, greed, brutality, laziness, lasciviousness. Peter Martyr solemnly chronicles the tradition of a country called "Inzignanin," the original inhabitants of which had been visited by men who had tails a meter long.[31] In the Arctic, Frobisher's crew captured a female "whom divers of our Saylers supposed to be eyther a devill, or a witch," so they plucked off her "buskins," found she was not

---

* The unpredictable conduct of the Indians from the white point of view is evident to anybody who will read through Samuel G. Drake, ed., *Indian Captivities or Life in the Wigwam*, New York, 1857, the woodcuts in which are themselves revelatory. In New England the Tarrantine Indians tied captives to trees and gnawed their flesh piecemeal from the bones. See J. Franklin Jameson, ed., *Johnson's Wonder-Working Providence*, New York, 1910, p. 149. After an unsuccessful attempt to hang a captive Indian, another made a hole in him and sucked out his blood. Charles H. Lincoln, ed., *Narratives of the Indian Wars*, New York, 1913, p. 41.

cloven-footed, and "for her ougly hew and deformity we let
her goe." [32] One native of that region, being captured by a
stratagem, "for very choler and disdaine he bit his tongue in
twaine," whereas others, to avoid being taken, committed
suicide by jumping into the sea.[33] At the other end of the
globe Lopez Vaz, a Portuguese, reported that the natives of
Tierra del Fuego were ten or eleven feet high. There were
rumors of headless men with eyes in their breasts and of
fierce Amazonian women. Obviously such creatures wor-
shiped the devil, practiced every diabolical art, and were
witches and wizards. Frobisher's crew were sure the Eskimos
"are great inchanters, and use many charmes of witchcraft." [34]
John Davis found them filled with a "devilish nature." [35]
Henry Hawks wrote that the witchcraft of the Indians was
such that when Europeans come near the seven golden cities
of Cíbola, "they cast a mist upon them, so that they cannot
see them." [36] John Hawkins found them "no such kinde of
people as wee tooke them to bee, but more devilish a thousand partes and are eaters and devourers of any man they can
catch." [37] Francis Drake, when he coasted along Brazil,
watched the Indians making fires, "a sacrifice (as we learned)
to the devils, about which they use conjurations, making
heapes of sande and other ceremonies, that when any ship
shall goe about to stay upon their coast . . . stormes and
tempests may arise, to the casting away of ships and men." [38]
The chief god they worship, reported Captain John Smith, is
the devil: "They say that they haue conference with him, and
fashion themselves as neare to his shape as they can imagine." [39] In this Protestant judgment Catholicism concurred.
Wrote Father Joseph Jouvency: "They call some divinity,
who is the author of evil, 'Manitou,' and fear him exceedingly. Beyond doubt it is the enemy of the human race, who
extorts from some people divine honors and sacrifices." [40]
And Father Pierre Biard agreed:

> . . . all this region, though capable of the same prosperity as
> ours, nevertheless through Satan's malevolence, which reigns
> there, is only a horrible wilderness. . . .[41]

They are, I say, savage, haunting the woods, ignorant, lawless and rude: they are wanderers, with nothing to attach them to a place, neither homes nor relationship, neither possessions nor love of country; as a people they have bad habits, are extremely lazy, gluttonous, profane, treacherous, cruel in their revenge, and given up to all kinds of lewdness, men and women alike. . . .[42]

The conflict of cultures was inevitable. When the white man tried to kidnap the Indian with the intent either of exhibiting him as a trophy, learning his language, or turning him into an interpreter, the Indian naturally grew suspicious and retaliated with whatever weapons he could command. When the Indian first roasted and ate a captured white man in order to acquire his knowledge or for ritualistic purposes sensible enough to the aborigine, the white man interpreted the act as the quintessence of diabolism. Against the superior military power and technological skill of the Europeans, the Indian could oppose only cunning and his knowledge of the land. Renaissance man—and this is particularly true of the Renaissance Englishman—found it difficult to understand how human beings (if they were human) could live without visible government, religion, or morality, and he therefore tended to assume that Indian culture, like all the rest of the world, was somehow organized under a king or an emperor with whom one could deal legally in matters of war and peace and the sale of land. Obviously the Indian had no concept of what to the Europeans were the elements of civil society; and he could fight the white man only by what the white man thought of as the basest treachery. The Machiavellian qualities in the European power struggle in some degree prepared the discoverers and the early colonists for some amount of bad faith, but not for the Indian usage of bad faith. Neither party to a treaty could understand what the word meant to the other.

What could the Indians be, except children of the devil? [43] On De Soto's expedition one Indian, visibly possessed by the devil, was subjected to exorcism by the friars.[44] As late as 1666

George Alsop in *A Character of the Province of Maryland* not only seriously advanced the proposition that the "Susquehanok" Indians had no other deity but alleged that every four years a child was sacrificed to the devil, who in return permitted the Indians to talk to him by raising a great tempest; [45] and Edward Johnson described their deity in some detail:

> It hath been a thing very frequent before the English came, for the Divell to appear unto them in a bodily shape, sometimes very ugly and terrible, and sometimes like a white boy, and chiefly in the most hideous woods and swamps . . . and since we came hither, they tell us of a very terrible beast for shape and bigness, that came into a wigwam toward the Northeast parts, remote from any English plantations, and took away six men at a time, who were never seen afterward. [46]

Who but the offspring of Satan, theologians to the contrary notwithstanding, would destroy even their male children because of their dreams, or cast away their daughters at birth and cause them to be eaten by dogs? [47] Or dispossess old women of such clothing as they had and shoot arrows at the pudenda? Or seize small children by the leg, throw them high in the air, and shoot them full of arrows before they reached the ground? [48] Or kill a trusting New Englander, his Bible in his hand, rip him open, and put his Bible in his belly? [49]

Cruelty begat cruelty, deceit was countered by deceit, and bad faith on the one side excused bad faith on the other. Although De Soto's expedition was, within reason, pacific in intention, the kidnaping of Indians by De Ayllón's expedition in 1521 had led to the massacre of some two hundred Spaniards by the Indians, and De Soto found himself the heir of a hostile attitude he could do nothing to overcome. The story of his expedition is one long tale of ambush, treachery, and revenge.[50] Thus, perhaps imitating Cortés and warned of the intention of the Chief Vitachuco to assassinate the Spanish leader, De Soto seized that Indian and thus set off a series of reprisals. Vitachuco and his fellow captives plotted against the Spaniards, and the chief attempted to strangle De Soto at high table, whereupon the captive Indians were massacred by the whites. The long struggle to overcome the Apalachee Indians, "gigantic in stature" and "very valiant and spirited" is a second chapter in the story, and the slaughter of both Indians and Spaniards at the burning of the Indian town of Mavila is a third—an episode that started an incipient mutiny in the remnants of De Soto's army. The Spaniards, working their way through difficult terrain, had to kidnap Indians for guides, the Indians retaliated by ambushing and assassinating the Spaniards, and the Spaniards countered on occasion by cutting off the hands and noses of Indians and sending them back to their villages as a warning. In the Pequot War of 1637, the burning and massacre of some hundreds of Indian men, women, and children trapped in the "fort" at Mystic, Connecticut—a massacre that continued until the English "grew weary"—drew no reproof from contemporary chroniclers but was on the contrary regarded as a signal proof of divine intervention. "The Lord," wrote Edward Johnson in his *Wonder-Working Providence* (1653), the first published history of Massachusetts, "was pleased to assist his people in this warre, and deliver them out of the Indians hands." As for the famous King Philip's War, which lasted two years, cost the lives of one-tenth of the adult males in the Massachusetts Bay Colony, and exposed two-thirds of the towns and villages to Indian raids, the contest was illustrated on the side of the Indians by the raping and scalping of women, the cutting off of fingers and feet of men, the skinning of white captives, the ripping open of the bellies of pregnant women, the cutting off of the penises of the males, and the wearing of the fingers of white men as bracelets or necklaces. Naturally the whites retaliated. When King Philip was finally shot, his head and hands were cut off and his body was quartered and hung on four trees. "The Providence of God wonderfully appeared" in this, wrote "R. H." in *The Warr in New-England Visibly Ended* (1677).[51]

The discovery that the Earthly Paradise was inhabited by

the offspring of Satan compelled Europeans to choose between two alternatives, neither of which proved successful.
Either you converted the Indians into children of Christ or
you exterminated them in a holy war.* The Mediterranean
peoples made more progress in converting the children of
Satan, the British in exterminating them. The long history of
American injustice to the red man springs from a profound
and brutal misunderstanding that passed into literary tradition, for, as Roy Harvey Pearce has shown,[52] the so-called Indian captivity narratives understandably passed from fact to
fiction. They became exercises in emotion, not historical records. The Indian long remained a figure of terror, a child of
hell, the evil being of *The Jibbenainosay* of Robert Montgomery Bird, the reason why Custer's massacre occurred and
why Kentucky was known as a dark and bloody ground. If
we put aside a few humanitarian successes like those of John
Eliot and the Quakers, a handful of documents like Eleazar
Wheelock's *Plain and Faithful Narrative of the Original Design, Rise, Progress and Present State of the Indian Charity-
School at Lebanon* (Boston, 1763) or William Smith's *Indian
Songs of Peace: with a Proposal in a Prefatory Epistle, for
Erecting Indian Schools* (New York, 1752)—and of course
Ramona and *A Century of Dishonor*—it is clear that the In-
dian was not sentimentalized until he became relatively harm-

---

* There is much truth in the assumption that, given the white man's
superiority in weapons, surprise, ambush, cunning, and deceit were the only
possible weapons left to the aborigines. But the Indian prowess with bow
and arrow (at least among certain tribes) made him a match for the European armed with crossbow and arquebus. Despite their armor the Spanish
under Coronado were kept out of the village of Tiguez by a great shower
of arrows. (F. W. Hodge, ed., *Spanish Explorers in the Southern United States*,
New York, 1907, p. 321.) The "Narrative of the Gentleman of Elvas" concerning De Soto's expedition says flatly that "Before a Christian can make a
single shot with either [crossbow or arquebus], an Indian will discharge
three or four arrows; and he seldom misses of his object. When the arrow
meets with no armor, it pierces as deeply as the shaft from a crossbow" (same,
p. 148); and according to the Inca the Spaniards more or less abandoned
armor for quilted cloaks (i.e. cloaks lined with blankets) as the only viable
protection against Indians who "fired so skillfully and close together that
they had hardly released one arrow before they had placed another in the
bow." (Varner, *The Florida of the Inca*, pp. 180, 236.)

less.* For most of North America throughout most of its history the Indian has been, like the rattlesnake, the alligator, and poison ivy, an inexplicable curse on Utopia. His tawny presence darkened the landscape, and his war whoop chilled the blood.

IV

In 1493 the New World dawned on the European imagination as a few small, delectable islands, any one of which was understandable in terms of a *hortus inclusus,* the walls of which sheltered the Earthly Paradise, or a bower of bliss, or the garden of eternal youth and spring, from the dark wilderness of the world. By 1607 the New World had stretched to an endless and confusing coastline running from Greenland and Baffin Bay through Gargantuan twistings and turnings to the Strait of Magellan and Tierra del Fuego. In any circumstances such geographical extension would have rendered untenable the concept of an isle of youth, verdancy, sunshine, and perpetual spring. But something more troubling than the interminable extension of the land occurred. That something was the discovery of the terror of nature in the New World. In that vast region the extreme thing seemed to happen more often than not. It turned out to be a land of the incredible, the immeasurable, the unpredictable, and the horrifying.

For example, the Elizabethan who read Richard Eden's translation of Peter Martyr (1555) found the New World a strange jumble of phenomena, the abnormal being especially prominent. He might, it is true, get reconciled to white Indians, tortoises so thick they stayed the course of the ships, mountains whereof some were of bright blue or azurine color

---

* The tendency to think that James Fenimore Cooper wrote about the noble savage arises from the obsession readers seem to have with that Byronic young man, Uncas, in *The Last of the Mohicans.* This is to overlook not merely Magua, and Indian John in *The Pioneers,* but also the disillusioned Indian portraits in *The Wept of Wish-ton-Wish, Wyandotté, The Oak Openings,* and other "Indian" novels by Cooper.

and others glistering white, peaks fifty miles high, the disappearance of the North Star, white and thick water, trees of
such bigness that sixteen men joining hands together and
standing in compass could scarcely embrace one of them, and
so on, but what of the many furious seas running with a fall
as if they were the streams of "floods," the whirlpools and
shelves along the shore and in the ocean, with many other
dangers and straits by reason of the multitude of islands, a
river hastening with so swift and furious a course that by the
violence and greatness thereof it drives back the ocean though
the sea be rough and enforced with a contrary wind? There
was, it was rumored, a gigantic lump somewhere in the middle of the earth, there were enormous tides and terrific light-
ning, there were men so huge that one of their feet was almost as long as two feet of a European, bats as big as doves, a
monster which, coming out of the sea, carried away a sailor
from the midst of his companions, a fish of such huge greatness that with a stroke of its tail it broke the rudder of a
brigantine, another that carried off ten men, a curlew as large
as a stork, apples that turned into worms, walking corpses,
and a monster as big as an ox, armed with a long snout like
that of an elephant and yet no elephant, of the color of an ox
and yet no ox, with the "house" of a horse and yet no horse,
with ears much like those of an elephant but not so open or
so hanging down, yet much wider than the ears of other
beasts. I assemble these details at random from a few pages
of a single book.[53] Let us go into more specific instances.

Even Columbus, that religious optimist, was occasionally
appalled by the unbridled forces of nature. Consider this incident from his third voyage:

> And in the night, when it was already very late, being on the
> deck of the ship, I heard a very terrible roaring which came
> from the direction of the south towards the ship. And I stayed
> to watch, and I saw the sea from west to east rising, like a hill
> as high as the ship, and still it came towards me little by little.
> And above it, there came a wave which advanced, roaring with
> a very great noise with the same fury of roaring as that of the

other currents, which, I have said, appeared to me as the waves of the sea breaking on the rocks. To this very day, I remember the fear that I had lest the wave should overwhelm the ship when it came upon her, and it passed by and reached the strait where it continued for a great while.[54]

Things like this did not happen in the tidy Mediterranean.

Other Europeans suffered other experiences equally terrifying. While the Jesuit Father Biard went to visit some Malouins on the island of Emeneic in the Saint John River in French Canada, when he was about a league and a half from his destination, twilight ended, night came on, and the stars appeared, "when suddenly, toward the Northward, a part of the heavens became blood-red: and this light spreading, little by little, in vivid streaks and flashes, moved directly over the settlement of the Malouins and there stopped. The red glow was so brilliant that the whole river was tinged and made luminous by it. This apparition lasted some eight minutes, and as soon as it disappeared another came of the same form, direction and appearance." The good father felt it was prophetic of something, he knew not what; the Indians said it meant war. "Everything was turned topsy-turvey; confusion, discord, rage, uproar reigned between our people and those of St. Malo. I do not doubt that a cursed band of furious and sanguinary spirits were hovering about all this night, expecting every hour and moment a horrible massacre of the few Christians who were there." [55] Let modern man murmur something about the Aurora Borealis if he will; then let him think himself backward to an era when witchcraft was everywhere and Satan roamed a wilderness, seeking whom he might devour.

Or consider the white terror of the north. In the month of July 1497, Sebastian Cabot found monstrous heaps of ice swimming in the sea, amid continual daylight.[56] During Martin Frobisher's first voyage a great island of ice fell apart, making a noise as if a great cliff had fallen into the ocean; during his second voyage, "in place of odoriferous and fragrant smels of sweete gums, & pleasant notes of musicall

birdes, which other Countreys in more temperate Zones do
yeeld, wee tasted the most boisterous Boreal blasts mixt with
snow and haile, in the moneths of June and July"; and on his
third he met "great Isles of yce lying on the seas, like mountaines," in "fogge and hidious mist" so thick the sailors in his
little vessels could not see one another.[57] Once

> the yce had so invironed us, that we could see neither land nor
> sea, as farre as we could kenne: so that we were faine to cut
> our cables to hang over boord for fenders, somewhat to ease
> the ships sides from the great and driry strokes of the yce: some
> with Capstan barres, some fending off with oares, some with
> planckes of two ynches thicke, which were broken immediatly
> with the force of the yce, some going out upon the yce to beare
> it off with their shoulders from the ships. But the rigorousnes
> of the tempest was such, and the force of the yce so great, that
> not onely they burst and spoyled the . . . provision, but like-
> wise so rased the sides of the ships, that it was pitifull to be-
> hold, and caused the hearts of many to faint.[58]

In Warwick Sound "truely it was wonderfull to heare and see
the rushing and noise that the tides do make in this place
with so violent a force that even our ships lying a hull were
turned sometimes round about even in a moment after the
maner of a whirlepoole, and the noyse of the streame no
lesse to be heard afarre off, then the waterfall of London
Bridge." [59] To Elizabethan ears this last comparison was not
an anti-climax. When one considers that the largest vessels
sent on these desperate seas were by our standards mere cock-
leshells, one's respect for the hardihood of the Tudor navy
vastly increases.

The earth was likewise unpredictable. "In the far north
there is great likelihood of Earthquakes or thunder: for that
there are huge and monstrous mountaines, whose greatest
substance are stones, and those stones so shaken with some
extraordinarie meanes that one is separated from another,
which is discordant from all other Quarries." [60] The Jesuits
attributed the extreme cold of Canada to the "wild and primitive condition of the land," which, because of the bound-

less forest, was never warmed by the sun, with the result that the snow and the water stagnated there "with no possibility of being consumed.* Thus, from these lands nothing can arise except cold, gloomy, and mouldy vapors; and these are the fogs when the wind ceases, and are piercing cold when they are put in motion and blown into a fury." [61]

In Middle America, at Darien, "when the slaves sprinkle the floor of the houses, toads spring into existence from the drops of water that fall from their hands, just as in other places I have seen drops of water changed into fleas," [62] and the climate was so insalubrious that Spaniards returning from Panama "are as yellow as though they suffered from liver complaint." Why this affliction in the midst of plenty? For Peter Martyr also informed Pope Leo X that in Panama cabbages, beets, lettuces, salads, and other garden stuff were ripe in ten days and that pumpkins and melons could be picked twenty-eight days after the seeds were sown. [63] Such was the paradox of the New World.

The terrain of South America also had its fearsome aspects. So great was the fury of the current of the Orinoco that "if any boat but touch upon any tree or stake, it is impossible to save any one person therein" and "no halfe day passed, but the river began to rage and overflowe very fearefully, and the raines came downe in terrible showers, and gustes in great abundance." Ralegh, from whom this is taken, saw far off a mountain of crystal like a white church-tower, over which

---

* The matter of the climate of Canada and the north is of particular interest. The first Lord Baltimore, who had visited Newfoundland in 1627 and again in 1628–1629, had been granted a large tract called Avalon, which he tried to colonize, but he had to give it up and founded Maryland in its place. He wrote the king: "Your Majesty may please to understand that I have fownd by too deare bought experience which other men for their private interests always concealed from me, that from the middst of October to the middst of May there is a sadd face of wynter upon all this land, both sea and land so frozen for the greatest part of the tyme as they are not penetrable no plant or vegetable thing appearing out of the earth untill it bee about the beginning of May, nor fish in the sea besides the ayre so intolerable cold as it is hardly to be endured. Bye meanes whereof, and of much salt water, my house hath beene an hospitall all this wynter, of 100 persons 50 sick at a tyme, my self being one and nyne or ten of them dyed." *Archives of Maryland,* Baltimore, 1885, Vol. III, pp. 15–18.

"there falleth . . . a mighty river which toucheth no part of the side of the mountaine, but rusheth over the toppe of it, and falleth to the ground with so terrible a noyse and clamor, as if a thousand great bels were knockt one against another. I thinke there is not in the world so strange an over-fall, nor so wonderfull to behold." ⁶⁴ Wonderful, indeed. Yet in that same strange continent a wind blows through the passes of the Andes "which is not very strong nor violent, but proceeds in such sort, that men fall downe dead, in a manner without feeling, or at the least, they loose their feete and hands: the which may seem fabulous, yet is it most true." This Jerome Costilla discovered, who lost his toes, "which fell off in passing the Desart of Chille, being perished with this ayre, and when he came to looke on them, they were dead . . . even as a rotten Apple falleth from the tree." Even weirder was the sight of the bodies of dead soldiers of Almagro's army lying "without any stinke or corruption" while a young boy kept alive in a cave nearby, feeding on dried horseflesh. "It is a strange thing, the quality of this cold ayre, which kils, and also preserves the dead bodies without corruption."

And there were still different terrors:

. . . the hot exhalations which engender in the inner concavities of the Earth, seeme to be the materiall substance of fire in the Volcans, whereby there kindleth another more grosse matter, and makes these shewes of flame and smoake that come forth. And these exhalations (finding no easie issue in the Earth) move it, to issue forth with great violence, whereby wee heare that horrible noise under the Earth, and likewise the shaking of the Earth, being stirred with this burning exhalation; Even as Gun-powder in mynes, having fire put to it breaks Rocks and Walls: and as the Chesnut laid into the fire, leapes and breakes with a noise, when as it casts forth the aire (which is contayned within the huske) by the force of the fire: Even so these Earthquakes doe most commonly happen in places neere the water or Sea. . . . There hath happened in Peru (the which is wonderfull, and worth to be noted) Earthquakes which have runne from Chille unto Quitto, and that is above a hundred leagues. . . . Upon the coast of Chille . . . there was so terrible an Earthquake, as it overturned whole Mountaines, and thereby stopped the course of Rivers which it converted into Lakes, it beat downe Townes, and slue a great number of people, causing the Sea to leave her place some leagues, so as the ships remayned on drie ground, farre from the ordinarie Roade, with many other heavie and horrible things.[65]

Hispaniola developed sharks, a bitter-sweet lake, divine miracles, and diabolical tricks duly set forth in the Third Decade of Peter Martyr. Oviedo describes crows "whose breath stinketh in the morning, and is sweete in the afternoone: the excrement which they avoide is a living worme" and tells of "Caterpillers, which shine in the night fiftie or a hundred paces off, only from that part of the bodie whence the legges issue: others only have their head shining. I have seene some a spanne long very fearefull." [66] The "crocodile" is again and again described, always in terms of loathing, as "a most fierce and cruell beast, although it be slow and heavie. Hee goes hunting and seekes his prey on the Land, what he takes alive, he drownes it in the water, yet doth he not eate it, but out of the water, for that his throate is of such fashion, as if there entred any water, he should easily be drowned. It is a wonderfull thing to see a combat betwixt a Caymant and a Tigre, whereof there are most cruell at the Indies." [67] This particular "Caymant" carried off a young Indian child and "sodainely plunged into the Sea" with it.

Equally alarming was a "cunning and ferocious animal" whose habitat was, apparently, Venezuela:

It is the size of a French dog and is very rarely seen. When twilight falls, it leaves its hiding-place in the woods and comes into the town, where it prowls about houses, wailing loudly. Those who are ignorant of the animal's subtlety would believe a child was being beaten, and many inexperienced people were deceived into incautiously going to the place where the imaginary child was weeping. The wild beast, lying in wait, then springs upon the unfortunate creature, and in the twinkling of an eye tears him to bits.[68]

Your only protection was to carry a burning torch and whirl
it around, upon seeing which the animal flees. It is seldom
seen in daylight.

And the sea, too, had its horrors. The Gilbert expedition, to
choose only one instance, beheld in the ocean "a very lion
to our seeming, in shape, hair and colour, not swimming
after the maner of a beast by mooving of his feete, but rather
sliding upon the water with his whole body (excepting the
legs) in sight. [He passed by the little fleet] turning his head to
and fro, yawning and gaping wide, with ougly demonstration of long teeth, and glaring eies . . . he sent forth a horrible voyce, roaring or bellowing as doeth a lion." Gilbert,
seeing this monster, rejoiced "that he was to warre against
such an enemie, if it were the devill." [69] But the early accounts
can furnish a whole menagerie, a weird aquarium of such
fearful creatures.

It cannot be argued that these terrors were found everywhere except in the future United States. The Coronado
expedition (1541) not only stumbled into the awe-inspiring
spectacle of the Grand Cañon, but ran into "sandbanks of
hot ashes which it was impossible to cross without being
drowned," where "the ground . . . trembled like a sheet of
paper . . . as if there were lakes underneath," so that "it
seemed wonderful and like something infernal," and also
into a hailstorm with hailstones as big as bowls or bigger, that
fell thick as raindrops.[70] The Narváez expedition started out
numbering six hundred colonists and soldiers, of whom only
four survived, and experienced terrific tempests during which
"we heard much tumult and great clamor of voices, the sound
of timbrels, flutes and tambourines as well as other instruments," and which lodged a boat in the treetops and disfig-
ured some of the dead bodies so that they could not be recognized, but when the pitiful survivors in their crazy boats
came to the mouth of the Mississippi, they were unable to
make for land, so violent was the current, and suffered a
wind that drove them further out to sea, not to speak of
other gigantic calamities.[71] De Soto found the same river so

vast that "a man standing on the shore could not be told, whether he were a man or something else, from the other side," and the gigantic force of the current, flowing turbidly, brought down huge trees; and off the Texas coast the mosquitoes were so numerous that the sails, which were white, appeared black with these insects at daylight, and it was a question whether the men could survive their bites.[72]

The details enumerated in these pages could be increased a thousandfold. I have not troubled to present what I have given in logical order or temporal sequence, preferring to suggest the illogical ways by which such things made their impression upon the European imagination. If the modern reader has acquired a feeling of a vague, rich jungle of repellent or terrifying things, animals, plants, and men, it is the impression he would have received, I suggest, had he been a literate European of the sixteenth or seventeenth century interested in reading about the new-found land. I suggest that this cloud of unpleasantness is one of the reasons why English colonial enterprise was so slow in getting under way. Between the cruelties of the Inquisition in Mexico—and on these one could read the reports of Job Hortop and David Ingram, in Hakluyt—and the cruelties of Satan and his savages, what room was there for the Englishman? Why should the Jacobean enterpriser bestir himself? Few expeditions returned any profit, many of them suffered disaster, and virtually all of them encountered something repellent in the way of climate, soil, wild beasts, wild Indians, or hostile whites. A powerful anti-image was formed.

Nor is the importance of this anti-image of the New World confined to the spacious days of great Elizabeth or those of her immediate successor. Modern literary theory, deeply influenced by the psychology of Freud and Jung, makes much play with the dark night of the American soul; and critics find such writers as Poe, Melville, Hawthorne, and Henry James more to their liking than they do writers like Franklin, Longfellow, Whittier, and Howells. This interesting revolution in taste springs from a sophisticated belief in myth, preferably primitive in tone. The myth-makers, however, do not go deep enough in time. If on the one hand the New World presented to the European Renaissance the possibility of that renewal of mankind that led the Jesuits to establish the almost perfect state in Paraguay and the Fourierists and their kind to create perfect commonwealths in Indiana, or on the Ohio or in the Middle West or in Texas, this obverse image, this other side of the coin, repelled and terrified, while it also fascinated, many minds. The unpredictable, the abnormal, the inhuman, the cruel, the savage, and the strange in terms of European experience were from the beginning part of the image of a land that was ours before we were the land's. The New World was filled with monsters animal and monsters human; it was a region of terrifying natural forces, of gigantic catastrophes, of unbearable heat and cold, an area where the laws of nature tidily governing Europe were transmogrified into something new and strange. Terror and gigantism have their attractions, psychologists say; and the Renaissance image of the New World was compounded of both positive and negative elements that attract and repel. We inherit the image, and its elements haunt us still.

—— ◆◆ III ◆◆ ——

Renaissance Culture and America

I

WE DO not think of the United States as having any connection with the Middle Ages. For one thing, 1492 is a date well within the confines of the Italian Renaissance. For another, it is impossible to know what is meant by *Medieval* and *Renaissance,* both terms having been refined by scholarship to the point of attenuation. Nevertheless, there were such phenomena as a feudal system, a society patterned on status rather than mobility, a culture organized under supernatural sanctions, and though the Renaissance might alter, it did not obliterate, this inheritance. The last enchantments of the Middle Ages hovered about the New World.

The Spain of Ferdinand and Isabella, Charles V, and Philip II, though in it the concept of feudalism yielded to that of a court nobility, was a country in which, or from which, individual adventurers of social status might depart on chivalric quests as Cortés did to fight Indians and as Don Juan of Austria did to fight Moslems, exploits paralleled by those of Captain John Smith. Although Spain and Portugal were Renaissance powers, they transferred a modified feudal system to their colonies, the original captaincies in Brazil being one instance, the *encomienda* system (though more faintly) a second, and the *ayuntamiento,* or medieval conception of the municipality, being a third. The British king,

7 1

James I, tried to establish in Nova Scotia a nobility based on feudal land tenure; and in the case of Virginia, Sigmund Diamond has traced the transition from a pattern of status to one of mobility. In Jamestown under Sir Thomas Dale every male colonist was a soldier, and every corporal, like a medieval yeoman, was responsible for seeing that none of his "Squadron" was absent "when the drumme shall call." Lord Baltimore also received his grant of Maryland on the feudal palatinate system. Sigmund Diamond points out that French Canada was a belated seventeenth-century experiment in feudalism, the seignorial system being an attempt to transplant the French feudal order to North America. "The landed seignior in Canada was entitled to many of the rights possessed by his counterpart in France—potential membership in the nobility; ceremonial rights like fealty and homage; judicial rights like holding private courts; and more lucrative rights such as the collection of rents and mutation fines, the imposition of labor services, and the monopoly of all milling." On the other hand the seigniors displayed little enthusiasm for installing mills, ovens, and the like because the fur trade was more profitable, so that the home government was ever and again urging them to create these instruments for the benefit of the *habitans*.[1] Moreover, vestiges of feudalism in the New World were crisscrossed by the growing commercialism of the sixteenth and seventeenth centuries. Colbert was an economic modernist in many ways, and the Virginia company was a joint-stock enterprise; yet medieval forms do not vanish by virtue of these truths, and if Diamond's conclusion be sound that in North America the need to recruit a voluntary labor force was the mother of liberty, we have the odd paradox that insofar as home governments imposed a quasi-medieval pattern upon their colonies, they unwittingly fostered the very "liberty" they were trying to keep down.[2]

The doctrine of the just price, the theory that usury is a sin, the notion of a social unit as a communal enterprise so managed that a common stock will take care of all the members—

notions like these may have had their origins in Greek, Latin, Jewish, and early Christian thought, but they are so strongly associated with medieval theory, we may justly range them under this rubric. These concepts and others like them colored New World colonization. The most important adaptation of medieval economic theory was the Jesuit communal state in Paraguay, established to Christianize the Guaraní Indians, the one signal success of its kind in history. Units in this commonwealth were organized on a semi-communal system of agriculture, mechanic arts, and public works, in an autonomous pattern under theological control, and so firm was the adherence to the theory of a just price that as late as 1901, if R. B. Cunninghame Graham is to be believed, Paraguayan Indians refused to undersell each other in the market-place.[3] When the king of Spain expelled the Jesuits from his dominions in the later eighteenth century, the commonwealth fell into ruin.

In North America a theory of communal economic responsibility seemed at first sight necessary and efficient, but at Jamestown, Plymouth, and other colonies it broke down quickly because free land was available to any enterpriser who would run off and exercise squatter's rights. The doctrine of the just price and a pejorative interpretation of interest as usury had longer lives. In Massachusetts Bay the gallant attempt of the Reverend John Cotton and his fellow ministers to maintain the doctrine of a just price was defeated in 1639 when Robert Keaine or Keayne of Boston was fined by the General Court for "notoriously" oppressing the buyer, only to have his fine reduced by the magistrates on the ground it was common practice elsewhere "for men to make use of advantages for raising the prices of their commodities." The minister denounced this kind of thing as un-Christian, but the General Court nevertheless rejected Cotton's legal code ("Moses his judicials") and adopted the "Body of Liberties" prepared by Nathaniel Ward, a clergyman of more liberal views.[4] Before we dismiss these vestiges of medieval economic (and religious) theory as a mere quaint footnote to American progress, let us remember that the Populist revolt of the nineteenth century and the support of farm prices in the twentieth are, if not results, at least curious parallels to the doctrine of a just price and of community responsibility for economic health.

Possibly more important is the concept of a theologically controlled, or at any rate a theologically centered, commonwealth. The transformation in Europe of the centrality of pope and emperor into the idea of *cuius regio, eius religio* is a complex problem. Neither theory was consistently held in the Old World. Américo Castro, in discussing Spain, too often considered to be medieval and rigid in matters of religion, can insist upon the extraordinary degree in that nation of religious tolerance and cross-fertilization among Moors, Jews, and Christians as late as the fifteenth century.[5] But the organization of the church, essentially medieval, was eventually transferred to the New World, and the creation of the Spanish Inquisition by the Catholic monarchs in 1480 narrowed the area of tolerance. When this was followed by the extension of the Inquisition to the Indies, the bishop of Porto Rico being the first American inquisitor-general delegate, it was inevitable that under Philip II a medieval *auto-da-fé* be held in the New World, as it was in Mexico in 1574. Doubtless the Inquisition was not as bad as it has been painted, but in Tenochtitlán, nevertheless, human sacrifice had been succeeded by the terrors of the secular arm, not relaxed until the time of the Spanish Bourbons. The narratives of Job Hortop, Miles Philips, David Ingram, and Robert Tomson show with what horror the Mexican Inquisition was regarded by the English.[6] If the Portuguese were more easygoing, Louis XIV did what he could to seal Canada against contamination by Protestants, so that French Canada became almost as much a theological commonwealth as Paraguay or New England.

How far this kind of thing is to be credited to the medieval inheritance of Western man may be debated. Certainly it does not represent the freedom of mind customarily asso-

ciated with the Renaissance. Nor should it be forgotten that
in Virginia the Anglican Church was, from the first planting,
the official church, remaining so until the acceptance by that
commonwealth of Jefferson's statute of religious freedom in
1785. Indeed, there was almost always some vestige of religious establishment in most of the English colonies. The
most famous example of a commonwealth dominated by
theology is of course the Massachusetts Bay Colony in the
seventeenth century. The philosophy and practice of New
England theology have been often analyzed, inevitably in
terms of the Protestant Reformation. But how far New England theological practice was medieval, how far it was colored
by the Renaissance, how far the Reformation was "modern"
—these are questions every specialist settles according to his
temperament and training. If New England orthodoxy lacked
the thumbscrew and the rack and had to content itself with
"pressing," hanging, and banishment, it was during the brief
years of its ascendancy the one consistent theocracy, aside
from Paraguay, in the Americas, nor should the intellectual
brilliance of New England theology conceal its essentially
medieval base. Not the tolerance of Rhode Island and
Pennsylvania but the intolerance of a *Historia contra Paganos*
is, one fears, more characteristic of the Bay Colony than the
ideals of Erasmus, more widely disseminated in New Spain.
So far as this attitude is medieval, it was a medievalism that
deliquesced under pressures of a thousand sorts. It remained
for a burgeoning Catholicism in the later nineteenth and
twentieth centuries to reinstate in American education the
scholastic philosophy.

Since a theocracy is impossible in this country under its
present constitution, these waifs and strays of medievalism,
once active on distant borders as in the case of Mexico, or
quaintly historical as in the case of Massachusetts, may seem
to have an antiquarian interest only. Yet we possess a continuing medieval inheritance, however shadowy, and this
inheritance creates its anomalies. Blessings have been invoked on human beings in many countries in many centuries

in many religious formulae. It is, however, a mark of the tenacity of one phase of medieval belief that in a twentieth-century republic governed by a constitution that never refers to the deity and that separates church and state, we cannot hold a commencement in a public high school or inaugurate a President without invoking God in a manner Saint Augustine and Saint Thomas Aquinas would not disapprove. We want our governors and teachers divinely inspired, whatever the Supreme Court may decide about prayer in the public school systems.

It may also be argued at this point that the Gothic revival in nineteenth-century American architecture, productive of such masterpieces as the "Glen Ellen" (Maryland) of Alexander Jackson Davis in 1832, Richard Upjohn's Trinity Church in New York City in 1846, James Renwick's St. Patrick's Cathedral in the same city and his more doubtful Smithsonian Institution (1846–1855) in Washington, and the original scheme for the University of Chicago in 1892–1893, is relevant. The same movement of course produced a great deal of pine Gothic in church architecture and of domestic Gothic sometimes buried under carpenter's frenzy, and all this may be claimed as proof of a continuing medieval inheritance. Moreover, there were published various poetical "lays" and narrative romances in the manner of Scott, not to speak of historical novels, nor should one forget the tournaments characteristic of "chivalry" in the Southern states, or the knights of this or that, now existing as fraternal orders, religious associations, and so on. The Ku Klux Klan has been traced to the Vehmgericht. But discontinuity intervenes, and I think it safer to trace all this kind of medievalism to the romantic movement, the vogue of Ruskin in America, and the popularity of Victorian Gothic architecture rather than to some subterranean connection with the actual medieval inheritance of the New World.

Of greater significance perhaps is the impressive record of medievalism in scholarship produced by American enthusiasm for German university scholarship and by the genetic explanation of institutions in a Darwinian and Spencerian universe. Henry Adams, who studied, however disdainfully, at Berlin and Dresden in 1858–1860, when he was appointed to a chair in medieval history at Harvard in 1870 threw himself, he said, into the arms of the Anglo-Saxons and published in 1876 his *Essays on Anglo-Saxon Law*. The historian of the Norman conquest, Edward Augustus Freeman, toured the country in 1881, preaching the theory that there were three Germanies—Germany proper, England, and the United States—and encouraged Professor Herbert Baxter Adams at the Johns Hopkins University to discover the roots of the New England town meeting in the depths of the Teutoburger forest. By 1894 Professor George Burton Adams of Yale (medievalism seemed to be a monopoly of people named Adams) brought out his admirable *Civilization during the Middle Ages*. In 1918 Professor Charles H. Haskins of Harvard published the first of a line of distinguished contributions, *Norman Institutions* (1918), followed by *Studies in Medieval Science* (1924) and *Studies in Medieval Culture* (1929). An important confluent was the enthusiasm of the Dante circle in Cambridge, originally assembled to hear Longfellow read his translation of the *Divine Comedy*, which was published in three volumes in 1867. Lowell's influential essay on Dante was included in *Among My Books* (1890), and Charles Eliot Norton's versions of *The New Life* (1892) and the *Divine Comedy* (in three volumes, 1892–1893) are a kind of climax to nineteenth-century medievalism. Meanwhile the art museums were collecting in that vast field. Interest in the history of the medieval culture waxes and wanes, but it reached a kind of double peak in the creation of the Medieval Academy of America in 1925 and of "The Cloisters" near Fort Tryon Park in New York City in the late 1930s. All this, however, did not affect the general life as did the communal system of the original settlements or the just-price doctrine, against which Keayne rebelled.

II

Our problem, however, is to inquire what the Renaissance meant to the New World, and eventually to the United States. Few Americans realize how large a fraction of American history lies in the sunlight or shadow of that great age. From 1492 to the establishment of Jamestown in 1607 is 115 years, a lapse of time equal to that between the inauguration of Washington in 1789 and the election of Theodore Roosevelt in 1904, or one-quarter of the total period of American history. When Columbus landed on Watling Island, Alexander VI was pope, Cesare Borgia would be made cardinal in 1493, and in 1494 Charles VIII was to invade Italy, an expedition that opened a period of misery for Italy and led to the northward spread of Renaissance ideas. When Jamestown was founded, *Antony and Cleopatra* was just being written, *The Alchemist* had not been produced, *Don Quixote* was but two years old, and the first opera that has come down to us, Monteverdi's *Orfeo,** had been sung only five years earlier. American history is more deeply rooted than most of us realize. In 1492 Copernicus was precisely twenty-one and had gone to the University of Kraków the previous year to study medicine, theology, mathematics, and astronomy; the world had to wait until 1530 for his *De Revolutionibus Orbium Coelestium.*

Renaissance influence upon American culture springs from several sources, but mainly from the great colonizing empires of the Mediterranean world and from Great Britain. The Portuguese influence was least, the Spanish influence the richest, the English influence the most immediate of these formative contacts. Historians have abandoned notions prevalent in the nineteenth century that the Spanish Empire in the New World was the product of cruel, unenlightened, lazy, or ineffectual men, albeit there were cruel, unenlightened, lazy, and ineffectual Spaniards, including some highly placed officials. The

---

* For his *Euridice* (1600) Peri wrote only the voice part and the bass except for the short ritornelli for three flutes. Monteverdi really scored his opera.

Spaniards invented a system of colonial administration unparalleled since the days of ancient Rome; in religion they launched the most sweeping missionary movement since the Germanic tribes accepted Christianity; and in the matter of race relations, though the Indians were unquestionably exploited and occasionally so oppressed that they rose in bloody rebellion against their conquerors, the Spanish government, in harmony with the church, adopted a theory, and often succeeded in practicing a policy, more enlightened than that of any other European power except Portugal. As for culture, the Spaniards transplanted dynamic forms of Renaissance art, thought, and institutions to the Americas with amazing quickness. Fascinating as a romantic figure, the conquistador makes but a transient appearance in colonial history. By the mid-sixteenth century the viceregal system, backed up by the Council of the Indies and the Casa de la Contratación in Spain, had substituted for the anarchy of slaughter—consider the bloody history of the conquest of Peru—a peaceful centralized administration that undoubtedly suffered from delay [7] and disobedience—"I obey but I do not enforce," ran a famous phrase—but that also, especially when improved in the eighteenth century, brought prosperity and progress to Latin America.[8] It would have been better for Spain, perhaps, if gold and silver had not existed so palpably in the New World; yet by 1650 the "Indies" supported about ten and a half million souls, of whom probably about 80 per cent were Indians living (at least the majority of them) conformably to the Spanish colonial system. What the population of British North America was in 1650 I do not know. Fifty years later it was about three hundred thousand, and in that part of the world the Indian and the white man were mortal enemies.

It was this Spanish culture, founded in medievalism, reshaped by the Renaissance, and transformed by the Baroque and by the Enlightenment, with which the English, after them the British and the British North Americans, and finally the citizens of the United States were incessantly in contact from the days of the Elizabethan admiral, Drake, to the days of the American admiral, Dewey. It deserves a little study, both because it is interesting in itself and because, as someone has written, in any broad view of the New World, the history of the United States, despite our appropriation of the term "American," is local history.

This is true both chronologically and topographically. The total superficial area of North, Central, and South America is over 15½ million square miles; the total superficial area of the United States proper is a little over 3 million square miles, or about one-fifth of the whole. Spanish sovereignty once extended as far north as the Carolinas on the Atlantic Seaboard and beyond San Francisco Bay on the Pacific Coast, embracing at one time or another the Carolinas, Georgia,[9] Florida, Alabama, Mississippi, Tennessee, Louisiana, Texas, New Mexico, Arizona, Arkansas, Oklahoma, Missouri, Kansas, Colorado, Utah, Nevada, Iowa, Nebraska, Wyoming, Idaho, Minnesota, the two Dakotas, and, on the Pacific Coast, California,[10] or parts of these states.* About two-thirds of the continental United States owes something to Spanish culture, if it be no more than the two thousand Spanish place names on our map. When the American Revolution ended, so much of the North American continent as was not allotted to the young republic was assigned to three imperial powers—France, which drew almost nothing, Great Britain, which retained Canada and various northern areas of the present United States (such as parts of Maine and the Oregon country), and Spain, which retained everything west of the Mississippi and south of the Oregon country (disputed among Russia, Great Britain, and Spain), and, in addition, Florida and a kind of no man's land south of the Tennessee and west of the Chattahoochee. North American contacts

* In 1780 a Spanish force hoisted their flag at or near Saint Joseph, Michigan, and in 1793 a Spanish expedition reached the Mandan country in North Dakota. The Spaniards at one time penetrated to Alaska. In the east the Spanish possession of Georgia was at one time a real threat to the Carolinas; not until 1702 did the English push the frontier back beyond the Saint John's River.

with Hispanic culture have been at once constant and intermittent, by way of the Caribbean and Central America, by
way of Florida, Alabama, Mississippi, and Louisiana, by
way of Mexico (however defined), and by way of the Pacific
Coast. Over a vast area Spain has sometimes done no more
than establish vague claims, but it has elsewhere left behind
perdurable testimony of its influence—the Spanish language
in New Mexico, the missions of California and the Southwest,
city plans for municipalities, a vocabulary for the cattleman,
and lasting fashions in art, music, architecture, and costume,
and habits.[11]

The inauguration of the viceregal system for the government of the Spanish colonial empire, essentially begun when
Antonio de Mendoza was appointed in 1529 (though he did
not reach America until 1535), marked the creation of a great
Renaissance empire in some sense on Roman lines, in some
sense on medieval lines, and in some sense on the lines of the
modern national state. Through his viceroys the king ruled
with a higher degree of absolutism in America than he ruled
with in Spain; and since the church in the New World, by
agreement with the Vatican, was under the direct control of
the crown except in matters of doctrine and religious discipline, the Renaissance theory of *cuius regio, eius religio* was
developed more consistently in the Spanish dominions than
it ever was in British North America. A caste system was
likewise created. At the bottom, after they came, were the
Negro slaves, above them the mass of Indians, and above them
the Spanish overlords in two groups—the commoners, and
the aristocracy of state and church. But the aristocracy was
also divided into two groups, the antagonism between which
was eventually to become an important force in the movement toward independence when the *criollos* of all classes
tended to unite against the *peninsulares*. The viceroys as
representatives of the crown naturally maintained a quasi-
regal state; and the crown naturally preferred administrators it could send out and recall, to colonials who might have
odd ideas about autonomy. The great offices were therefore

monopolized by the *peninsulares*—that is, by Iberians. The utmost dignity to which the native-born *criollo* could in most cases aspire was a post in some municipal council *(cabildo)*, although for him movement upward in the ecclesiastical hierarchy was perhaps easier than in that created by the secular state.[12]

This caste system was complicated by another element. Aztec and Inca societies had likewise been organized on a caste pattern and ruled by an "emperor." While unions between Spanish common soldiers and Indian females produced *mestizos*, the Spanish nobility in the colonies did not think it beneath them to marry into the ranks of what they construed to be the nobility of empires they had conquered; * and some of the children of these upper-class unions rose in time to become influential administrators, writers, priests, artists, and architects, occasionally going to Spain and there becoming part of the peninsular nobility.[13] The most celebrated of such personalities was probably the Inca Garcilaso de la Vega. Such unions were rendered more natural by the atmosphere of chivalric honor Spanish authors managed to cast over the history of the imperial conquests. Despite prohibitions, there was a steady flow of romances of chivalry into the Spanish colonies; [14] and, as John Van Horne has shown, the Indian as an enemy, not being a Protestant, seems not to have suffered in Spanish narrative poetry the degradation suffered by heretic Englishmen. On the contrary, he is dowered with the attributes of a brave, spirited, and patriotic foe, as if he were a knight of the Round Table or a cavalier at the court of Charlemagne.[15] In this connection it is illuminating to remember that Voltaire thought a speech by the Indian cacique Colocolo in Canto II of Part I of Ercilla's *La Araucana*,[16] the epic *par excellence* of Spanish-Indian warfare, surpassed anything in Homer, a judgment that seems excessive. But one finds oneself meditating on the solitary case of the marriage of the "princess" Pocahontas to the middle-class

---

* For example, Juan de Oñate, the conqueror of New Mexico, married Isabel Tolosa Cortés Montezuma, a descendant of both Cortés and Montezuma.

John Rolfe, in contrast to this intermingling of races in Spanish America. In Brazil, of course, racial intermingling was even greater.

To the eye of the cultural historian this Renaissance culture has a curious sense of timelessness, though it changed with the changing years. An important cohesive element was ceremony, the more necessary, Spaniards thought, because the barbaric splendors of the Incan and Aztec courts were never quite forgotten. By 1748, the date of the celebrated official visitation of the "Indies" by Jorge Juan and Antonio de Ulloa, ceremony had become consecrated by time, and their description of viceregal splendor of Lima (which could be paralleled at Mexico City) still has its fascination.

> For the safety of his person and the dignity of his office, he [the viceroy] has two bodies of guards; one of horse, consisting of 160 private men, a captain, and a lieutenant: Their uniform is blue, turned up with red, and laced with silver. This troop consists entirely of picked men, and all Spaniards. The captain's post is esteemed very honourable. . . . The 2d is that of the *Halbadiers* [*sic*] consisting of 50 men, all Spaniards; dressed in a blue uniform, and crimson velvet waistcoats laced with gold. These do duty in the rooms leading to the chamber of audience, and private apartments. They also attend the vice-roy when he appears in public, or visits the offices, and tribunals. The only officer of this body is a captain, whose post is reckoned very eminent.

This may be a little like the look of the stage in the first act of *Carmen* but it is nonetheless impressive.

When a new viceroy arrived on the Pacific coast, litters, mules, and booths were made ready for him and his entourage. He formally notified Lima of his arrival, traveled to Callao incognito, lodged there at the viceregal palace, which was "adorned with astonishing magnificence," and the next day received in stately order all the officials, the corporations, the professors, the priests, and so on. The second day he lumbered in his coach to a place halfway between Callao and Lima, where his displaced predecessor met him, embraced him, and yielded to him his staff of office. On the day of the new viceroy's entrance into Lima "the streets are cleaned, and hung with tapestry, and magnificent triumphal arches erected at proper distances. At two in the afternoon the vice-roy goes privately to the church . . . which is separated by an arch and a gate from the street, where the cavalcade is to begin."

A splendid procession was then formed, the viceroy and his retinue on horseback, the university professors in their gowns, the magistracy in crimson velvet robes, and innumerable other corporations and official bodies, each properly garmented. The procession went through the streets to the great square before the cathedral, where the new royal representative was met by the archbishop and the chapter, a Te Deum was sung after all had been seated in their proper order, the procession re-formed, the viceroy went on to his palace in Lima and was there "conducted to an apartment in which a splendid collation is provided, as are also others for the nobility in the anti-chambers [sic]." The following day there were other ceremonial visits, masses, and dinners, the viceroy being everywhere attended "by all the nobility, who omit nothing to make a splendid figure on these occasions." There were five days of bullfights, disputations by university students, a contest among poets for prizes, and other festivities, and, say the reporters significantly, "these ceremonies, which greatly heighten the magnificence of this city, are so little known in Europe, that I shall be excused for enlarging on them." [17] Obviously ceremony, as Bacon said it should be, was a mode of social control.

The viceroys, the missionary orders, and the secular clergy became patrons of art and learning in less than half a century after Columbus's landing. The ideas of Erasmus and Sir Thomas More were taught in Spanish America long before the ideas of Ramus were taught at Harvard College; and as early as 1537 Fray Juan Graces, bishop of Tlaxcala, wrote Pope Paul III from Mexico about his pleasure in finding Indian children quite as teachable as white children, able to learn Latin, Castilian, and other subjects. (Harvard was to graduate its solitary Indian alumnus, Caleb Cheeshahteaymuck, in 1665.) The priority of universities is as much a matter of zealous dispute as protocol in a foreign office; Santo Domingo claims precedence by reason of a papal bull of 1538 which gave university standing to a Dominican school on that island. As early as 1536, however, a college for the sons of Indian chiefs (Santa Cruz de Tlatelolco) was founded by the Franciscans; the University of Mexico (which had twenty-three chairs by the end of the seventeenth century) dates from 1553, the University of San Marcos in Lima from 1572. At the request of an archbishop the first printing press in the New World was set up in Mexico in 1539 by one Giovanni Paoli, a century before Stephen Day started his printing plant in Cambridge. The first printed book in the Americas is said to be Fray Juan de Guevara's *Christian Doctrine,* written in Huasteco; and the great Fray Bernardino de Sahagún, a true son of the Renaissance, produced his valuable *Historia General de las Cosas de la Nueva España* in Castilian and Náhuatl between 1540 and 1569. When in 1585 a forlorn little band of Englishmen were trying to stick it out on Roanoke Island, three hundred poets were competing for a prize in Mexico City. In 1604, three years before Jamestown, Bernard de Balbuena or Valbuena produced his poem in eight cantos, a prologue, and an epilogue, *Grandeza Mexicana,* to celebrate the beauty of a great city, the loveliness of its gardens, the splendor of its buildings, the attractiveness of its women, and the aristocratic quality of its men.[18] In the last quarter of the seventeenth century the University of Mexico boasted of Carlos de Sigüenza y Góngora, mathematician, poet, historian, archaeologist, philosopher, another son of the Renaissance; and in 1651 was born that amazing genius Sor Juana Inez de la Cruz, poet, prose-writer, dramatist, scientist, scholar, musician, folklorist, mystic, and wit, who is said to have matched her knowledge and her quickness against twoscore university professors and won. Indeed, as late as 1802, when the scientific-minded Jefferson was

President, the great Alexander von Humboldt announced that there was no city in the Western Hemisphere, including the United States, that had such large and solid scientific institutions as did the Mexican capital.

Anglo-Saxon response to this stately and brilliant culture was long hostile and negative. Elizabethan gentlemen-adventurers leading piratical expeditions into the Caribbean occasionally, it is true, met with grave, traditional Spanish courtesy and sometimes responded in kind; but in general the Anglo-Saxons were bewildered, exasperated, or contemptuous of Spanish Catholicism, Spanish stubbornness, the slow pattern of Spanish colonial life, governed by the necessity of referring all important decisions to some remote central authority. Successors of the Elizabethan seadogs continued this attitude.[19] The American backwoodsman and riverman, anxious to open the mouth of the Mississippi for trade, and to smuggle contraband past the *guarda costa*, could make little or nothing of the dilatoriness or the obstinacy of Spanish officialdom in New Orleans or the Floridas. The same blank incomprehension led Andrew Jackson into some highly dubious * military and political actions.[20] Stephen Austin's difficulties in Texas arose in part from the fact that Mexican officials in Texas, heirs of the Spanish system, had to refer every problem to Mexico City; and in California the long and mounting tension between "Americans" and *"caballeros"* exhibits the same kind of misunderstanding between two cultures, two religions, two worlds. But in cultural history a relation of negation is sometimes as important as one of assent.

---

* The Americans built Fort Crawford on the Spanish frontier, then faced the necessity of provisioning it by way of the Escambia River, which runs into Pensacola Bay. This required permission for American goods to pass through Spanish territory unhindered and untaxed. Local Spanish officials could only say they were there to enforce the law, and advise the Americans to refer their problem to the governor-general in Havana, though some supplies were allowed to pass "in the name of humanity." Matters went from one annoying episode to another until the American commander, Gaines, wrote a letter to the Spanish commandant, which, says the judicious historian Bassett, "for raw and undignified manner ought to make any courteous American blush to this day."

Before 1898 the most vivid encounter between the Yankees and the culture of Hispanic America was the Mexican War. Casual reading among books by such American observers as left their impressions in print seems to show two or three standard responses to the relics of the Spanish Renaissance: curiosity about ceremony, stock pathos evoked by ruins, interest in the exotic, and bewilderment at the backwardness of Mexicans, crossed with respect for the bravery of the Mexican soldier and disgust with alleged Mexican cruelty. Even before the forties, Edward Thornton Tayloe, a member of the legation staff of Joel R. Poinsett, the first American minister to Mexico, after preparing himself by reading Mexican history and such authorities as Humboldt, recorded in detail the ceremonies celebrating the anniversary of Mexican independence (which clearly descend in part from the viceregal days), horror at the treatment of criminals in Vera Cruz in 1825, the contrast between the splendor of the cathedral in Mexico City and filthy streets "thronged with the dirtiest, the most diseased, deformed and half naked wretches you can imagine," and the "tattered grandeur" of a *hacienda* he visited. He rejoiced in the expulsion of the friars and found a good many absurdities in Mexican Catholicism, but he was not militantly Protestant.[21] Albert M. Gilliam, "late consul to California," a sentimental and silly person, was violently opposed to Santa Anna and to the church, but, traveling in Mexico in 1843, he allowed his thoughts to "revel" in the country's early history, seriously believed that rich Spaniards in the old days paved the streets between their houses and the baptismal font with bars of gold and silver when their children were baptized, and in Vera Cruz rhapsodized after this sort:

> There can be beheld the broken columns and fallen dome of a proud and lofty church, where once pealed the notes divine of a solemn organ. Indeed, ruin and decay may be seen in all,— in whatever direction the eyes may be turned. . . . How impressively does the scene of this place remind the looker-on of the vanity and futility of all human things; and how melan-

choly the reflection to him who stands on the spot and medita-
tively contemplates over the falling dwellings and palaces;
where once the Spanish *belle,* with her tuned guitar, sweetly
warbled her touching notes in the ears of her lover;—falling
into heaps of mouldering rubbish.

It is not clear whether the lover or the building falls into
rubbish, but "tuned guitar" is a neat phrase. Gilliam knew no
Spanish, a deficiency that did not prevent him from including in his volume of *Travels* a lengthy and hostile biography
of Santa Anna, in an appendix.[22]

Brantz Mayer, secretary to the American legation in 1841–
1842, was a far more intelligent man who devoted a great
deal of space to Mexican antiquities, attended a ceremony
over which Santa Anna presided with dignity, exclaimed
over the brutality of the Mexican civil war, cock-fighting, and
the treatment of prisoners, pungently described the *lépero*
class of the Mexican proletariat, did not care for the church,
and urged Santa Anna to model himself upon George Washington. He, too, admired cathedrals, and, apologizing for
being rude, nevertheless firmly asserted that the priesthood
served both God and Mammon. But he admired Santa Anna's
regiments, had nothing but "kindly recollections of the
people, and none but favorable impressions of the mass of
a society, in which I had been taught to believe that I should
be held in utter antipathy as a heretical stranger," and
thought that Mexico would improve only after ridding itself of "Spanish bigotry" and through European immigration. His sympathetic book concludes with a prophetic warning against foreign intervention.[23]

These writers precede hostilities between the United
States and Mexico. William W. Carpenter, a member of a
Kentucky regiment of volunteers, was captured by the Mexicans and on the whole had little good to say of them, even
though he was protected by various nationals of that country,
including a priest, during his incredible captivity, escape,
and wanderings. But E. Kirby Smith, stimulated by the fact
that the American force landing at Vera Cruz followed

Cortés's ancient route to Tenochtitlàn, writes from the castle
of Perote in 1847 about the ruins of an old "palace": "The
inhabitants know nothing of its history and it has evidently
been abandoned for centuries. . . . Here knights have armed
for the battle and celebrated their victories on their return.
Here blushing beauty has listened to the amorous tale. . . .
Where are they all now?" His mind has obviously been
colored by Sir Walter Scott.[24] Thomas B. Thorpe pays tribute
to the architecture of the cathedral at Monterrey, "a curious
mixture of the Grecian and Moorish," which he found pleasing, but dwells at length upon the "dreadful appearance"
of the halls of justice and the prisons with their "crowded
grated windows" that give "fearful evidence of the narrow
cells within, and the hopelessness of escape, except in death,"
and reports that a "lone Mexican sentinel" gave "additional
repulsiveness to the building." *He* has an air of having read
Melmoth the Wanderer.[25] Dr. Richard M'Sherry could find
no other explanation of Mexican defeat than the absence of
a bourgeoisie. Mexico lacked, he avers, "the first element of
national greatness, *i.e.,* a people." He found "aristocracy and
dregs," but "the sturdy middle class, the bone and sinew, ay,
the *vital element,* exists not here." While we are continuing
our fantasy about reading, his view of a people vaguely suggests Michelet.[26] It is, however, interesting to find only mild
hostility to Catholicism in most of these accounts and to note
that the relations between the invading armies and the Mexicans seem curiously amiable. But the reconciliation of a Renaissance inheritance, however decayed, and a doctrine of
Yankee progress was clearly difficult.

Part of the ambiguity arises from notions of Americanism
on either continent. Latin American thinkers have their
own mystique of Americanism. Not the conquest of a New
World by industry, but the fusion of two great peoples into
a new race of men is the point of view of an Americanist
such as the Mexican Alfonso Reyes (1889–1959), so much a
man of the Renaissance even in the twentieth century,[27]
Mariano Picón Salas said, that, along with Ortega y Gasset

and Miguel de Unamuno, he must be reckoned one of the few universal men of our time. Reyes' *Vision of Anáhuac* (1915) is a prose poem, a meditation on the strength and splendor of the Aztecs, his "Thoughts on the American Mind" (1939) ignores industrial expansion to talk about the cultural mission of American man: "My feeling [is] that the American mind is called upon to fulfill the highest complementary function: that of establishing syntheses, even though they be of necessity provisional; that of applying the results quickly, testing the truth of the theory on the living tissues of action. In this way, just as European economy now has need of us, so will the mind of Europe need us, too." Why? Because Latin American culture is by the very law of its being international, yet deeply rooted. Like José Vasconcelos he thinks of Latin Americans as the "cosmic race." He argues that "our America" should rededicate itself to the dream the discovery gave rise to among the thinkers of Europe: the dream of Utopia. His essay, "The Position of America," is an analysis of the elements of the new culture he sees being shaped.[28] This may look like William James, but Reyes' language is not the language of pragmatism nor that of the cold war, and it is perhaps significant how few of our writers —Mary Austin and Waldo Frank are among this minority [29] —are willing to grant Alfonso Reyes and his compatriots the premises from which he argues.

III

American response to the transplanted Renaissance tradition in New Spain has not been wholly negative. The great edifices of the Spanish colonial empire—cathedrals, palaces, the houses of the rich, the government structures, the fortifications, and the missions—were, many of them, built in a great period of Spanish architecture [30] and are, despite earthquake, war, and neglect, the most nearly perdurable remains of Hispanic colonial culture. In Santo Domingo the original architecture was thoroughly Spanish, but as the empire spread, as the work of the friars was extended, Indian craftsmen were trained to imitate plateresque, *mudéjar,* baroque, and rococo ornamentation, often harmonizing it with their own traditions, as is evident in Peru. Wandering Anglo-Saxons admired these rich and powerful structures in the West Indies, Mexico, Central America, along the Pacific Coast, and elsewhere; and in those portions of the United States that were once parts of Spain some of these structures still stand—the Cabildo in New Orleans, the Cathedral of Saint Augustine (burned in 1887 but rebuilt) in Florida, the Spanish missions in Texas, the Southwest (see Pl. V), and California. As one moves northward from Mexico, ornamentation on these buildings decreases, and on the old Spanish frontier the mission was often a fort as well as a church, a hospital, a school, and a hostelry. Sometimes, as in Arizona, adobe replaced brick and stone. But the beauty of the buildings that remain has had its effect upon American taste. The Santa Barbara mission in California is incomparable; the ornamentation by Huisar * of the façade of the mission at San José, Texas, is a lasting treasure; the lines of even so simple a structure as that at San Juan Bautista in California are simple and functional.[31] They have stirred the North American imagination.

The so-called Spanish revival in American architecture of the twentieth century is in part a renewal of Renaissance and baroque forms. Not all North American "Spanish" architecture is either Spanish or architecture, as the decoration of night clubs, "circus" movie houses, and cheaply built apartments and hotels immediately testifies. Yet the courthouse at Pima, Arizona, and the tower of the California building in Balboa Park in San Diego (Pl. VI) are examples of Spanish revival amply justified by site and tradition. When one moves to a somewhat more gaudy example of the plateresque (at least I think that was the intent), as in a Tampa theater, the

---

* Huisar or Huicar seems to have been a descendant of the architect who designed the Alhambra, or a major part of it.

problem of the commercial arises, as it did, far more amusingly, with the construction of the Roxy Theater in New York, since demolished. Roxy's was a magnificent example of commercial Spanish, some parts of which, like the curate's egg, were very good indeed. As for "domestic" Spanish, Renaissance or otherwise, a walk through any unit of suburbia will reveal examples of architecture styles that go back at least to the Spanish Habsburgs.

North American interest in the great painters of Spain [32] owes little or nothing to the Spanish colonial empire and in fact melts into the general vogue, both popular and scholarly, of Renaissance painting in the United States that virtually begins with the generation of Washington Allston. Spanish American painting from the sixteenth century forward is virtually unknown to North Americans until the period of Orozco in Mexico. Without passing aesthetic judgment on the comparative worth of this art, one may note that altar pieces and official portraits were the principal kinds of painting in demand in the Spanish empire. The twentieth-century vogue of Orozco and his compeers does little for countries south of Mexico and seems to be part of the enthusiasm for popular, primitive, or "revolutionary" themes that have nothing to do with the Spanish Renaissance. The vogue of Aztec, Incan, and Mayan decorative motifs, like other revaluations of "native" art (the Navajo rug is an example), likewise has little connection with the Renaissance world, however grateful the moderns may be to ecclesiastics who preserved as much of the native cultures as they did. But when we pass from painting and the graphic arts generally to music, the problem is a little more complicated.

Spanish music is compounded of many simples—Arabic rhythms, Oriental *fioriture,* the music of the gypsies, the influence of Flemish composers in sixteenth-century Spain, the vogue of the Italian madrigal in the peninsula, the invention of the *zarzuela* (Spanish equivalent of the *opéra comique),* Spanish interest in organ music and organ-building, the vogue of the guitar (especially in its earlier form) among the aristocracy, and enormous debates about the theory and practice of musical composition. When some portion of the art was transferred to the New World, music was soon involved with African rhythms, the Negro (and Indian) love of percussion instruments, primitive religious rites involving music and dancing, and much else. On top of this extraordinary mixture the eighteenth-century colonists imported European opera as a kind of status symbol, composing operas of their own—in 1708, for example, Mexico City heard a *Rodrigo* and in 1711 a *Parténope* by "native" composers such as Fray Manuel Zumaya. If one puts aside recent interest in "early" music which includes the compositions of so characteristic a Renaissance composer as Tomás Luis de Victoria (ca. 1549–1611), a contemporary of Palestrina, born in Old Castile and dying in Madrid, North American interest, despite the vogue of such musicians as Albéniz and Falla, has been most strongly colored by traditional "folk" music from the Caribbean and Mexico and by Latin American dance music, the vogue of the tango and the rumba being representative. Whether one has in mind compositions like "La Bamboula," "Le Bananier," "Ojos Criollos," and "La Noche de los Trópicos" of Louis Moreau Gottschalk [33] or "El Salon México" of the living Aaron Copland, the impulse seems to come from folk rhythm, popular music, or dance tune. But the components of this art of the people are not necessarily ethnological only; there is some reason to believe that musical and rhythmic elements and instrumentation transmitted from Renaissance Spain have here undergone an astonishing change, so that when the North American hums something about steel guitars, he may be paying unconscious tribute to the empire of the Habsburgs.

In literature the problem is less complex but equally interesting. The "black legend" [34] of Spanish cruelty and Catholic perfidy intermingled with tales of the buccaneers and Caribbean piracy to produce a vast sub-literature of the type that led Tom Sawyer, the Black Avenger of the Spanish Main, to stand with folded arms and look his last as the raft neared Jackson's Island. *Ramon, the Rover of Cuba, and Other Tales* "by the author of 'Evenings in Boston,' " published in New York in 1843, is representative: "Any reader may perceive," says the preface, "that Ramon's pictures are drawn from the life." Occasional daring minds in seventeenth- and eighteenth-century North America—among them Cotton Mather, Samuel Sewall, Thomas Jefferson, and Joel Barlow[35] —were aware of humanistic culture in Spain and her colonies, but the common assumption that Las Casas was a reliable historian made it impossible for the Americans to be receptive.

The creation of the republic, however, somewhat altered historical values. The Mathers' concept of the providential ordering of history by a Calvinist deity passed into the concept of the ordering of history by natural law superintended by a God who was certainly Protestant and might be deistical but who was somewhat more generous-minded than His predecessor. Poets, philosophers, historians, and moralists were compelled to reassess the meaning of Renaissance Spain to American development. Nobody nowadays reads Barlow's *The Vision of Columbus* (in 1807 reworked but not improved as *The Columbiad*), but Barlow tried to consult "authorities," he tried to show history as the outcome of cosmic law, and since Isabella was instrumental in sending Columbus on his voyage, he had to re-estimate a woman who was a monarch, a Catholic, and a Spaniard but who was likewise an instrument in founding the United States. Together with the widely read histories of the Scotchman, William Robertson,[36] *The Vision of Columbus* may be said to inaugurate in the United States the literature of the "great subject." The great subject was the discovery, exploration, and conquest of the New World, and, though the primary focus was for a time on Columbus,[37] historians could not ignore Renaissance Spain.

One of the curious elements in American culture is that although American knowledge of the Spanish colonial world was virtually a blank in the British colonies, in the first half of the nineteenth century Spanish Renaissance history becomes a central theme in the American romantic movement. If we skirt such minor matters as Cotton Mather's curious *La Fe del Christian . . . Ambiada a los Españoles* (Boston, 1699), Samuel Sewall's curiosity about Spaniards, John Adams's knowledge of Spanish, Jefferson's longing to know more about Latin America, and the influence of *Don Quixote* on Brackenridge's *Modern Chivalry* (1792–1815), we come to the astonishing success of Washington Irving in creating the American image of late medieval and Renaissance Spain. If he was not the first American to do so, he was the first American writer of importance to study in the Spanish archives. In 1826, at the instigation of Alexander Everett, Irving went to Madrid to translate Navarrete's study of Columbus. He had the vast advantage of daily intercourse with Obadiah Rich, the distinguished bibliographer, and the genius to see that a mere translation would not suffice. He therefore wrote *The Life and Voyages of Columbus* (1828), *The Conquest of Granada* (1829), *The Companions of Columbus* (1831), *The Alhambra* (1832), and such oddments as conclude *Wolfert's Roost* (1855). These books are triumphs of an informed romantic imagination. If America had no dim, rich, historic past, Spain would serve.

Although Irving was no seaman, no economist, no anthropologist, and no political historian, his *Columbus* is still a major book. *The Companions of Columbus* is inferior, but the *Granada* and *Alhambra* volumes create the imaginative context for the later studies of Bancroft, Motley, and Prescott. If, as Merriman holds, the age of chivalry lingered into the time of Charles V, Irving intuitively seized upon this truth. For him Spain has a chivalric landscape like that of the *Orlando Furioso*. He writes of Spain in terms of a fated race, fatal loves, and knightly honor. The fated race is of course the Moors, the leaders of whom from time to time shine with unexampled splendor as paladins. Thus in the *Alhambra* Ismael ben Ferrag, king of Granada, routed a Christian army in a mountain pass, and in the panic two Christian princes, Don Pedro and Don Juan, were slain. The body of Don

Pedro was carried from the field; that of Don Juan was left in the defiles of the mountains.

> His son wrote to the Moorish king, entreating that the body of his father might be sought and honorably treated. Ismael forgot in a moment that Don Juan was an enemy, who had carried ravage and insult to the very gates of his capital; he only thought of him as a gallant cavalier and a royal prince. By his command diligent search was made for the body. It was found in a barranco [ravine] and brought to Granada. There Ismael caused it to be laid out in state on a lofty bier, surrounded by torches and tapers, in one of these halls of the Alhambra. Osmyn and other of the noblest cavaliers were appointed as a guard of honor. . . . Ismael wrote to the son . . . to send a convoy for the body, assuring him it should be faithfully delivered up. In due time, a band of Christian cavaliers arrived for the purpose. They were honorably received and entertained by Ismael, and, on their departure with the body, the guard of honor of Moslem cavaliers escorted the funeral train to the frontier.[38]

This is a far cry from the black legend.

But if Irving is the pioneer romantic interpreter of Spain, his more powerful and scholarly contemporaries and successors—Bancroft, Motley, Prescott, and, in another bracket, Parkman—are wedded to a "progress" theory of history that forever misreads Catholic culture. They exalt great men, if they are on the right side; they create great villains, who are of course on the wrong side; and they pass nineteenth-century moral judgments on men of the sixteenth and seventeenth centuries.[39] In his excellent study, *History as Romantic Art*,[40] David Levin has analyzed and exhibited their formulae, which increase rather than diminish the black legend. In these books Philip II becomes one of the great historical villains, an invention by Christopher Marlowe surrounded by personages out of Italianate melodrama. Cortés and Pizarro are men of destiny who destroy empires because "progress" demands their passing, and for this purpose Machiavellian stratagems are suggested to them by the friars, by the Inquisition, or by the inherent fact that they are

Catholics and Spaniards. When, however, William the Silent resorts to Machiavellian devices, Motley passes them over—history is on William's side. Yet heroic endurance, whether by Spaniard, Indian, or anybody else, is always admired, nor does the age of chivalry pass from the picture. These writers stamped their image of Renaissance Spain upon the American imagination. Modern scholarship by Roger Bigelow Merriman, Clarence Haring, Lewis Hanke, and others struggles to correct their picture. The painstaking volumes by Charles Lea—*The Moriscoes of Spain* (1901), *The History of the Inquisition in Spain* (4 volumes, 1906–1907), and *The Inquisition in the Spanish Dependencies* (1908)—have not altered the unfavorable image.

That Renaissance Spain and its empire are explicable in terms of romanticism becomes a tenet of faith among American fictionists ranging from Cooper with his dull *Mercedes of Castile* (1840) to Francis Marion Crawford, whose *In the Palace of the King* (1900) contains an unforgettable picture of Philip II as a human spider. The conflict of Spaniard and Aztec produced Robert Montgomery Bird's *Calavar* (1834) and *The Infidel* (1834), Lew Wallace's *The Fair God* (1873), and Thomas A. Janvier's entertaining *The Aztec Treasure House* (1890), a boy's book undeservedly neglected, but in none of these, nor in Simms's *The Damsel of Darien* (1839), Mary Johnston's *1492* (1922), Hergesheimer's *The Bright Shawl* (1922), nor in any other American novel does one feel that the depths of Spanish character have been plumbed as the depths of German character are really sounded in the *Buddenbrooks* of Thomas Mann. Nor are the poets, including Freneau, Bryant, and Longfellow, any subtler. We have to wait on Archibald MacLeish's *Conquistador* (1932) for adequate insight, and Mr. MacLeish is the first to say that he has pillaged the incomparable narrative of Bernal Díaz. The one enduring venture into understanding Spain is Ticknor's *History of Spanish Literature* (1843), even though a Unitarian is not good on mysticism.

IV

Spain is typical of the Mediterranean powers, which organized their empires on a system of centralized authority, whereas the British colonies on the mainland had but a loose connection with the crown and grew up in fits of absence of mind. The Mediterranean pattern, moreover, involved paternalism to an extent that makes the Dutch in New Amsterdam, amiably satirized by Irving, avuncular in comparison. For example, William Bennet Munro collects the story of a busybody in France, who wrote the colonial *intendant* in Canada, saying that a bake oven should be established in each seigneury and the *habitans* required to bring their dough to it to be made into bread. The *intendant* had to remind the home office that in the cold Canadian winters the dough would be frozen stiff if the inhabitants had to proceed from their scattered dwellings to a central bakehouse.[41] Without entering into the vexed problem whether Roman Catholicism is as democratic as other faiths, one may observe that in the Catholic colonial empires royal control from a distance did little to energize democracy in the modern sense, and that to this day the flavor of political life differs in portions of New Mexico, Arizona, Texas, Louisiana, and other regions once a part of Spain or inhabited by displaced French Canadians, from democratic political behavior in, say, Oregon.

A central problem in Renaissance colonial government was how, across the vast ocean and with slow and irregular communications, any distant authority could uniformly assert its control over naval expeditions, armies, settlements, churches, and trading posts likely to break out into "liberty." An important mode of control was, as I have intimated, ceremony as an articulation of power. Forms of religion in that age demonstrated an inward and spiritual grace by an outward and visible ceremony; forms of political authority, disdaining the anonymity of republican virtue, required that the ruler or his representative be immediately cognizable, the "admiral" or the captain evident at once by virtue of ceremony and costume designed to impress the beholder with the might and magnificence of rule. A U. S. Grant virtually unrecognizable in slouch hat and worn uniform, a Thomas Jefferson tying his horse to a legendary fence before being inaugurated would have been unthinkable in an age that had known the Field of the Cloth of Gold [42] and that had invented the ceremonial reception of a new viceroy. Even in the British colonies custom or sumptuary edict prescribed dress, decoration, and decorum in order that within the social hierarchy order could be made permanent. This, with the intuition of genius, Hawthorne saw, as he makes evident in the second chapter of *The Scarlet Letter.*

Renaissance kings did not loll on their thrones, nor did dukes, tyrants, captains, and governors sit easily in their seats of power. Ceremony became an instrument. The chapter in Burckhardt's *Civilization of the Renaissance in Italy* entitled "The Festivals" is here illuminating; so also is any thoughtful examination of the pictures assembled in J. Lucas-Dubreton's *La Renaissance italienne: vie et mœurs au xvᵉ siècle.*[43] The opening chapters in Lewis Einstein's *Tudor Ideals* show the same belief in ceremony among the English. A monarch could not be married, nor a general return victorious, nor a ruler be inaugurated without pageantry. Even civic festivals took the form of *trionfi;* even carnivals involved allegories of religion, mythology, history, and power. What was true of the Mediterranean world was true of England. The consolidation of the Tudor kingdom was marked by an increase of ceremonial. A royal "progress" involved an enormous pattern of expense, mythology, poetry, and protocol. Elizabeth required her courtiers to sink to the ground like Byzantine flatterers when she entered the room. Shakespeare cannot bring a king on stage without a "sennet" and appropriate attendance; if he comes on alone, we know he has lost his power. Bacon devotes a serious essay, "Of Ceremonies and Respects" to this important problem, declaring: "Not to use Ceremonies at all is to teach Others not to use them againe; And so diminisheth Respect to himselfe: Especially they be not to be omitted to Strangers and Formal Natures." [44]

The pageantry of ceremonial form was inevitably transferred to the New World, as we have seen in the case of the viceroy at Lima. When Columbus went ashore at Guanahani, his captains beside him, the royal standard was displayed, the banners of the expedition were unfurled, one bearing an F and the other a Y for Ferdinand and Isabella, and over each initial there was displayed a crown and on the reverse a cross. After all had come ashore, the crews knelt, they gave thanks, they embraced the ground with ceremonial tears, and two notary publics solemnly recorded the words and the ceremony. In part this was legally necessary to the act of taking possession, but in part also it restored a firm pattern of authority to an expedition that had been constantly threatened by mutiny.

Similar solemn acts characterized other landings. Cortés, not knowing whether he was an arch rebel, and facing mutiny in his forces, having landed on the Mexican coast, ingeniously solved his difficulty by announcing his readiness to establish a colony (Villa Rica de la Vera Cruz). He appointed the usual municipal officers, resigned into their hands the commission he had received from Velásquez in Cuba, and then, at the request of the very officials he had created, accepted their ceremonial appointment as captain-general and chief justice. Thus strengthened by "legality," he went immediately to work, subduing mutiny by putting many of the rebels in irons. Who could oppose this representative of empire, ceremonially created? By transforming a military expedition into a royal civic community, he secured, as Prescott acutely observes, an effectual basis for future operations and a formula to justify his acts.[45] Again, when Cortés returned from his unfortunate expedition into Honduras, he passed under triumphal arches and over roadways strewn with flowers, the municipality of Mexico City went out to greet him, a cavalcade escorted him to the convent of Saint Francis for a solemn thanksgiving, and then brought him to his palace.[46] In summing up the character of Cortés, Bernal Díaz writes:

> In his appearance, manners, transactions, conversation, table, and dress every thing bore the appearance of a great lord. His cloaths were according to the fashion of the time. . . . He wore on his finger a ring with a very fine diamond, and in his cap, which according to the fashion of that day was of velvet, he bore a medal. . . . His table was always magnificently attended and served, with four major domos or principal officers, a number of pages, and a great quantity of plate both gold and silver.[47]

How else could one impress the mutinous world with the notion that power is power?

Nor is all this mere Spanish flourishing. Observe Lord De La Warr landing to restore order at Jamestown in 1610:

> Upon his Lordship's landing at the South gate of the Pallizado (which lookes into the River) our Governour [Sir Thomas Gates] caused his Company in armes to stand in order, and make a Guard: It pleased him, that I [William Strachey] should beare his Colours for that time: his Lordship landing, fell upon his knees, and before us all, made a long and silent Prayer to himselfe, and after, marched up into the Towne, where at the Gate, I bowed with the Colours, and let them fall at his Lordship's feete, who passed on into the Chappell, where he heard a Sermon by Master Bucke our Governours Preacher; and after that, caused a Gentleman, one of his own followers, Master Anthony Scot his Ancient, to reade his Commission, which intituled him Lord Governour, and Captain Generall during his life, of the Colony and Plantation in Virginia. . . . After the reading of his Lordships Commission, Sir Thomas Gates rendred up unto his Lordship his owne Commission . . . after which, the Lord Governour, and Captaine Generall, delivered some few words unto the Company, laying many blames upon them for many vanities, and their Idlenesse, earnestly wishing, that he might no more finde it so, least he should be compelled to draw the sword of Justice. . . .

De La Warr had the church repaired, and in it the colonists were required to hear two sermons on Sunday and one on Thursday. Every morning at the ringing of a bell about ten o'clock each man addressed himself to prayers, and again at four o'clock before supper.

> Every Sunday, when the Lord Governour, and Captaine Generall goeth to Church, hee is accompanied with all the Counsailers, Captaines, other Officers, and all the Gentlemen, and with a Guard of Holberdiers in his Lordships Livery, faire red cloakes, to the number of fifty, both on each side, and behinde him: and being in the Church, his Lordship hath his seate in the Quier, in a green Velvet Chaire, with a Cloath, with a Velvet Cushion spread on a Table before him, on which he kneeleth, and on each side sit the Counsell, Captaines, and Officers, each in their place, and when he returneth home againe, he is waited on to his house in the same manner.[48]

Ceremonial was not, however, inevitably solemn. When Champlain and Poutrincourt returned to Port Royal after a hazardous expedition southward by sea, they were met by Neptune, six tritons, a sound of trumpets, the thunder of cannon, and a great deal of verse, all arranged by that incorrigible, if exiled, child of the Renaissance, Lescarbot. Thus was a *trionfo* staged in Nova Scotia.[49]

Ceremonial continued to symbolize power through the colonial period in British North America and into Washington's administrations. The ceremonies at Washington's republican court, like his triumphal tour to New York, were, to be sure, strongly tinctured by a theory of Roman virtue, but it must not be forgotten that one of the foundations of Renaissance ceremony was a return to Rome. Not until the administrations of Jefferson did political ceremonial definitely recede. Thereafter for a time, because a plain people wanted no truck with aristocratic folderol, foreign visitors to the United States were alternately delighted and scandalized by the simplicities of American public life. The assassinations of Lincoln and Garfield, however, succeeded in rousing public attention to the need of guarding the chief magistrate; and the celebration of the Philadelphia Centennial Exposition (1876) and the World's Columbian Exposition (1893) required elaborate ceremonials as a mode of asserting the majesty of the republic. In the South, moreover, the tourney never died out. The false Renaissance splendor of the Mardi Gras balls in New Orleans, like the fancy dress balls of the Gilded Age, restored the Renaissance court in republican America and brought even the *trionfo* to prominence in a society that neither knew nor cared about the origins of its playthings. By the end of the nineteenth century and in the twentieth, publicity has taken over in matters ranging from the Pasadena Rose Parade to the Mummers festivity in Philadelphia. Modern presidential inaugurations are an awkward compromise among folksiness, military might, and the demands, however belated, of a *trionfo*. But perhaps the most astonishing reversal and return is in the American academic world. Until late in the last century students were graduated in nonacademic garb while a faculty costumed like preachers looked on. Indeed, as late as 1917 the University of Texas refused to recognize academic garb at academic ceremonies. Today, however, at every American commencement any campus bursts into pseudo-medieval and pseudo-Renaissance ceremonial splendors—indeed, even high-school seniors and children in kindergarten do not feel they are "graduated" unless they wear cap and gown.

But while the uses of ceremonial are important components of the social and political history of all the colonies, one should not exaggerate. Despite the joyous activities of Lescarbot, French Canada, for example, experienced virtually no transfer of Renaissance culture as a whole. Up to 1665 there were only about two thousand Frenchmen in the colony, so that when Colbert's program of expansion was launched, not only did he have to begin all over again, but also Canada was shaped under the Sun King and not under Francis I. Nothing in the Canadian winter could justify the erection of the type of château one associates with the joyous loves of Henri IV, nor did church architecture, that great gift of the Renaissance to the Spanish New World, develop anything of real merit in seventeenth-century Canada. Indeed, an authoritative study shows that between 1615 and 1665, of the twenty-eight known examples of church architecture in New France only nine were in stone. In the eighteenth century, to be sure, one can trace some faint influence of the baroque on church interiors, but this seems to be subdued to neo-classicism.[50] As for the graphic arts, music, and literature in French Canada, the Renaissance contribution in each case seems to be negligible.

Something of the same is true of architecture in the English colonies. The first dwellings were transplanted from England of the seventeenth century and are half medieval, half Jacobean, but the American colonies developed no shadowy parallel to Hampton Court, no faint echo of Grinling Gibbons, no paintings that can be put under a Renaissance rubric. There was in fact no real aristocracy in the colonies to bring in the viceregal splendor of New Spain, and no great Indian empire to destroy and imitate, however impressive public ceremonial became in wilderness terms. Music, too, though the Puritans praised it and the Virginians practiced it, was necessarily of the simpler sort—psalms, "vayne and triflyng ballades," some dance tunes like "Sellinger's Round," and the like. The few instruments of which we have record are simple and easily transportable—the bass viol, the early violin, the virginals, and perhaps the lute. Gilbert Chase, an authority, finds in the library of William Brewster of Plymouth a copy of Richard Alison's *The Psalmes of David in Metre . . . to be sung and plaide upon the Lute, the Orpharyon, Citterne, or Base Violl . . .* (London, 1599), and points out that Alison was an important composer of the Elizabethan period, but the fact, useful in correcting popular notions of Puritan bigotry, scarcely indicates a rich musical life.[51]

Political forms aside, the great link between Renaissance England and the mainland colonies was the art of writing and the scholarship upon which that writing was based. If it be true that Hakluyt's *Principal Voyages of the English Nation* be the prose epic of the English race *(Purchas His Pilgrimes* is, as it were, the *Odyssey* to Hakluyt's *Iliad)*, it is also true that the earliest writing about Virginia, New England, the other mainland colonies, and about future British possessions in the West Indies is part of this epic. Once Jamestown was founded, the recorders of its history, Captain John Smith among them, share the attitudes, the values, and the prose styles of the late Elizabethan and the Jacobean ages. I have elsewhere [52] made a particular analysis of Virginian writing in the seventeenth century; it should here suffice to quote two representative passages that illustrate its ties with English Renaissance prose. The first, from *The Proceedings of the English Colonie in Virginia* (Oxford, 1612), is a sentence put into the mouth of the Indian Ocanindge: "If hee haue offended you in escaping your imprisonment, the fishes swim, the fowles flie, and the very beastes striue to escape the snare and liue: then blame not him for being a man." The second is from a letter by John Rolfe, the husband of Pocahontas, to Sir Thomas Dale:

> Thus when I had thought I had obtained my peace and quietnesse, beholde another, but more gracious tentation hath made breaches into my holiest and strongest meditations; with which I haue bin put to a new triall, in a straighter manner then the former: for besides the many passions and sufferings vvhich I haue daily, hourely, yea and in my sleepe indured, euen awaking mee to astonishment, taxing mee with remisnesse, and carelessnesse, refusing and neglecting to performe the duteie of a good Christian, pulling me by the eare, and crying: why dost not thou indeuour to make her a Christian? And these haue happened to my greater wonder, euen when she hath bin furthest seperated from me, which in common reason (were it not an vndoubted worke of God) might breede forgetfulnesse of a farre more worthie creature.[53]

So far as style is concerned, these are clearly passages by a contemporary of Ralegh, Thomas Hooker, and Florio, the translator of Montaigne.

The impulses behind much colonial writing in British
North America in its earlier phases have been analyzed by
Moses Coit Tyler, still the leading authority on colonial
American letters; [54] and the labors of scholarship have shown
what weighty libraries were shipped to both Virginia and
New England in the earlier seventeenth century. Upon the
learning of the Renaissance and the Reformation as this
was understood at, say, Cambridge University, the curriculum of Harvard College, once the notorious Eaton was got
rid of and Henry Dunster took over, was shaped; that is to
say, upon the liberal arts, the so-called three philosophies,
and the learned tongues. Learning, even in the case of Nathaniel Ward's satirical *Simple Cobbler of Agawam* (1647),
was so naturally a component of colonial prose in seventeenth-century New England, one notices its absence rather
than its presence. Even John Josselyn, admirable observer
and nature-writer (he who brought something by "Mr. Francis Quarles, the poet" to the Reverend John Cotton), cannot avoid a learned quip in his description of the Puritans
as "like Ethiopians, white in the teeth only; full of ludifi-
cation, and injurious dealing, and cruelty." [55] No colony
in North America had in it more learned men than did Massachusetts Bay, and no colony produced a more constant
stream of writing—history, theology, biography, sermons,
journey-books, political tracts, verse. Leading British authors
of the right sort were quickly imported, some of whom served
as models. Moreover, the sources of learning were not in
Great Britain alone; appeal was made to the Continent, Calvin's *Institutes* being but one among many Continental titles.
Latin was commonly read by those with any pretensions to
writing. And it is true that particular passages in this literature have the amplitude of Spenser, Sidney, Ralegh, and the
great Hooker. The British colonists in general, and the New
Englanders in particular, continued to be far more intimately
bound up with the intellectual life of the home country than
were the French in Canada with the France of Louis XIV.
But one faces a real difficulty in making a distinction. The

English Renaissance had no sharp terminal date, not even 1660, inasmuch as *Paradise Lost* was published in 1667. Nevertheless, most of the seventeenth century differs in tone and interest from the spacious days of great Elizabeth, and this difference becomes apparent after the publication of the King James Bible and the performance of *The Tempest* at court, both in 1611. It is virtually impossible to imagine a New England Puritan exclaiming:

> O, wonder!
> How many goodly creatures are there here!
> How beauteous mankind is! O brave new world,
> That has such people in't!
> —Act V, Scene i

The New England mind simply did not work this way. Its new world was for the saints, not for lovers, and it failed to find most of mankind beauteous. Because New Englanders came in the lag of the Renaissance, not in its noon, their view of the universe was more like that of John Donne than it was like that of Francis Bacon—always with particular exceptions. Moreover, though copies of Spenser, Milton, Quarles, and others appeared in American libraries in the seventeenth century, New Englanders were cut off from the stage —the great glory of the English Renaissance—so that Marlowe, Shakespeare, Ben Jonson, and the rest were not real forces in their culture. Seventeenth-century New England writing, often of the highest acuity as argument and of greater breadth and vigor than most of us know, began in the Renaissance, but it did not linger there.

V

Although down to the Federal period leading Americans occasionally went on the grand tour—Charles Bulfinch, for example, visited England, France, and Italy at the age of twenty-two—and though one hears occasionally rumors of a Renaissance painting's being owned by a wealthy American before James Jackson Jarves formed his collection, direct contact between Renaissance culture, however defined, and the rising American republic diminished and virtually disappeared with the Revolution. One can of course argue that the obvious Palladian components of "colonial" and "Georgian" architecture represent a continuing influence. The history of the Italian city republics and the books of their historians were, as we shall see, an important influence upon the revolutionary leaders and the members of the Constitutional Convention, nor did some knowledge, however slight, of such Renaissance authors as Machiavelli, Cervantes, and Shakespeare [56] totally vanish.* But a more dynamic approach to Renaissance culture, particularly in the fine arts, had to wait upon the awakening of romantic interest in Italy among the Americans of the nineteenth century.[57]

Like Goethe in his passion for Italy, Americans of means, particularly if they came from the northern states, longed for the colors of the South. Mediterranean culture held for them the allurements of a classical past made familiar by textbook and poetry, the allure of *banditti,* peasantry, ancient families, and crimes of passion that Italian opera and romantic fiction made thrilling, the attraction of famous libraries, and, of course, the appeal of art collections that compounded religion, classical antiquity, and imputed idealism, and sensuous appeal the American did not know at home. Italy therefore drew writers as various as Cooper and Hawthorne, Longfellow and Henry James, and such artists as Washington Allston, Horatio Greenough, Thomas Crawford, and W. W. Story. The Italian vogue was the resultant of many forces. One was the imaginative appeal of Byronism. Had not Byron admired Daniel Boone and "The Dying Gladiator," the

---

* It seems almost incredible that standard instruction in Shakespeare in school, college, and university did not begin until after the middle of the nineteenth century. Not being required, he was eagerly read outside of class. Out of 175 undergraduates at Harvard in 1807, 99 subscribed to a Boston edition of Shakespeare.

mournful Colosseum and the cynical tale of *Beppo?* Another, if opposite, force was the enormous appeal of Mrs. Anna Brownell Jameson, whose eminently proper sentiments about medieval and Renaissance art are expressed in *Memoires* [sic] *of the early Italian Painters and of the Progress of Painting in Italy from Cimabue to Bassano* (1845). This but preluded a mighty triptych: *Sacred and Legendary Art, Legends of the Monastic Order,* and *Legends of the Madonna,* all followed by *The History of Our Lord as Exemplified in Works of Art* (1864). Mrs. Jameson was originally published in London, but her works were quickly imported or pirated, and in the 1890s were edited as a whole by Estelle M. Hurll and republished in revised and enlarged form in Boston.[58] Mrs. Jameson was informative. Her works are still in demand in public libraries. She was wholesome, she was on the side of the angels, and the nude embarrassed her. To the influences she released, coupled with the appeal of John Ruskin, the Americans owe the many sepia prints of Guido Reni's "Dawn" that used to hang over library shelves and on the walls of American schoolhouses. When in *The Marble Faun* Hilda spends her blameless life conscientiously copying Renaissance paintings, her scruples before the supposed portrait of Beatrice Cenci and before anything "base" beautifully reflect Mrs. Jameson.

One had, indeed, to walk a narrow way between Catholicism and paganism. On the one hand Renaissance masterpieces were frequently devout yet idolatrous; on the other hand they were brilliantly painted but sensual. When Charles Eliot Norton reported on art in his *Notes of Travel and Study in Italy* in 1859, he wrote in the preface that he did not hesitate "to express myself strongly in regard to . . . the corrupt doctrines of the Roman Church and methods of the Papal Government," and after reviewing some of the Renaissance masterpieces in Rome, faithful shadow of Ruskin that he was, he remarked: "The decay of the vital forces of a people may be altogether concealed for a time from the eyes of outside observers by shows of splendor, by lustre of genius, brilliant, though perverted, and, indeed, by actual advance in material development, corresponding in some measure to the loss of spiritual energy. Such was the case in Italy during a great part of this time [the Renaissance]. . . . Living was both easier and more civilized . . . but living is not life." [59]

The basis of a less ethereal attitude toward Renaissance culture was laid by James Jackson Jarves, who began collecting Italian painters in the 1850s but whose difficulties in disposing of his collection illustrate the naïveté of the earlier American attitude. He showed his paintings in New York City in 1860 and again in 1863. They were then sent to Boston, where nobody seemed to know what to do with them. Eventually 119 were sold to Yale through the generosity of that great admirer of Ruskin, Augustus Russell Street. Another group eventually found a permanent home in the Cleveland Art Museum. Jarves's own theories were laid down in several volumes, among which *The Art Idea* (1864) is characteristic: he desired idealism but he also recognized the power of Renaissance work. It is a mark of the rapidity with which American scholarship about art matured that only thirty years after the appearance of *The Art Idea* Bernard Berenson brought out his *The Venetian Painters of the Renaissance,* the first of a distinguished line of specialized studies that marked B. B. as an international authority! [60]

In that interval the American captain of industry took over the attributes and activities of the Renaissance merchant prince as a collector of books and art and as a patron of architects, decorators, and painters. An elder generation, among whom W. W. Corcoran and W. T. Walters, both of Baltimore, and Alexander White of Chicago are characteristic, made collecting respectable, whether as a status symbol or as an expression of a genuine culture. The millionaire generation, among whom one can number Senator William A. Clark, Henry Clay Frick, Isabella Gardner, John G. Johnson, Martin A. Ryerson (who discovered El Greco for Americans), Charles Phelps Taft, and Thomas Fortune Ryan, bought even more splendidly and established opulent galleries that eventually became public institutions. The fabulous success of the Huntington family, of William Randolph Hearst, and of John Pierpont Morgan is part of American folklore, and the gap between the uncertainties of Hearst and the surer taste of J. P. Morgan [61] is, in a way, an index of continuing uncertainty in taste. But lavish buying in turn induced increasing sophistication among art dealers, museum directors, advisers to the rich,* and mature scholars. Scholarship in Renaissance matters could in the twentieth century be based upon such great American libraries as the Huntington, the Morgan, and the Folger. The founding of the Renaissance Society of America in 1954 and of its line of distinguished publications, the creation of Dumbarton Oaks in Washington, a benefaction of the Bliss family, as a school of Byzantine studies, and the taking over by Harvard University of I Tatti in Florence as a center of Renaissance scholarship show how the wheel has come full circle. Italy, which produced Columbus but which had small part in colonizing the New World, is now a central theme in Renaissance scholarship in the United States.

The parallel between the mercantile patron of the arts in Renaissance Europe and the American millionaire is further substantiated by the curious outburst of activity in housing the wealthy in buildings modeled on French châteaux and Italian palaces. It is not true that Fifth Avenue was at one time "lined" with such structures, as rumor declared it to be, and the problem of determining what part of these magnificent mansions derived directly from European originals and what part from studies at the École des Beaux-Arts, to which American architects increasingly turned after the

---

* Berenson advised Isabella Gardner, Samuel P. Avery advised W. T. Walters and W. H. Vanderbilt, and William M. Laffan advised Morgan, in their purchasing.

Civil War, is a nice question in architectural history. When William Henry Vanderbilt spent three million dollars on a block-long residence from 51st to 52nd Street on Fifth Avenue, the style, said a contemporary critic, "for those who are particular about a style" "may be called Italian Renaissance," but for William K. Vanderbilt's house, just to the north of it, Richard Morris Hunt deliberately followed the Château de Blois and two fifteenth-century houses at Bourges, intending, it appears, a sixteenth-century French mansion for nineteenth-century American living. "Biltmore" at Asheville, North Carolina, created by Hunt for the Vanderbilts (1896), is another piece of French Renaissance; and as for "The Breakers" at Newport (Pl. VIII), it outshone the Medici. The effect of this opulence upon such a cultivated European as Paul Bourget was to stagger him. He recorded going to a Catholic church in New York that struck him as a "club of prayer" decorated with copies of Madonnas by Andrea del Sarto and Raphael; he observed that *"l'interminable suite des habitations luxeuses qui bordent cette cinquième avenue proclaime cette folle abondance,"* among these *"vastes constructions"* being *"une gentilhommière française du seizième siècle"* and a residence in the style of Louis XIII; and at Newport, *"une ville d'été,"* whither he went to see how the Americans housed themselves, Aladdin's lamp, apparently, had created residences in the style of Queen Elizabeth, in the style of the French Renaissance, in the style of the Trianon, and in a good many other styles besides— *"l'argent surtout."* [62] McKim, Mead and White, of course, became the "formal champions" of Renaissance style in America, one of their results being the lovely façade of the Boston Public Library. But any history of architecture will reveal the rise and fall of this passion for the Renaissance among the rich, and show pictures of the Villard house, the University Club in New York, and other examples of our enthusiasm. Domestic enthusiasm for the French Renaissance style can still be found in the residential districts of Boston, Chicago, Cleveland, and other cities, though these houses are rapidly disappearing. For that matter many a decayed "opera house" in still smaller cities will in its dusty decoration and faded elegance document the wide, if evanescent, extent of Renaissance influence upon both public and private architecture in the United States before World War I.[63]

────◆ IV ◆────

Renaissance Man in America

I

EXPLORERS, conquerors, leaders of expeditions, founders of colonies, and governors of colonial empires in the New World from 1492 to 1620 were men of the Renaissance, products of that strange and fascinating mélange of tradition and change, cynicism and idealism, belated remnants of the medieval universe and startling anticipations of modernity that has challenged the imagination of mankind by producing personalities as varied as those of Leonardo da Vinci, Cesare Borgia, Shakespeare, Torquemada, Bacon, Philip II, and Queen Elizabeth. Our notion of the significance of this truth in American history is, however, not precise.

The Renaissance ideal of man as commonly presented in the schools is that of the Renaissance gentleman, an ideal charmingly set forth in Castiglione's *Il Cortigiano* (1528), Englished by Sir Thomas Hoby in 1561; in Sir Thomas Elyot's less colorful *The Book Named the Governor* (1531); and in Spenser's *The Faerie Queene* (1590–1596). The seventeenth century in England saw the doctrine continued in such books as Henry Peacham's *The Compleat Gentleman* (1622) and Richard Brathwaite's *The English Gentleman* (1630), "containing sundry excellent rules, or exquisite observations, tending to direction of every gentleman, how to demeane or accommodate himselfe in the manage of pub-like or private affaires." Such titles are part of an extensive library of courtesy books that comes down into our own time, that experiences a boom after any great social upset, and that is devoted in a rather simple-minded way to the proposition that "manners makyth man." Scholarship, a little book-bound in this particular, has contented itself with the educational theories and the doctrines of egalitarianism or caste set forth in this library.[1] It has assumed an interpretation based upon a theory of liberal education and has not inquired with particularity into the relation between the doctrine of the gentleman and the practice of leadership.

And this has been natural. The Virginia or South Carolina aristocrat, the New England Brahmin, the well-bred Pennsylvanian representative of a Main Line family, and others like them are American types as characteristic as the hillbilly and the squatter, types which take away from the United States the sting of Mrs. Trollope's charge that democracy breeds boorishness and must ever do so. Even if historical forces did not thus make for a defense of the gentleman in America, the Renaissance doctrine of the *uomo universale* is attractive in its own right. Who but must admire the well-rounded man (commonly thought of as just emerging from youth), proficient in every art and skill, yet never proficient to the point of vocationalism, learned without pedantry, a poet, a courtier, a dancer, a musician, a Latinist, a lover, one perfect in such physical exercises as riding, fencing, leaping, swimming, running, and wrestling, but somehow never breaking into vulgar sweat? Even those who have never read Castiglione are familiar with the ideal as it is set forth in Ophelia's moving lament:

> O what a noble mind is here o'erthrown!
> The courtier's, soldier's, scholar's eye, tongue, sword!
> The expectancy and rose of the fair state,
> The glass of fashion and the mould of form,
> The observ'd of all observers.
> —*Hamlet*, Act III, Scene i

Lady Percy's description of her dead Harry but reinforces the lineaments of this admirable type:

> . . . by his light
> Did all the chivalry of England move
> To do brave acts; he was, indeed, the glass
> Wherein the noble youth did dress themselves.
> . . . in speech, in gait,
> In diet, in affections of delight,
> In military rules, humours of blood,
> He was the mark and glass, copy and book
> That fashion'd others.
> —*2 Henry IV*, Act II, Scene iii

Here, however, is no image of the contemplative life; and it is perhaps a mark of long-run Renaissance influence upon the United States that among the great names in American history virtually none is notable for the *vita contemplativa*. On the other hand, the soberer seventeenth century emphasized among the characteristics of the *uomo universale* those that related to the life of thought somewhat more and those related to the life of action somewhat less. Milton, in his *Of Education* (1644), is in point, since in that tractate we find the end of learning is not merely to "repair the ruins of our first parents," but also to acquire "a complete and generous education," which shall fit a man to "perform justly, skilfully and magnanimously all the offices, both private and public, of peace and war." The Miltonic essay is better remembered for its gigantic pattern of study than for the fact that Milton did not neglect military exercises and wrestling ("wherein Englishmen are wont to excel"), after which the pupils were to "unsweat" themselves to "the solemn and divine harmonies of music." But if physical exercise was not neglected in Milton's scheme, it is still true that his chief interest lay in a bookish education, just as it is true that most of those who have written about the gentleman in America have been more interested in his reading and breeding than in the ethics of his public activities.[2]

The theory of Castiglione (the Hoby translation, thought Ascham, if "advisedlie read, and diligentlie folowed" for a year in England would do a young man more good than three years in Italy) was not without its influence in America. Activist persons of general culture can be found. Bernal Díaz del Castillo, though without "family," is perpetually concerned with his own style and actions and with those of others, and records with pleasure chivalric deeds by Cortés and his companions. Cortés himself was a courtier, a lover, a poet, an orator, a captain, and a governor. Champlain, who rose from nothing, became an admiral, a mathematician, a theorist of navigation, a skillful painter, and a cartographer; in his old age he had someone at the table read in the morning from a historian and in the evening from the biography of a saint. Captain John Smith trained himself for knight-errantry, warred against the Mohammedans, put three Turks' heads on his coat-of-arms, was sufficiently a lover to attract the amorous interest of a lady in Constantinople, was a discoverer, a horseman, a navigator, a statesman, a general, and a scholar so trained in Renaissance ideals as to imitate the classical historians by putting formal speeches into the mouths of Powhatan and himself. The following short passage from the "Epistle Dedicatory" of the *True Travels, Adventvres and Observations of Captain Iohn Smith* (London, 1630) has the right Renaissance ring and might have come from Federico de Montefeltro in *Il Cortigiano:* "Many of the most eminent Warriers, and others; what their swords did, their penns writ. Though I bee never so much their inferiour, yet I hold it no great errour, to follow good examples; nor repine at them, [who] will doe the like." [3] Doubtless the spirit of Sir Thomas Elyot rather than that of Castiglione reigns in the careers of Governor Bradford of Plymouth and Governor Winthrop of Massachusetts Bay, yet each exemplifies in decent measure the universalism of the ideal.

Later examples of the persistence of the *uomo universale* can be found. Here is the Reverend Cotton Mather descanting on the virtues of Captain Josiah Winslow in 1725:

> As he was a Young Man of a Beautiful Countenance; of an Hail and Firm Constitution of Body, which enabled him to act with much Vigour, and undergo the Hardships of the War; So he was a Pleasant and Spritely Witt; of a Sweet Disposition; Of a Free and Generous Temper; Modest and Bashful in his Behaviour, Full of Life; and full of Love to every One: Of so condescending a Spirit, that it sometimes drew him into Inconveniences: Obedient and Respectful to his Superiors; Kind to all; Far from Insulting over his Inferiors; which gained him great Respect from those that were Acquainted with him; and especially of the Souldiers that were under him; He was so far from taking any Advantage, that in their Streights and Difficulties, he has given sometimes to Poor Fellows that were in Necessity the Cloathes off his Back, to supply them.[4]

Somewhat more attuned to religion in Jonathan Edwards' eulogy is the portrait of the Reverend David Brainerd, missionary to the Indians; yet the traits of the Renaissance gentleman are still evident. Brainerd

> was a singular Instance, of a ready Invention, natural Eloquence, easy flowing Expression, sprightly Apprehension, quick Discerning, and very strong Memory; and yet of a very penetrating Genius, close and clear Thought, and piercing Judgment. He had an exact Taste: His Understanding was (if I may so express it) of a quick, strong and distinguishing scent. His Learning was very considerable: He had a great Taste for Learning; and applied himself to his Studies, in so close a Manner when he was at College, that he much injured his Health. . . . He had an extraordinary Knowledge of Men, as well as Things . . . a great Insight into human Nature . . . a peculiar Talent, at accommodating himself to the Capacities, Tempers and Circumstances of those he would instruct or counsel. . . . He expressed himself with that exact Propriety and Pertinency, in such significant, weighty, pungent Expressions; with that decent Appearance of Sincerity, Reverence and Solemnity, and great Distance from all Affectation . . . that I have scarcely ever known parallel'd.[5]

This is not, to be sure, Castiglione or Sir Thomas Elyot, but it is not so remote from their doctrine as to be unrecognizable.

In Virginia in the same century we have William Byrd— "Col. William Byrd, of Westover, in Virginia, Esq.ᵘ "— who wrote love letters like Petrarchan sonnets, collected books, plunged twice a day into the river in winter to harden his body, was a herbalist, a surveyor, a student of philosophy, government, divinity, the classical past, and contemporary literature, and who became a member of the Royal Society. Of a greater eighteenth-century Virginian it has been said that he was the last Renaissance man. Certainly Jefferson's manifold interests—architecture, government, agriculture, the physical sciences, education, travel, the earth sciences, anthropology, law, philosophy, invention, and much else—eminently qualify him. Nor was he without a charming amorous skill, as certain of his letters testify. In 1787, even before Jefferson had visited Europe, the Marquis de Chastellux described him in terms equally satisfactory to the Renaissance ideal and to eighteenth-century philosophy:

> An American, who without ever having quitted his own country, is at once a musician, skilled in drawing; a geometrician, an astronomer, a natural philosopher, legislator, and statesman. A senator of America, who sat for two years in that famous Congress which brought about the revolution; and which is never mentioned without respect, though unhappily not without *regret;* a governor of Virginia, who filled this difficult station during the invasions of *Arnold,* of *Phillips,* and of *Cornwallis;* a philosopher, in voluntary retirement, from the world, and public business, because he loves the world, inasmuch only as he can flatter himself with being useful to mankind; and the minds of his countrymen are not yet in a condition to bear the light, or to suffer contradiction.[6]

Doubtless other candidates for the description *uomo universale* in American terms will occur to the reader; yet after Jefferson and his generation it is harder to know who they are. So powerful a notion ought not, one thinks, to vanish from American culture, but it is difficult to trace its specific influence in the nineteenth and twentieth centuries. A biographer of Samuel F. B. Morse, painter, inventor, politician, and (dare one add?) crank, calls him an American Leonardo, but admirable as Morse was in many ways, he seems to me less significant than Joseph Henry (1797–1878), playwright, pedagogue, surveyor, professor of mathematics and natural philosophy, scientific research worker in electricity who both anticipated and paralleled Faraday, member of the Princeton faculty, president of the American Association for the Advancement of Science and of the National Academy of Sciences, and first secretary (that is, director) of the Smithsonian Institution; or George Perkins Marsh (1801–1882), linguist, lawyer, scholar, leading diplomat, railroad commissioner, traveler, and author of, among other books, *Man and Nature, or Physical Geography as Modified by Human Action* (1864; revised as *The Earth Modified by Human Action*), one of the few great philosophical scientific works by an American, which stands at the "fountainhead of the conservation movement"; or the second secretary of the Smithsonian, Spencer Fullerton Baird (1823–1887), zoologist, ornithologist, linguist, ichthyologist, administrator, conservationist, and writer; or *his* successor as secretary, Samuel Pierpont Langley (1834–1906), astronomer, engineer, architect, physicist, wit, pioneer in the study of solar and lunar radiation, pioneer in aerodynamics, and unsung—and misunderstood—hero of "mechanical flight." Such figures seem to be nearer the type of the *uomo universale.*

But of course a cultural puzzle remains. Does the American notion of the "all-around man" owe anything to Castiglione, or was it the product of the working assumption that republicans, busily engaged in creating a perfect new society, must *e theoria* produce human beings possessing flexibility of talent? American education, strongly colored by religion in the colonial period, was at the beginning of the national period rededicated by theorists to republican virtue, but the duties of the citizen as outlined in essays from the early republic do not make up the same bundle of attributes as those of Renaissance man. Doubtless an enthusiasm for the point of view of Matthew Arnold later put selections concerning a gentlemanly culture into freshman reading books, but nineteenth- and twentieth-century doctrines of the gentleman, implicit or explicit in the writings, say, of the elder Holmes, Santayana, Robert Grant, and Ellery Sedgwick, show that the tradition has weakened, has become thin, genteel, and academic. In one sense the *uomo universale* loses effectiveness in the national period. In another sense he survives.*

II

He survives in part because in the later nineteenth century the genteel tradition of the cultured gentleman was clearly the aim of liberal education—one thinks of James Russell Lowell, Woodrow Wilson, and Charles Eliot Norton. He is perhaps transmogrified into the "all around" American. Yet even in the years when Theodore Roosevelt was preaching to the effete sons of the ivy colleges the virtues of the strenuous life, the American was not, except in unusual circumstances such as the Civil War, called upon to endure outrageous suffering or to display martial proficiency. It is mainly in the period of exploration and settlement that endurance and combat become primary virtues; and since the wilderness and the sea afforded small opportunity for bookish theoric, a certain physical vibrancy in the Renaissance

---

* It may be thought that more attention should be paid to the many-sided Franklin in this discussion of the phases in America of the *uomo universale*. But the basis of Franklin's activity is characteristically utilitarian, not cultural in the sense of gentility or of the gentleman. The "apostle of modern times," "the first civilized American" (titles given Franklin by two biographers) was in fact viewed by the court at Versailles as a natural man of genius rather than as the product of sophisticated cultivation. His case, however, perfectly illustrates the difficulty of distinguishing the evolution of types of culture.

ideal was echoed in the New World as the more gentle aspects were not. In the *Cortigiano* Duke Guidobaldo de Montefeltro is praised for bearing his "manye and diverse calamities" "with such stoutnesse of courage, that vertue never yeelded to fortune. But with a bold stomacke despising her stormes, lived with great dignitie and estimation among all men: in sicknesse, as one that was sounde, and in adversitie, as one that was most fortunate." Count Ludovico's contribution to the discussion includes advice to the gentleman that he "shew him selfe most fierce, bitter, and evermore with the first." "In everie place beside," he says, "lowly, sober, and circumspect, fleeing above all things, bragging and unshamefull praysing himselfe: for therewith a man alwaies purchaseth himselfe the hatred of the hearers." And Federico cannily advises that "where the Courtier is at skirmish, or assault, or battaile upon the lande, or in such other places of enterprise, he ought to worke the matter wisely in separating him selfe from the multitude, and undertake notable and bolde feates which hee hath to doe, with as little company as he can, and in the sight of noble men that be of most estimation in the campe, and especially in the presence and (if it were possible) before the very eyes of his king or great personage he is in service withall." [7] The two leading elements in these injunctions are physical endurance and courage, and an invitation to flout discipline in order to show off one's personal prowess in the interests of glory. The men of the Renaissance were members of a fiercely competitive culture, the more competitive by reason of the close proximity of death; and this total situation was immediately paralleled in the New World. In the courtesy books justice, prudence, temperance, fortitude, courtesy, and liberality are the canonical components of the gentleman: in the wilderness fortitude and cunning had survival values not so evident in temperance and courtesy.

Individual prowess was both cause and consequence of the thirst for glory. Glory was the reward of physical prowess, to be recorded by literary men. The dedication of Richard Eden's *A treatyse of the newe India* (1553) is characteristic:

> Wherby we maye perceue such magnanimitie to haue ben in our predicessours, men of noble and stout courage, yat they thought it not sufficiente in their life time to deserue prayse and honour, except the same might also redounde to theyr posteritie, yat they might therby bee encouraged to do the like. Whyche thing truely hath ben ye cause, yat in al ages noble enterprises haue ben commended, and such as haue attempted ye same, haue bene honoured.
>
> . . . yet sure I am that aswel they which set forth or take vpon them this viage, as also they which shal hereafter attempt ye lyke, may in this smal boke as in a little glasse, see some cleare light, not only how to learne by the example, dammage, good successe, and aduentures of other, how to behaue them selues and direct theyr viage to their most commoditie, but also if dew successe herein shoulde not chaunce according unto theyr hope and expectation (as oftentimes chanceth in great affaires,) yet not for one soyle or fal, so to be dismayed as with shame and dishonor to leaue wyth losse, but rather to the death to persist in a godly, honeste, and lawful purpose, knowing that whereas one death is dewe to nature, the same is more honourably spent in such attemptes as may be to the glorye of God and commoditie of our countrey, then in soft beddes at home, among the teares and weping of women.[8]

Such was the characteristic formula, whether the Latins were undertaking New World enterprises for the glory of the Virgin, the saints, the Holy Catholic Church and the rulers of Spain or Portugal, or whether the Protestants proclaimed the wonders of Oriana,* the virtues of the Bible, the grandeur of the French monarchy, or the greatness of the English maritime tradition.[9] Glory was so often associated with death as to lead the modern reader to murmur something about the

---

* Characteristic is John Speed, who in the *Historie of Great Britaine* (1611) celebrates "the Court of Queen Ceres, the Granary of the Western world, the fortunate Island, the Paradise of Pleasure and the Garden of God." Camden called Elizabeth "the Queen of the Sea, the North Star, the restorer of naval glory."

Freudian death wish; but glory was also a Janus-faced idol in another sense, for it called at once for self-aggrandizement and self-sacrifice.

Ramusio, as we have seen (translated by Hakluyt), thought the effort of Sebastian Cabot to reach Cathay by the Northwest Passage an enterprise that "would be the most glorious, and of most importance of all other that can be imagined to make his name great, and fame immortall, to all ages to come, farre more then can be done by any of all these great troubles and warres which dayly are used in Europe among the miserable Christian people." Thus Edward Haye announced that "in this last age of the world (or likely never) the time is compleat"; and that if a leader's "motives be derived from a vertuous & heroycall minde, preferring chiefly the honour of God, compassion of poore infidels captived by the devill, tyrannizing in most woonderfull and dreadfull maner over their bodies and soules; advancement of his honest and well disposed countreymen, willing to accompany him in such honourable actions," and various other motives, he would undertake "an action . . . not to be intermedled with base purposes." Thus Ralegh, after solemnly announcing in *The Discoverie of Guiana* that "the way of deceit is not the way of honor or good opinion," boasts in the next pages of tricking the Spaniards into the belief that "I was bound onely for the reliefe of those English which I had planted in Virginia," and declares a little later that "I shall willingly spend my life" in searching for an empire so great that "whatsoever prince shall possesse it, that Prince shall be Lord of more golde, and of a more beautiful Empire, and of more Cities and people, then either the King of Spaine, or the great Turke." Perhaps there is an ironical connection between this confusion of moral principles and the declaration of Ralegh's lieutenant, Laurence Keymis, writing of the second voyage to Guiana and promising to "remove all fig-leaves from our unbeliefe," that "we cannot denie that the chiefe commendation of vertue doth consist in action." [10]

The ambiguities of glory were, as I have said, intermingled with death. Perhaps the emotional climax of Gilbert's *Discourse* is this passage: "That he is not worthy to live at all, that for feare, or danger of death, shunneth his countries service, and his owne honour: seeing death is inevitable, and the fame of vertue immortall." [11] Frobisher, caught in the ice, "not opening his eares to the peevish passion of any private person, but chiefly respecting the accomplishment of the cause he had undertaken (wherein the chiefe reputation and fame of a Generall and Captaine consisteth) and calling to his remembrance the short time he had in hand to provide so great a number of ships their loading, determined with this resolution to passe and recover his Port, or else there to burie himselfe with his attempt." John Janes wrote of John Davis's third voyage that "At length our Captaine by whom we were all to be governed, determined rather to end his life with credite, then to returne with infamie and disgrace, and so being all agreed, wee purposed to live and die together, and committed our selves to the ship." Lister, one of the captains in the Earl of Cumberland's voyage to the Pacific in 1586, informed a naval council off the Straits of Magellan: "My accompt is this, that he that dieth for this yeere is excused for the next, and I rather choose death, then to returne in disgrace with my lord." Keymis, it will be recalled, committed suicide rather than go back to England after his disasters in Guiana; and were it not tedious, innumerable other instances of this marriage of glory and death could be compiled from the literature of exploration. Let one more suffice: the quaint "conceit" with which Edward Haye prepares the reader for Gilbert's death as that worthy transferred from the *Golden Hinde* to the *Squirrel:* "The evening was faire and pleasant, yet not without token of storme to ensue, and most part of this Wednesday night, like the Swanne that singeth before her death, they in the Admiral, or Delight, continued in sounding of Trumpets, with Drummes, and Fifes: also winding the Cornets, Haughtboyes: and in the end of their jolitie, left with the battel and ringing of dolefull knels." [12]

The proximity of death added intensity to the pursuit of glory and a special fierceness to the quarrels that pursuit aroused. Wrote Peter Martyr: "But for the jealousy of the Spaniards, who can never agree amongst themselves in their keen dispute about honours, all these countries would already be conquered. How each is the declared enemy of his companions in this dusty squabble of ambition, which blinds them: how nobody can endure to be commanded by the others, I have already sufficiently explained." [13]

Death and jealousy likewise were commonplace enough among the English. Lewis Einstein in his invaluable *Tudor Ideals* points out that gentlemen volunteers became a kind of English fashion, a parallel to the Italian *condottieri*, and that scarcely a foreign campaign from Spain and Hungary to France and the Low Countries but Englishmen participated in it. Toward the end of Elizabeth's reign the country was full of idle soldiers without discipline, fiercely thirsting for glory and contemptuous of dying, and he quotes Thomas Churchyard to the effect that "the last reward of a soldier is death; this do I desire as a man that have made choice though unworthy of that profession. I covet to die like a soldier and a true subject." [14] The indiscipline, the melodramatic changes of fortune in the careers of Albuquerque, Columbus, Cortés, De Soto, Champlain, Ralegh, and Captain John Smith substantiate Einstein's general truth. The thirst for fame, the avidity, the murderous jealousy, the amorality, the contempt for life evident among the explorers of the New World were first exhibited and afterward matured upon the battlefields of Europe. There is truth in Randolph Adams' comparison of Champlain to Caesar, and it may be, as he says, that Champlain was more deeply and sincerely concerned with the glory of France than ever Caesar was with that of Rome, but both men lived in a cloud of conspiracies, and Champlain was merely more fortunate in not being assassinated.[15]

III

Charmed as we are by Castiglione, Sir Thomas Elyot, and Edmund Spenser, we forget an even more powerful tradition of individual conduct for Renaissance man, that enunciated by Commynes in his *Memoirs* (1498/1524) and elaborated by Machiavelli in *The Prince* (1513) and the *Discourses on Livy*. Castiglione's was the grammar of conduct merely, Machiavelli wrote the grammar of power; and the discovery and exploration of new lands, the extension of empire, the seizure of command, and in some cases the creation of whole armies and navies (as by the buccaneers of the West Indies) were problems of power, not of politeness. Charmed likewise by romantic legends of Jamestown and idealized versions of the Pilgrims and the Puritans, we fail to realize that the world of Columbus and Cortés, Gilbert and Ralegh, Champlain and La Salle was the world of violence and cunning Machiavelli despairingly analyzed. The conduct of leaders in the New World was curiously like the conduct of leaders in the Old; and if Machiavelli had known as much about the performance of Europeans in America as he knew about the performance of Italian rulers, he could have drawn his illustrations quite as richly from the one case as he did from the other.

The murky world of the fifteenth and sixteenth centuries has also been concealed by the politeness of textbook writers, so that the bloodthirstiness of the Spaniards in the New World and the frequent treacherousness of white man and Indian in North America seem inexplicable to the modern reader. But the Renaissance was, in both hemispheres, all in one piece. Both Commynes in the fifteenth century [16] and Machiavelli in the sixteenth look out on a world in which the problem of leadership is not a question of what rulers should do in order to be good but of what rulers must do in order to survive.* Cruelty is old, but in the West cruelty as an

---

* Like Machiavelli, Commynes separates the ethical domain from that of

intellectual and scientific component of leadership may be said to begin with the Emperor Frederick II, who after 1231 sought to destroy the feudal order and transform his subjects into a people without will to resist. For this purpose he created a mercenary force of Saracens experienced in slaughter and deaf to Christian pleas. Fourteenth-century Italy, of course, produced even bloodier rulers. Thus Giangaleazzo Visconti on one occasion left Milan under pretext of making a pilgrimage, swooped down on his unsuspecting uncle, got rid of him, forced his way back to Milan, captured the government, and gave the place over to plunder. His son, Giovanni Maria Visconti, in 1409, when the starving populace begged for peace, set fierce hunting dogs upon the Milanese and caused his mercenaries to slaughter the people. He was himself assassinated in the church of San Gottardo. The infamous Ezzelino da Romano erected eight prisons in Padua, two of which contained three hundred captives apiece, and though his executioners were always busy, his prisons were always full. Once he captured eleven thousand Paduans, only two hundred of whom survived his dungeons. He took Friola and caused the entire population to be deprived of eyes, noses, and legs, and on another occasion he walled up a princely family and starved them to death. Galeazzo Maria Sforza fed *his* prisoners on human excrement or buried them alive. He, too, was assassinated on the way to church. Francesco Sforza, when young, married a rich heiress, the Countess of Montalto, who bore him a daughter; both mother and child were poisoned by an aunt who seized the inheritance. During the invasion of Italy by Charles VIII all the houses in the vicinity of Assisi were leveled, the peasants, unable to till their fields, turned to murder, stags and wolves overran the area, and beasts grew fat on human bodies. Ferrante, the ruler of Naples, had his opponents embalmed and kept in the costumes they wore in

action, and the most frequently recurring adjective in the *Memoirs* is *saige,* in the sense of crafty.

life; some of his victims had been killed as they left the royal table. At Ferrara in 1452 a princess was beheaded for adultery with her stepson, and subsequently the bastard son of a bastard of the family sought to wrest the crown from Ercole I, who is said to have poisoned his wife on discovering that, instigated by her brother, Ferrante of Naples, she was about to poison *him*. Doubtless legend has exaggerated the crimes of the Borgias, but they were nonetheless evil. Cesare, Machiavelli's hero, employed one Remirro de Orco, a cruel and able man, to restore order in the Romagna; then, when order was restored, he seized his agent, cut his body in half, and displayed it in the public square with a bloody knife at its side. The treachery of Senigallia is famous; the "guests" were strangled.

The history of the royal house of Scotland in the fifteenth and sixteenth centuries is a long and tedious tale of kidnaping, conspiracy, assassination, poisoning, and treachery, nor should the romantic glamour of Mary Stuart conceal the tawdriness of the story. The history of royalty in fifteenth-century England is not much better, nor are the Tudors a great moral improvement. Indeed it has been said that Henry VIII is the incarnation of Machiavelli's *The Prince*, having an elastic conscience, a passion for efficiency, profound hypocrisy, and an iron will. Hired *bravi* were familiar in England, as when Lord Oxford set a gang of them on Sidney; and, as one scholar suggests, the poisoning of the foils by Laertes in the final act of *Hamlet* probably seemed natural enough to the original audience. Einstein, who makes the observation, sagely remarks that in the emergence of the free personality in the Renaissance, an unchecked bridle was initially given to the prince's authority, with the resulting suppression of those who lost his favor. Loss of office and of property followed as a matter of course (one thinks of Cortés forcing himself to the side of the Spanish monarch and exclaiming that he had given Spain more land and wealth than any other), and death in a shorter or longer time followed as a frequent consequence, as in the case of Sir Walter Ralegh.[17] I refrain from itemizing Spanish atrocities in the Netherlands, wholesale butchery in Ireland, and such characteristic episodes as the burning in Scotland of Dunbar and all its citizens by the English in 1544.

In *The Prince* Machiavelli set himself the problem of studying power and leadership. How can these be stabilized in a world of treachery, mutiny, greed, assassination, and hypocrisy? He turned against the idealism of the humanists and had only contempt for Utopias. He sought a continuing principle of cohesiveness amid the anarchy of Italy. Ordinary ethics, he thought, may do for ordinary occasions and ordinary men, but the leader—the prince—is *a fortiori* not an ordinary man. If leadership is to survive, and survive it must if society is to exist, it must not merely understand how to maintain itself, it must ceaselessly extend its power, even if in so doing it becomes both ruthless and hypocritical. The ruler not only may but on extraordinary occasions ought to do what would be wrong for ordinary men to do. He must disregard the reproach of being thought cruel if through cruelty he is able to keep order. He who quells disorder by a few timely examples will in the end prove more merciful than he who from leniency permits things to take their course and so result in bloodshed. The cruel acts of the leader may, indeed, hurt individuals, but leniency may ruin the state. Let the leader acquire if possible a reputation for generosity, but let him not fear accusations of cruelty or bad faith. Everyone knows it is praiseworthy to keep faith and live uprightly, yet there have been great princes who have known how to overreach men by cunning and who have accomplished great things for themselves, their families, and the state by getting the better of those who trusted merely to honest dealing. Indeed, a prudent leader neither can nor ought to keep his word when to keep it is hurtful to him, especially if the causes that led him to pledge his word have been removed. Of course, if all men were good, this would be bad advice, but since men are dishonest and weak and do not keep faith with the leader, the leader need not keep faith with them. No prince has been censured for taking extraordinary measures to constitute a kingdom or found a republic, but a prince may be despised if he seems to be fickle, irresolute, or cowardly. He must so bear himself that greatness, courage, wisdom, and strength appear in his actions; and though it is good to be both feared and loved, if one must choose, it is better to be feared. Men are either to be caressed or annihilated—they forget more easily the death of their fathers than they do the loss of their property. In sum, the leader must study both the lion and the fox. There is, however, always one incalculable component in the algebra of power, and this is Fortune. God and Fortune govern the world—Machiavelli is, after all, a Catholic—but Fortune is the ruler of half our actions. Into the relation between God and Fortune, Machiavelli apparently does not care to inquire.

Such in summary is this influential book, a complete breviary for conquest.* It is reinforced from Roman history in the *Discourses,* and it has troubled the world ever since 1513. I have used the words "prince," "ruler," and "leader" interchangeably. Cesare Borgia was never a prince in our sense of the term, but his actions parallel or anticipate those of the *conquistadores,* the principal difference being that he was operating in the Old World and they in a new environment. It is precisely the novelty of the environment or, more strictly, the distance of the new environment from the old that makes Machiavelli illuminating in the matter of discovery, exploration, and conquest.

---

* It is important not to be misunderstood. It may be interesting that there are 400 direct references to Machiavelli in Elizabethan literature and that *The Prince* was not translated into English until 1640, but the problem I am attempting to deal with is explication of actual conduct, not one of literary source material.

IV

If centers of power in Europe of the Renaissance were themselves unstable, they could not mysteriously impart to the expeditions they sent out a stability not known in the homeland. We who are used to instant communication by radio or telephone with distant parts of the world can scarcely imagine the lonely insecurity of the commander of an expedition sent across the vast Atlantic in the ships of the period to conquer, explore, or settle. His crews were crowded together in the stinking vessels, living on salt meat and bad beer. His sailors were ignorant and superstitious; his soldiers took instant advantage of any weakness; his gentlemen companions were often insanely jealous of him and secretly determined to carve out estates or accumulate riches on their own. Members of the expedition were not necessarily his own countrymen. If emergency arose, he could not appeal to the distant authority of the sovereign, and even if he could, the royal court being commonly divided in counsel, instructions, when they were belatedly received, were likely as not to be ambiguous. Commanders had therefore to compel loyalty largely by cunning and personal force. Nothing is more revealing than the appearance in Hakluyt or Purchas of articles of agreement among the several captains or masters of ships composing a fleet supposedly under unified command, instructions designed to keep to a plan of campaign and to prevent desertion. A typical one is the "Articles and orders to be observed for the Fleete, set downe by Captaine Frobisher Generall, and delivered in writing to every Captaine, as well for keeping company, as for the course." [18] Notwithstanding (this was in 1578), "the Thomas of Ipswich the night following lost company of the other Shippes, and afterward shaped a contrary course homeward, which fell out as it manifestly appeared, very much against their Captaine Master Tanfields minde, as by due examination before the Lordes of her Majesties most honourable privie Counsell it hath since bene prooved, to the great discredite of the Pilot Cox, who specially persuaded his company against the opinion of his sayd Captaine, to returne home." [19]

Insubordination, mutiny, conspiracy, and rebellion appear with monotonous regularity in the accounts of the discovery, conquest, and settling of the New World. On his first voyage Columbus had to contend with mutiny in his crew and rebellion in the captains of his three ships, and even after the discovery, an event that, one thinks, might have unified morale, Martín Alonso Pinzón on November 22, 1492, sailed off in the *Pinta* without asking anybody's leave and did not rejoin his chief in the *Niña* until January 4, 1493. Columbus had to swallow his wrath. The second voyage was under somewhat better control, though discipline was still imperfect, and he planted his second colony on Hispaniola. But from the third voyage he wrote the sovereigns a letter chronicling virtual civil war among the Spaniards:

> When I went on the voyage to Paria, I found almost half the people in Española in revolt [led by Roldan], and they have made war on me to this day, as if I had been a Moor, and at the same time there has been a serious conflict with the Indians. It was then that Ojeda [Alonso de Hojeda or Ojeda] came and he endeavored to put the seal on this state of affairs, saying that Their Highnesses [Ferdinand and Isabella] had sent him with promises of gifts and franchises and wages. He gathered a great following, for in all Española there are few who are not vagabonds, and there is no one with a wife and children. This Ojeda troubled me greatly and it was necessary that he should be sent away, and he went, declaring that he would speedily return with more ships and men. . . . At this time one Andrian attempted to revolt as before but Our Lord would not permit his evil purpose to be carried into effect . . . owing to his ingratitude, I was not able to save him, as I had intended to do. . . . This Andrian . . . sent Don Fernando [de Guevara] to Xaragua to assemble some of his followers, and there was there a dispute with the alcalde, whence arose a deadly quarrel.[20]

Andrian was one Andria de Moxico, a young man of good family, a follower of the mutinous Roldan, who was angered

by Columbus's treatment of his cousin, Hernando de Guevara. When the treason of Hernando de Guevara against
Columbus was revealed, Columbus ordered him to be
hanged, and when he did not even then confess his treachery,
caused Hernando to be hurled to death from the walls of
Concepçión, the fort he had built on that island.*

As it has been inferred that this anarchy sprang from a
special weakness in Columbus, it is well to note that mutiny
and treachery plagued other leaders. After Balboa had painfully conveyed the material for four ships across the Isthmus
of Panama in order to navigate the ocean he had discovered,
he was ordered back by the jealousy of Pedrarias (Pedro Arias
de Ávila), taken to Panama, and incontinently hanged.
Magellan had to crush a formidable mutiny in April 1520;
and Sir Francis Drake, on the same spot on the coast of
South America, had both to try and to execute Thomas
Doughty for plotting against him. The bloody history of
Peru is a monotonous tale of treachery, civil war, and slaughter among the Spaniards themselves; not until Pedro de la
Gasca in 1548 massacred the remaining forces of the Pizarro
family and slew all but one of the family itself was there
order in the colony. In Colombia in 1535 Alonso de Lugo,
the son of the governor of New Granada, led a party inland
which failed, partly out of mutiny and partly out of his own
rapacity. Alonso eventually fled the scene. A nobleman
named Pedro de Ursuá tried to reach the fabulous El Dorado
by crossing the Andes from Peru. He took with him his
mistress and a lieutenant named Lope de Aguirre. Dissension broke out almost at once. On New Year's Day, 1561,
Aguirre caused Pedro de Ursuá to be murdered. He then
killed the mistress, Dona Iñez, on the ground that she was a
burden to the expedition; after that he renounced his allegiance to the Spanish monarch and slaughtered all the mem-

---

* Roldan was but temporarily checked and was later involved in further
conspiracies against the admiral and Bartholomew Columbus. Vincent Yañez
Pinzón also misbehaved.

bers of the party who would not do likewise. The rest committed every atrocity against the Indians and took to murdering one another. A remnant reached the mouth of the Orinoco, captured the island of Margarita, and tried to invade Venezuela. Aguirre was finally put to death by the royal governor.[21]

English annals are somewhat less bloody, but the pattern of indiscipline is the same. In 1576 the bark *Michael,* part of Frobisher's third expedition, "conveyed themselves privily away from him, and returned home, with great report that he was cast away." [22] On John Davis's third voyage to the north bad blood developed between the crews of the *Sunshine* and the *Elizabeth.* The *Sunshine* people wanted to go catch fish and return home safely, but the master did not wish to leave the *Elizabeth* and told the captain of that vessel "hee was afrayd his men would shape some contrary course while he was asleepe." [23] Davis left two ships on the fishing grounds after "taking their faithful promise not to depart untill my returne unto them," but after only sixteen days the two vessels "departed for England, without regard of their promise: my selfe not distrusting any such hard measure." [24] On the fatal expedition of Sir Humphrey Gilbert "the Vizeadmirall forsooke us, notwithstanding we had the winde East, faire, and good." Sickness was the excuse but, says Edward Haye, "the reason I could never understand," a desertion the more ironic since every ship had sailed with sealed orders, not to be opened until they were well clear of the Irish coast, "lest any of the company stealing from the fleet might bewray the same." Once arrived at Newfoundland, while the loyal men were doing their best on shore,

> others of another sort & disposition were plotting of mischiefe. Some casting to steale away our shipping by night, watching oportunitie by the Generals and Captaines lying on the shore: whose conspiracies discovered, they were prevented. Others drew togither in company, and carried away out of the harbors adjoyning, a ship laden with fish, setting the poore men on

shore. A great many more of our people stole into the woods to hide themselves, attending time and meanes to returne home by such shipping as daily departed from the coast.[25]

Sickness and death on this as on other expeditions encouraged desertion and mutiny. The voyage of Charles Leigh and "divers others" to Cape Breton is a long tangle of quarrel and treachery in both French and English ships, each nation having its own mutinies to suppress and each attempting to pillage the ships of the other.[26] The voyage of Andrew Barker of Bristol in the *Ragged Staff* to the Caribbean is a tale of disaster, the central contention being between Barker and his master, Philip Roche. This culminated in a duel. In the Gulf of Honduras William Coxe, apparently an early buccaneer, captured the ship and "with violence" put Barker and certain others on shore. There Barker fought a second duel with a German named Weiborn, in which both were wounded; then he begged to come on board again. The request was refused, and sixty Spaniards surprised Barker and eight of his men on shore and slaughtered them. Coxe and his crew left this anchorage, went to another island, and split up a chain of gold belonging to the dead captain.[27] Sailors on the *Delight,* confronting the terrors of the Strait of Magellan in 1589–1590, understandably grew fearful, and "divers of our company raising dangerous mutinies: we consulted, though somewhat with the latest, for the safeguard of our lives to returne while there was some small hope remayning: and so set saile out of The Streight homeward about the 14. of Februarie 1590." Hakluyt prints the impressive document drawn up by the rebellious crew.[28] These are but representative instances, chosen at random.

In situations like these the leader, if either he or his men or some part of them were to survive, had to be both lion and fox in the best manner of Machiavelli. Far from civilization for months and years at a time, living in a climate he did not understand, enduring indescribable miseries (consider De Soto, Laudonnière, and the Jesuit fathers in Canada), growing more and more accustomed to the brutality of treacherous native enemies and the jealousy of his own men, compelled to kill or be killed, the New World leader did not have to read the *Discourses* to learn that founders of states must assume that all men are bad and will always, when they have a free field, give a loose rein to their evil inclinations, or that the wise founder of a commonwealth must endeavor to acquire an absolute and undivided authority, or that you cannot subject men to hardships unless you hold out rewards or, without danger, deprive them of the rewards you have promised. These commonplaces of the grammar of power they learned by experience. Cortés, Pizarro, and even Captain John Smith could have told Machiavelli that he who sets up as a tyrant and slays not Brutus and he who creates a free government and slays not the sons of Brutus, can never maintain himself.[29] Among them Machiavelli's complaint that neither prince nor citizen resorts to the example of the ancients was unnecessary; they did not need Machiavelli to tell them how to survive, they were practicing the Machiavellian precepts on their own.

Cortés is the greatest example of Machiavellian man in the New World. Ruthless, determined, polished, insubordinate, he was a profound student of human nature. When the news reached him that Velásquez had revoked his commission to go to Mexico, he sailed secretly away before the official messengers could catch him up, gathering supplies through misrepresentations along the Cuban coast. He landed in Mexico, founded Vera Cruz, and received from his self-created *cabildo* the commission to do what he was going to do anyway. But this made it legal. He fought the Tlascalans three times, then joined them as an ally against the Aztecs, burning his ships in order that shipmasters, pilots, and seamen would have to go with him and not run away. He flattered his troops with classical orations. He received five tax-gatherers sent by Montezuma to collect tribute and demand twenty sacrificial victims from the coastal Indians, then ordered the local chief to refuse the demand and imprison the tax-collectors, and after that, took them from the jail, assuring them he was saving their lives, and sent two of them back to Montezuma with a message of friendship as from one potentate to another. At Cholula his Indian mistress, Marina, informed him of an Indian plot to murder the Spaniards; whereupon Cortés, like Cesare Borgia, lured the chief and a company of his followers into an enclosure, taxed them with treachery, when they blamed it all on Montezuma, pretended to be infuriated by this imputation on his "friend," and massacred three thousand Indians. Arriving at Tenochtitlán, after a decent interval he seized Montezuma through treachery, left the city to fight off Narváez's men just landed at Vera Cruz, persuaded them to join him, and returned to find that his lieutenant had slaughtered some Aztec nobles during a ritualistic dance and that the city was in arms. To induce the Aztecs to lay down their weapons, Cortés compelled Montezuma to address them—that prince was then stoned by his own people. The Spaniards were driven out during the Noche Triste; returning, they destroyed as much of the Aztec empire as they could. When Cortés discovered a conspiracy among his own officers to overthrow him, he hanged the leader from the window bars of his own lodging. The one unintelligent act of his career, if one judges it by Machiavellian standards, was the execution of Guatémoc and Tetepanquetzatl, the lord of Tlacopan, during the march to Honduras to put down the rebellion of Olid. The expedition almost starved to death, and some of the Mexican allies roasted one of their dead companions and ate him; Cortés, to show his contempt for this, commanded one of the starving men to be burned alive. His men grumbled at the meager distribution of the spoils they had won and accused Cortés of hoarding gold; yet they followed him. This is the same man of whom Bernal Díaz says that he was most affable with his captains and comrades, that he could talk Latin with the lawyers, that he made songs, spoke quietly, and prayed each evening with a book of hours in his hand.[30] Let it be remembered that some of the Spaniards had served in Italy under Gonsalvo di Cordova and may have seen Cesare Borgia himself.

The career of Cortés gives us a full-scale example of Machiavellian man in the New World, but it is not sole and singular. Ponce de León, made governor of Porto Rico in 1509, was superseded through a court intrigue, whereupon he waged a civil war against his successor, simultaneously putting down an Indian uprising with great cruelty. Francisco Pizarro, a bastard of enormous determination, courage, ruthlessness, and egotism, started the conquest of Peru with 62 horsemen and 106 infantry. Like Cortés he lured the leading Indians by fair words into massacre, seized on the ruling Inca by strategy, then strangled him, rooted out the leading natives by the measures Machiavelli advises, and was murdered in 1541 by the followers of Almagro (whom he had executed for mutiny), leaving a legacy of blood to the dominion he had established.

The contrasting qualities of Pámfilo de Narváez and Hernando de Soto, though both of them came to grief, illustrate the Machiavellian problems of weakness and strength. Narváez sailed from San Lucar de Barrameda on June 17, 1727, to conquer Florida in five ships carrying some 600 colonists and soldiers. He seems to have been entirely incompetent and thoroughly selfish. Waiting at Santo Domingo for 45 days to procure matériel and horses, he lost 140 deserters, lured away by the colonists. After a succession of disasters in Florida, he did not know what to do, and most of his mounted men "commenced secretly to plot, hoping to secure a better fate for themselves by abandoning the Governor and the sick," though some men of gentle blood remained loyal, if not to Narváez, at least to the concept of loyalty. Sailing from the "Bay of Horses" in incompetently constructed boats, he and his men were enticed ashore and assaulted at night by Indians who had seemed to be friendly. Narváez, hit in the face by a stone, was rescued by the remnants of his force and carried to a boat while 50 other

Spaniards ("not one among us escaped injury") three times fought off the Indians. What was left of the crazy flotilla was carried away from land by a wind from the north and by the force of the Mississippi River where it enters the gulf. Narváez displayed his usual incompetence. Cabeça de Vaca, who was in charge of one boat, observed two others, drew near, and discovered that one of them carried Narváez, who weakly asked Cabeça de Vaca what should be done. Cabeça de Vaca thought they should join together, but the governor denied all aid to Cabeça de Vaca's boat, he refused to allow his oarsmen to help Cabeça de Vaca by throwing out a tow-line, and his final injunction was "that it was no longer a time in which one should command another; but that each should do what he thought best to save his own life; that he so intended to act; and saying this, he departed with his boat." The reader has some satisfaction in learning that Narváez was thereupon carried out to sea and never seen again.

Equally unfortunate, Hernando de Soto yet commanded the admiration of his chroniclers and followers, even when he was wrong. Though the *Narrative of the Gentleman of Elvas* makes it clear that in the author's opinion De Soto, when he had the chance, should have retreated to the seacoast, he writes; "The Governor then resolved at once to go in quest of that country, and being an inflexible man, and dry of word, who, although he liked to know what the others all thought and had to say, after he once said a thing he did not like to be opposed, and as he ever acted as he thought best, all bent to his will." The Inca Garcilaso de la Vega, who wished he might attain "the classic eloquence of the greatest Caesar" in chronicling the heroic deeds of De Soto and his men, deeds which were "much nobler than those of the Greeks, Romans and peoples of other nations," is loud in his praise of De Soto as a great captain. Desiring to capture Capafi, an Indian chief, "now that he felt him so within reach, [De Soto] fought like the very valiant soldier he was. As a good captain, he gave courage to his men by calling their names aloud, and when he did so, they made such a tremendous onslaught upon their foes and wounded them with such ferocity and cruelty as almost to annihilate them." When a small contingent returned to the main body from a side expedition, De Soto "welcomed his captain and soldiers as would a loving father, joyfully embracing and questioning each of them individually as to how he felt and how he had withstood the journey." Even when matters were steadily growing worse, "It was a matter of the greatest joy for the soldiers to witness the fine attitude the Governor himself demonstrated toward his men in this affliction [of hunger] by strengthening and helping them to endure their hunger as if he were not privileged in any way and were the least of them all." Both writers join in eulogizing him after his death and burial in the Mississippi. Says the Gentleman of Elvas:

> The next day, the twenty-first of May, departed this life the magnanimous, the virtuous, intrepid captain, Don Hernando de Soto, Governor of Cuba and Adelantado of Florida. He was advanced by fortune in the way she is wont to lead others, that he might fall the greater depth: he died in a land, and at a time, that could afford him little comfort in his illness, when the danger of being no more heard from stared his companions in the face, each one himself having need of sympathy, which was the cause why they neither gave him their companionship nor visited him, as otherwise they would have done.

And the Inca writes admiringly:

> Severe in punishing transgressions of military science, he pardoned others freely. He esteemed highly those of his soldiers who were strong and brave, and he personally was most courageous, in fact so courageous that wherever he entered a battlefield fighting, he cut a path through which ten of his men could pass . . . he was always the first or the second to rush forth at the alarm . . . in those assaults which the enemy made by night, he was the first and never the second.

Here are Machiavelli's Fortune and his lion. But the Inca is also not unaware of the fox. Describing a sea fight between a

Spaniard and a Frenchman in the harbor of Santiago, from which the Frenchman stole away by night, the Inca's comment is that "after all, the observance of one's word in such cases is very stupid, for it is a characteristic of wise men to change their minds, particularly in war since things pertaining to war are unstable and peace is uncertain, and since the ultimate end one seeks in war is simply to emerge victorious." For this reason he records without reproach various tricks by which De Soto lured Indians into his power.[31]

Hampered by ambiguous restrictions, Ralegh's third Guiana expedition was sent out by James I at the same time that James was conciliating the Spanish court; the king apparently let the Spaniards know the details of Ralegh's plan, in a mutiny in Guiana his son was murdered, the remnants of the expedition returned, and Ralegh was confined to the Tower and later executed, the victim of the game of power. The story of alternating French and Spanish settlements in Florida is a story of weakness crisscrossed with ruthless leadership and massacre. The history of Jamestown from 1606 to 1610 is, by comparison with the conquest of Mexico or of Peru, very small beer, yet the tale of a struggle for power is like. On the island of Nevis, John Smith was charged by Wingfield with mutiny and a gallows erected for his judicial murder; at Jamestown, Wingfield was deposed from the presidency of the council on charges of misgovernment, he and Kendall were accused of plotting to run off to England and Kendall was shot, Ratcliffe and Gabriel Archer tried to escape and were prevented, Newport and Ratcliffe plotted to keep John Smith out of the colony so that the Indians would kill him, and Ratcliffe was imprisoned. He later died, a captive of the Indians, who tied him to a tree, roasted him, and let their women scrape the flesh from his bones during the process. Out of these charges and countercharges John Smith emerges as the strong ruler who saves the colony by strength and cunning, deliberately deceiving the Indians when policy requires that he do so. Later governors—Sir Thomas Dale and Lord De La Warr, for example—have to follow his policy of "thorough" if the "unruly sparks, packed off by their Friends . . . poor Gentlemen, broken Tradesmen, Rakes and Libertines, Footmen and such others . . . fitter to spoil or ruin a Commonwealth, than to help to raise or maintain one" were to survive. The Indians massacred a third of the settlers in 1622, partly in retaliation for the hideous massacre of Indians by the settlers.

Doubtless at this distance it is easy to misunderstand the criminal codes of the seventeenth century, reading into them barbarities that were taken for granted in a ruder age; yet an examination of the account of Gates's men when they were shipwrecked on Bermuda shows how necessary was a policy of ruthlessness. Set to work to build a vessel that would get them off the island, some men mutinied and were punished by being marooned on a lonely islet until they grew heartily sick of one another's company. Then one Stephen Hopkins stirred up a second mutiny, for which he was pardoned. Next, Henry Paine stole for still another set of mutineers and struck the captain of the guard when he was exposed for doing so. He was sentenced to be hanged, confessed all, and asked to be shot. This was done. His fellow mutineers fled the camp. And it is notorious that in 1621 some tried to flee from Jamestown but were captured, hanged, shot, or broken on the wheel. Dale had to be the same kind of strong man that Captain John Smith had been.[32]

Nor is the Virginia case exceptional. Maryland was plagued by intrigue and rebellion from its beginnings. Here is Governor Harvey writing Secretary Windebank on December 16, 1634:

> This faction I find greate cause to suspect is nourished from England for this Summer came letters to Capt: Matthewes who is the patron of disorder as your Honor will understand by the bearer hereof Lieutenant Evelin (and by his comportment in other matters as your Honor will finde in these papers) upon the reading whereof hee threw his hatt upon the ground scratching his head and in a fury stamping cryed a pox upon Maryland, many Letters and secrett intelligences hee and the

rest of the Councell have especially Claybourne and many meetings and consultations. . . .

Forty years later it was the Jesuits who were plotting "to over terne Engl^d, with feyer, sword and distractions" and "the Maryland Papists" intended "to drive us Protestants to Purgatory within our selves in America, with the help of the French spirits from Canada . . . O Treachery plainly discovered out of the Cabinet of Popish Maryland, wch opened further out starts a Number of Grievances, which prognisticat an absolut ruyn and subversion of the king's Maj^ty's loyall subjects in Maryland." Propaganda, this, but the point is, surely, the climate of opinion it represents. "Soe it is," wrote Charles Carroll from Saint Marys in 1689, "that neither Catholique nor honest Protestant can well call his life or estate his own." And Richard Jones wrote Samuel Groome at the same time that "the long soard in the Rables hands is our masters." [33]

John Hammond was by no means enthusiastic about the life in Virginia or Maryland. Of Virginia under Dale he wrote:

> Then were Jayls emptied, youth seduced, infamous women drilled in, the provisions all brought out of England, and that embezzlled by the Trustees (for they durst neither hunt, fowl, nor Fish, for fear of the Indian, which they stood in aw of), their labour was almost perpetuall, their allowance of victuall small, few or no cattle, no use of horses nor oxen to draw or carry, (which labours men supplyed themselves) all which caused a mortality; no civil courts of justice but under a Marshall law, no redresse of grievances, complaints were repaied with stripes, moneys with scoffes, tortures made delights, and in a word all and the worst that tyranny could inflict or act, which when complained of in England, (but so were they kept under that it was long ere they would suffer complaints to come home) . . .

As for Maryland, "Twice hath she been deflowred by her own Inhabitants, stript, and made deformed," [34] and that part of the difficulty lay in the lawless character of the settlers in his majesty's North American colonies is evident from a petition of the mayor of Bristol in England to the king:

> Among those who repair to Bristol from all parts to be transported to his majesty's Plantations beyond seas, some are husbands that have forsaken their wives, others wives who have abandoned their husbands, some are children and apprentices run away from their parents and masters, oftentimes unwary and credulous persons have been tempted on board by menstealers, and many that have been pursued by hue-and-cry for robberies, burglaries or breaking prison, do thereby escape the prosecution of law and justice.[35]

One glaring instance of the resulting disorder, this time occasioned by the Dutch, happened in 1648:

> Those men of trade came a Shoare with their goods where they traded with the Indians and frequenting soe much with the Indian women till they gott the Country dutyes otherwise called the Pox and so they named that place the Whorekill. That is in English the whores Creeke, whereupon they returned home and entered againe a second time . . . they went some ten or twelve miles higher where they Landed againe and traded with the Indians trusting the Indians to come into their Stores a Shoare, and likewise aboard of their sloope drinking and debauching with the Indians till they were all at last barborously murdered and so that place was Christined with their blood and to this day called the Murderers Kill that is Murderers Creeke.

On still a later visit the Dutch went up higher, built a fort, and "lived without government until 1652."[36]

This sort of thing has of course been dismissed as propaganda or as not reflecting the true quality of colonial life. But the lawlessness of the frontier would seem to be a well-established truth, as life in the early years of Australia with its convicts and remittance men, in New Zealand, in California during the Gold Rush, in Nevada in the days of its silvermine prosperity, in the rush to the Klondike, and in other well-attested historical areas and eras amply testifies; and though the "quality" and the bourgeoisie certainly also migrated to the New World, the point is the need for control by the Machiavellian strong man even through lynch law and vigilantes, if necessary. The seventeenth-century situation in North America was often of this kind, made worse, one conjectures, by distance from royal (or proprietary) authority and, during the English Civil Wars, by confusion in the home government. Witness Bacon's Rebellion in Virginia.

V

Nothing, however, more richly exemplifies the Machiavellian theory of leadership as compounded of sagacity, cruelty, and intelligent deceit than does the history of buccaneering during the seventeenth century in the Caribbean. It was then, and earlier, and is now, virtually impossible to distinguish among privateering, piracy, and buccaneering, and the literature on this fascinating topic is confused by romanticism, by the fact that in the nature of the case few of the men concerned left records behind them, and by the truth that the court records give only the cases of those who were tried and condemned, pardoned, or found innocent. I shall come in a moment to piracy. Let us look at the buccaneers.

The word itself comes from the killing of wild cattle for their hides and meat by the so-called *gens de la côte,* stateless men without wives, who presently took to the sea as privateersmen, buccaneers, or pirates. Drake and Hawkins had set an example for raids in peace or war upon the Spaniards; and the buccaneers, who were in effect seamen and soldiers following sea *condottieri* of their own·election, profited from this precedent under such leaders as Pierre Legrand, L'Ollonais, Michel le Basque, Bartholomew the Portuguese, Mansfield, and the great Henry Morgan. Buccaneering developed amid, and contributed to, the rich anarchy of that part of the world, product of the four-cornered struggle of Spain, Holland, France, and England for the sugar islands and the mineral wealth of the Spanish New World. The weakening power of Spain invited attack, but the other three powers could not agree among themselves as to the distribution of the spoils.

The buccaneers, who founded their own pirate republic on the island of Tortuga, were virtually a fifth power with their own army and navy, now hiring out to some European crown, now operating on their own, always feared by Spain and perpetually distrusted by the governments that employed them. They were forced to cruelty and cunning as instruments of aggrandizement and plunder, and their leaders maintained control by the personal ascendancy that comes from superior strength, recklessness, opportune generosity, and the crafty use of terror. Leadership was, paradoxically, constitutional: no expedition set out until articles of agreement had been drawn up and assented to, the various members having fractions of the booty to be seized given to them at the end of the expedition in proportion to their rank, responsibility, wounds, or even death—in which case their portion was assigned to a designated comrade. Every buccaneer was assumed to have erased his allegiance to a European sovereign by crossing the Tropic of Cancer and being accepted into the republic.

In their earlier history the buccaneering groups chose their own leaders, but when in the contests for empire the powers discovered the usefulness of this fierce soldiery, their leaders commonly received commissions from some crown and agreed to give the royal governor who issued their commissions a tenth of the plunder. At the height of their strength, from 1640 to about 1680, the buccaneers could muster fleets of eight, ten, twelve, and twenty sail and expeditions of from four hundred to two thousand fierce fighting men. They did not, of course, always wait on formal declarations of war to seize shipping or plunder towns; and their historian assures us that between 1655 and 1671 the buccaneers sacked eighteen cities, four towns, and more than thirty-five villages (all Spanish), some of them eight times.

The considerable town of Porto Bello was plundered once, Panama twice, and Campeche three times; when a town was plundered, it was usually burned unless ransom was offered. Captives were tortured to extort ransom. Cruelty bred cruelty; in retaliation for much torture and robbery, the Spaniards, when they captured Providence Island (at one time a hopeful Puritan settlement), made thirty-three Englishmen prisoners, clubbed them to death when they were too feeble to work, and carried off three captains to Panama, where they languished, chained, in dungeons for seventeen months.

Such men could be controlled only by personal prowess, extreme daring, and ruthless cruelty. Pierre Legrand, a Norman, began his career by capturing a Spanish vice-admiral, part of the annual *flota,* from a boat containing only twenty-eight men. He caused a hole to be bored in his own vessel so that it must sink (one remembers Cortés burning his ships), thus compelling his followers to conquer or perish. Esquemeling in his *Buccaneers of America* describes a certain "Rock Brasiliano," who roasted Spaniards alive, despoiled the dead, and beat the wounded to death. Having captured a Spanish ship, L'Ollonais ordered the crew under hatches and had them decapitated, one by one, as they came on deck. He made no account, says Esquemeling, of murdering ten or twelve Spaniards in cold blood; and in the capture of Gibraltar (near Maracaibo), seeing his men hesitate, he made them a speech that, one imagines, Bernal Díaz would approve: "We must either defend ourselves like good soldiers, or lose our lives with all the riches we have got. Do as I shall do, who am your Captain. At other times we have fought with fewer men than we have in our company at present, and yet we have overcome greater numbers than there possibly can be in this town. The more they are, the more glory we shall attribute unto our fortune, and the greater riches we shall increase unto it." The buccaneers assented, and he continued: " 'Tis well; but know ye withal that the first man who shall show any fear, or the least apprehension thereof, I will pistol him with my own hands." He captured the town by tricking the Spaniards, let most of his captives starve to death, and returned eventually to the pirate republic on the island of Tortuga. Do not the mood, the appeal to wealth and glory, and the reference to fortune make one think of Machiavelli? [37]

The buccaneers were adventurers from every class of European society who fled to the West Indies to avoid trouble, to save their lives, or because the innumerable dissensions of Europe—the Civil Wars in Great Britain, the Thirty Years' War in Germany, the troubles in France inherited from the religious wars and typified by the Fronde—drove them out to recoup their wasted fortunes. They were mainly men without families. Jamaica became the home of discontented soldiers, their rebelliousness increased by the habit of dumping criminals and exiles on the West Indies. Typical is the career of Sir Henry Morgan, who was kidnaped in Bristol as a boy, was sold as an indentured servant to a man on Barbados, ran away, joined the buccaneers, and rose through Machiavellian genius to such a pitch of fame that he sacked Porto Bello and received the thanks of the Council of Jamaica in 1671, sacked Panama, returned to England, and was knighted in 1674—a career more incredible than that of Captain John Smith. The long account of the siege of Porto Bello in Esquemeling reads like a chapter from Schiller's *The Thirty Years' War*—and, indeed, a good way to comprehend this incredible part of New World history is to read *Wallensteins Lager* and realize that we are dealing with the contemporaries of the Piccolomini.[38]

Nor is all this as remote from influencing the history of the United States as at first sight it seems to be. From the days of Elizabeth down into the nineteenth century pirates, buccaneers, filibusters, freebooters—the terms are virtually interchangeable—haunted North American waters both as bases for their operations, areas in which to plunder, rob, and burn, and as markets for the disposal of their goods. Pirates entered into profitable relations with merchants in Boston,

New York, and other ports, and found both Chesapeake Bay and the coastal waters of the Carolinas useful to their trade. As early as 1611 it is said that one Captain Easton had forty vessels under his command for the plunder of shipping off Newfoundland, nor was he without rivals. Colonial governors sometimes connived at piracy; and in the Carolinas, for example, members of the governors' councils had to be dismissed from their posts because of their friendly relations with pirate leaders. Karraker, in one of the few scholarly treatments of the subject,[39] basing his study upon archives in Great Britain and here, finds good reason to cast moral doubt upon the origins of certain mercantile fortunes in the colonial period. A typical case illustrative of the difficulty in drawing lines concerns a petition from a merchant named Perry on behalf of one Edward Davies and others jailed in Jamestown. The petition came to the attention of the Privy Council. Davies and his companions had spent some time in the South Seas, "procuring" plate and other goods. Resolved to spend the rest of their days "honestly and quietly," they went to Philadelphia and then to Virginia, where they were seized by the captain of the *Dumbarton* and jailed for piracy —the problem was how to get them out again. By 1700 American waters had become so infested with piratical enterprise that one observer described the situation as being like that of a state of war.

Armed conflict occurred. In 1689 a British garrison at Fort Loyal, Falmouth, Maine, deserted, decided to turn pirates, and had to be captured. In 1700 a fleet of buccaneers under the command of the famous (or infamous) La Paix appeared in Chesapeake Bay, was attacked by colonial forces under the command of Governor Nicholson, and defeated: twenty or thirty pirates were killed, some were hanged after the encounter, and about ninety were sent to England for trial.[40] The capture of Stede Bonnet off the Carolina coast and of Blackbeard off Ocracoke Inlet, both in 1718, is famous in legend. The story of Captain Kidd will never be cleared up to everybody's satisfaction—awarded £150 by the Royal

Council of New York for services rendered, he was then commissioned by Lord Bellomont to fight the pirates; a list of
leading piratical captains having been given him, he departed,
possibly turned pirate himself, came back to enrich his benefactor, whom he perhaps deceived a second time, was captured, sent to England, and hanged in 1701. It is hinted that
he was put out of the way to conceal the relations of leading
men in England and North America with the pirates.[41] There
are records of New England trials for piracy in 1653, 1672,
1674, 1675, 1689, 1690, 1704, 1723, 1724, 1765, and (incredibly) as late as 1834. The list is incomplete and of course does
not include trials of pirates in New York, Charleston, and
other places. The court records show that those who were
hanged were commonly young men in their twenties—a lad
of fourteen was had up in one of these trials and let go—and
the hanging of pirates, sometimes in chains, was an important
public spectacle, some pirates grimly observing that being
preached at by clergymen increased the terrors of death. Yet
a Captain Nelson of Prince Edward Island is said to have
spent his declining years in respectable retirement in New
York City, one Francis Dole lived with his wife in Charleston
at the end of the seventeenth century, and of course Jean
Lafitte helped Andrew Jackson to defend New Orleans
against the British! [42]

The pirate and the buccaneer have left two indelible
legends in the American mind. One, an embodiment of Byronism, is that the pirate is a romantic figure flying the Jolly
Roger, commanding his crew with a glance of his eye, compelling his captives to walk the plank, falling in love with
beautiful women, whom he sometimes treats with distinguished courtesy, and professing an understandable philosophy of life. Such books as *The History of the Pirates,* published at Hartford, Connecticut, in 1835, and *The Pirates
Own Book,* first printed in Boston in 1837 and recently (1924)
reissued by the Marine Research Society of Salem, are of
this general character, which eventuates in the fiction of
Robert Louis Stevenson and the pictures of Howard Pyle.

There seems to be little in what is actually known of a short and brutal life to justify romance. Pirate captains customarily came to power by trickery, murder, mutiny, or some other form of seizure, maintained control over their crews only for brief periods of time and through Machiavellian devices, and died on the gallows, in sea fights, or by assassination at the hands of rival marine *condottieri,* and so on.

The other element in legend is that which leads historians and social reformers to characterize the operations of big business, particularly after the Civil War, by such phrases as piracy, buccaneering, robber barons, the big barbecue, and associated terms. Not all these words go back to the high seas, of course, but enough of them thus originated to show a sneaking regard among the Americans for the unchecked individualism of piracy, the gross satisfaction of a power lust through a code (as in the case of the buccaneers) invented by the trade ("to go on the account" was the term used to describe someone taking up piracy) and held to be superior to ordinary morality or ordinary law. The pirate appealed, in a sense, to natural law, he survived by a combination of force and cunning, and the Social Darwinists of the later nineteenth century in another sense merely translated his code into more elegant terms. There was of course a basic difference: despite legends of buried pirate treasure, most pirates accumulated no permanent wealth, whereas, during the period of the great barbecue, American business leaders, dedicated though they were to ruthless exploitation, were also dedicated to amassing enormous fortunes that would endure.

VI

The lack of any definitive study of the vogue of Machiavelli in North America seems to indicate that *Il Principe* had no such influence as the cult of the gentleman. But the central issue is, as I have said, not one of influence [43] but of conduct, and it seems unlikely that the powerful traditions we have been discussing died out and left no aftermath. What happened was that the Machiavellian theory of power, so far as the mainland colonies were concerned, seemed to split into two parts. One has to do with terror as an instrument of policy, and the other with cunning.

The Indians were an eternal problem on the frontiers. Until late in the history of the United States their numbers were forever exaggerated, and struggling states (such as Kentucky and Tennessee) or straggling settlements (the Virginia frontier or the Connecticut Valley in the seventeenth century, for example) seemed to be perpetually contesting with enormous, shadowy forces, always untrustworthy, always irresponsible, always cruel. From the beginning the English and after them the Americans continued to attribute to amorphous Indian tribes all the qualities of sovereignty, permanent political organization, and "polity" familiar to Europeans. They could not comprehend that an Indian "emperor," "king," sachem, chief, or even tribal council had no power to alienate land, agree to a treaty, or bring to justice in the white man's court honorable savages who had avenged themselves by scalping white families. Inevitably the Indian was charged with bad faith, and the charge was exacerbated by the well-known cruelties of Indian warfare and the ritualistic torture of prisoners. Since the Indian did not keep faith with the white man and since he was powerful, the white man need keep no faith with the Indian and was justified in outwitting him by cunning, fraud, superior power, and cruelty as an instrument of power.

The experiences of two colonies are illuminating. The massacre of white settlers by supposedly "friendly" Indians in the Virginia of 1622 set off a long series of merciless retaliatory performances by the whites on the all too familiar pattern of the *lex talionis.* Half a century later, raids by the Susquehannock Indians on the frontiers of Maryland and Virginia demanded retaliation, and Nathaniel Bacon arose not merely to put down the Indians but to seize, or at any rate manipulate, political power in the colony itself. The history of Bacon's Rebellion, notably the actions of Governor Sir William Berkeley, becomes in miniature another example of Machiavellianism. He continually attempted to deceive Bacon, he continually failed to keep his word, and when, after Bacon's death, Berkeley triumphed, his victory was characterized by the senseless hanging of the chief followers of the dead rebel (including one Anthony Arnold, who was obviously insane) and the confiscation of their estates, all after the terror pattern of sixteenth-century Italy. That England, or at least its monarch, had advanced beyond terror and confiscation as instruments of policy, at least temporarily, is evident in the famous remark of Charles II that the old fool had taken more lives in that naked country than the king had taken in England for the murder of his father.

The New England colonies were likewise caught in a trap. Striking back at the perpetual encroachments of the whites, Indians fought in the only way they knew how to fight—by ambush, massacre, torture, and arson, all provocations enough. But rather more than the Virginians did, the New Englanders attributed such bloody business as King Philip's War to Satan and regarded their own strategy of terror as part of a holy crusade. This is evident, for example, in Samuel Penhallow's *History of the Wars of New-England* (1726); the author apologizes for asking the reader to peruse "the story of a *barbarous War*," but justifies what was done by an appeal to religion: "I might with *Orosius* very justly entitle this History, *De miseria hominum,* being no other than a Narrative of *Tragical Incursions* perpetrated by Bloody *Pagans* . . . Monsters of . . . Cruelty . . . implacable in their Revenge, as they are terrible in the Execution of it." [44] The pagans are apparently loosed by a Protestant God and frontier settlements are massacred as a punishment for human backsliding (the logic of this escapes the modern reader), but God also permits the white men to surround, surprise, burn alive, and massacre most of the Pequot nation in 1637.

The *in terrorem* principle obviously weakens in modern America, though one is compelled to reflect upon gang warfare in Chicago, the Heinz-Daley copper fight in Montana, and the assassination of Huey Long; but the use of fraud to maintain either a single person or a group in political control does not pass so quickly. A series of interesting studies has been made of the behavior of a group determined to fasten something like the feudal system or manorial control upon the southern mainland colonies, in parallel, apparently, to the like system of control in the British West Indies.[45] Entrepreneurs streamed out of Stuart England to the islands and to protected places on the North American coast to create, if they could, manorial estates on the European model. A great effort, beginning in 1660, was made by Clarendon, Shaftesbury, Albemarle, Carteret, and others of a small group that eventually included Governor Sir William Berkeley to monopolize political power by what any finer conscience would denominate as fraud. This group were members of the Privy Council, which they controlled, they dominated the East India Company and the African slave trade, and they managed for some years every important political and economic interest of Restoration England in Great Britain and abroad, if William E. Dodd is to be believed. They passed, or caused to be passed, the Clarendon Code (1662–1665), which not merely penalized dissent but compelled unity in Great Britain, the North American colonies, and the West Indies, or was intended to, and they created and enforced the Navigation Acts of 1660 and 1663 that gave a monopoly of the carrying trade to English shipping and brought money into the pockets of the dominant group.

Sir William Berkeley went from Virginia to London in the summer of 1661 as the mouthpiece of the Virginia planters to resist commercial restraint, but the group seems to have taken him over. He received £2000 from the king, was made one of the eight lords proprietor of all the region from Virginia to Florida, and agreed that this territory should be divided into tracts of 48,000 acres each, to be presided over by a landgrave or duke in order that the manorial (and feudal) system might be maintained. Lord John Berkeley became joint overlord with Carteret of the provinces of New Jersey; other court favorites were granted some six million acres between the Rappahannock and the Potomac. When Berkeley returned to Williamsburg, he had to keep the House of Burgesses in line, and this he succeeded in doing for some time by the simple process of having no new elections except to fill a vacancy. This policy, indeed, was one of the causes of Bacon's Rebellion, which somewhat alleviated the fraudulent manipulation of power; yet Berkeley's widow was the wealthiest person in the colonies after his death and became virtually governor of South Carolina, where in 1692 the vote was limited to freeholders. Families became dominant in Virginia, in Maryland, and in South Carolina, and it is interesting to see how family domination was maintained. One instrument was the fraudulent acquisition of land. Thus Philip Ludwell brought 40 immigrants into Virginia and was therefore entitled to 2000 acres for his trouble; it was a simple matter, after securing a land patent, for him to add a zero to each figure and thus become the proprietor of 20,000 acres. Alexander Spotswood, though he encouraged immigration, acquired some 85,000 acres "by means not always above question," says the sober *Dictionary of American Biography;* more bluntly, he got two parcels of 20,000 acres and 40,000 acres under a "borrowed" name. Famous is the case of one Jacob Stoner, who secured land in the names of his cows. By 1696 a royal commission complained that the dominant caste had procured such large grants of land, there was no waste land to be taken up by indentured servants on their release.

How was this managed? The historian of Virginia, Philip Alexander Bruce, in a famous passage makes it clear:

It is not going too far to say that the members of the Council appropriated to themselves all those higher offices of the Colony which were attended with the largest salaries, or presented the most numerous chances for money-getting. They deliberately disregarded the fact that the concentration of these offices in so few hands brought about serious damage to the public interests whenever the Councillor was required by his incumbency of two separate positions to perform two sets of duties really in conflict with each other; a Councillor, for instance, was called upon to pass upon the correctness of his own accounts as collector; as collector, he was obliged, for his own enlightenment as a judge of the General Court, to inform himself of all violations of the Navigation Acts; as a farmer of the quit-rent, he practically owed the success of his bid to himself as a Councillor; as escheator, who was a ministerial officer, he took and returned the inquisitions of escheats to himself as a judicial officer, and as such, passed upon points of law coming up in his own inquisitions.[46]

Add that the chief planter in any county was likely to be the commander of the militia, sheriff of the county, the principal justice of the peace, and representative in the House of Burgesses, if not a member of the Governor's Council, and the smooth working of the system becomes evident. Machiavelli, one surmises, would have admired it. The Virginia system developed many virtues in the way of hospitality, culture, and intellect; nevertheless, at the end of the seventeenth century about one hundred families *were* Virginia.

How fully and with what polish these families controlled the colony is evident in one of the most extraordinary instances of peculation in all American history—the famous "Robinson affair" in Virginia. John Robinson (1704–1766), graduate of William and Mary and member of the House of Burgesses from King and Queen County, became in 1738 both speaker of the House and treasurer of Virginia, positions he held until his death in 1766. He was so obliging to his friends as to have looted the colonial treasury of more than £100,000—an enormous sum in that age. One way of doing this was to recirculate paper notes he was legally required to burn. Edmund Pendleton, who tried to settle the estate, said this was due merely to his "goodness of heart and benevolent disposition," attributes that would not have passed muster as public defense in the days of Boss Tweed. The "first men" of the colony could not or would not pay up on demand, and as late as 1789 the problem of repayment was still pending. Among the curiosities of the case was the appointment to committees of inquiry of distinguished Virginians who had benefited from the transaction. The coherence of an elite group could not further go; and part of the difficulty faced by a man like Patrick Henry was that the elite group instinctively tended to close their ranks against a new power-figure in Virginia.[47]

For Machiavellianism assumed finesse more often than it did brutality, and one speculates on the modes by which a small elite class retained a monopoly of real estate and of political power in New York, the Carolinas, and elsewhere. The South Carolina aristocracy were landowners to whom the proprietors had made enormous grants of the most fertile acres environing Charleston; these same landowners, many of them councilors and assemblymen, took advantage of the interim between the fall of the proprietary regime and the purchase of the colony by the crown to appropriate some eight hundred thousand additional acres under old patents; and Herbert L. Osgood points out that the local magnates "stopped at nothing" to protect their interests, imprisoning unfriendly surveyors and preventing newcomers from acquiring either land or political influence.[48] In the eighteenth century likewise enormous grants were made to "Protestant settlers" in Augusta County, Virginia, which once ran to the Pacific (in theory) and out of which various states or rather parts of states were later formed. Between 1743 and 1760 the Virginia Council granted forty-three tracts amounting to more than three million acres to groups of elite "realtors"— the Loyal Land Company, the Ohio Land Company, the Greenbrier Company—the associates of which were the leading families of Virginia. Attempts by the crown to control this orgy of acquisition were resented, the resentment mounting into what one historian calls a "pre-revolutionary revolt in the Old Southwest."[49] And the system maintained itself. In antebellum Nashville young bloods, though they held to the European code of honor, walked impudently in and out of church during service, keeping their hats on until they reached the family pew. They developed thirst, gambling, a scorn of commercialism, and an easy belief that wealth and political wisdom were connecting virtues. Their women came to scorn the domestic arts. Yet by shrewd political manipulation they long remained dominant. Says one scholar: "In general . . . public ideals were established by the parvenu aristocracy of the larger slave-owners . . . political control was exercised by office-seekers, aspiring to rank with the upper classes, who achieved a regimentation of opinion among the masses by appealing to their ignorance and prejudices." [50] They may or may not have read Machiavelli; but the principles of control were not unlike those in *The Prince*. And of course the same thing was true of the manorial system in New York.

John Adams never visited the Southern colonies, but he knew politics, he watched the Southern delegates to the Continental Congress; and Page Smith, his biographer, has dug up a letter of March 23, 1776, to Horatio Gates, in which Honest John laments the reluctance of the Southern colonies to form a republican government, which can be done only on "popular principles," "abhorrent to the inclinations of the barons of the South, and the proprietary interests in the middle colonies, as well as to that avarice of land which has made upon this continent so many votaries of Mammon that I sometimes dread the consequences." [51]

It cannot of course be argued that chicanery was confined to the Southern colonies or that the possession of vast estates and political power was *ipso facto* an evil thing.[52] In New York, for example, the monopoly of land and of political power was long the basis of an "aristocracy" that controlled elections in city and state, that restricted the franchise to obedient renters and their ilk, and that exhibited the usual scramble for additional land [53] until the anti-rent struggle brought in the constitution of 1846 and public opinion forced the great proprietors to sell their manors to the farmers. The difficulty of tracing the history of ideas is graphically illustrated by the attitude of James Fenimore Cooper to this shift

toward democracy. Believing both in government by a gentleman class and in the sacredness of contract, he wrote his anti-
rent trilogy—*Satanstoe* (1845), *The Chainbearer* (1845), and
The Redskins (1846)—to trace the acquisition, management,
and dispossession of such an estate. He was of the opinion
that "the proprietors thought but little of their possessions as
the means of *present* support, but rather maintained their
settlements than their settlements maintained them; looking
forward to another age, and to their prosperity, for the rewards of all their trouble and investments." He was led to
this by personal considerations—the struggle of his father to
develop the Cooper estate, and his own lesser but vigorous
interest in a farm called "The Chalet." *The Crater* (1847)
shows in miniature what happens when "democracy" takes
over from gentlemanly control; and the wheel comes full
circle when we find the novelist setting up a definition of the
gentleman that has many of the characteristics of Castiglione's
courtier: "In addition to the great indispensables of tastes,
manners, and opinion, based on intelligence and cultivation,
and all those liberal qualities that mark his caste, he cannot
and does not stoop to meannesses of any sort. He is truthful
out of self-respect, and not in obedience to the will of God;
free with his money, because liberality is an essential feature
of his habits, and not in imitation of the self-sacrifice of
Christ; superior to scandal and the vices of the busybody, inasmuch as they are low and impair his pride of character rather
than because he has been commanded not to bear false witness against his neighbor." And Cooper, or the fictitious
Littlepage for him, says he reveres the Christian but never
meets a gentleman "without feeling how vacant and repulsive
society would be" without him.[54] Not unnaturally, unscrupu-
lousness, cunning, force, and fraud are in Cooper's fiction
attributed to demagogues.

On the other hand the acquisition of land from the public
domain of state or nation by the railroads, notably in the
West, seems to many to indicate the continuance of a tradition of finesse, fraud, and force, though the assumption has

been disputed.[55] In *The Octopus* (1901) the utter defeat of the embattled ranchers by the unscrupulous Pacific and South-western Railroad, represented by Shelgrim, Gerard, S. Behrman, and the pliable Genslinger, editor of the Bonneville *Mercury*, organ of the road, is conducted along Machiavellian lines, not omitting murder direct and indirect. Toward the end of the book Presley, the *raisonneur*, concludes at least temporarily that "men were naught, death was naught, life was naught; FORCE only existed—FORCE that brought man into the world, FORCE that crowded them out of it to make way for the succeeding generation, FORCE that made the wheat grow, FORCE that garnered it from the soil to give place to the succeeding crop." This may be, indeed, the "mystery of creation," "primordial energy flung out from the hand of the Lord God himself," as Presley says. I do not know whether Norris read Machiavelli, and commentators on him are naturally somewhat obsessed with his relation to French naturalism and Darwinian evolution; nevertheless, it would be a nice exercise in logical discrimination to distinguish this concept of force from Machiavelli's concept of power. The ruthlessness of power, often based on the fraudulent acquisition of property, real and otherwise, becomes a standard theme in later American fiction, as in Robert Herrick's admirable *Memoirs of an American Citizen* (1905),[56] and Dreiser's "trilogy of desire," *The Financier* (1912), *The Titan* (1914), and *The Stoic* (1947), together with many another novel of exposure, naturalism, or reform—consider, for example, Jethro Bass's manipulation of the New Hampshire legislature in *Coniston* (1906) by Winston Churchill, a bloodless, yet sinister parallel to some of the actions of Cesare Borgia. But all this is matter for later discussion, the point being that Machiavellianism, whether as finesse, fraud, or force, has long been a standard component of American political life.

---·➤ V ➤·---

The Colonial Idea in England

I

As time drifted on, the mist of uncertainty that shrouded South America, the Caribbean, and North America in a vague blur known as the Indies or the New World slowly lifted; and when the outlines of the North American continent became clearer to English seamen and to Tudor and Stuart monarchs, a colonial impulse began to stir. Before passing to this specific theme, however, it is well to be reminded of a profound difference between the concept of imperial expansion under the Spanish crown and the curious and tentative beginnings, half private, half official, of English expansion overseas to the New World. In the Caribbean and on the Spanish Main the dynamism of royal power found its center in the municipality, or *cabildo,* a semi-autonomous unit partly medieval in political structure, striving to be a city, and often in fact becoming one, as the history of Santo Domingo, Havana, Panama, and Vera Cruz demonstrates. The *cabildo,* under the crown, possessed or directed administrative, judicial, and military powers and activities, served as a base for further conquest, and was a market for provincial trading and international wares, a collecting point for the king's revenue, and a center of religious authority, since it was commonly the seat of a bishop. This concept was alien to English experience. English settlements, tentative and timid on the Maine coast, or fumbling and ill-directed at Roanoke Island, Jamestown, or Cape Cod, were clearly not of this order. If one inquires why, when the Spanish were planting "colonies" at the end of the fifteenth century, the English waited until after the opening of the seventeenth to create colonies of their own, one is forced back upon important historical and political considerations.

The Tudor kings did not lack enterprise, but their hands were full, of necessity or design, with other problems. In the first place Henry VII had to consolidate his little kingdom, conciliate or repress dissatisfaction, and rescue his treasury from bankruptcy. In the second place Henry VIII was temperamentally more interested in the Field of the Cloth of Gold and in being a European power than he was in the cold wilderness of North America; and his political, matrimonial, and theological troubles were many and vexing. In the third place, until James I ascended the English throne, Scotland was a hostile power, the Welsh were commonly unbiddable, and the Irish would not be subdued. In the fourth place English foreign trade at the opening of the sixteenth century was largely in the hands of Mediterranean and Baltic merchants, and the process of repossessing that trade for English merchants and English shipping was long, arduous, and complex. In the fifth place there was a sheer lack of money and men, despite the cry of overpopulation, as any student of Elizabeth's tortuous policies, foreign and domestic, soon comes to realize; and when the English eventually found enough risk capital (to which the sale of the monasteries contributed), a steady income from the Muscovy trade was more attractive than wild and mutinous adventures on the shores of Newfoundland or up the Orinoco. In the sixth place the reports brought back by those who, like Frobisher and Davis, had sought a Northwest passage comparable to the Baltic were uninviting—so much so that a document such as Gilbert's *Discourse of a Discovery for a New Passage to Cataia* (1576) had to expend a good deal of rhetoric to prove that life in that part of the New World was not as bad as it had been painted. Finally, once the Protestant religion had been established and England found herself pitted against the most powerful Catholic power in the world, the sixteenth-century Caribbean offered a fine fusion of patriotism, plunder, and salvation, immensely appealing to mercantilist adventurers who thought of economic wealth principally in terms of bullion.

The terms customary in sixteenth- and early seventeenth-century writing about overseas settlements were "colony" and "plantation." These were novel words. There is little or no evidence that English thought about colonization was influenced by Greek or Roman theory, which is not cited in the literature until late.[1] Jamestown was of course a Stuart counterpart of a Greek colony in the Aristotelian sense that its inhabitants could be reached by the voice of a single herald, and it developed a military garrison vaguely like that of a Roman *colonia*, but the parallel is accidental. In Middle English the word "colonie," like its medieval Latin counterpart, referred to a settlement of agricultural laborers associated with a particular portion of the earth's surface, but this is not an appropriate term for Tudor settlements. English plantations in Ireland were not known as colonies. The earliest discoverable appearance of "colony" in the sense of a settlement in a new or foreign country politically dependent upon the parent state seems to be in a Scottish document of 1548–1549; its first appearance in English proper is in Eden's translation of Peter Martyr in 1557. According to the *New English Dictionary*, Bacon in 1622 was the first to use the verb "to colonize." Even "plantation" in the sense of a foreign colony appears relatively late, the first recorded instance being in Hooker's *History of Ireland* (1558). The late appearance of these terms suggests that, despite the activity of the Spaniards, the Portuguese, and the French, English thinking about the nature of a colony had to begin virtually *de novo*.

There were nevertheless historical and foreign precedents that seem to have colored English thought. The Roman and the Scandinavian conquests of Britain, not to speak of the Norman conquest, furnished examples. Not only did Virginia and New England employ a warrior-settler type of occupier (as Pennsylvania, for example, did not), but propagandists recognized the validity of the historical appeal. Thus the Reverend William Crashaw in *A Sermon Preached in London before . . . his Maiesties Counsell for . . . Virginea, Febr. 21, 1609* (London, 1610) roundly urged that "stately houses, costly apparell, rich furniture, soft beds, daintie fare, dalliance and pleasures : . . are not the meanes whereby *our forefathers* conquered kingdomes, subdued their enemies, conuerted heathen, ciuilized the Barbarians, and setled their common-wealths." [2] And William Strachey, in his "Praemonition to the Reader" in *The Historie of Travaile into Virginia Britannia* (written about 1613), is explicit about the Romans and the "Scots":

> Had not this violence and this injury bene offred to us by the Romans (as the warlike Scots did the same, likewise, in Caledonia, unto the Picts), even by Julius Caesar himself, then by the emperour Claudius . . . who reduced the conquered partes of our barbarous iland into provinces, and established in them colonies of old souldiers . . . we might yet have lyved overgrowen satyrs, rude and untutred, wandring in the woodes, dwelling in caves, and hunting for our dynners, as the wild beasts in the forrests for their praye. . . .[3]

But all this is remote, rhetorical justification; what is more pertinent are the colonies of the Hanseatic cities in the Baltic and of the Italian city republics, notably Venice and Genoa, in the Levant. By establishing outposts in the Aegean islands, at Athens, in the Black Sea, in Egypt, and elsewhere, Venice, for example, tounded trading posts or *fondachi*. Over them the influence of the metropolis was supreme. The original grant permitting their creation in a foreign country was obtained by the metropolis, buildings were erected at public cost, and magistrates were appointed by the home government. These magistrates were responsible in Venice to a body somewhat like the (later) English Board of Trade and

Plantations. Venetian laws were carried into the *fondaco*, the trade of which was monopolized by the mother city. Associated with the creation and management of such a colony and its commerce was a joint-stock company, a fourteenth-century invention by which state action could be conveniently concealed as private enterprise.

Because of the prestige of Italian commercial theory in Renaissance Europe, and because trade relations between England and Venice were often close, the *fondaco* idea may fairly be said to have influenced Tudor thought about colonies. Like the *fondaco*, the English settlement was often the product of joint-stock enterprise chartered by the state (the crown). The governor, "admiral," and council (if there was one) were appointed by the crown, removable by the king, and expected to follow specific instructions from the home authorities. English law (or "rights") was usually carried into the settlement by express provision of charter or patent, colonial trade was monopolized by the mother country, and in their earlier years English settlements expected forts, storehouses, churches, and other public structures to be put up at government expense. Indeed, the treaties settlers made with Indian "kings" suggest the analogy of Venetian agreements with foreign powers. From the point of view of the crown the creation of a settlement that would send wealth home was an overriding consideration; and since risk capital in England was found in the cities, the cities, with the approbation of the crown, had their relations with the new project—as, for example, in the case of the "London Company." The first colonial administrators were at once military chiefs, ambassadors, judges, and commercial agents. In general this concept of planting a settlement * explains the almost immediate development of conflict between the colonial "administration" dutifully enforcing the *fondaco* concept, and colonists primarily interested in the private ownership of land and in private profits.[4]

---

* The English "factory" in India is an analogous case.

II

More immediate, however, was the example of Ireland; and the struggles of sixteenth-century Englishmen to subdue the wild Irish and to strengthen imperial rule profoundly colored the concept of a plantation, influenced the appeal of "promotion" literature, and created certain important misconceptions about the New World.

Before the accession of Henry VIII, English power in Ireland had sunk to the lowest ebb in history. In rebuilding his empire Henry at first attempted conciliation as a means to draw the natives into civilized life that would benefit trade. But the Irish proved recalcitrant, a combination of conciliation with coercion seemed necessary, and only by the ruthless suppression of rebellion did Lord Grey manage to govern Ireland without undue bloodshed until 1540. After Henry's death disaffection became chronic and desolation spread.[5] Though the English monopoly of gunpowder gave an overwhelming superiority to the royal forces,* it became evident that mere military forays could not hold that country. If Ireland had never existed, the English in America would probably have refused to sell firearms to Indians who were "naked and unarmed, destitute of edged tools and weapons," but the immediacy with which English colonists were instructed to keep the natives unarmed suggests the pertinence of Irish experience. Of course the regulation was frequently violated.

The idea of English plantations in Ireland became even more prominent during the reign of Elizabeth. One may note that Irish anarchy carried with it three important corollaries. One was that the Irish service was unpopular. It was "well known to be the most miserable war for travail, toil

---

* The tract issued on behalf of Sir Thomas Smith's proposed colony of Ards in County Down, for example, is emphatic in declaring that a few hundred footmen and horsemen could keep the Irish in subjection.

and famine in the world," said one observer in 1598; and in
1599 Sir John Dowdall wrote Cecil that "most part of the
army . . . seem beggarly ghosts, fitter for their graves than
to fight a prince's battle. The report hereof so works in mens
minds that they had as lief go to the gallows as to the Irish
wars." The reasons for this unpopularity were many—bad
pay, insufficient provisions, incompetent leadership—but a
leading one was the character of Irish warfare. That warfare
was compounded of ambush and treachery. The Irish, wrote
Gainsford in *The Glory of England* (1618), "will plash
down whole trees over the passes, and so intricately wind
them, or lay them, that they shall be a strong barricade, and
then lurk in ambush amongst the standing wood, playing
upon all comers as they intend to go along. On the bog they
likewise presume with a naked celerity to come as near our
foot and horse as is possible, and then fly off again, knowing
we cannot or indeed dare not follow them." [6]

The second result of Irish conflict was the desolation of
the country. The island acquired the reputation of being a
desert. Everyone is familiar with Spenser's description of
the starving Irish, but Spenser's was not the only one. In
1575 Sir Henry Sidney wrote the Lords of the Council about
Offaly and Leix, where English plantations had been attempted, that the land was "spoiled and wasted, by the race
and offspring of the old native inhabitors, which grow great,
and increase in number; and the English tenants decay, both
in force and wealth. . . . They are daily so spoiled and
burned, the charges they have been at, and their daily expenses they be at, to defend themselves, so weakeneth them,
as their state is to be pitied." In 1598 Chief Justice Sir William Saxey said in a letter to Cecil that Munster had been left
desolate by Irish rebels. He described "infants taken from
the nurses' breasts, and the brains dashed against the walls;
the heart plucked out of the body of the husband in the view
of the wife, who was forced to yield the use of her apron to
wipe off the blood from the murderer's fingers; [an] English
gentleman at midday in town cruelly murdered, and his

head cleft in divers pieces; divers sent into Youghal amongst the English, some with their throats cut, but not killed, some with their tongues cut out of their heads, others with their noses cut off." In 1599 an official minute declared that "we see by manifold experience, what madness it is for a Deputy or General to lead royal forces against naked rogues in woods and bogs, whom hounds can scarce follow, and much less men. Their ordinary food is a kind of grass. Neither clothes nor houses, generally, do they care for. With this their savage life are they able to wear out any army that seeketh to conquer them." The writer compares the wild Irish to wolves and foxes. And in Fynes Moryson's *Itinerary* (1617) one reads of "a most horrible spectacle of three children . . . all eating and gnawing with their teeth the entrails of their dead mother . . . the common sort of the rebels were driven to unspeakable extremities." [7] He reports that old women caught, killed, and ate little children.

It appeared that a race capable of these atrocities was little better than bestial. Said William Thomas in *The Pilgrim: A Dialogue on the Life and Actions of Henry VIII* (1552):

> . . . the wild Irish, as unreasonable beasts, lived without any knowledge of God or good manners, in common of their goods, cattle, women, children and every other thing . . . nor yet any justice executed for murder, robbery, or other like mischief; but the more force had ever the more reason. And hereof it followed that because their savage and idle life could not be satisfied with the only fruit of the natural unlaboured earth, therefore continually they invaded the fertile possessions of their Irish neighbours that inhabited the . . . English Pale.[8]

Sure, Sir Henry Sidney wrote the queen in 1567,

> there was never people that lived in more misery than they do, nor as it should seem of worse minds, for matrimony among them is no more regarded in effect than conjunction between unreasonable beasts. Perjury, robbery, and murder counted allowable. . . . I cannot find that they make any conscience of sin, and I doubt whether they christen their children or no; for

neither find I place where it should be done, nor any person able to instruct them in the rules of a Christian; or if they were taught I see no grace in them to follow it; and when they die I cannot see they make any account of the world to come.[9]

Spenser returns to the ancient Scythians to find a parallel to Irish barbarism:

There bee other sortes of cryes all so vsed amongst the Irishe, which savoure greatlie of *Scithian:* barbarisme, as theire Lamentacions at theire burialls, with disparefull outcryes and ymoderate waylinges . . . since I latelie spake of theire manner of cryes in ioyninge battaile, to speake also somewhate of the manner of theire Armes and arraye in Battaile . . . And first of theire armes and weapons, amongst which theire broade swordes are proper *Scithian:* . . . Also theire shorte bowes and little quivers with shorte bearded arrowes, are verie *Scythian.* . . . Moreover theire longe broade sheildes, made but of wicker roddes which are commonlie vsed amongst thee . . . Northerne Irishe. . . . Likewise theire goinge to battayle without Armour on theire bodies or heades, but trusting onelie to the thicknes of theire glibbs [matted hair over the eyes], the which they saye will sometymes beare of a good strooke, ys meere salvage and Scythian . . . besides theire confused kynde of march in heapes without any order or arraye, their Clashinge of swordes togeather, their fierce rvnninge vpon theire Enemies, and theire manner of feighte, resembleth altogeather that which is redd . . . to haue bene vsed of the Scythians.

. . . so haue I sene some of the Irishe [drink] not theire Enemies but frindes bloode, as namelie at the execution of a notable tratour. . . . I sawe an old woman . . . tooke vpp his heade whilst he was quartered and sucked vpp all the blood running there out sayinge that the earth was not worthie to drincke yt, and therewith also steeped her face and brest and tare her haire cyringe and shriking out most tirriblie.[10]

The point is not the bias or inaccuracy of such reports; the point is that this picture of Ireland and the Irish preceded or accompanied the voyage literature having to do with the New World, that English experience with one wild race conditioned their expectation of experience with another, and that the deep popular disfavor into which Irish expeditions fell inevitably prejudiced colonial enterprise in North America.

For, point by point, these observations are paralleled in writing about the American Indians. Take the matter of ambush. The Jacobean reader of Hakluyt's translation of a narrative of the De Soto expedition, *Virginia Richly Valued* (1609), discovered that Indians are "a people so warlike and so nimble, that they care not a whit for any footemen. For if their enemies charge them, they runne away, and if they turne their backs, they are presently upon them. . . . They never stand still, but are alwaies running and traversing from one place to another; by reason whereof neither crossebow nor arcubuse can aime at them; and before one crossebowman can make one shot, an Indian will discharge three or foure arrowes; and he seldom misseth what hee shooteth at." Or he might read of the bloody treachery at Mavila, or the burning of De Soto's horses at Chicaca.

. . . for all their faire and cunning speeches, they are not overmuch to be trusted, for they be the greatest traitors of the world, as their manifold most craftie contrived and bloody treasons, here set down at large, doe evidently prove. They be also as unconstant as the wethercock, and most readie to take all occasions and advantages to doe mischiefe. They are great liars and dissemblers; for which faults oftentimes they had their deserved paiments. . . . To handle them gently . . . will be without comparison the best; but if gentle polishing will not serve, then we shall not want hammerours and rough masons enow, I meane our old soldiours trained up in the Netherlands.[11]

This summary view of the Indians might be a discussion of the wild Irish.

If Spenser said the Irish scarcely knew the purpose of clothing, John Smith pictures the Indians "couered with the skinnes of wilde beasts," wearing "large mantels of deare skins not much differing in fashion from the Irish mantels," adorning themselves with "a dead Rat tied by the tail" or with live snakes that "often times familiarly would kiss [their] lips." The leggings of the New England savages reminded the author of *Mourt's Relation* of "Irish trouses," and Thomas Morton declared that the "Natives of New England are accustomed to build them houses much like the wild Irish." Spenser describes the Irish "cryes in ioyning battaile"; listen, now, to John Smith: "Vpon the first flight of arrowes, they gaue such horrible shouts and screeches, as though so many infernall helhounds could not haue made them more terrible." William Morrell in *Nova Anglia* could make Indian warfare clear only by comparing it to that of the Irish; and in 1637 Roger Williams, writing to John Winthrop, threatened that if the Indians were not kindly used, they might "turne wild Irish themselues." [12] In sum, America was uncomfortably like Ireland.

A single instance will illuminate the unhappy parallel. Sir Humphrey Gilbert regularly put men, women, and children to the sword in Ireland; [13] in Virginia Sir Thomas Dale dealt mercilessly with the Indians and all who consorted with them:

> Sr Tho: Dale haveinge allmoste finished the foarte, and settled a plantacyon in that p'te dyv^rs of his men being idell, and not willinge to take paynes, did runne away unto the Indyans; many of them beinge taken againe, Sr Thomas in a moste severe manner cawsed to be executed, some he appointed to be hanged, some burned, some to be broken on wheels, others to be staked, and some to be shott to deathe, all theis extreme and crewell tortures he used, and inflicted upon them, to terrefy the reste for attempteinge the lyke, and some wch robbed the store, he cawsed them to be bowned faste unto trees, and so starved them to deathe.

Indians bringing food were treated as spies: "Some of them Sr Tho: Gates cawsed to be apprehended and executed for a terrour to the reste, to cause them to desiste from their subtell practyses." [14] Doubtless the Spaniards, the Portuguese, and the French were equally brutal in a cruel and brutal age, but the doctrine that the only good Indian is a dead Indian first

took shape, it would appear, in the doctrine that the only
good wild Irishman is a dead wild Irishman.

While Ireland was being terrorized into "civilitie," dis-
charged soldiers, returning to England, filled the land with ill
reports of Irish life, just as disgruntled sailors and settlers,
returning from some ill-starred New World venture, spread
unfavorable reports about America. The two regions played
into each other's hands. The misfortunes of the New World
echoed the misfortunes of the Old; the situations were too
much alike not to strengthen the assumption that colonial experience was everywhere of a piece. Unable to comprehend
the Brehon laws, the English simply decided that the wild
Irish were savages; unable to understand Indian "polity,"
they reached a like conclusion. Used to savagery in the one
place, they looked for it, they provoked it, in the other.

III

The transfer of experience and ideas, expectation and emotional attitude from the struggle to "plant" Ireland to the
endeavors toward colonizing North America was made easy
by the fact that many of the leading proponents of American
colonization, many of the "adventurers," and many of the
actual leaders in New World ventures had had connections,
sometimes unfortunate, with Irish affairs. Among the more
famous names are those of Sir Humphrey Gilbert, Sir Walter
Ralegh, Sir Francis Drake, Sir Ferdinando Gorges, the Earl
of Southampton, Captain Ralph Lane, Lord De La Warr,
Chief Justice Popham, Captain Christopher Carleill, and Lord
George Carew, many of whom were also authors or instigators
of influential "reports" on the New World. Sir Humphrey
Gilbert had a military career in Ireland. After his raid on
Nombre de Dios, Sir Francis Drake spent some time with
Essex in Ireland, from which he emerged in 1575 to plan his
circumnavigation of the globe. In January 1598/9 Sir Fer-
dinando Gorges was named sergeant-major of the army in

Ireland; and though he seems not to have served, he must have learned something about Irish affairs. The Earl of Southampton went to Ireland in 1599 and again in 1600 on missions semi-military and semi-political, and during the parliamentary session of February–May 1624 he appeared as an authority on Irish affairs and was a member of the committee to consider the defense of that island. In the same epoch Lord De La Warr not only fought under Essex but was knighted by the Irish lord deputy. Gorges, Southampton, and De La Warr were, of course, members of the Council of Virginia. Lord George Carew, a member both of the Council and of the Virginia Company, fought under Sir Henry Sidney in Ireland during the seventies, held a succession of important Irish posts in the eighties, and rose to even greater distinction in the Irish establishment at the close of the century. In 1603 he retired as Lord Justice for Ireland, but he revisited the country in 1610 to survey the Ulster settlements.[15] Bacon's report to James I entitled "Certain Considerations Touching the Plantation in Ireland," dated 1606, praises Chief Justice Popham for his successes in the Munster plantations. Ralegh, of course, received a grant of 12,000 acres in Ireland and settled a large number of English families in Cork and Waterford about 1594. Ralph Lane was mustermaster in Ireland in 1592 and submitted a project for musters in Ireland to the English authorities while he held that appointment.[16] Captain Christopher Carleill served in Ireland in 1584 and again in 1588. Lord (formerly Captain) Chichester, another prominent Irish official, served with Carew on the committee to draw up a frame of government for Virginia. In general it can be demonstrated that a considerable number of the incorporators and "adventurers" of the original Virginia Company had an active interest in Irish plantations.

The doctrine that a plantation had to be, in its origins, a military establishment, and the excuse that native sloth made invasion and settlement necessary were, in addition to the misinterpretation of the "wild" inhabitants, the most important notions developed by the Irish experience and transferred to the New World. Equally important was the idea that the subjugation of, or through, a colony implied a system of feudal tenure. Having in mind the experience of over a century, Bacon thus proposed that the title of Earl of Ulster be added to that of the Prince of Wales, and that an Irish nobility be created, based on Irish landholding. He sketched a council in residence in Ireland and a council in London for governing the plantations. He argued likewise that there was no necessity for the undertakers to execute their duties in person, their kinsfolk, servants, and tenants sufficing, and said that settlement must take the form of towns. The parallels to early colonial theory regarding America are obvious.[17] In the case of Nova Scotia, for example, Sir William Alexander in 1621 received a royal patent for all the land between New England and Newfoundland, and on the express analogy of the Ulster settlement of 1609 (which carried into effect Bacon's proposal of an Irish nobility) Alexander was authorized to set up the scheme of the Knights Baronets of Nova Scotia. For the sum of 300 "merks" (150 pounds sterling) any person approved by Sir William and the king might receive a patent of nobility of the Nova Scotia establishment, and 6000 acres of land. On this land it was his duty to establish settlements. One hundred thirteen such baronets were created, though most of them, through the payment of fines, were released from the necessity of providing settlers. Wars with France and the exchange of New World possessions between France and Great Britain stopped the operation of the scheme, but in making propaganda for his colony Alexander and his associate, Sir Robert Gordon of Lochinvar, addressed themselves mainly to the upper classes. Before one decides that so "aristocratic" a program sprang from the pedantry of James I, let him remember that it was in some such fashion that Ulster was subdued. Let him also recall the case of George Calvert, who owned 2300 acres of land in County Longford, became Lord Baltimore on the Irish establishment, was a member of the

Virginia Company, acquired "Avalon" in Newfoundland, and asked for and received Maryland as a county palatine on terms his settlers later denounced as giving him more autocratic powers than were possessed even by the crown.[18]

A succession of schemes, a program of propaganda for planting Englishmen on territory wrested from the wild Irish began as early as 1551. Anti-Irish gossip had to be offset by effective propaganda, the formula for which set the pattern of American "promotion literature." Thus *A Letter sent by T. B. Gentleman unto his very frende Mayster R. C. Esquire, wherin is conteined a large discourse of the peopling and inhabiting the Cuntrie called the Ardes* (1572) not only outlines the mode of settlement that was to be tried at Jamestown, but anticipates many arguments concerning the New World. The climate and fertility of the country are praised, and private possession of land is promised. "How say you," inquires the author, "have I not set forth to you another Eutopia?" Prospective colonists are assured the land is empty and "lacketh only inhabitants, manurance, and pollicie." Three familiar themes appear: England was never so full of people, "and the dissolution of Abbayes hath done two things of importance heerin. It hath doubled the number of gentlemen and marriages, whereby commeth daily more increase of people, and suche younger brothers as were wonte to be thruste into Abbayes, there to liue (an idle life), sith that is taken from them must nowe seeke some other place to liue in." Again: "To inhabite and reforme so barbarous a nation as that is, and to bring them to the knowledge and law, were bothe a godly and commendable deede, and a sufficiĕt worke for our age. . . . Let us, therefore, vse the persuasions which Moses vsed to Israel, they will serve fitly in this place, and tell them that they shall goe to possesse a lande that floweth with milke and hony." And finally: ". . . it shall be furnished with a companie of Gentlemen and others that will liue frendly in felowships togither reioysing in the frute and commoditie of their former trauaile, which (through noble courage) for estimatiō sake, and the loue of their owne countrey the[y] first enterprised, deseruing . . . to be crowned with garlands of honours and euerlasting fame." Unemployment and overpopulation, the missionary motive, and a union of profit and fame—experience taught the persuasive quality of these arguments.

In 1589 another characteristic pamphlet [19] shows the deep unpopularity of the plantation idea and the persistent desire to make emigration attractive through propaganda. Robert Payne in his *Brife description of Ireland* attempted to soften current prejudice against the wild Irish. He found the better sort of people "very ciuill and honestly giuen," said that most of the kerns and gallowglasses had been slain in the Desmond rebellion, and described the remaining Irish as harmless, idle folk like English beggars. They hated the Spaniards because of the Spaniards' "monsterous cruelties in the West Indians"—a note that is to recur in the American material. Ireland is incomparable; and he praises Irish forests, stone and mineral wealth, wild fowl, seafood, hunting, and agricultural plenty. "You may keep a better house in Ireland for L. li, a yeere, then in England for CC. li. a yeere." The author admits there had been fraudulent men among previous "undertakers" in Ireland, who "enticed many honest men ouer, promising them much but performing nothing, no not so much as to pay their seruants, and workmen wages." But of course *his* undertakers, "many good knights and gentelmen of great worship," are worthy men. Much of the pamphlet seeks to allay popular fears. Any one of six million English, says the writer, "is good innough for three wetherbeaten spainerds whom a fewe of our frostie nightes will make shrinke like rotten sheepe. yet thus much I must say for them, if almightie God for our contempt of his holye worde hath giuen them power against vs, as hee did the frogges against the Egiptianes, Then is there no force able to resiste them: (without that) I see no cause why we either in England or in Ireland should feare them." Other documents on the Ulster "plantations" enumerate various "commodities" and do what they can to make emigration attractive; [20] yet a survey of 1618–1619

showed only 1974 families in the six counties of Ulster, confessed to humiliating failure, and failed to foresee the success
of the English plantations in the 1620s, when such wealthy men
as Sir Christopher Hatton possessed princely estates comparable to those of "King" Carter in Virginia later.[21] Blame for
failure and delay was placed upon the character of the emigrants. "Ireland for these many years hath been the receptacle
for our English runagates, that for their misled lives in England, do come running over into Ireland. Some for murder,
some for theft; some that have spent themselves in riot and ex-
cess are driven over for debt, some come running over with
other men's goods, some with other men's wives, but a great
number now lately, that are more hurtful than all the rest, and
those be recusants." Thus wrote Barnaby Rich in *The Irish
Hubbub* (1617).[22]

Precisely as in a later century the name Canada or Australia was likely automatically to evoke the image of a remittance man, a ne'er-do-well, a runaway, or a criminal, so the
Irish experience predetermined the image of the character
of emigrants. Maryland, because of the Baltimores, is especially illuminating in this context. Thus in 1655, in "Virginia and Maryland, or The Lord Baltamore's printed Case,
uncased and answered," it was hotly charged that the proprietor "now admits all sorts of Religions, and intended even
2000 Irish, and by his own Letters clears and indemnifies
one, that said, Those Irish would not leave a Bible in Maryland." [23] Of the Newport-Gates-Somers "supply" sent to
Virginia even earlier, William Stith wrote in his *History of
Virginia* that "a great Part of this new Company consisted of
unruly Sparks, packed off by their Friends, to escape worse
Destinies at home. And the rest were chiefly made up of
poor Gentlemen, broken Tradesmen, Rakes and Libertines,
Footmen, and such others, as were much fitter to spoil or
ruin a Commonwealth, than to help to raise or maintain one."
This "seditious and distracted Rabble hath laid one of the
finest Countries in *British America,* under the unjust Scandal
of being a mere Hell upon Earth, another *Siberia,* and only

fit for the Reception of Malefactors, and the vilest of the People. So that few People, at least few large Bodies of People, have been induced, willingly to transport themselves to such a Place. . . ." [24] The custom of transporting felons to Virginia began, he thinks, with King James. Stith's acrid paragraphs go back to John Hammond's *Leah and Rachel* (1656) and earlier records, Hammond writing, for example, as we have seen: "Then were Jayls emptied, youth seduced, infamous women drilled in, the provisions all brought out of England, and that embezzlled by the Trustees." [25] A minor but illuminating incident in this part of the world in 1648 I have already cited in Chapter IV.[26] In this episode on the Delaware Bay and River the Dutch replace the English, but the compound of sordor, treachery, and cruelty is again woven into a single whole, the origins of which are, in large measure, from Tudor Ireland.

IV

But it is time to turn to the positive side of the picture and to examine the promotion literature in English of the early colonial period. It must not be forgotten that, whatever the power of the printed or written word among the upper and middle classes, the majority of Englishmen could not read—a fact that calls for severe scrutiny of certain hasty inferences sometimes drawn from this propaganda. Obviously the obligation laid upon this literature was to destroy the unfavorable image of colonizing and substitute a more alluring one. The literature was in this successful, inasmuch as colonies were founded, were nourished, and grew, and it has also had the unintended success of coloring all American origins with glamour.

Promotion literature [27] falls into several distinguishable categories. The most impressive is the formal treatise on colonization, of which there are two sorts: treatises which, anticipating settlement, theorized, from inference or from the example of others, about the character of the potential colony; and treatises which drew felicitous inferences from English experience, once it had begun. The first type is mostly a sixteenth-century product, as in Hakluyt's *Discourse of Western Planting* (1584); the most illustrious example of the later type is probably Bacon's essay *Of Plantations* (1625). Secondly, one may associate with this type the general prefaces or other introductory matter in collections of voyages or reports on colonial enterprises. The various volumes of the second edition of Hakluyt's *Principal Navigations* (1598–1600) have such prefaces, and the introductory pages to William Vaughan's ("Orpheus Iunior") *The Golden Fleece* (1626) and John Hammond's *Leah and Rachel* (1656) are of this sort. A third type is the official request to government for a patent, or the request plus the patent, published to persuade "adventurers" to invest and settlers to migrate; examples can be found in Brown's *Genesis of the United States,* and the "Instructions to the Colonists by Lord Baltimore" (1633) are of this order.[28] A fourth type, often quoted in this study, is the reports of exploratory voyages. These commonly stress the economic plenitude of the new settlement, the healthiness of its situation, and the gentleness of the natives. Thomas Hariot's *A Briefe and true report of the new found land of Virginia* (1588) may be put in this category. In the fifth place the circulation of material having both official sanction and a personal tang is part of the picture, as in the "Coppie of a letter from Virginia . . . to the Councell of Virginia here in England," and such pamphlets as Robert Johnson's *Nova Britannia* and *A Trve Declaration of the estate of the Colonie in Virginia* (1610), a "confutation of such scandalous reports as haue tended to the disgrace of so worthy an enterprise." This was published "by aduise and direction of the Councell of Virginia." [29] A sixth type, emanating from official authority, includes publication of the official laws and of regulations concerning the acquirement of land, both intended to assure the settler of the morality and good order of the enterprise, such as William Strachey's *Lavves Diuine, Morall and Martiall* of "Virginea Britannia" (1612).[30] Seventh is that cleverest form of company-inspired propaganda, the official sermon on such an occasion as the departure of an important person for the colony, which appealed to the middle class and corrected wild talk in the taverns; an instance is Robert Gray's *A Good Speed to Virginia* (1609), dedicated to the Virginia Company. Finally, there is the personal report by an interested observer, such as Edward Winslow's *Good News from New England* (1624).

What are the chief themes of this promotion literature? One I have already touched upon in connection with Mediterranean colonial enterprise—the appeal to glory and heroism; and in English promotion literature, in apparent contradiction to what I have earlier remarked about the lack of influence of the Roman or Greek colony upon English theory, the sanction of antique heroism is frequently invoked. Thus Robert Johnson concluded his *Nova Britannia* (1609) by saying: "It would be my griefe and sorrow, to be exempted from the company of so many honourable minded men, and from this enterprise, tending to so many good endes, and then which, I truely thinke this day, there is not a worke of more excellent hope vnder the Sun, and farre excelling (all circumstances wayed) those Noble deedes of *Alexander, Hercules,* and those heathen Monarks, for which they were deemed Gods among their posterity." [31] John White appealed to Roman example: "It is reported that when *Annibal* lay before *Rome,* it discouraged him much in his hopes of taking the Citty, that at the same instant there marched out of the Citty at contrary gates under their colours an Armie of souldiers towards the sea, to be shipped & sent over for a supply into *Spaine;* for it argued the *Romans* feared him not. . . ." Let the English therefore send out colonies.[32] Crashaw appealed to Romulus and Remus as instances of the difficulty of founding a new nation; and William Strachey, in his *Historie of Travaile into Virginia Britannia* (it is true the work was not published until 1849), called upon the English to meditate upon antique virtue:

> It is read that Themistocles hearing of the great victory that Melciades [Miltiades] had obteyned on the playne of Marathon, said, that that report would not lett him take any rest; and Julius Caesar wept at the sight of Alexander's image (who had at the yeares of twenty-four obtayned the name of Great), and cryed out: "Am I not miserable, that have done nothinge worthy of memory, and yet this prince at these yeares hath executed so many notable thinges?" Shall these, for the smoake of momentary glory, breake out thus passionate and forward? and shall not we, for the glory of our God be as affectionate [i.e., eager] and ambitious? [33]

But these Renaissance flourishes conceivably were less compelling than appeals to Christian virtue. Sir Robert Gordon prophesied that all Christian after-ages would "eternize" the "shining brightnesse" of such men as Drake, Ralegh, Amadas, White, and others.[34] Robert Gray in his sermon proclaimed that "the name, memorie and actions of those men doe only liue in the records of eternitie, which haue emploied their best endeuours in such vertuous and honourable enterprises, as haue aduanced the glorie of God, and inlarged the glorie and wealth of their countrie," and that therefore the fame of the Virginia Company would last as long as the sun and the moon.[35] Nor was Captain John Smith unpersuaded of the value of a Christian sanction:

> If he haue but the taste of virtue and magnanimitie, what to such a minde can bee more pleasant, then planting and building a foundation for his Posteritie, gotte from the rude earth, by Gods blessing and his owne industrie, without preiudice to any? If hee haue any graine of faith or zeale in Religion, what can hee doe less hurtfull to any: or more agreeable to God, then to seeke to conuert those poore Saluages to know Christ, and humanitie, whose labors with discretion will triple requite thy charge and paines? [36]

"Our forefathers," wrote Robert Johnson, "not looking out in time, lost the prime and fairest proffer of the greatest wealth in the world, and wee taxe their omission for it, yet now it falles out, that wee their children are tryed in the like, there being yet an excellent portion left, and by Diuine prouidence offered to our choice." [37] Thus Protestant divinity paralleled the appeal of the Spanish crown, the Roman Catholic Church, and Las Casas.

The imperialism of the English, the Dutch, the Danes, and the Swedes, and the renewed energy of the French in the seventeenth century ran up against the established empires of Portugal and Spain, and in the case of England added religious rivalry to the rivalry for space. A second leading theme in the literature is, therefore, expansionism and the English right to empire. The examples of the Spanish and the Portuguese empires, wrote Peckham, should "minister just cause of incouragement to our Countreymen, not to account it so hard and difficult a thing for the subjects of this noble realme of England, to discover, people, plant and possesse the like goodly lands, and rich countreys not farre from us . . . not a little animate and encourage us to looke out and adventure abroad, understanding what large Countreys and Islands the Portugals with their small number have within these few yeeres discovered, peopled and planted." [38] His doctrine echoed through scores of tracts, pamphlets, sermons, and the like vehicles of propaganda. Every part of the New World had its eager advocates, the idea being to "gaulle yhe King of Spain as yt wolde dyuerte hys forces, yhat hee troublethe these partes of Chrystendome wyth," [39] and the persistent search for a Northwest Passage, like the persistent search for strategical colonies in the New World, was part of expansionist psychology arising in no small measure from fear and hatred of Spain. This theme gave Hakluyt one of his most splendid passages:

. . . it can not be denied, but as in all former ages, [Englishmen] have bene men full of activity, stirrers abroad, and searchers of the remote parts of the world, so in this most famous and peerlesse governement of her most excellent Majesty, her subjects through the speciall assistance, and blessing of

God, in searching the most opposite corners and quarters of the world, and to speake plainly, in compassing the vaste globe of the earth more then once, have excelled all the nations and people of the earth. For, which of the kings of this land before her Majesty, had theyr banners ever seene in the Caspian sea? which of them hath ever dealt with the Emperor of Persia, as her Majesty hath done, and obteined for her merchants large & loving privileges? who ever saw before this regiment, an English Ligier in the stately porch of the Grand Signor at Constantinople? who ever found English Consuls & Agents at Tripolis in Syria, at Aleppo, at Babylon, at Balsara, and which is more, who ever heard of Englishman at Goa before now? what English shippes did heeretofore ever anker in the mighty river of Plate? passe and repasse the unpassable (in former opinion) straight of Magellan, range along the coast of Chili, Peru, and all the backside of Nova Hispania, further then any Christian ever passed, travers the mighty bredth of the South sea, land upon the Luzones in despight of the enemy, enter into alliance, amity, and traffike with the princes of the Moluccaes, & the Isle of Java, double the famous Cape of Bona Speranza, arive at the Isle of Santa Helena, & last of al returne home most richly laden with the commodities of China, as the subjects of this now flourishing monarchy have done? [40]

This, to be sure, is the Elizabethan age speaking out loud and bold, but the carry-over into the Stuart monarchy was dynamic, so much so that the valuation put on colonies even as late as the time of Charles II placed English plantations in the West Indies ahead of the mainland colonies because they were better bases for intercepting Spanish trade.* It must not be forgotten that to intercept the Spanish treasure fleet was

---

* To break the power of Spain it was less necessary that Virginia and New England be settled than it was to take military possession of convenient ports, islands, and river-mouths. Hence the persistent attempt to establish an English colony in Guiana (1604–1606, 1609, 1610–1611, 1613, 1617, 1620–1623). Bermuda was acquired in 1609; and portions of the West Indies fell into English hands—Saint Christopher in 1624, Nevis in 1628, Montserrat and Antigua in 1632. The colony on Barbados was planted in 1627 and by 1640 had a population of 18,000. From 1631 to 1635 English Puritans persisted in the endeavor to found a Puritan colony on Providence Island off the Mosquito Coast.

somehow to create economic wealth in one's own country; European thinking about trade was strictly mercantilistic.[41]

V

The attempt to rival the heroes of Plutarch, the call to convert the heathen, and the desire to expand the bounds of empire were, in the main, Renaissance values common to all the colonizing powers. We come closer to the English situation *per se* when we analyze the problem of population, the special appeal for trade, and the peculiar moral sanction on the English expressed in the promotion literature.* That England was actually suffering from a glut of population at the end of the sixteenth century may be doubted, but that scores of writers thought the country was overcrowded is clear enough—alarm over social dislocation is one of the commonest notes in Tudor literature. The sixteenth century, as somebody has said, lived in terror of the tramp; and the sociological appeal of colonial promotion literature was alike to those fearful of anarchy, the socially dispossessed, and those fearful of being uprooted by the enclosure movement, the sale of the monastery lands, or the shifts in population by reason of the wool trade or some other rising industry. No appeal is more constant in the literature. Thus Gilbert, among the eight numbered reasons of "commodities" that "would ensue," once he found the Northwest Passage, declares: "Also we might inhabite some part of those countryes, and settle there such needy people of our countrye, which now trouble the common wealth, and through want here at home are inforced to commit outragious offences, whereby they are dayly consumed with the

---

* In what follows I purposely confine most of my illustrations to those from the earlier material. Propaganda for the Carolinas, Pennsylvania, or Georgia commonly paralleled that for Virginia and New England, but played up the economic appeal and the real-estate appeal.

gallowes." [42] In his *Divers Voyages* Richard Hakluyt lamented
that the prisons were "pestered and filled with able men to
serue their Countrie, which for small roberies are dayly
hanged vp in great numbers" ("twentie at a clappe" in Roch-
ester), who ought to be sent to the colonies and there use-
fully employed. [43] In his *Discourse of Western Planting* he
lamented that idle soldiers go "up and downe in swarms for
lack of honest intertainment" and could be used against
"stubborne Savages" who "shal refuse obedience to her Maj-
estie." [44] "Look seriously into the land," preached William
Symonds, "and see whether there be not just cause, if not
a necessity, to seek abroad. The people, blessed be God, do
swarm in the land." [45] And the great John Donne thought
that colonization "shall redeeme many a wretch from the
Lawes of death, from the hands of the Executioner, upon
whom, perchance a small fault, or perchance a first fault, or
perchance a fault heartily and sincerely repented, perchance
no fault, but malice, had otherwise cast a present and igno-
minious death." [46] Patrick Copland that same year (1622)
praised the officers of the city of London, "who seeing this
Cittie to be mightily increased, and fearing lest the ouer-
flowing multitude of inhabitants should, like too much
bloud in the body, infect the whole Cittie with *plague* and
pouertie," urged "the transporting of their ouer-flowing multitude into *Virginia*." [47]

Plantations were not merely to relieve the surplus population, they were to reform criminals, albeit there were those
who asked for criminals in order that a particular colony
might be held, and inconsistently complained of the kind of
colonist they got.[48] Thus Hammond, in his *Leah and Rachel*,
though he paints a vivid picture of lawlessness at the beginning of his account, finds the Virginians undergoing a sea
change into something new and strange, having become "generally affable, courteous and very assistant to strangers," theft
"seldom or never committed . . . and although Doores are
nightly left open (especially in the Summer time), Hedges
hanging full of Cloathes, Plate frequently used amongst all

comers and goers (and there is good store of Plate in many houses) yet I never heard of any losse." [49]

The myth that the American Adam came to the New World and lost his innocence should, in some sense, be reversed; he came here to regain virtue. Francis Higginson wrote with pleasure that in New England children of five can set out corn, and exclaimed:

> Oh what a good worke might you that are rich do for your poore brethren, to helpe them with your purses onely to convey them hither with their children and families, where they may live as well both for soule and body as any where in the world. . . . For when you are once parted with England you shall meete neither with taverns nor alehouse, nor butchers, nor grosers, nor apothecaries shops to helpe what things you need, in the midst of the great ocean, nor when you are come to land, here are yet neither markets nor fayres to buy what you want.[50]

A letter from the Virginia Company to the City of London in 1609 expresses the wish to "ease the city and suburbs" of the idle:

> And if the inmate . . . shall demaund what may be theire present mayntenance, what maye be theire future hopes? it may please you to let them Knowe that for the present they shall have meate, drinke and clothing, with an howse, orchard and garden, for the meanest family, and a possession of lands to them and their posterity, one hundred acres for every man's person that hath a trade, or a body able to endure day labour, as much for his wief, as much for his child, that are of yeres to do service to the Colony, with further particular reward according to theire particular meritts and industry.[51]

Forty years later in *A Perfect Description of Virginia* we read that "All kinds of Trades-men may live well there, and do gaine much by their labours and arts," that youths of sixteen and upward are wanted for apprentices and servants, "then to have Land given them, and Cattel to set them up," and that there is room for "thousands of these kinds of young boyes and maydens." [52] The legend of the cleansing West begins, it is clear, not at the Mississippi but in London.

The results were inevitably contradictory. On the one hand the mainland colonies had to be pictured as a vast improvement over England, as Hammond does in *Leah and Rachel*:

> The Country is very full of sober, modest persons, both men and women, and many that truly fear God and follow that perfect rule of our blessed Saviour, to do as they would be done by; and of such happy inclination is the Country, that many who in England have been lewd and idle, there in emulation or imitation (for example moves more than precept) of the industry of those they finde there, not onely grow ashamed of their former courses, but abhor to heare of them and in small time wipe off those stains they have formerly been tainted with.[53]

On the other hand the literature is filled with complaints about the unruliness, lack of discipline, insubordination, and want of common sense exhibited by the common man during not only the period of exploration but also that of first settlement. We have already had some glimpse into the mutinous spirit of early Jamestown. Sir Ferdinando Gorges complained of the "idle proceedinges" of his colony on the New England coast, which "have mutch prejudcialld the publique good, deviding themselves into factions, each disgracing the other." English fishermen on the Maine coast were "worse than the very Savages, impudently and openly lying with their Women, teaching their Men to drinke drunke, to sweare and blaspheme the name of *GOD*, and in their drunken humour to fall together by the eares." And Edward Winslow complained of Weston's colony that among the causes of the "overthrow and bane" of plantations, the irresponsibility of those who send out men "endued with bestial, yea, diabolical affections" was important.[54] It was all very puzzling. The writer of promotion literature was inevitably caught between liberty and authority—between the need of creating a small, quasi-feudal military garrison and trading post to keep order, and the appeal of laissez-faire principles, by which, abandoning any sort of communal responsibility, the settler could make his private fortune. Inevitably, however, the psychology of real-estate promotion won out; typical is R. Rich's *Newes from Virginia:*

> To such as to Virginia
>   Do purpose to repaire;
> And when that they shall hither come,
>   Each man shall have his share,
>
> Day wages for the laborer,
>   And for his more content,
> A house and garden plot shall have,
>   Besides 'tis further ment
>
> That every man shall have a part,
>   And not thereof denied
> Of generall profit, as if that he
>   Twelve pounds, ten shillings paid.[55]

The concept of communal enterprise gave way to obstreperous individualism.

But was it lawful to intrude upon the savages? Was it right to claim sovereignty over lands that conceivably belonged to the Emperor of China, or, if not to him, then to the Emperor Powhatan? The Spanish and the Portuguese had had their ethical problem solved for them by the pope; the Protestant English not only had no pope but desired to oust the Spaniards from as much of the New World as they could, at the same time assuring settlers it was lawful for them to colonize. They appealed therefore to the law of nature and to the Bible, intermingling the two appeals. And inasmuch as the English were obviously the successors of the Chosen People as the Spanish were not, the argument, especially as against the Indians, was comforting.

"Their land," wrote Robert Cushman, "is spacious and void," the Indians "do but run over the grass, as do also the foxes and wild beasts"; wherefore, "as the ancient Patriarchs therefore removed from straiter places unto more roomthy . . . so it is lawful now to take a land, which none useth; and make use of it." [56] God, argued John Winthrop, gave the earth to man—"why then should we stand starving here for places of habitation?" [57] John White held the same opinion:

> If it were then the minde of God, that man should possesse all parts of the earth, it must be enforced that we neglect our duty, and crosse his will, if we doe it not, when wee have occasion and opportunitie. . . . It cannot be denied but the life of man is every way made more comfortable, and afforded a more plentiful supply in a larger scope of ground, which moves men to bee so insatiable in their desires to joyne house to house, and land to land, till there be no more place . . . the husbanding of unmanured grounds, and shifting into empty Lands, enforceth men to frugalitie, and quickneth invention: and the setling of new States requireth justice and affection to the common good: and the taking of large Countreys presents a naturall remedy against couetousnesse, fraud, and violence.[58]

Even Thomas Morton of Merry Mount fame ironically reproduced the argument—God had swept away "heapes" of savages "for the propagation of the Church of Christ." [59]

For a new Canaan had been appointed for English Protestants, and to the Elizabethan or Jacobean Englishman there was no disharmony between the argument for individual gain and the argument of religious glory. In 1578 Anthony Parkhurst wrote Hakluyt that God would prosper His faithful if they would but obey His commands:

> Such is the malice of wicked men the devils instruments in this our age, that they cannot suffer any thing . . . to proceed and prosper that tendeth to the setting forth of Gods glory, and the amplifying of the Christian faith, wherein hitherto princes have not bene so diligent as their calling required. . . . I trust God hath made you an instrument to increase the number, and to moove men of power, to redeeme the people of Newfoundland and those parts from out of the captivitie of that spirituall Pharao, the devil.[60]

If the Indians could not be converted "Apostolically, without the helpe of man" nor "meerely imperiallie, when a

Prince, hath conquered their bodies, that the Preachers may feede their soules," but only "by way of marchandizing and trade," then let the English "buy the pearles of earth" and sell "the pearles of heauen." [61] Why not? Adam and Noah, said the Reverend John Cotton, were told to multiply and replenish the earth, and God directs the migrations of people which follow. "This may teach us all where we doe now dwell, or where after we may dwell, be sure you looke at every place appointed to you, from the hand of God: wee may not rush into any place, and never say to God, By your leave; but wee must discerne how God appoints us this place." [62] There was, however, no doubt that God appointed Massachusetts Bay for His holy colony.

Scores of tracts enforced similar arguments. In his sermon of 1609 the Reverend William Crashaw had waxed eloquent in italics:

> The Israelites had a *commandement* from God to dwell in *Canaan,* we haue *leaue* to dwell in *Virginea:* they were *commanded to kill* the heathen, we are *forbidden to kill them,* but are commanded to *conuert* them: they were *mighty* people, ours are *ordinarie:* they *armed,* ours *naked:* they had *walled townes,* ours haue scarce *houels* to couer them: that land flowed with *milke and honie,* our[s] abounds with as *good or better:* they sent men to search *that,* so we to search *this:* they brought of the *commodities,* so haue we: many *slandered* that countrey, so they doe of ours: more *beleeued* the slander then the trueth, and so they doe in ours: yet some stoode boldly for the *trueth,* and so there doe in ours, and better then those that doe depraue it.[63]

If English beginnings were poor and small, Crashaw pointed out that the Israelites went down into Egypt but seventy souls and increased to six hundred thousand. And the stately John Winthrop not only agreed that Christians have warrant to occupy waste lands, following Biblical precedent, but appealed to the law of nature: "That which is common to all is proper to none. This savage people ruleth over many lands without title or property; for they inclose no ground, neither have they cattell to maintayne it, but remove their dwellings as they have occasion." [64]

Doubtless these arguments were inconsistent. How appeal to the law of nature, which gives the earth to all men, and simultaneously insist that therefore you have the right to bring any portion of the earth that is "waste" under your dominion? How reconcile the appeal of a laissez-faire existence beyond the wildest dreams of the Jacobean world with the argument that "the setling of new States requireth justice and affection to the common good"? Why if the appeal to antique virtue was proper to the English at the end of the sixteenth century, was "the Portingales time . . . out of date"? [65] How reconcile praise of the "constant resolutions" and "incomparable honour" [66] of the Iberians with casting them in the role of "Midianites" to be overcome by that stout Gideon's band, the English? [67] The Elizabethans and the Jacobeans, like us, found no difficulty in entertaining two or more contradictory notions at one and the same time; they resolved these inconsistencies as John White resolved them toward the conclusion of his *The Planters Plea:* "If in the Worlds infancy, men out of an ambitious humour, or at present for private advantages and expectation of gaine, thrust themselves out from their owne dwellings into parts farre remote from their native soyle; why should not we conceive, that if they doe this for a corruptible crowne; that the desire and expectations of an incorruptible . . . may as strongly allure such as by patient continuance in well-doing seeke immortalitie & life?" [68] The complex origins of the colonial idea in England, the immense and contradictory elements that contributed to its growth and that led to the planting of mainland colonies of Englishmen in the New World show not only that the pristine image of a new Eden had already been criss-crossed with darker shades of doubt and selfishness, but require us also to be cautious in adopting simplicistic notions that an American dream somehow mysteriously broke down in the nineteenth or twentieth century. Insofar as the origins of the American idea go back to the planting of the first mainland colonies by the English, these origins are as conflicting, inconsistent, and difficult to identify as the components of other great episodes in the history of Western man. "America" did not descend directly from Eden.

VI

The Useful and the Good

I

AFTER the Renaissance of the South, the Renaissance of the North, which pursues analogous aims but bears the Reformation in its bosom. The bright colors of the Mediterranean world, the chiaroscuro of brilliance and blackness that is Spain and Italy, the half-African energy and languor of Portugal fill the vision for a time, then make way for the soberer cultures, the more familiar products, the temperate landscapes of northern France, the Low Countries, the Germanies, and the British Isles. To the subtle, half-pagan, and wholly sensuous charm of Botticelli, Leonardo, Correggio, and the Venetians succeed Dürer, who had reached only his maturity when Columbus sailed; Holbein, who was twenty when Luther affixed his ninety-five theses to the church door in Wittenberg; and, by and by, Frans Hals, Rubens, and Rembrandt. On the one side the *terribilità* of Michelangelo; on the other the "Melancholia" of Dürer, which, created in 1514, followed the completion of the central vault of the Sistine Chapel ceiling by four years. In the Renaissance of the South mythological subjects express a nostalgic idealism, as if the direct heirs of the antique world were imaginatively returning upon their birthright; but the same themes in the North, painted by Rubens or, more rarely, by Rembrandt, exist, so to speak, in present time and are clothed in present flesh—the warriors vigorous and immense, modeled on the men who resisted Alva, the women less nude than unclad, so that we may see what good food and drink produce in beautiful plumpness. Portraits in the South mirror personality; in the North they express character. Pictures by Gerard Douw, de Hooch, Vermeer, and Maes lovingly insist upon tangible things in a bourgeois universe as the fading glories of Venice yield to the splendor of Antwerp, that "flower of the world," which, when it vacates pride of place, gives way not to Genoa, Cadiz, Seville, or Lisbon but to Amsterdam. In vain does Charles V, perhaps the last monarch to believe in universal empire, struggle to restore a lost medieval unity, in vain does Philip II endeavor to stamp out heresy; the tough Protestant spirit overcomes him, the mercantile navies of the North check and turn back, as it were, the chivalry of the South. Feudalism retreats eastward to the plains beyond the Elbe; in the Low Countries, in England, in France, even in Scandinavia the merchant class comes more and more to determine policy. The trade of the North is in necessities, and the Mediterranean triad of olive oil, wine, and "corn" seems exotic to countries trafficking in salt fish, lumber, woolens, and naval stores. The movement of culture is from Francis I to Colbert, from Sir Thomas More to Bacon, from Paracelsus, who, said his enemies, died drunk, to William Gilbert, the discoverer of the earth's magnetism, and William Harvey, the discoverer of the circulation of the blood.

The colonization of Latin America was, despite its superior humanity in race relations, the unexpected efficiency of its administration, and the dazzling richness of its special culture, the product of a dying feudal order that momentarily prolonged itself in the New World. The colonization of North America, despite odd claims to unlimited feudal dominion based upon the voyages of Madoc, Prince of Wales, the notion that Powhatan was an emperor something like Genghis Khan, and royal largesse in the matter of granting unmapped lands to undeserving courtiers, was a product of the capitalist spirit expressed in joint-stock enterprises and asserting a Protestant ethic as the viceroyalties of Mexico or Peru asserted a Catholic and Iberian view of the world. Out of the British mainland colonies developed the mightiest industrial nation of the twentieth century, and historical curiosity is naturally excited to inquire into the origin and development of the American capitalist economy. Unfortunately no historical inquiry is more involved. Debate turns upon the meaning of "wealth," "calling," "capitalism," the "capitalist spirit," and associated words, and the disputants are determined, it sometimes appears, not to understand each other's terms.[1] The principal questions at issue are at once theological, moral, and intellectual; and if we begin cautiously and far away, we may ask why and how, if work was a curse laid upon Adam and his descendants forever, diligent labor was transformed not merely into a virtue but also into a Christian virtue. Are good works necessary for salvation or are they a proof of salvation, and does the desire to pursue them flow from either the hope or the conviction of salvation? What is the relation of one's "calling" to his eternal destiny? If it is impossible to give alms to the poor without having the wealth to give away, is not profit-making proof of God's benevolence, and if it is, why should the particular case of interest ("usury") be condemned? And—perhaps the central issue—did not Protestantism with its emphasis upon individual judgment favor individual enterprise (and therefore capitalism) to an extent and in a way that Catholicism did not? Inasmuch as all the great tools of modern business were invented in Arabian or Catholic lands, Protestant historians are naturally inclined to stress the link between theological and economic individualism.

This dispute between religion and trade, between theology and business enterprises arises in part out of the slow surrender by the church to the secular state not merely of the controls but also of the norms governing commerce, profit-making, and investment. In the nineteen-twenties, whatever the dispute among theologians and economic historians,

there was among the then popular historians no real problem. For example, Van Wyck Brooks derived American culture from two symbolic figures—Jonathan Edwards, the
idealist who dominated the campus, and Benjamin Franklin,
the utilitarian (with whom Weber began) who dominated
the stock exchange. To Charles and Mary Beard, to Vernon
Louis Parrington, and to Frederick Jackson Turner, the explanation was likewise simple: economic motives, if they did
not utterly determine men's desires, were more often para-
mount than not, and Beard in particular turned the Constitution of the United States into a protection erected by wealthy
men, much as later, in the slaughterhouse cases, the fourteenth
amendment was turned into a device that protected corporations. Men were not led as by an invisible hand, in pursuing
their own ends, to bring happiness to society as a whole.[2] Today we may envy this simplicity but it is impossible to share
it.

To reconcile God and Mammon, the practice of piety and
the accumulation of riches, is an old ethical dilemma, direc-
tives for solving which descend from the ancient Jews, Aristotle, and the medieval church. After 1450 subsistence farms
in Western Europe began to make way for capitalist farming:
under the Tudors the gentry acquired land and influence
and accumulated risk capital; in France the nobility of the
robe began to gain on the nobility of the sword; and in English seaports, in the Low Countries, and along the Baltic the
capitalist bourgeois, commonly Protestant, fulfilled with enthusiasm the duty laid on the middle class perpetually to
rise. All of Europe, to be sure, burned with energy, but by
and by it appeared that what was conquered by the sword
had to be paid for by the purse, that the banker might be a
more powerful personage than the baron, and that the merchant, less picturesque than the conqueror, was more likely
to succeed. Catholics were presumably neither more nor less
worldly than Protestants, the Venetian merchant was quite as
shrewd as the merchant in London, and the Protestant perhaps did no more than combine into a new dynamic practices

and traditions already approved by a theology that was itself changing. Nevertheless, the spirit of capitalism seems more strongly rooted in the Protestant confessions than it was in Catholic faith.

The abolition of monasticism in Protestant lands lessened the value of the contemplative life as a road to salvation. After Luther and Calvin the vast question of what constitutes a church became central to all the Protestant faiths, but the Protestants, having given up the confession as a mode of periodically relieving the soul of its sense of guilt, were thrown back, so to speak, upon individualistic performance. One must strive in this world. God calls upon His faithful to believe in Him, He calls upon them to do His work in the world—how shall their belief be evidenced except by action? Even if salvation lie in faith, not works, the necessity of working is not obviated. Indeed, the testimony of faith *is* in working, so that even he who feels he is damned is obligated to work at his calling, for the glory of God. To believe otherwise would be to impute unrighteousness to the Almighty. The wicked may flourish like the green bay tree—that is in God's hand. But the righteous may not therefore fall idle. Seest thou a man diligent in business? He shall stand before kings. Even if all those who stand before kings because of their diligence are not therefore righteous, the righteous are not to be less diligent than the wicked.

Three central issues emerged. The first concerns the doctrine of one's calling. Every man (the theory was usually discussed in masculine terms) has two callings: one, a divine call, a summons to God through Christ that may, it is hoped, end in salvation; the other, to his station in life, his particular occupation, profession, skill, or vocation—in short, what he is good for. Not to ascertain what one's true vocation in this world is and, having found it, not to labor in it are to betray the purpose for which God sent one into living society. In the second place, God is the great governor of the commonwealth. He has arranged the trades and the vocations, the arts and the sciences into an orderly pattern that in the long run will prepare the earth for His Kingdom; wherefore the duties of practical life are as much a part of one's Christianity as duties of any other sort. Therefore the conscientious discharge of the responsibilities of trade is at once evidence and result of Christian virtue. Energy became the index of the Christian character, and insofar as the Christian energetically pursues his calling, God will prosper him unless something else intervenes. What is that something else? This was the third, and greatest, problem. Like the ancient Jew, the Christian was directed to prosper. But prosperity means wealth, and wealth corrupts, wealth is evil. If to the Puritan the monkish eremite betrays God by retreating from the world that God has made, the Puritan was also aware that affluence might lead one into the City of Destruction, from whose sloth, negligence, chambering, wantonness, and vainglory Bunyan directed the Christian to flee. How was one simultaneously to gain riches and avoid the temptation inherent in them? By the doctrine of stewardship, which implied the stern self-discipline Protestantism imposed upon its followers. The qualities that made for success in commerce— sobriety, frugality, thrift, the credit-making virtues—were they not Christian virtues also? Business could be conducted with the high seriousness of religion; the self-sufficiency of the Protestant soul could be translated into the self-sufficiency of the moral tradesman. A thousand sermons, treatises, and essays adjured, warned, guided, and exhorted the Protestant middle class to get wealth, yet remain ascetic, grow rich but not relax their spiritual energy—Richard Baxter's *Saints Everlasting Rest* (1650), from which Weber draws, Richard Steele's *The Tradesman's Calling* (1684), which Tawney cites, Defoe's *The Compleat English Tradesman* (1725–1727), more worldly than either. Historians examine what Augustine, what Aquinas, what the medieval Jew,[3] what Luther, what Calvin, what "painful Perkins," what a thousand others contribute to the doctrine that a businessman may be godly. Their investigations fascinate the reader, but it is here sufficient to remember that, however the doctrine of the gospel of wealth was put together, it became identified with the Protestant ethos, and that the New England colonies, New Amsterdam, Quaker Pennsylvania, the Swedes in Delaware, even Maryland (save for a brief period) were Protestant.[4] Indeed, south of the Potomac, though there were worldly planters, there were more members of the middle class, and the Scotch-Irish in the Great Valley and in the Carolinas were as pawky Christians as was Bailie Nicol Jarvie in *Rob Roy*. In American experience the ethos of Jonathan Edwards and the ethos of Benjamin Franklin are complementary, not opposed.

II

Colonial enterprise was everywhere undertaken to make money for somebody. Even at the risk of repeating the obvious, it must be emphasized that Spain, which reshaped European economy by sluicing the precious metals of the New World into the Old, Holland and France, which sought to monopolize the North American fur trade, and the Pilgrims and the Puritans, who, though they founded holy commonwealths, had to deal with joint-stock "companies" in England, were not ignorant that a business world exists. Private gain and easy real estate were central themes in English colonial propaganda. What crossed the Atlantic into the British mainland colonies was not, then, capitalism, but a theological sanction upon the credit-making virtues. These became so fully amalgamated with Christian values in the United States, they were taken as axiomatic. Christianity meant activism, not withdrawal from the world, so much so that when nunneries and monasteries were built in the United States they were thought to be un-Christian because they were un-American. Even in the Catholic Church few Americans have chosen the mystical way of life; the great figures are builders and shapers such as Bishop England and

Cardinal Gibbons. There is no prominent North American equivalent to Saint John of the Cross or Sor Juana de la Cruz, not even Mother Cabrini. Despite Jonathan Edwards, Jones Very, and the vogue of Zen Buddhism, the American way is not contemplative. Characteristic of our contemporary business ethic was the publication in 1959 of twelve essays entitled *Business and Religion: A New Depth Dimension in Management,* but though one article is by a Jesuit priest, one is by Reinhold Niebuhr, and one is by Kenneth E. Boulding, who passes the Protestant ethic in review, the central quality of the collection is fear of definition. The author of the opening essay wants to spell religion with a small "r." [5] Neither Luther nor Calvin, neither Saint Ignatius nor Leo IX, neither Cotton Mather nor Henry Ward Beecher wanted to spell religion with a small "r," and the problem of how Protestant activism moves from Calvin's *Institutes* to *Business and Religion* with a small "r" (dare one add with a big "B"?) is the question before us.

The doctrine of the two callings is plainly set forth in a book much read in seventeenth-century Massachusetts, William Ames's *Conscience with the Power and Cases thereof, Divided into five Bookes.* Chapter V of Book Two concerns "effectual vocation" or entrance into "saving grace." Vocation in the secular sense is discussed in Book Five, all the divisions of the inquiry being supported by Scriptural texts, which I here omit. One reads that "Hee which hath so much power, and gifts bestowed on him, by God that hee may live laudably in some honest calling, if hee abstaine from all employment willingly, hee cannot bee quitted from sinning greivously," the reasons being:

> First, It is the ordinance of God, that every one by helping others in some particular calling, should glorifie God. Secondly, Every one hath received his talent, or some part of a talent from God to that end: which cannot bee buried or hid without sinne; Thirdly, Idlenesse is too bee flied [*sic*], as the mother and nurse of many vices, especially of evil thoughts, desires, curiosities, and wicked contrivements. Fourthly, the Glory of

God, publique and private wellfare, as also the peace of conscience, may and ought to bee sought by some honest calling.

How know that one's calling is honest? Scripture and good
sense will distinguish socially useful employments from idle
ones. The qualities for approved employments are skill, "by
which every one perfectly knoweth those things, which properly belong to his owne vocation"; attention to his own business; diligence; wisdom "in observing, taking, and using
rightly opportunity"; courage and constancy in overcoming
difficulties; "moderation in the desire of gaine, and care of
wished success"; and of course "a religious sanctifying of all
our labours." Ames is suspicious of poverty, both the "coun-
terfeit" kind practiced by monks and "true" poverty, which,
though it be sent by the Almighty, is a miserable state. Riches
are neither good nor bad, but if they increase through the
providence of God, the mind must be fortified against the
vices in their train, especially covetousness, which can, however, be fended off by "frequent and serious meditation on
the vanity of riches." He admires an honest frugality, but also
declares that "wee must helpe others with those things which
doe overabounde with us." [6]

We have seen in the case of Captain Keayne and "Moses
his judicials" [7] the inevitable conflict between business ethics
and traditional theological controls; nevertheless the enunci-
ation of the doctrine of the callings was not pretermitted.
Thus Cotton Mather in *Two Brief Discourses. One Directing
a Christian in his General Calling; Another Directing him in
his Personal Calling* (1701) tells his readers: "Acknowledge
thy *Dependence* on the glorious God, for thy *Thriving* in
the World," quotes Deuteronomy 8:18, and adds: *"Riches* are
not always to them who are sharpest at inventing the most
probable Methods of coming at it. Be sensible of this; The
way to succeed in our Enterprizes, *O Lord, I know the way
of man is not in himself."* [8] The next year the Reverend John
Danforth of Dorchester, preaching on *The Right Christian
Temper in every Condition,* said: "God hath given us Tem-
porals to Enjoy, to some more and some less; now our Duty

is to be satisfyed with them, accounting them enough for us, and best for us, for the Present time: We should therefore suck the sweet of them and so slack our Thirst with them, as not to be Insatiably craving after more." [9] The Reverend William Cooper in *Jabez's Character and Prayer A Little Consider'd and Improv'd, in a Sermon to a Society of Young Men in Boston* (1716) exhorted them to remember that religion does not mean a sour face and to think that God sometimes honors the pious with His favors.[10] In 1719 the better-known Benjamin Colman was more explicit. God, he said, "fits persons for the days and for the places which he allots unto them; and by a differing Genius directs and inclines one to this calling and abode, and another to that," and "when the Merchant has hous'd his stores, and the husbandman gather'd in his . . . still both depend on the continued watch of Divine Providence, to preserve their substance. . . . And . . . when they open their stores for sale, they still depend on the direction of Providence in their dealings with men." [11] That same year an anonymous pamphleteer insisted that "The Wise Creator and Governour of all things *fitted* and *adapted* Man for *Work,* and *Business.* . . . So far as we are thus *Industrious* we are obedient to God, profitable to our selves, useful to our Neighbours, advantagious to Posterity." [12] Said the Reverend Thomas Symmes of Bradford in 1720: God "requires and expects, that every Man should *abide in his Calling,* and *seek to* excel in his own Sphaere, in the Improvement of all his Endowments and Enjoyments for the Honour of GOD, his Bountiful Benefactor, and the Interest of his Prince and Country." [13] One could go on indefinitely. As late as 1774 the Reverend Moses Dickinson, in *A Sermon Delivered at the Funeral, of the Honorable Thomas Fitch, Esq; Late Governor of the Colony of Connecticut,* announced that idleness is a sin "testified against in the holy scriptures," one that "contradicts the end of our creation," and declared that "the employment that we are occupied in, should not only be lawful, but it should be what we are fitted for." [14]

But the direct line from pulpit to counting-house was subject to deflections. One such was caused by the problem of paper money, currency depreciation, and rampant mercantilism arising after virtually every war between Great Britain and France in the eighteenth century, a problem that blurred theology and patriotism and transferred the sanction of acceptable commercial conduct from divinity to public law.[15] Another was the necessity of widening the argument in an agrarian economy more and more conditioned by physiocratic theory, so that the farmer as well as the merchant would be encouraged to work with God. Thus in 1774 we find Richard Wells writing: "THE genius of America is agriculture, and for ages to come must continue so. An extensive wilderness to the westward will long receive the gradual overflowing of population; and the Manufacturer of Great-Britain will never meet with a formidable rival in the shape of an American Farmer, so long as he can purchase the cloathing of his family with the produce of his fields." But the farmer must be providentially guided: "OUR fields, through the wonted providence of the great Lord of the soil, produce their usual crops—our barns expand with the pressing load of unnumbered sheaves; and a joy 'like unto the joy of harvest' spreads serenity of countenance through . . . ten thousand families." The biblical quotation is from Isaiah 9:3 and reminds us that the Americans, like the Jews, regarded themselves as a chosen people prospering with herds and flocks and corn.[16] The third great force of deviation was the gradual secularization of culture in the eighteenth century; and it is one of the ironies of history that the leading document in this rubric is by no less a theologian than the Reverend Cotton Mather, author of *Bonifacius. An Essay Upon the Good,* again and again reprinted under the title *Essays To Do Good,* after its original appearance in 1710. This book, said Franklin, gave him a turn of thinking that influenced the principal events of his life.

Bonifacius [17] is, so to speak, a series of half-secular, half-holy generalizations on a theme earlier developed by Mather:

"Acknowledge thy *Dependence* on the Glorious God, for thy *Thriving* in the World." [18] After gravely ridiculing the fashion of prefaces and dedications, the book sets forth a topic ostensibly furnished by the British ambassador to the Duke of Brandenburg, to the effect that a capacity to do good makes doing good a duty. The work is addressed to various classes in a community. We are still, in one sense, in the hands of a theologian, for we read that "an *Holy Heart* will cause a man to do Good Works" and that the motto on the gates of the Holy City is: "None but the Lovers of Good Works to enter here." But it soon becomes evident that Mather is more concerned with the affairs of this world than with the New Jerusalem. He lays down directions for reading, for the education of children, for the management of servants, and for the conduct of various vocations—directions that in the sequel were to condition American culture. Read good books, he commands, not "the *Devils Library*" of "foolish *Romances,* or *Novels,* or *Playes,* or *Songs,* or *Jests that are not convenient,*" and for several generations Americans were to shun fiction on the ground that it was immoral and told lies. Wise, however, in the ways of children (the "Slavish, Raving, Fighting way of Education" he condemns), Mather would "endeavor for my *Children* . . . the *Daughters* as well as the *Sons,*" that they "have so much Insight into some *Skill,* which lies in the way of *Gain* . . . that they may be able to Subsist themselves." Servants, like children, are to read only improving books, not "Pestilential *Instruments of Wickedness.*" Neighbors are to be cheerfully dealt with unless they need to be admonished for their sins. Education should be purged of Greek and Latin "Vain Fictions, and Filthy Stories," to be replaced by "Books containing Grave Sayings, and things that may make them truely Wise and Useful in the world." (One thinks of the McGuffey readers.) If they wish to master the tongue, let young scholars turn profitable sentences into Latin. Let magistrates be pious, physicians be not soulless research men but "Sollicitous, to *Find Out,* and *Give Out,* something very considerable for the

Good of Mankind." Merchants who tithe themselves commonly prosper, as do lawyers who abhor a *"Dirty Cause."* In sum, though Mather did not realize it, he could be quickly translated into a merely secular ethic.[19] Nor is he to be justly accused of hypocrisy. He was aware of the risks the doctrine ran: "There is one thing in the Condition of many *Rich Men* which cannot be with sufficient Horror thought upon. *Great Estates,* like to *great Rivers,* often are swelled by Muddy Streams running into them. Some of the *Wealth* is *Ill-gotten Wealth. Dishonest Gain* has increased it. *Unfair* and *unjust* Things have been done in the amassing of it. A *Restitution* is now requisite; A *Restitution* as far as the Robber is able; either to the *wronged parties,* or if they can't be found, in *Deodands:* Without This, their Sin remains *unrepented* of, and GOD will be a *Revenger."* [20]

Evidences of a translation of this doctrine from theology to utilitarian theory are to be found in literature before Franklin, but this great name symbolizes the substitution in the eighteenth century of benevolent deism for a Christian God and of empirical experience for theology. Classic statements by him are such things as "Rules for a Club Established for Mutual Improvement" (1728), "Articles of Belief and Acts of Religion" (1728), "Hints for Those That Would Be Rich" (1736), "The Way to Wealth" (1758), and of course the *Autobiography,* left incomplete at Franklin's death, the text of which is something of a puzzle.[21] The "Articles of Belief" announce the existence of "one supreme, most perfect Being," who is to be loved and adored and who presides over the credit-making virtues. The "Hints for Those That Would Be Rich" stresses prudent investments, points out the unprofitableness of being idle, selling and buying on credit, and waste in "any unnecessary Household stuff, or any superfluous thing." "The Way to Wealth" (also known as "Father Abraham's Speech" and as the "Preface to *Poor Richard Improved"*) is the classic compounding of Americanized proverbial wisdom concerning frugality, thrift, industry, and obvious virtue. But by its personal touch the *Autobiography* not only shows Franklin's doctrine in action; it is also a text studied by hundreds of thousands of Americans. It has become our secular Bible.

Who does not know this seemingly candid record of Franklin's "Errata" in morals and finance, of his steady climb to wealth as printer, tradesman, inventor, and investor, of his successes as a public servant who had learned to avoid words like "certainly" and "undoubtedly" in order that he might the more easily prevail? Who does not know his list of virtues and his attempt at a daily calendar of success or failure in practicing them? Some passages are as familiar as the Declaration of Independence:

I began now gradually to pay off the Debt I was under for the Printing-House. In order to secure my Credit and Character as a Tradesman, I took care not only to be in *Reality* Industrious and frugal, but to avoid all *Appearance* of the Contrary. I drest plainly; I was seen at no Places of idle Diversion; I never went out a fishing or Shooting; a Book, indeed, sometimes debauch'd me from my Work; but that was seldom, snug, and gave no Scandal; and to show that I was not above my Business, I sometimes brought home the Paper I purchas'd at the Stores, thro' the Streets on a Wheelbarrow. Thus being esteem'd an industrious thriving young Man, and paying duly for what I bought, the Merchants who imported Stationery solicited my Custom, others propos'd supplying me with Books, I went on swimmingly. . . .

My circumstances . . . grew daily easier. My original habits of frugality continuing, and my father having, among his instructions to me when a boy, frequently repeated a proverb of Solomon, "Seest thou a man diligent in calling, he shall stand before kings, he shall not stand before mean men," I from thence considered industry as a means of obtaining wealth and distinction, which encourag'd me. tho' I did not think that I should ever literally *stand before kings*, which, however, has since happened; for I have stood before *five*, and even had the honour of sitting down with one, the King of Denmark, to dinner. . . .

We have an English proverb that says, *"He that would thrive, must ask his wife."* It was lucky for me that I had one

as much dispos'd to industry and frugality as myself. She assisted me cheerfully in my business, folding and stitching pamphlets, tending shop, purchasing old linen rags for the papermakers, etc., etc. We kept no idle servants, our table was plain
and simple, our furniture of the cheapest. For instance, my
breakfast was a long time bread and milk (no tea), and I ate it
out of a twopenny earthen porringer, with a pewter spoon. But
mark how luxury will enter families, and make a progress, in
spite of principle; being call'd one morning to breakfast, I
found it in a China bowl, with a spoon of silver! They had been
bought for me without my knowledge by my wife, and had
cost her the enormous sum of three-and-twenty shillings, for
which she had no other excuse or apology to make, but that
she thought *her* husband deserv'd a silver spoon and China
bowl as well as any of his neighbors. . . .

My list of virtues contain'd at first but twelve, but a Quaker
friend having kindly informed me that I was generally thought
proud . . . I determined endeavoring to cure myself, if I could,
of this vice or folly among the rest, and I added *Humility* to
to my list. . . . I cannot boast of much success in acquiring the
reality of this virtue, but I had a good deal with regard to the
appearance of it.

Franklin was a genius to whose sagacity we owe all sorts of
creations from bifocal spectacles to the American Philosophical Society, and perhaps the very existence of the republic.
The comfortable estate he acquired through his practice of
the credit-making virtues enabled him to spend his later years
in the service of his country and set an example for the ty-
coons of the age of business later. Nevertheless, his story is
always told from his point of view that does not exclude
evidence of hypocrisy and snobbery (I dined with the King of
Denmark). One wonders, however, about the satisfactions of
life Mrs. Franklin experienced, timidly buying a china bowl
and a silver spoon to get some touch of color into a house
filled with cheap furniture, taking her husband's illegitimate
son into her family and bringing him up, and staying home
all the years Franklin lived in Europe standing before kings
and having his little flirtations with Madame d'Houdetot

(whom he thought it would be nice to meet again in heaven). The debit side of Franklin's doctrine is not merely that it denies any importance to aesthetic experience; it also encourages both explicitly and implicitly a dreary self-regard and a drearier hypocrisy. These qualities are to appear over and over again in American novels concerning businessmen.

The union in Franklin's prose of the credit-making virtues and the doctrine of deism did not prove a permanent liaison. Even in the later eighteenth century ministers (it is true, of increasingly liberal faith) continued to urge that a Christian God smiled upon industry, frugality, and charity. "Self-Love," preached the Reverend Samuel Cooper in 1753, "is at least as necessary to the Support and Happiness of the World as social," but "Mutual Benevolence" is like "the great Law of Gravitation, by which all Particles of Matter . . . attract each other," whereas "Idleness" remains, as before, "the Nurse of Vices; the Enemy of Self-Enjoyment; and destructive at once both to the Bodies and Souls of Men," something that "hebetates" the mind.[22] A gospel society, said the Reverend Ebenezer Pemberton after the outbreak of the Seven Years' War, would be an ideal state in which "Every one content with his Lot, would rejoice in the Prosperity of his Neighbour.—The Great would command without Haughtiness, and Inferiors submit without Murmuring—The Rich would employ their superfluous Wealth, to relieve the Miseries of the Poor; and the Poor gratefully acknowledge the Kindness of their Benefactors," and God would distinguish a thrifty, "wise and vertuous People, by temporal Blessings." [23] We cannot pause for everything, but we may note that by 1784 George Washington had become the Joshua of the West, Jesus was to reign, and in the United States, declared the Reverend George Duffield, one of the chaplains of Congress, "far removed from the noise and tumult of contending kingdoms and empires . . . shall the husbandman enjoy the fruit of his labour; the merchant trade, secure of his gain; the mechanic indulge his inventive genius; and the sons of science pursue their delightful employment." [24] By 1795 the Reverend John M'Knight was urging that "idleness, prodigality, dissipation, and luxury are the bane of republicanism and of liberty; and the scenes and amusement which tend to foster these, are the hot beds of vice, from which such noxious vapors arise." [25] Almost at the close of the century the Reverend Joseph Lathrop urged that Christianity is useful in our present life, since it "enjoins industry, frugality, temperance, sobriety and self government on the individual; and justice, peace, truth, fidelity and benevolence on the citizen and neighbour," [26] and thus recaptured the Benjamin Franklin virtues for theology. Exhortation was undoubtedly necessary: in her study of mercantile practices in New York on the eve of the Revolution, Virginia D. Harrington found that "constant attempts were made to pass goods off for better than they were. . . . Even the most reputable merchants raised the proof of rum by adding spirits and 'mended' poor wine by coloring it"— though she of course finds with Franklin that "a reputation for fair dealing demanded a certain amount of honesty." [27]

III

That one has a duty to pursue one's calling and in that pursuit an expectation that he will prosper under the sanction of the Almighty, whether Calvin's God or the God of Benjamin Franklin, was a belief that did not disappear in 1776. But the notion became immensely involved with considerations arising out of the American Revolution, the early years of independence, and the currents and counter-currents of the Napoleonic age. The new country was called upon to decide its destiny during years more complicated than any other period in Western history until now. Were we to become an agrarian republic, a land vaguely after the manner of ancient Israel and the bucolic poets, and so avoid or minimize the corruption of municipal wealth? Or, driven forward by necessity and desire, were we to encourage manufactures to such an extent (but to such an extent only) as would fill our own needs, yet avoid both the national rivalries of Europe and the importation of unrepublican luxuries? Or was it wiser for us, given our infinite resources in materials and our unexampled freedom to experiment, to mobilize ingenious men, industrialize quickly, and, ever expanding, eventually dominate the world? We who know the answer of history find it difficult to realize the confusion and the clamor in the debate. Yet from 1775 to 1825 here was a central issue, involving the possibilities of national misery or happiness, problems of republican virtue, theological issues (*were* we a chosen people? a Christian nation?), the direction of our diplomacy and, above all, the vast enigma of the unpredictable conduct of Europe from 1789 to 1815, and beyond.

However one may nowadays smile at the spread-eagle rhetoric of the writers, three characteristic utterances from the last successive decades of the eighteenth century throw light on the emotions of the age. The first is from the *Royal American Magazine* for January 1774, and is part of an "Address of AMERICA'S GENIUS, to the PEOPLE in the AMERICAN WORLD":

> AMERICA blossoms as the expanding rose, and rises like the towering cedar; every morning the sun views her encreased fame, and each new day extends her domain and adds new glories to her crown.—Here the streams of wealth, the beams of science, the stars of wisdom, the light of virtue, and the sun of liberty, will all unite their rays, and form the sublime circle of human splendor and felicity. . . . The time is coming, when the knee of empires and splendid kingdoms will bow to your greatness and supplicate favour of your liberal and peerless Majesty.[28]

Here is Tench Coxe pleading for manufactures in 1787:

> How numerous and important then, do the benefits appear, which may be expected from this salutary design! It will consume our native productions now encreasing to super-abundance—it will improve our agriculture and teach us to explore the fossil and vegetable kingdoms, into which few researches

have heretofore been made—it will accelerate the improvement
of our internal navigation and bring into action the dormant
powers of nature and the elements—it will lead us once more
into the paths of virtue by restoring frugality and industry,
those potent antidotes to the vices of mankind and will give us
real independence by rescuing us from the tyranny of foreign
fashions, and the destructive torrent of luxury.[29]

And here in the late 'nineties is a panorama of the American
empire sketched by a Philadelphian:

The industrious labourers and mechanics are the sinews, the
bones and the marrow of every community. Riches and honour
are only an appendix to the book of life. We can live without
them: particularly in this wide extended empire, whose uncultivated forests and fertile plains, invite the uplifted *ax* and the
furrowing *plough*. . . . The tide of population continues to
flow over the *Appalachian* mountains; nor will it cease to flow
until that vast "wilderness becomes like *Eden*." [30]

The problem of one's calling inevitably became involved
with doctrines of republican virtue. For example, as early as
February 1776 the Congress urged upon the colonies that
they create societies for the promotion of manufactures,
partly from motives of economics, partly because home manufactures would insure simplicity of taste. Such societies were
founded, their titles commonly including the adjective "useful," as in the New Jersey Society for Establishing Useful
Manufactures and the Pennsylvania Society for the Encouragement of Manufactures and the Useful Arts, both dating
from the 'eighties.[31] Obviously the utilitarian argument differs basically from the providential theory of Cotton Mather,
but the outcome is much the same. Meanwhile the southern
colonies, or at least some of them, were exposed to the doctrines of Mandeville, for so I interpret a writer in the *Maryland Gazette* in 1746, who said that riches are of no value
"unless used in such a manner, as to supply the Delicacies
and Conveniences of Life; for by that Means, the Labourer
is encouraged in Industry, Money circulates, and the Society
reaps Benefit by it; but Treasure can be of no Use either to

the Possessor, or his Neighbors when hoarded up in Chests and strong Boxes." [32]

By the end of the Napoleonic period interdenominational church groups, participating in the religious revivalism arising out of the reaction against the French Revolution and its aftermath, were establishing national societies that fused utilitarianism, patriotism, the encouragement of business enterprise, the Protestant ethic, and a theory that religion is a stabilizing force, into a single whole. The American Education Society, organized in Boston in 1815, ostensibly subsidized ministerial students; the formal purposes of the American Bible Society, the American Tract Society, the American Sunday School Union, and the American Home Missionary Society, all founded by 1826, are indicated in their names. But a careful student of their publications has pointed out that they were commonly launched by the well-to-do, who felt it their duty to "bridge over the dangerous chasm between the rich and the poor." A spelling book published by the American Sunday School Union contains this gem:

> It signifies not what our stations have been,
> Nor whether we're little or great;
> For happiness lies in the temper within,
> And not in the outward estate,

a doctrine that was somehow supposed to keep down ebullient radicalism. It was solemnly stated that "the Gospel is the most economical police on earth," and the theory of the stewardship of wealth and the duty of the poor to be content in that station of life to which providence had called them was stated over and over again.[33] To this vulgarization the finely wrought doctrines of Calvin had been brought.

Addressing the New York Athenaeum on December 14, 1824, Henry Wheaton made a wide survey of our potential national greatness, took example from the "simultaneous revival of letters and liberty in Italy" (by which he meant Dante, Michelangelo, and Cosimo de' Medici), and got around to a general theory of commerce, which, it seems,

will not insure national greatness unless it be accompanied
by wisdom. American commerce "out of her abundance,
[must] contribute something to the still nobler object of
improving the higher and better part of our nature . . . and
the exaltation of the national character, by that superiority
which the general sentiment of mankind has regarded as the
chief title to distinction." [34] But how was wisdom to accompany commerce? The genius of America would show the
way. Under tyranny, proclaimed a speaker in Troy, New
York, the "mechanic arts advance but slowly, because under
such governments the human faculties are cramped. . . . It
is in free States, that they find their favorite abode. There,
the human mind exerts itself without the restraint of fear;
its faculties go out freely and cheerfully in every direction,
in search of good. . . . Under the patronage of liberty, they
supply every department of society, and every want of life." [35]
Solomon Lincoln declared in 1826:

> It is delightful to look around us and to witness the rapid de-
> velopment of our national resources—giving strength and en-
> ergy to the character of our government—the wide extension
> of our territory—the salutary effect of wise, mild and equal laws
> —the activity of enterprise—and the excitement which the rich-
> est rewards give to cultivate industry, and to cherish talent:
> science lending her aid to the arts—the inventive powers of
> man tasked to strike out new paths in which to emulate the im-
> provements of the old world. . . . All—all—made happy in
> the repose of honourable peace.

Our ancestors, not insensible of the "value of practical learning," acted wisely, he said, in "cherishing the useful, rather
than the elegant arts." [36]

But it was not in Fourth of July oratory only that merchants were urged to combine virtue and profit. The great
Francis Wayland, president of Brown University for twenty-
eight years and in his youth a student under the Reverend
Moses Stuart, who, at Andover Theological Seminary, was
said to have trained more than fifteen hundred ministers,
published in 1835 *The Elements of Moral Science* and in

1837 *The Elements of Political Economy,* works that went through innumerable printings. *The Elements of Moral Science* is divided in two parts, each scrupulously worked out. The second part is entitled "Practical Ethics." Wayland believed in the moral sense, he argued that conscience can be progressively cultivated, and he made the heart of his system the assertions that happiness consists "in the *gratification of our desires within the limits assigned to them by our Creator*" and that "our *greatest happiness* is to be obtained, not by the various modes of self-gratification, but by simply seeking the good of others, and in doing the will of God from the heart." How was this applicable to business? "I may gratify my love of wealth by industry and frugality, while I conduct myself towards every other man with entire honesty. . . . Every individual is created with a desire to use the means of happiness which God has given him in such manner as he thinks will best promote that happiness; and of this manner he is the sole judge." The right of property is fundamental, something upon which "the very existence of our race, depends," and, indeed, "the first steps that were taken in the recovery of Europe from the misery of the dark ages, consisted in defining and establishing the right of property upon the basis of equitable and universal law," a statement that may or may not refer to the Protestant Reformation. "The seller, or merchant, is supposed to devote his time and capital to the business of supplying his neighbors with articles of use. For his time, risk, interest of money, and skill, he is entitled to an advance on his goods; and the buyer is under a correspondent obligation to allow that advance, except in the case of a change in the market price." The seller "has no right to appeal to the fears, or hopes, or avarice of the buyer. This rule is violated when, in dealings on the exchange, false information is circulated for the purpose of raising or depressing the price of stocks. It is violated by speculators who monopolize an article to create an artificial scarcity. . . . The case is the same when a salesman looks upon a stranger who enters his store, and deliberately calculates how he shall best influence and excite and mislead his mind, so as to sell the greatest amount of goods at the most exorbitant profit." The taking of interest is justified, and the rate should not be fixed by law in most cases. If people fail in business, it is usually by reason of "causeless, reckless speculation, by childish and inexcusable extravagance, or by gambling and profligacy." Anticipating William Graham Sumner, Wayland flatly states: "The control of society over the labor of the individual, over his religious opinions, over his personal expenses, and over various other innocent acts can work nothing but evil." [37]

A whole library was created on this topic. In 1844 Henry Ward Beecher, the most powerful Protestant preacher in the mid-century, published his influential *Lectures to Young Men,* in which one reads that idleness is the road to ruin and a hearty industry the road to happiness—"the applause of conscience, the self-respect of pride, the consciousness of independence, a manly joy of usefulness, the consent of every faculty of the mind to one's occupation, and their gratification in it . . . a happiness superior to the fever-flashes of vice in its brightest moments. I never knew an early-rising, hard-working, prudent man, careful of his earnings, and strictly honest who complained of bad luck." Whatever European "radicals" might say, whatever the miseries of unemployment even in America, Beecher argued it was folly to denounce wealth, the love of which God had implanted in every man.[38]

It is fascinating to watch the secularization of the doctrine. Francis Bowen in the *North American Review* in 1851, reviewing Gilbart's *A Practical Treatise on Banking,* commented on the chapter regarding "the moral and religious duties of banking companies," which "from its simplicity and directness, and the large range of Scripture illustrations . . . is well calculated to advance the high end which its author had in view"; in 1855 Andrew Preston Peabody in the same magazine said the mercantile life of the late Amos Lawrence showed "the controlling influence of Christian

morality . . . in all things"; and in 1856 Thomas Wentworth Higginson, reviewing various biographies of merchants, remarked that commerce is the chief estate and controlling power in "the several nations of Christendom," and
admired Thomas Handasyd Perkins both for being a self-
made man and for his Christian benevolence.[39] Then between
1886 and 1899 Andrew Carnegie published in various magazines twelve articles later collected as *The Gospel of Wealth*
(1900), in which the benevolism is retained but from which
the religious sanction virtually vanishes. The first chapter,
"How I Served My Apprenticeship," tells the story of a self-
made man, and in the light of his progress from poverty to
riches Carnegie could later assure the students at Cornell:
"I can confidently recommend to you the business career as
one in which there is abundant room for the exercise of man's
highest power, and of every good quality in human nature.
. . . The business career is . . . a stern school of all the
virtues." As early as 1868 Carnegie wrote a memorandum to
himself, vowing not to allow his personal income to rise above
$50,000 a year, the rest of his earnings to be devoted to
benevolence, for there is "no idol more debasing than the
worship of money." The book ardently preaches the doctrine of stewardship: "Surplus wealth should be considered as
a sacred trust to be administered by those into whose hands it
falls, during their lives, for the good of the community,"
holds that "neither the individual nor the race is improved
by almsgiving" of an indiscriminate sort, and exemplifies
powerfully Cotton Mather's doctrine in *Bonifacius*. Yet, possibly because Carnegie was descended from Scottish radicals,
his references to Christianity are sparing and sometimes
ironical, as in his treatment of the parable of the talents, and
in *The Gospel of Wealth* the Protestant ethic has become
thoroughly secularized.[40] Perhaps the most ironic comment
on this philosophy is found in *A Connecticut Yankee in King
Arthur's Court* (1889).

What Carnegie preached to his fellow millionaires Orison
Swett Marden (1850–1924) proclaimed to the common man.

He read Samuel Smiles's *Self-Help* (1859) as a boy and shaped his life by the gospel of perseverance. He attended Boston University and the Harvard Medical School, and by working hard at catering and hotel management left college with $20,000. The panic of 1893 wiped out his fortune but not his incredible optimism. He published *Pushing to the Front* in 1894, founded a magazine entitled *Success* (1897), went bankrupt in 1912, and started all over again in 1918. His book *Success* (1897) and another volume, *He Can Who Thinks He Can* (1908), are characteristic of the thirty or more titles he produced. These are said to have sold by the millions of copies in twenty-five languages. The Protestant ethic is here about as attenuated as it can be. The first chapter of *Success,* entitled "Enthusiasm," informs the reader that Jesus was an enthusiast, but so were Saint Paul, Harvey, Galileo, Fulton, S. F. B. Morse, Columbus, Bunyan, Agassiz, Raphael, and J. M. W. Turner. Earnestness is the key. "Fortune always smiles on those who roll up their sleeves and put their shoulders to the wheel." No one, he says flatly, "worships poverty today." Marden preaches a doctrine of plenitude crossed with a theory of the goodness of evolutionary competition. He would like "to fill every young man with utter dread of poverty—its shame, its constraint, its bitterness." If there were no impulse to make money, "whence would come the discipline which industry, perseverance, tact, sagacity and frugality give? . . . To succeed today you must concentrate all the powers of your mind upon one definite goal and have a tenacity of decision which means death or victory." There is a curious story toward the end of the volume about Christ as the friend of the earnest man. Here, as in Marden's other preachments, we learn that tenacity is a function of character. "Strength of character is a thing which must be wrung out of obstacles overcome. Life is a great gymnasium, and no man who sits in a chair and watches the parallel bars and other apparatus ever develops muscles or endurance." [41] No doubt. But nothing can be farther from, say, Saint Francis of Assisi.

In a series of lectures at universities, addresses a cut above Marden, Albert Shaw in *The Outlook for the Average Man* (1907) showed himself aware, as Marden was not, of changing social conditions, the disappearance of traditional economic landmarks, and the anxiety of young men about their prospects. New meanings must be found for success. But he argued that opportunities were still great, he restated the gospel of self-discipline and the love of work. Money must never be the direct object to be sought. Work must absorb the mind. "I hope that the young men in our colleges will be Utopian enough to believe in a future state of economic society in which each man will be more free than now to render service to the community according to his special abilities, while in return the supply to all useful workers of their ordinary needs will become more and more a matter of easy assurance, and therefore much more in the background than now." As of old, industry, skill, and character were essential to that high degree of efficiency that would alone assure success. Shaw took in not only business but the whole range of the professions, arguing that "there will be corresponding increase in the opportunity to earn honorable renown by the full devotion of one's talents to the social good in any chosen field." He was a genuine idealist, but he refused to discuss the relation between Christianity and a business career, resting content in a general glow about the diffusion of wealth through earnest endeavor. "The more energetically you turn your attention to the further development of the resources of wealth lying all about you, working in the right spirit and under modern conditions of fair play, the better it will be for everybody in the community." This, clearly, is the Protestant ethic minus theology.[42]

But the great proponent of life as a moral gymnasium was Teddy Roosevelt in such books as *American Ideals* (1897) and *The Strenuous Life* (1900); and on this doctrine *Hunting Trips of a Ranchman* (1885) and *The Rough Riders* (1899) were, so to speak, laboratory reports, the one on a personal, the other on a national scale. The mystical, the contempla-

tive had no place in his universe. Chance plays some part, but
by and large success is the result of application and character; and if Roosevelt seems far removed from Calvin, one
remembers William Allen White's statement that he came
straight out of the Old Testament—be good and you will be
useful and should be happy. A fellow can best help other
fellows "not by almsgiving, but by joining with [them] in an
intelligent and resolute effort for the uplifting of all."
Muscular Christianity closes what Calvinism began:

> I preach to you, then, my countrymen, that our country calls
> not for the life of ease but for the life of strenuous endeavor.
> The twentieth century looks before us big with the fate of many
> nations. If we stand idly by, if we seek merely swollen, slothful
> ease and ignoble peace, if we shrink from the hard contests
> where men must win at hazard of their lives and at the risk of
> all they hold dear, then the bolder and stronger peoples will
> pass us by, and will win for themselves the domination of the
> world. Let us therefore boldly face the life of strife, resolute to
> do our duty well and manfully; resolute to uphold righteous-
> ness by deed and by words; resolute to be both honest and
> brave, to serve high ideals, yet to use practical methods.

If this was as obvious as a billboard, the Franklinian emphasis upon the practical fuses with vigorous Christianity and
social Darwinism. The bases of the country, Teddy thought,
were laid deep in material prosperity coming from thrift,
business energy, and enterprise, and he proposed to honor
simultaneously the captains of industry, Abraham Lincoln,
and U. S. Grant.[43]

The universality of business in the United States, wrote
the British traveler G. W. Steevens, had its murderous side,
for "in America the man who fails in business has failed in
the one thing there is to do." [44] But he had been anticipated
by Nathaniel Hawthorne:

> It is the iron rule in our day to require an object and a purpose
> in life. It makes us all parts of a complicated scheme of progress,
> which can only result in our arrival at a colder and drearier re-
> gion than we were born in. It insists upon everybody's adding

somewhat—a mite, perhaps, but earned by incessant effort—to an accumulated pile of usefulness, of which the only use will be, to burden our posterity with even heavier thoughts and more inordinate labor than our own. No life wanders now like an unfettered stream; there is a mill-wheel for the tiniest rivulet to turn. We go all wrong, by too strenuous a resolution to go all right.[45]

That appeared in *The Marble Faun* in 1860.

IV

The image of a Christian tradesman suggests some pamphlet by Defoe or character sketch by Richard Steele, and reminds us that the businessman has not commonly been the subject of biography until recent times. Funeral eulogies were naturally concentrated upon the virtues of the deceased, and there were American mercantile biographies that centered upon eccentrics such as Stephen Girard.[46] At the other end of the temporal spectrum modern business biographies principally deal in the economic outlook and commercial practices of the subject and his public interests, minimizing his church connections as earlier biographers did not. Therefore the actual working of the Mather-Franklin doctrine of the useful and the good can best be seen in the lives of nineteenth-century American businessmen. In that period the assumptions about one's calling were so powerful as to color even the accounts of Stephen Girard, who forbade anybody in clerical garb to set foot in the college he founded and who named his vessels after French skeptics, but who nevertheless is given all the credit-making virtues. The first great collection of business biographies in the United States was Freeman Hunt's *Lives of American Merchants* (2 volumes, 1855–1857), which praises Franklin, gives a history of commerce, stresses the fact that Americans are superior to the British because they show no hypocrisy about being a nation of shopkeepers, and collects admiring accounts, by various hands, of such men as Thomas Handasyd Perkins, Nicholas Brown, Samuel Ward, Jonas Pickering, Abbott Lawrence, John Jacob Astor, Judah Touro, and many more.* Not being a Christian, Touro might have been expected to offer difficulties, but he is described as an "Israelite without guile," has a proper religious upbringing, and is extensively mourned at his death. John Jacob Astor, it seems, was "trained from childhood in the practice of rising early and giving a portion of his first waking hours to the Bible and Prayer-book, a practice kept up in after life, and, as he often declared, the source of unfailing comfort and pleasure." "A class thus educated by toil and the Bible," sternly adds the biographer, "is equal to all the best offices of ordinary life." [47] All the figures in the collection are distinguished by habits of early rising, diligence, honesty, shrewdness, and religious conviction (except, of course, Girard), all are opposed to indiscriminate almsgiving, and all are famous for public-spirited charities— Girard College, the Perkins Institute for the Blind, the Astor Library, and so on. It is significant that Hunt, for nineteen years editor of the first American magazine devoted to commerce, *Hunt's Merchant's Magazine*, published *Worth and Wealth: A Collection of Maxims, Morals and Miscellanies for Merchants and Men of Business* (New York, 1857), a kind of informal and jolly *summa* of the theory and practice of the useful and the good.

One could accumulate innumerable other practical instances of the working of the doctrine. Thus William E. Dodge, known as the Christian merchant, "loved," says his biographer, "to transact business for God at the same time that he transacted business for himself." He was one of the founders of the Union Theological Seminary.[48] Jay Cooke could confront calmly the panic of 1873 because he "took the plain facts of the Christian faith, believed them unquestioningly,

---

* The merchant, thought Hunt, "provides for, civilizes, and Christianizes his fellow-men." The merchant biographies arose from Hunt's conviction that the merchant, "accused of lacking culture," was quite as reputable as the politician.

wove them into his daily life, so they were veritably a part of himself, and wished not for more." He had "no doubt that he was appointed and sustained by a higher power." [49] Cooke once proposed to Phillips Brooks to convert the whole United States at Cooke's expense; and when one of his agents in financing the Northern Pacific, a man named Wilkeson, told a prospective investor that he believed in the project as he believed in God, he was presumably echoing the opinion of his employer. Whatever one may think of this odd union of theism and the railroad business, Cooke was a deeply religious man (he was a Sabbatarian) with a high sense of social responsibility.[50] Grounded in Calvinism, Cyrus Hall McCormick wrote in 1845 that "business is not inconsistent with Christianity, but the latter ought to be a help to the former, giving a confidence and resignation, after using all *proper means*." He established what became the McCormick Theological Seminary to assist providence, since "Providence has seemed to assist me in our business"; and he fought off theological liberalism with the money he had gained from selling his reaper.[51] Commodore Vanderbilt claimed the maxims of the Bible were implanted in him in youth,[52] though there are those who have wondered. Henry Clay Frick was steeped in Franklin's *Autobiography* and was so impressed by William George Jordan's *Self-Control: Its Kinship and Majesty* that he bought many copies of it to give away.[53] If he lacked the religious motivation of some of his contemporaries, he shared their interest in intelligent philanthropy. Of Carnegie I have already spoken.[54]

But perhaps it will bring things to a climax to concentrate on the career of John D. Rockefeller.[55] He had a difficult boyhood, for his father was a failure, but from the beginning he was firmly religious, believing in a simple, unshaken Baptist doctrine of good works and faith and in the virtues of thrift, industry, and competitive enterprise. Accomplishment, he once said, is the goal of every man who tries to do his part in the world. He was a devotee of Franklin, at least as he understood Franklin, but where Franklin had visualized only

the competition of merchant with merchant and tradesman
with tradesman, Rockefeller lived in a more savage world,
one in which traditional competition was more wasteful than
not; and in backing the trust as a form of corporate enterprise, he regarded himself as under providence moving toward the good. If to his contemporaries Standard Oil became
not only a myth but a monster, a Machiavellian entity as unscrupulous, hypocritical, and cruel as ever a prince was supposed to be, it was just too bad. The law of the jungle was a
fact of life. What was the difference, indeed, between the
narrowness of the Puritan turned Baptist and the self-seeking
of Standard Oil? Scholarly attempts to persuade us of the
culture of English Puritanism lead us to forget the simple
delight in sheer destruction that Scott understood when he
wrote *A Legend of Montrose* and Macaulay caught in "The
Battle of Naseby":

> Oh! evil was the root, and bitter was the fruit,
> And crimson was the juice of the vintage that we trod.

In one sense Rockefeller was a reversion to type. Allan
Nevins concludes that though he was a business genius, he
was a man without fire or gusto, without a kindling fraternal
concern for people casually met. God had prospered him,
God destroyed his competitors, and there developed in the
mind of this unpredictable genius (like Henry Ford a cross
between the country banker and Napoleon) a mystical belief
that God had commanded him to gain wealth that might be
used for the welfare of mankind—the old doctrine of stewardship. Thence eventually developed the long list of Rockefeller family philanthropies—the University of Chicago, the
General Education Board, the Rockefeller Medical Foundation, the Rockefeller Foundation, and the rest. His life
vibrated among three points—his home, his office, his church.
Troops of Sunday-school workers were invited to his home in
Cleveland—home of the man who was the principal devil in
Henry Demarest Lloyd's *Wealth against Commonwealth*
(1894); foreign missionaries touched the heart that the plight

¶Epistola Christofori Colom: cui etas nostra multū debet: de Insulis Indie supra Gangem nuper inuentis. Ad quas perquirendas octauo antea mense auspicijs τ ere inuictissimi Fernandi Dispaniarum Regis missus fuerat: ad Magnificum dñm Raphaelem Sanxis: eiusdem serenissimi Regis Tesaurariū missa: quam nobilis ac litteratus vir Aliander de Cosco ab Dispano ideomate in latinum conuertit : tertio kal's Maij. M·cccc·xciij· Pontificatus Alexandri Sexti Anno primo.

Quoniam suscepte prouintie rem perfectam me cōsecutum fuisse gratum tibi fore scio: has constitui exarare: que te vniuscuiusq; rei in hoc nostro itinere geste inuentecq; ad/ moneant: Tricesimotertio die postq; Gadibus discessi in mare Indicū perueni: vbi plurimas insulas innumeris habitatas bo/ minibus repperi: quarum omnium pro foelicissimo Rege nostro preconio celebrato τ verillis extensis contradicente nemine pos/ sessionem accepi: primeq; earum diui Saluatoris nomen impo/ sui: cuius fretus auxilio tam ad hanc:q ad ceteras alias perue/ nimus. Eam vo Indi Guanahanin vocant. Aliarum etiā vnam quanq; nouo nomine nuncupaui. Quippe aliā insulam Sancte Marie Conceptionis· aliam Fernandinam · aliam Dysabellam· aliam Johanam· τ sic de reliquis appellari iussi. Quamprimum in eam insulam quā dudum Johanā vocari dixi appulimus: iu xta eius littus occidentem versus aliquantulum processi: tamq; eam magnā nullo reperto fine inueni: vt non insulam: sed conti nentem Chatai prouinciam esse crediderim: nulla tñ videns op/ pida municipiaue in maritimis sita confinib? preter aliquos vi/ cos τ predia rustica: cum quorz incolis loqui nequibam quare si mul ac nos videbant surripiebant fugam· progrediebar vltra: existimans aliquā me vrbem villasue inuenturum. Deniq; ridēs q longe admodum progressis nihil noui emergebat: τ bmōi via nos ad Septentrionem deferebatq; ipse fugere exoptabā: terris etenim regnabat bruma: ad Austrumq; erat in voto cōtenderer

I. First page of the first Latin edition (Rome, 1493) of the letter of Christopher Columbus describing the New World, written in February 1493, during his homeward voyage in the ship *Nina*.

II. Woodcut from one of the Italian editions (Florence, 1493) of the letter above, showing the landing of Columbus in the New World. King Ferdinand, on his throne in Spain, watches Columbus disembark.

III. Produced at Augsburg between 1497 and 1504, this woodcut was among the earliest pictorial representations of American Indians. "They . . . also eat each other, even those who are slain, and hang the flesh of them in the smoke."

IV. Jan Mostaert's "Landscape in the West Indies," painted sometime before 1555 or 1556, and also referred to as "An Episode of the Conquest of America," is the first full landscape of the New World.

v. The mission of San Xavier del Bec ("The White Dove of the Desert"), near Tucson, Arizona, founded in 1692. The beauty of such buildings, created in a great period of Spanish architecture, has had its effect upon American taste.

vi. The tower of the California Building, erected in Balboa Park, San Diego, for the California Pacific International Exposition, in 1915, is an example of Spanish revival architecture justified by site and tradition.

VII. William Henry Vanderbilt's block-long Italian Renaissance house, at Fifth Avenue and 51st Street, with the mansion of William K. Vanderbilt, designed by Richard Morris Hunt in sixteenth-century French style, adjoining it at 52nd Street. Both houses were erected at the end of the 1870s.

VIII. An aerial view of "The Breakers," the summer "cottage" built for Cornelius Vanderbilt in 1893-95 at Newport, Rhode Island. Erected at enormous expense out of materials brought from France, Italy, and Africa, it outshone the palaces of the Medici in opulence.

IX. The colossal marble statue of George Washington by Horatio Greenough, originally intended for the national Capitol, is the masterpiece of the classical school of American sculpture.

Smithsonian Institution, Washington, D.C.

X. The Court of Honor at the World's Columbian Exposition, Chicago, 1893, with the 75-foot figure of "The Republic," by Daniel Chester French, done in the classical style, in the foreground.

XI. In "Kindred Spirits" (1849), Asher B. Durand showed the poet William Cullen Bryant and the painter Thomas Cole on a rocky ledge in the Catskills, discussing the glories of that wild nature whose sublimity was a favorite theme of the Hudson River School of artists.

XII. Albert Bierstadt, in paintings such as "The Valley of the Yosemite" (1866), strove to record the grandeur of the West; his immense panoramic views suggested an inhuman wilderness of shimmering light and melodramatic darkness.

of small refiners of oil could not reach; and only when Washington Gladden denounced "tainted money" in 1905 was any effort made to make it clear that all Rockefeller had wanted to do in a Christian way was to end disorder and waste. If the story that God told him to give his money to the University of Chicago is sheer legend, it is myth with a grain of truth. One director of a Rockefeller corporation said that all the meetings opened with prayer and that one chair was kept empty to honor Jesus. It seems to have occurred to nobody that the symbol might be ambiguous.

The doctrine of the useful and the good under providence has, then, been long a governing force in American commercial life. Dr. Sigmund Diamond, in a monograph entitled *The Reputation of the American Business Man*,[56] after studying the obituary notices that followed upon the deaths of Stephen Girard, John Jacob Astor, Cornelius Vanderbilt, John P. Morgan, John D. Rockefeller, and Henry Ford, finds a predictable criterion governing a century of American values. The criterion is that of the useful and the good. The dead man made money because God intended him to be useful to society. What social good did he intend with the money he had made? The money was made through the Franklin virtues of thrift, shrewdness, hard work, inventiveness; the good must be example as well as benevolence. Henry Ford may have been the last representative of this tradition—who knows?—but the words of Horace Mann, addressed to the Boston Mercantile Library Association in 1849, were pertinent in the world of the Tin Lizzie. Wealth is valuable only as a contribution to human welfare, and it is therefore the duty of all good Americans "by diligence in business, abstinence in pleasures, privations even . . . to seek to attain a competence."

Whether the doctrine lives on into the welfare state is precisely the question under debate.[57] On the one hand much of the Protestant ethic has been absorbed into the business ethos and comes out as "responsibility," "adjustment," the capacity to direct without seeming to, and the capacity to go through the forms of, say, a committee meeting patiently while in fact dominating the committee under the aegis of "leadership." On the other hand not only is business honesty now enforced by statute in ways it was not so enforced during earlier decades, but also the concepts of truth in advertising, honest goods, and institutional repute reinforce Franklin's doctrine that honesty *is* the best policy. Perhaps the most significant areas of contemporary American activity for a career open to the talents and to industry are those industries and occupations that cannot seem to secure enough technically trained personnel to fill their incessant demands; and any scrutiny of the want ads inserted by employers in such newspapers as *The New York Times* or in trade journals, professional periodicals, and circulars sent to colleges, institutes, and universities reveals a return upon the doctrine that bright and honest capacity is welcome. What has dropped out is any reference to God.

Roman Virtue

I

THE New World was no part of the Roman empire. Americans do not, like Europeans, drive over highways originally laid down for the legions of Caesar, nor in the midst of cities or on some nearby hill see ruined temples from the time when Zeus was the father of gods and men. The legal system of the United States owes little or nothing directly to Roman law. No battered statues are dug up in America as they are dug up in Greece or Israel or Italy, and we see no weathered arches resembling that of Titus in Rome, no Colosseum, no ancient theater still in use like that of Herodes Atticus in Athens, no palace ruins such as the palace of Diocletian at Split, nor, though the Spaniards built churches on sites dedicated to the worship of savage gods, do we have in the New World any temple like the Pantheon erected by Agrippa and later converted into the church of Santa Maria Rotunda. Despite the success of American scholarship in the classical academy in Rome, with the agora in Athens, or on the site of Nestor's palace near Pylos, we do not know antiquity directly. We no longer characteristically study the ancient tongues. Greek has disappeared from most public education; Latin has shrunk to a shadow of its importance in the days when the founding fathers read it fluently; and though the vogue of courses in translation and of general education has restored a certain pale vitality to the Greeks, it has done less for the Romans. For these and other reasons the notion that the classical past has exerted an important influence on the culture of the United States seems to many absurd.

Yet evidence of that influence lies all around us. Many villages, towns, and cities have either classical names such as Rome, Troy, Athens, Syracuse, Ithaca, Utica, Alexandria, or Augusta, or names compounded, sometimes uncouthly, out of one or more classical elements, as Thermopolis, Minneapolis, Itasca, or Spotsylvania. Our streets are sometimes known as Euclid Avenue, Appian Way, Acadia Drive, or Phaeton Road. The names of the states occasionally reveal classicism, as in the cases of Pennsylvania, Virginia, and Georgia. The American college occupies something called a campus, a word that came into American English in this sense in 1774. Fraternities and sororities display Greek letters standing for words known only to the initiate, as if the Eleusinian mysteries were still operative. Certain categories of students in high school and college are sophomores, juniors, and seniors; the first of these Latinate derivatives dates (in this country) from 1726, the third from 1651, and the middle term from some period in between.

Constitutionally we are not a democracy but a republic; that is, a *res publica,* a phrase referring to the commonweal, which in the sense of a government by elected representatives came into English in the seventeenth century. The head of the government, despite efforts to entitle him high mightiness, protector, regent, or serenity, is a president, from *praesidens,* this sense of the term dating from 1783. The national legislature is not a parliament, a *rath,* a meeting of the estates, nor a general assembly but a congress, from *congressus,* a coming together. The English term first appears in 1768 but was not used to mean a legislative assembly until 1775. The upper house is not a *gerousia,* a *boule,* a council of ancients, a house of lords, or a chamber of deputies, but a senate, from *senatus,*[1] a gathering of older and presumably wiser men. The congress meets not in a parliament house, a state house, a palace, or a government house but in a capitol, a word originally designating a citadel or temple on a hilltop, like the temple of Jupiter Optimus Maximus which stood on the Capitoline Hill in Rome. Our first two political parties were Federalists and Republicans, terms originating in the Latin language; our present ones are Republicans and Democrats, the second term coming from the Greek. The fact that these classical derivatives were fresh in their time indicates they were deliberately adopted. Even today, as somebody has observed, many of our liveliest political words are from the Latin, as in the cases of quota, moratorium, referendum, and propaganda.

The great seal of the United States bears an eagle, a bird suggested by the eagle of the legions, the difference being that the American eagle is a bald eagle and not a Roman one. It clasps an olive branch in one talon, a sheaf of arrows in the other, emblems of peace and war not common in this country before the Revolution, and having classical connotations. The figure is surmounted by an enigmatic Latin phrase, *E pluribus unum.* On the obverse is a truncated pyramid over which is a triangle in a glory with the eye of God in the triangle, and above this one reads: *Annuit coeptis*—he has favored our beginnings. Below the pyramid is *Novus ordo seclorum*—a new order of the ages. On the base of the pyramid, not in Arabic numerals but in Roman for greater dignity, is MDCCLXXVI, when the new order of the ages began. Both Latin phrases hint at the desire of the founding fathers to renew in 1776 an ancient virtue.

Our coinage, largely the creation of Jefferson, is decimal coinage, self-consciously alien from the coinage of the mother country, whose pounds, shillings, and pence Americans nowadays find it hard to calculate. It was early agreed that our hard money would not show the head of any living president, partly because Roman coins had displayed the heads of deified emperors. The first coinage law (1792) directed the mint to put the eagle on several coins and on their other sides (this in a country that did not recognize goddesses) a figure of Liberty. The goddess persists. Sometimes she stands, sometimes she sits, sometimes she shows only her head, or her head and shoulders, and sometimes she is known as Columbia, but she is always a goddess. She is clad in classical garments; and on her head, or near her on a pole or standard she sometimes clasps, is a Phrygian cap, worn in Rome by liberated slaves. On the Roosevelt dime this cap is on her head and has sprouted wings; bored with the cap, she may have borrowed her new headdress from Mercury, messenger of the gods. Most dimes show on the obverse the *fasces,* a bundle of rods tied together around an ax, the head of which protrudes from the bundle. This was borne before the Roman lictor as an emblem of his legal power, the ax for beheading, the rods for scourging. The heads of historical personages, when they appear on the money of the United States, are seen in profile, or, more rarely, in three-quarters view, as were the heads on the coins of the ancient world. On the Jefferson nickel, for example, Jefferson is portrayed in profile, and on the obverse is an image of Monticello, a "Greek" building surmounted by a Roman dome. The Lincoln penny shows Lincoln in profile, and the obverse is an image of the classical shrine in Washington that honors him. The American quarter-dollar displays Washington in profile; the obverse holds an eagle. But on the silver dollar Liberty appears with her Phrygian cap and a laurel wreath; the eagle is again on the other side. It is perhaps a mark of our classical enthusiasm in coinage that the English phrase, "In God we trust," did not appear on American coins until 1864.

This classical iconography has long persisted. When the American Academy of Arts and Sciences was founded in Boston in 1780, a great seal was necessary; and the great seal fused classical mythology, the topography of Boston, and the hope of the country. The principal figure is Minerva. At her right is a field of Indian corn, the native grain of America, and the prospect on the right is bounded by a hill crowned with oaks. On the declivity of the hill toward the sea are the outskirts of a town. About the feet of Minerva are several "instruments of husbandry." On her left are a quadrant and a telescope, a prospect of the sea, a ship steering toward the town, and overhead the sun is rising above a cloud. Over the whole is the motto: *Sub libertate florent.* The committee which approved the seal thought it represented the situation of a new country, depending on agriculture but attending to the arts, commerce, and science. The sun rising above the cloud was the rising sun of America, and the Latin motto was supposed to indicate that the arts and sciences flourish best under liberty.

Holger Cahill has studied emblems of unity and freedom in various objects in the Metropolitan Museum; he finds that in typographical vignettes of the earlier nineteenth century the figure of Liberty is commonly surrounded by symbols of agriculture or manufacture, or appears, somewhat unclassically, with railroad trains or steamers in the background. Commonly she is given a cornucopia, and it is sometimes difficult to determine whether she is Liberty, Justice, Columbia, or Prosperity. Thus a silver medal of about 1852 shows a female figure extending a wreath, the liberty cap on a pole, and on the left side of the goddess a plow, a cornucopia, a caduceus, and on her right a spinning wheel, a sheaf, and various other objects. Occasionally she turns into a comely Indian but she commonly retains her classical profile. I have seen somewhere an "America Guided by Wisdom," the goddess this time without her liberty cap but holding the shield of the United States, a cornucopia at her feet, her costume "classical," her foot in a Roman sandal, while Mercury points to a fleet, Ceres sits at Mercury's feet, and Minerva instructs America while the sun breaks through the clouds. Business letterheads of the nineteenth century combine classical gods, goddesses, and motifs, with factories, railroad trains, machines, and other evidences of prosperity. A weathervane of about 1885 in the Edison Institute of Technology in Dearborn shows Columbia holding the American flag; and of course the climax of this sort of thing was French's enormous statue of "The Republic," seventy-five feet high, designed for the Court of Honor at the World's Columbian Exposition (Pl. X), a smaller replica of which (only twenty-four feet high) now stands in Jackson Park, Chicago. It is remarkable in what degree the public iconography of the nation—the statues that crown the domes of state capitols, the figures of justice in our courthouses, the emblems of peace, or plenty, or progress, or some other general ideal—are classical females in a republic that was never part of Greece or Rome.

Most state legislatures meet in capitols, though in the East a few do not. Twenty states exhibit Latin mottoes on their great seals; for Arkansas, *Regnat populus;* for Colorado, *Nil sine numine;* for Kansas, *Ad astra per aspera;* for Mississippi, *Virtute et armis;* for Missouri, *Salus populi suprema lex esto;* for North Carolina, *Esse quam videri;* for Virginia, *Sic semper tyrannis.* Perhaps the most extraordinary among these is the motto of Michigan: *Si requaeris peninsulam amoenam, circumspice.* The great seals of American cities frequently display Latin mottoes, and so do some of the sham heraldic devices invented by sedate business firms or those desiring to emphasize class appeal. College diplomas began as Latin documents and long remained so; when in 1961 Harvard College abandoned Latin for English on its diplomas the graduates thought their dignity was being lowered. College seals or coats of arms or emblems frequently display Greek or Latin phrases. Of these the best known is possibly *Veritas* at Harvard. *Veritas,* as interpreted by James Russell Lowell in his great "Commemoration Ode" of 1865, became patriotism or *amor patriae:*

> Many loved Truth, and lavished life's best oil
>   Amid the dust of books to find her,
> Content at last, for guerdon of their toil
>   With the cast mantle she hath left behind her.
>   Many in sad faith sought for her;
>   But these, our brothers, fought for her,
>   At life's dear peril wrought for her,
>   Testing the raptured fleetness

Of her divine completeness;
    Their higher instinct knew
Those love her best who to themselves are true,
And what they dared to dream of, dare to do;
    They followed her, and found her
    Where all may hope to find,
Not in the ashes of the burnt-out mind,
But beautiful, with danger's sweetness round her.

This passage, which virtually enrolls Horatius at the bridge among the Harvard alumni, equates *veritas* in its highest aspect with *virtus*,* or love of the republic.[2] The idea is that of Montesquieu.

That the young nation should have accepted a set of classical coordinates to particularize components of its government and its republican culture is less astonishing than its failure to do so would have been. To western man between the fall of Constantinople (1453) and the fall of Napoleon (1815) the classical past was perpetually a catalytic agent, a dynamic force so wonderful and so elusive that generation after generation of thinkers recast Greece and Rome in their own images. If the humanists did not literally rediscover antiquity, they remolded it, they energized it, they caused it to shine upon the horizon of European culture with a golden splendor. Quite as important as the speculations of Leonardo or the discoveries of Galileo were the rediscoveries of Homer and Plutarch, Lucan and Livy, Ovid and Virgil, or the reassessment of these authors and of others. The study of writers from the ancient past, the collecting and evaluation of gem and coin, statue and inscription, the discovery, assembling, editing, and interpreting of manuscripts revealed a

* The implied assumption that Roman *virtus* has some connection with war and victory is as old as America. For example, Samuel Cooper, preaching to the Ancient and Honourable Artillery Company of Boston (Boston, 1751), remarked that the Romans had particular marks of honor to reward the bravery of their soldiers, that love of country led the Romans to conquer others, and that the love of mankind is superior to a narrow love of country, for "we cannot in this applaud their Virtue." He also deplores a tendency among the ancient Greeks to banish those who won the admiration of their people.

world at once timeless and flexible, elusive and permanent, a lost Utopia of the west inhabited by noble beings—Aspasia, Pericles, Marcus Aurelius, Horatius, Cato, Cornelia, Caesar, Harmodius, and Aristogeiton—men and women capable of creating republics and extending empires, writing tragedies and concocting satires, codifying wisdom and anticipating modernity. They were the wisest and most beautiful of mankind.

Two examples from the extremes of this period will illustrate the compelling power of antiquity. In 1472 Ivan III married Sofia, the only niece of the last emperor of Byzantium, Constantine Paleologus, and so prepared Russia for the concept of Moscow as the third Rome and of its ruler as Czar or Caesar. At the other end of the temporal spectrum, in 1789, the Cincinnatus of the West, the Father of his Country, George Washington, took his oath of office on the balcony of the "classical" United States building in New York City and became president of a new republic eight times as large in area as the republic of Rome when Rome included all of Italy. Washington's journey from Mount Vernon to New York had been through a succession of "classical" arches, allegorical structures commonly displaying the Roman eagle in some form or other, or through choirs of maidens offering him laurel crowns. Between the revival of the concept of Caesar and that of Cincinnatus, what range and variety of interest, of style, of invention, of philosophy, of political theory created or colored by antiquity! Grammar was reinvented, philology was born, the theory of politics took on new meaning, the major languages of Europe were, so to speak, reorganized, history was rewritten, art and architecture were transmogrified, printing acquired the whole range of classical antiquity for its province, the stage was transformed (consider the change from *Gorboduc* to *Antony and Cleopatra!*), modern criticism began, modern music was founded, the science of aesthetics was created—all matters in which the cult of the classics had a major part. In Elizabethan literature alone the greater number of translations are directly or indirectly ver-

sions of Greek and Latin authors. Spenser wishes to fashion
a gentleman after the precepts, modified, to be sure, of
Aristotle, and portrays English rustics conversing as he
thought Roman or Greek shepherds might have talked. Six
of the thirteen tragedies of Shakespeare are from the ancient
world, Marlowe writes *Hero and Leander,* Ralegh's *History
of the World* comes down to the period when Macedonia became a Roman province, and Ben Jonson turns into a kind of
Horatian legislator for the muses of England.

From the Renaissance through the Enlightenment the cult
of classicism presents three great, intermingling aspects—the
phase of discovery, the phase of emulation, and the phase of
codification and control. Probably it is impossible for us to
comprehend the excitement of discovery in fifteenth-century
Europe, an excitement paralleling and sometimes surpassing
that aroused by the discovery of the New World. When somebody asked Cirisco de' Pizzicolli why he wore himself out by
incessant journeyings after fragments of antiquity, he responded, "I go to awake the dead." Demetrius Chalcondylas
fled from Byzantium to Rome in 1447; a pupil wrote, "It
seems to me that in him is figured all the wisdom, the civility,
and the elegance of those famous and illustrious ancients."
Raphael begins a letter on the need for systematically mapping
Rome by referring to the divinity of the spirits of antiquity.
The "Laocoön" was dug up in 1506. The pope placed the
Apollo Belvedere on a marble base in 1523 when the Vatican
Museum was begun. Ghiberti· wrote of a marble found at
Padua: "This statue, when the Christian faith triumphed, was
hidden in that place by some gentle soul, who, seeing it so
perfect, fashioned with art so wonderful, and with such
power of genius, and being moved to reverent pity, caused a
sepulchre of bricks to be built, and there within buried the
statue, and covered it with a broad slab of stone, that it might
not in any way be injured." [3]

In the nature of things the North Americans could not participate in the excitement of discovery except later, intermittently, or by proxy. Of course when time had ripened their

culture and their wealth, we sometimes find a kind of sur-
rogate for discovery. For example, Jefferson sent back to
Richmond from Paris his designs for the Virginia capitol, a
building to be "simple and sublime . . . copied from the
most precious mode. of antient architecture remaining
on earth." When he wrote this he had not seen the Maison
Carrée at Nîmes, but when he did visit it in 1787 he wrote
Madame de Tessé: "Here I am . . . gazing whole hours at
the Maison quarrée, like a lover at his mistress. . . . From
Lyons to Nismes I have been nourished with the remains of
Roman grandeur . . . I am immersed in [antiquities from
morning to night]. For me the city of Rome is actually [exist-
ing in all the splendor of its] empire." [4] We owe to an American poet that supreme phrase about the ancient world,

> The glory that was Greece
> And the grandeur that was Rome.

Possibly an unconscious yearning to be thought of as having
a portion in antiquity and therefore of the world community
is shown by the popularity among wealthy Americans of
such works of art as Piranesi's etchings of the ruins of Rome,
or by Healy's charming, if sentimental, picture of Longfellow
and his daughter Edith under the arch of Titus (1869), or by
the vogue of Italy among both American tourists and American artists of all sorts in the nineteenth century, an appeal
created partly by Renaissance art and partly by the allure of
the lone mother of dead empires. Byron had enormous
vogue [5] in the United States. In one sense the admirable
work of American classical scholars and archaeologists in
Italy and the eastern Mediterranean continues the excitement
of discovery. On the other hand it is important not to exaggerate; and the ambiguous responses of Hawthorne and Mark
Twain to classical remains in Italy remind us that Americans
were also characteristically glad to be free of the tyranny of
the past.[6] But our non-classical contemporary world cannot
quite comprehend the long, continuing emotional thrust of

antiquity into the United States, not quite validated by
Elizabeth Taylor in *Cleopatra*.

II

Emulation of the classical past or, more strictly, emulation
of the actions of heroic figures in Plutarch or the classical
historians was a force in the period of exploration and settlement, as previous chapters have hinted—so much so that the
attentive reader of Cawley's study of the imaginative impact
of the voyagers upon the Elizabethan imagination comes by
and by to feel that poetry and the stage were bathed in an
atmosphere of antique virtue.[7] In addition to the instances I
have cited in earlier chapters a pair of additional passages
from Hakluyt are too characteristic to be overlooked. In
the "Epistle Dedicatorie" to the first volume of the second
edition of the *Principal Navigations* he quotes a speech of
the elder Scipio to Cornelius Scipio Africanus on love of
country, and in the similar epistle for the second volume is
more explicit in his application:

> These and the like Heroicall intents and attempts of our
> Princes, our Nobilitie, our Clergie, & our Chivalry, I have in
> the first place exposed and set forth to the view of this age, with
> the same intention that the old Romans set up in wax in their
> palaces the Statuas or images of their worthy ancestors; whereof
> Salust in his treatise of the warre of Jugurtha, writeth . . . I
> have often heard (quoth he) how Quintus maximus, Publius
> Scipio, and many other worthy men of our citie were woont to
> say, when they beheld the images and portraitures of their an-
> cestors, that they were most vehemently inflamed into vertue.[8]

We who languidly read in school anthologies Drayton's "To
the Virginian Voyage":

> You have Heroique Minds,
> Worthy your Countries Name,
> That Honour still pursue,

cannot comprehend this excitement.

Captain John Smith felt it, however, so much so that *The Proceedings of the English Colonie in Virginia* (1612), which, though coming from several hands, forms the second part of *A Map of Virginia* and was put together, whether by Smith or under his supervision, in twelve books, is like a prose Aeneid. In this narrative Aeneas-Smith transplants to unknown shores a divinely guided people and is opposed by Powhatan, like Turnus, a hero of equal eminence. Each is surrounded by lesser heroes and weaker men, each nation appeals to its own deities, each side utters appropriate orations on friendship, political power, the nature of greatness, authority, and ethics, and speeches of defiance and "pollicie" are virtually classical essays. Aeneas-Smith is wily in diplomacy, skilled in utterance, a ruler, a warrior, a lawgiver, a man above ordinary passions (Pocahontas was "the very Nomparell" of Powhatan's kingdom, but Smith "ever much respected her"). Almost singlehanded he defeats hundreds of warriors, he receives a mysterious wound in the hour of his triumph, and he is removed from the scene. The narrative is single and whole. Some eighteen set speeches are placed in the mouths of the chief contenders, ten being allotted to Smith, five to Powhatan, and three to lesser Indians. Thrice the great king Powhatan pictures his own grandeur. He addresses the invaders in the spirit of Calgacus in the *Agricola;* and in such an utterance as the following speaks like an antique Roman or a Greek:

> Captaine *Smith,* you may vnderstand that I, hauing seene the death of all my people thrice, and not one living of those 3 generations but my selfe, I knowe the difference of peace and warre better then any in my Countrie. But now I am old, and ere long must die. My brethren, namely *Opichapam; Opechankanough,* and *Kekataugh,* my two sisters, and their two daughters, are distinctly each others successours. I wish their experiences no lesse then mine, and your loue to them, no lesse then mine to you: but this brute from *Nansamund,* that you are come to destroy my Countrie, so much affrighteth all my people, as they dare not visit you. What will it availe you to take that perforce, you may quietly haue with loue, or to destroy them that provide

you food? What can you get by war, when we can hide our provision and flie to the woodes, whereby you must famish, by
wronging vs your friends? And whie are you thus iealous of our
loues, seeing vs vnarmed, and both doe, and are willing still to
feed you with that you cannot get but by our labours? Think
you I am so simple not to knowe it is better to eate good meate,
lie well, and sleepe quietly with my women and children, laugh
and be merrie with you, haue copper, hatchets, or what I want,
being your friend; then bee forced to flie from al, to lie cold in
the woods, feed vpon acorns roots and such trash, and be so
hunted by you that I can neither rest eat nor sleepe, but my
tired men must watch, and if a twig but breake, everie one crie,
there comes Captaine *Smith:* and then must I flie I knowe not
whether, and thus with miserable feare end my miserable life,
leauing my pleasures to such youths as you, which, through
your rash vnadvisednesse, may quickly as miserably ende, for
want of that you never knowe how to find? Let this therefore
assure you of our loues, and everie yeare our friendly trade shall
furnish you with corne; and now also if you would come in
friendly manner to see vs, and not thus with your gunnes and
swords, as to invade your foes.[9]

All this redounds to the credit of Captain Smith, but such
language was never spoken by a guttural Indian and recorded
by a stenographer at Jamestown. Possibly the Reverend William Simmonds revised the whole thing in London. But the
point is not accuracy or authorship, the point is the quality
of the antique world here imputed to the speaker—

In utrumque paratus,
*Seu versare dolos seu certae occumbere morti.**

---

* But the Romans were not always admired. The Reverend Richard Salter
declared in New London in 1768: "Nor do I conceive a man truly great, who,
out of vain glory and worldly views, is led to do some great things: nay,
that Roman spirit so often commended and extolled, which appears to be
influenced only by the prospect of fame, riches, honours, and authority, which
not only ceased to exert itself for the public good, when it met with ingratitude and injustice, neglect and contempt; but shrank, and shrivel'd up
into a mean, dastardly fear, or self-love, that made them run upon the
sword, as their only refuge and relief; is far from deserving the encomiums
given it, that christians should be rather cautioned against it, and taught to
treat it with the contempt and abhorrence it deserves." *A Sermon, Preached
before the General Assembly of the Colony of Connecticut, at Hartford* . . .
New London, 1768, p. 20.

It seems probable that other histories written in the earlier colonial period—those of Bradford and Winthrop come to mind—may owe something to the *annales* formula of historians of antiquity and that biographical sketches in them, together with the biographies, too frequently pious, of New England worthies, may be indebted to similar sketches of personalities in Sallust, Suetonius, and other standard Latin or Greek historians, including Plutarch. It is also true that the Boston Latin School (1635) and Harvard College (1636) and their successors in the colonial and provincial eras made a kind of core curriculum out of Latin and Greek. Thus in 1642 the rule for entering Harvard ran: "When any Schollar is able to Read Tully or such like classicall Latine Authour ex tempore, & make and speake true Latin in verse and prose, suo (ut auiunt) Marte, and decline perfectly the paradigmes of Nounes and verbes in yᵉ Greeke toungue, then may hee bee admitted into yᵉ Colledge, nor shall any claime admission before such qualifications." [10] The president of Harvard could address a graduating class in 1677 as *liberi liberaliter educati*—gentlemen educated like gentlemen.[11] The assiduity of scholarship has turned up an impressive variety of Latin and Greek books in library lists from the seventeenth and eighteenth centuries.[12] Closer examination of these lists, however, suggests that it is one thing to be exposed as a boy to the paradigms of "nounes and verbes," to read books of divinity in Latin, and to own some of the standard secular authors from antiquity, and another thing to be possessed of the spirit of republican Greece or Rome or be charmed by Virgil and Horace. Samuel Eliot Morison, the historian of Harvard, rejoices that even in the seventeenth and eighteenth centuries Oxford and Cambridge recognized Harvard degrees, and an able cultural historian of Virginia, Louis B. Wright, after analyzing library holdings, declares that "the classics . . . maintained their high place in the cultural aspirations and ideals of the gentry." [13] But it has also been remarked that the classical learning of the Virginia gentry was sometimes exhausted when they had named their slaves

Pompey, Caesar, Julia, and so on. Theology, pedantry, and codification likewise set in. Learning has its ugly side; and when one of the most notable of Harvard graduates, Cotton Mather, could produce in all good faith so craggy a passage as this:

> . . . at the same time, you should familiarize yourself with the *Style* of some Authors, whose *Latin* cannot but ever Charm you with its Elegancies. On this Occasion, I am as far from inviting you into the Gust of *Lineacre*, as great a critic as most we have had for the *Latin Tongue*, who, *Ciceronis dictionem, numquam probare potuit, nec sine fastidio audire;* As I am, from inviting you into the *Ciceronian* Bigotry of a *Bembo*, or, to be as afraid as *Longolius* was of useing the Word, *Possibile*,[14]

the modern reader feels he is some distance from genuine classicism. However valuable the *Manuductio ad Ministerium* may have been for the training of ministers, antiquity had to get out from under the theologian and the pedagogue. To construe Cornelius Nepos or the fables of Phaedrus (or even Homer) in the grammar schools did not inevitably lead to the understanding of classical antiquity. The seventeenth century and the first quarter of the eighteenth therefore mark a pause in the rhythm of the doctrine of Roman virtue.

A new age begins with the second quarter of the eighteenth century, an age of increasing secularization, of, in the American sense, "sophistication," and of this sophistication American interest in the classics partakes. The forces at work were many—the ending of Queen Anne's War (the War of the Spanish Succession) in 1714, a slow increase in the latitudinarian spirit of American Protestantism, an imperceptible growth in Socinianism, Arminianism, Arianism, and rational theology, private tutoring, the development of library societies, a wider diffusion of reading, easier communications with Europe, emigration, the steady growth in the secularization of the colleges. When Leverett became president of Harvard in 1708 theological dominance there began to diminish, and a like diminution began slowly to show itself at William and Mary (1693), Yale (1701), Princeton (1714),

Columbia (1754), Rutgers (1766), and Dartmouth (1769), whatever the original evangelical thrust of the institution. Michael Kraus has suggested that European representations of the Indians after the manner of the Greeks had the important consequence of placing life in America alongside of Greek life, at least as Greek life was interpreted by writers fashionable in the later eighteenth century, and that a kind of Indian-Graeco-Roman-American personality developed.* He quotes this interesting passage from *The Gentleman's Magazine* of 1745: "When I consider the coolness and bravery with which they [the colonials] marched to action [against Louisburg], and their return from victory to their several occupations, I take into my mind the great image of the ancient Romans leaving the plow for the fields of battle, and retiring after their conquests to the plow again." [15] It is possible also that a shift in acceptable theories of history altered the colonial view of antiquity, for the transition from an illogical fusion of divine guidance and Fortuna in Machiavelli to an illogical union of providence and natural causes in Robert Beverley and William Hubbard is presumably no more difficult than a transition to a cyclical theory of history † that

---

* So far as the continuing Roman image of the Indian is concerned Cadwallader Colden, *The History of the Five Nations*, New York, 1727, writes this: "The *Five Nations* are a poor Barbarous People, under the *darkest Ignorance*, and yet a *bright* and *noble Genius* shines thro' these *black Clouds*. None of the greatest *Roman Hero's* have discovered a greater Love to their Country, or a greater Contempt of Death than these *Barbarians*, have done, when Life and Liberty came in Competition: Indeed, I think our *Indians* have out-done the *Romans* in this particular; for some of the greatest *Romans* have Murder'd themselves to avoid Shame or Torments . . . VVhereas our *Indians* have refused to Dye meanly with the least Pain, when they thought their Country's Honour would be at stake, by it, but gave their Bodies willingly up to the most cruel Torments of their Enemies" (iii). He admired Indian eloquence, found that sachems distribute all the presents and plunder they acquire in war, said that each Indian nation is an absolute republic and that their present state exactly shows "the most *Ancient* and *Original Condition of almost every Nation*" (ix–xvii).

† A typical instance of the confusion between liberty as an absolute and the cyclical theory is found in William Smith's *Sermon Preached in Christ-Church, Philadelphia . . . before the . . . Free and Accepted Masons of the State of Pennsylvania, On Monday December 28, 1778 . . .* Philadelphia, 1779, which opens with a rhapsodic address to liberty and goes on this way: "The EGYPTIAN, the BABYLONIAN, the ASSYRIAN, the PERSIAN Empires;

simultaneously commanded the Americans to avoid the luxury of the ancient world and to progress as Christians and republicans.[16]

New wealth in the colonies had to house itself, and in the little American cities of Salem, Boston, New York, Philadelphia, Baltimore, Charleston, in towns and villages where lived the new-rich local squire, or on Pennsylvania farms and Southern plantations, modernity in the shape of classicism overtook not only the crudities of frontier housing but traditional Jacobean modes as well. Houses we now vaguely call "colonial" began to appear in the second quarter of the century. Forgetting the technical complexities of the architectural transition from Wren to Robert Adam, we may label most of them Georgian and pass over the first, second, and third phases of a development that brings us beyond the Seven Years' War. Georgian architecture breathed the spirit of a secular classicism; it was well ordered, symmetrical, stately, formal, and secure; it was the architecture of gentlemen who had tamed the wild energies of the Renaissance and the baroque into something precise and well bred, into the expression of a decorous and polite intelligence. These mansions dot the Atlantic seaboard at irregular intervals. Examples are, the Wentworth Gardner House in Portsmouth (1760), the Royall house in Medford (1737), the Lee house in Marblehead (1768), "Waynesborough" in Paoli (1721), "Cliveden" in Germantown (1761), "Woodlands" in Philadelphia (1770), "Homewood" near Baltimore, the date of which does not seem to be precisely established, the famous "Westover" in Virginia (1730–1734). There are many more. Domestic Palladianism, at first clumsy and uncertain, grows more and more refined as manuals of housing are imported;

---

the *Commonwealths* of ATHENS, of SPARTA, and of ROME, with many more of later Date—Where are they now? 'FALL'N—FALL'N—FALL'N' the weeping Voice of History replies! The Meteors of an Age, the Gaze of one Part of the World; they rose—they blaz'd awhile on high—they burst and sunk again, beneath the Horizon, to that Place of Oblivion, where the pale Ghosts of departed Grandeur fleet about in Lamentation of their former Glory!" This descent into oblivion is somehow to be prevented by following the poverty and disinterestedness of Cincinnatus.

and by and by Peter Harrison—Christ Church in Cambridge (1761) and the Touro Synagogue in Newport (1762–1763)— can almost support himself as an architect. Eventually colonial classicism echoes and reproduces the pure, chaste line of Robert Adam; it prepares the way for the classicism of the republic. The road from Faneuil Hall (1741) and the Philadelphia State House (Independence Hall, 1733–1741) to the capitol at Richmond, to Monticello, and to buildings of the so-called classical revival of the early nineteenth century, evidenced, say, in Girard College, Philadelphia, is not tortuous; one hesitates only to establish how much is Greek, how much is Roman, and how much is British or Continental fashion. The continuing dynamic element is clearly classicism for a governing elite, a classicism evident in their wallpaper, their doorways, their furniture, their fireplaces, their manners, and their social values.[17]

Educational reformers might fulminate against the classics —Franklin, who in 1744 proudly published James Logan's translation of Cicero on old age, as the "first Translation of a *Classic* in this Western World," [18] compared the classic tongues to a *chapeau bras,* a hat carried under the arm but never put on the head. But when the Reverend Richard Peters preached at the founding of Franklin's academy in Philadelphia, he innocently demonstrated how secularism had taken over, for, declaring that "the learned Languages" are but "a small Part of Education," he said also that "It is no inconsiderable Part of the Plan, that whilst the Pupils in the *Latin* and *Greek* Schools are taught the grammatical Construction of the Classicks, it is intended Lectures shall be read to those who are forward enough in their Learning, wherein the Subject Matter of each Author will be explained and illustrated, and his Style, Spirit and Elegance, pointed out; so that they may be apprehended, tasted, admired, and, it is hoped, well imitated by the Pupils in their Compositions." [19] That fiery periodical, *The Independent Reflector,* edited in New York by William Livingston and his friends, took a reserved view of classicism and gave "great Offence" to some readers by its "Latin mottos"; nevertheless a modern edition of this magazine (which appeared 52 times between November 30, 1752, and November 22, 1753), shows about 100 Latin or Greek tags, quotations, names, or allusions scattered among 345 pages of text. This is as if Walter Lippmann should quote Shakespeare in every third column. Livingston, though he denied that Latin and Greek were essentially "useful as preparatory to real and substantial knowledge," inconsistently called upon the testimony of Plato, Aristotle, Lycurgus, and other "ancient politicians" to show that "the Education of Youth" was the principal "Duty of the Magistrate" rather than a duty of the church.[20] In fact, those who lived in the Georgian houses accepted the classics as part of a gentleman's culture and hoped that somehow something modern might emerge. This is interestingly evident in the case of Edmund Pendleton of Virginia, for example, who, a posthumous child, had had only two years of formal schooling, but who, determined to rise in Carolina County (which he did), taught himself Latin and when he was admitted to the bar surpassed most of his fellow practitioners in his ability to translate it.[21]

What emerged more immediately, to continue well past the American Revolution, was an ideal curious among men we are taught to regard as activists—an ideal of retreat, the model of which was Horace's Sabine Farm. That poet's little house and little fields, the garden that yielded its adequate wine, the fountain of Bandusia, the flocks and herds, the site that was never too hot or too cold, a hospitable place for friends and not without the hope of female companionship— here was a model for the American gentleman amid "rural scenes," whether on the Potomac, the Schuylkill, or Narragansett Bay, or in the foothills of the Appalachians. Colonial poets—Mather Byles, William Livingston, Benjamin Church, Benjamin West, Nathaniel Evans—versified this rural ideal, not forgetting even an American Lalage. Characteristic is Livingston's "Philosophic Solitude; or, The Choice of a Rural Life. A Poem by a Gentleman educated at Yale College," which in 1747 pictured the delights of a country house, tranquillity, friendship, the calm contemplation of nature, a good library, good wine, and an understanding female friend—

> With her I'd spend the pleasurable day,
> While fleeting minutes gayly danc'd away.

This was no mere literary concept, but one that influenced the fathers of the republic. When in 1773 John Adams conceived that his public career was over, he wrote: "In this situation I should have thought myself the happiest man in the world, if I could have retired to my little hut and forty acres, which my father left me in Braintree, and lived on potatoes and sea-weed for the rest of my life. My resolutions to devote myself to the pleasures, the studies, the business and the duties of private life are a source of ease and comfort to me that I scarcely ever experienced before." In February 1774 he bought the paternal homestead and the accompanying farm from his brother, set to dreaming of rural improvements, and eight years later wrote from The Hague: "Oh peace! when wilt thou permit me to visit Penns-hill, Milton-hill, and all the blue hills? I love every tree and every rock upon all those mountains. Roving among these, and the quails, partridges, squirrels, etc., that inhabit them, shall be the amusement of my declining years." In 1784 he told Mrs. Warren that he envied her rural occupations at Neponset Hill, and that "My little farm is now my only resource and books for amusement, without much improvement or a possibility of benefiting the world by my studies." When William Smith pronounced a eulogy over General Montgomery, killed at Quebec, he found it admirable that his hero "chose a delightful retirement upon the banks of Hudson's river, at a distance from the noise of the busy world! . . . In this most eligible of all situations, the life of a country gentleman, deriving its most exquisite relish from reflections upon past dangers and past services, he gave full scope to his philosophic spirit, and taste for rural elegance." Franklin advised Dr.

John Fothergill to retire to a villa, give himself repose, delight in viewing the operations of nature, gather his ingenious friends about him, and enjoy his library. This was in 1764. In 1785 he admired a song called "The Old Man's Wish," and enumerated a warm house in a country town, an easy horse, some good authors, ingenious and cheerful companions, a Sunday pudding, stout ale, a bottle of burgundy, and control of one's passions as the *summum bonum* of old age. Washington's attachment to Mount Vernon is of the same order, as was Madison's attachment to Montpellier, and, of course, Jefferson's love for Monticello. After he left the White House, Jefferson wrote Kosciusko:

> I am retired to Monticello where, in the bosom of my family, and surrounded by my books, I enjoy a repose to which I have been long a stranger. My mornings are devoted to correspondence. From breakfast to dinner, I am in my shops, my garden, or on horseback among my farms; from dinner to dark I give to society and recreation with my neighbors and friends; and from candle light to early bed-time, I read. My health is perfect; and my strength considerably reinforced by the activity of the course I pursue . . . I . . . feel, at length, the blessing of being free to say and do what I please.[22]

Foreign travelers did not miss the point: here were antique simplicity and calm. For example, Brissot de Warville, a great admirer of Honest John, whom he visited in 1788, wrote of "the celebrated Adams; who, from the humble station of a school-master, has raised himself to the first dignities. . . . He has, finally, returned to his retreat, in the midst of the applauses of his fellow-citizens, occupied in the cultivation of his farm, and forgetting what he was when he trampled on the pride of his king, who had put a price upon his head, and who was forced to receive him as the ambassador of a free country. Such were the generals and ambassadors of the best ages of Rome and Greece; such were Epaminondas, Cincinnatus and Fabius." [23] Instances of the ideal of the Sabine farm could be indefinitely multiplied.*

---

* Not long after the Revolution, John Drayton in *A View of South Caro-*

We have, to be sure, got a little away from Horace, but we
are on the trace of a second classical ideal, this time the doctrine of simplicity and frugality found in the ancient republics, particularly republican Rome.[24] Obviously here was
reinforcement for non-importation agreements, the building
up of simple, honest American industry, the capitalizing of
and propaganda for the sturdy rural ethos imputed to the
colonists and to the new nation, once it shook itself free from
British control. Coupled with this was the warning that
luxury had ruined Greece, Rome, and many another state,
and even the insinuation that Europe was deliberately cor-
rupting America by exporting this mysterious commodity to
the New World.[25]

Thus in 1757 *The American Magazine,* published in Philadelphia, denounced luxury and appealed to republican
Rome and ancient Sparta, imploring Americans to study the
virtues of the Antonines; and a writer who called himself
"The Antigallican" enumerated forms of luxury (mostly
French) ranging from ostentatious buildings to masquerades,
rejoiced that this "detach'd quarter of the globe" was still
a stranger to luxury, and quoted Horace to prove that only
"the blotches and imposthumes of human nature" are supported by it. In 1763 the Reverend East Apthorp, preaching
on the peace treaty that ended the Seven Years' War, con-
gratulated the colonies on their good fortune, remarked that
Americans could always find sufficient employment *"in agriculture* and a *simple commerce,"* feared "an *iniquitous* and
excessive Trade, and an inundation of wealth and luxury,"

---

lina (Charleston, 1802), described the "elegant and expensive country seats"
of the Caroline gentry. Elegance and expense are scarcely Horatian, but the
spirit is like: "At an early period gentlemen of fortune were invited to
form these happy retreats from noise and bustle; the banks of the Ashley,
as being near the metropolis of the state, was first the object of their attention . . . here elegant buildings arose which overlooked grounds, where art
and nature were happily combined. Gardeners were imported from Europe;
and . . . soon the verdant lawn spread forth its carpet . . . and nature
drawn from her recesses, presented landscapes, diversified and beautiful, where
winds had not long before shook the trees of the forest." The Sabine villa
has turned "elegant," but the notion of philosophic felicity remains.

and appealed to Horace and Isaiah. John Adams, writing his *Dissertation on the Canon and Feudal Law* in 1765, implored his fellow countrymen to remember "how often were the people cheated out of their liberties, by kings, decemvirs, triumvirs, and conspirators" and generally proclaimed the importance of republican frugality. In 1766 Jonathan Mayhew adjured American women to continue in "the spirit of the Roman matrons in the time of the commonwealth." Freneau, joining with H. H. Brackenridge to write "The Rising Glory of America," in which they praised the Horatian ideal of such Romans as Fabricius and Camillus, who

> love a life
> Of neat simplicity and rustic bliss,
> . . . from the noisy Forum hastening far,

in his first published poem, "The American Village" (1772), not only lauded Horatian simplicity but charged that Britain had been corrupted by luxury as America had not:

> Thus fell the mistress of the conquer'd earth,
> Great ROME, who owed to ROMULUS her birth,
> Fell to the monster Luxury, a prey,
> Who forc'd a hundred nations to obey.
> She whom nor mighty CARTHAGE could withstand,
> Nor strong JUDEA's once thrice holy land
>
> . . . .
>
> She, she herself eternal years deny'd,
> Like ROME she conquer'd, but by ROME she dy'd:
> But if AMERICA, by this decay,
> The world itself must fall as well as she.

The Royal American Magazine, which in 1774 thought America "blossoms as the expanding rose and rises like the towering cedar," called upon Europeans to blush "whom the circling cup of luxury intoxicates," since, "unfit to cultivate Ohio's banks," they could not share the virtue of the colonials. Benjamin Rush's *Oration . . . Containing, An Enquiry into the Natural History of Medicine among the Indians in North America* (1774) is an amalgam of warnings against effeminacy and luxury and of descriptions of Indians and early Pennsylvanians in Roman terms: Philadelphia hospital records show, he said, "the encroachments of British diseases upon us." [26] The almanacs hammered away at the difference between republican simplicity and European luxury during both the American and the French Revolutions. What could be more like a republican Roman than George Wythe as described by Andrew Burnaby in the 1790s? Wythe, "who, to a perfect knowledge of the Greek language, which was taught him by his mother in the back woods, and of the ancient, particularly the Platonic philosophy, had joined such respect for the divine laws, such philanthropy for mankind, such simplicity of manners, and such inflexible rectitude and integrity of principle, as would have dignified a Roman senator, even in the most virtuous times of the republic." [27] That the United States won its independence from Britain because the latter was effeminate and corrupt was plain as day to a writer in Cork in 1801:

> While the arms of Rome were employed in subjecting the States of Italy, while these states (with resources similar to those of their rivals,) and with equal capacity in war, continued . . . to keep her martial genius on the wing, by retarding the career of her ambition; her internal temperament was sound, and her strength and vigour properly supported, but when her fortunes and her arms had overcome every obstacle—when the nations who opposed her were extinct or become tributary to her power —when the luxurious spoils of Asia and of Egypt began to be displayed in the triumphs of Rome, the Republic sickened and sunk under its own weight. In the subsequent periods of the empire . . . the Provinces . . . asserted their liberty and erected the ensigns of rebellion. The invasion of the Barbarians was but an *alternative,* a natural series of events would have compleated the dissolution. Rome contained within her own bosom the seeds of destruction. . . . The preceding description may suggest some of the causes which operated in the order of things, to separate the United States from Great Britain.[28]

III

From the agitation over the Stamp Act through the years of Revolution, the adoption of the Constitution, and the tumult of the French Revolution, classicism remained a powerful force, whether for propaganda, historical precedent, warning, or the theory of a republic. Probably the cult of antiquity among the Americans was never as sophisticated or as somber as it was among the French; [29] undoubtedly, although the populace and populist leaders did not lack catchwords from antiquity, classicism was principally a force among an elite minority; * and possibly the friends of classical studies now overestimate its influence in the eighteenth century. But patriotism as a concept in the period requires a moment of analysis. The word comes from the Greek *patrios,* concerning one's fathers, which in turn has something to do with *patris,* meaning fatherland. In the little Greek republics the land to which one was emotionally attached was a circumscribed area, just as the Latin *patria* refers not to a nation but to a neighborhood, a village, an estate, a farm. In the twentieth century Willa Cather makes illuminating use of this truth in *My Ántonia* when she has the Latinist Gaston Cleric explain to Jim that in Virgil's *Georgics* the line

Primus ego in patriam mecum . . . deducam Musas

means that Virgil wants to bring the muses into the little rural neighborhood on the Mincio where his father's fields sloped to the river and the old beech trees stood with their broken tops. The American Constitution was not the creation of mere land-grabbers and financiers with an economic

---

* The withdrawal of Tory Loyalists from America greatly reduced the number and influence of the gentry for a time, but the weakening or loss of control by an elite was but temporary. Up to the administration of Jackson the presidents of the United States were invariably gentlemen having a considerable tincture of classical learning in their cultural backgrounds and ideals.

ax to grind, Charles Beard to the contrary notwithstanding;
it was the creation of *patria*-minded persons, including Washington, who wrote in 1797: "I am once more seated under my
own Vine and fig tree, and hope to spend the remainder of
my days, which in the ordinary course of things (being in my
Sixty-sixth year) cannot be many, in peaceful retirement,
making political pursuits yield to the more rational amusement of cultivating the Earth." [30]

In the Constitutional Convention urban values were in
some sense represented by the Pennsylvania group, eight in
all, of whom seven came from Philadelphia, and by Hamilton, the solitary signer from New York. The South Carolina
contingent, Rutledge, Charles Pinckney, Charles Cotesworth
Pinckney, and Pierce Butler, were all from Charleston, but
the South Carolina gentry were characteristically country
gentlemen who wintered in the city; and most of the rest—
two from New Hampshire, two from Massachusetts, two
from Connecticut, four from New Jersey (including William
Livingston, who lived at "Liberty Hall"), five from Delaware, three from Maryland (Baltimore was to that state as
Charleston was to South Carolina), two from Virginia, three
from North Carolina, and two from Georgia—came from
village, agrarian, or plantation backgrounds. To them the
classical notion of *patria* was immediate and real. I do not
have in mind only the stately pillared porch of Mount Vernon, since a village culture also nourished an *amor patriae*,
and the village norm was preferable to the "corruptions" of
the city. Here, for example, is Jeremy Belknap addressing his
fellow citizens at the conclusion of his *History of New
Hampshire* in terms of *patria*, in terms, in fact, of an expanded Horatian ideal:

> Were I to form a picture of a happy society, it would be a town
> consisting of a due mixture of hills, valleys and streams of wa-
> ter: The land well fenced and cultivated; the roads and bridges
> in good repair; a decent inn for the refreshment of travellers,
> and for public entertainment: The inhabitants mostly husband-
> men; their wives and daughters domestic manufacturers [i.e.,

makers by hand], a suitable proportion of handicraft workmen, and two or three traders; a physician and lawyer, each of whom should have a farm for his support. A clergyman of any denomination, which should be agreeable to the majority, a man of good understanding, of a candid disposition and exemplary morals; not a metaphysical, nor a polemic, but a serious and practical preacher. A school master who should understand his business and teach his pupils to govern themselves. A social library, annually increasing, and under good regulation. A club of sensible men, seeking mental improvement. A decent musical society. No intriguing politician, horse jockey, gambler, or sot; but all such characters treated with contempt.[31]

Such a situation, he concludes, would be the most favorable to "social happiness" this world can afford.

Unless we comprehend that eighteenth-century America cherished this ideal, we cannot understand the power of Greece and Rome in the Revolutionary period. For example, the president of Princeton, John Witherspoon, lived in a country seat he called Tusculum, after Cicero's villa; he contributed to the *Pennsylvania Magazine* under the pseudonym of Epaminondas; he said: "I have in view the sages and legislators of antiquity, who acquired so much renown by establishing systems of policy and government for different states"; and he helped to train James Madison, Aaron Burr, ten cabinet officers, twenty United States Senators, thirty or more Congressmen, twelve governors, thirty judges, and fifty state legislators.[32] Obviously his doctrine did not include Roman imperialism as a goal. Only in such an epoch could Thomas B. Hollis write from London in 1788 to Joseph Willard: "Our papers mention that there is an intention of having the Olympic Games revived in America. All her friends wish it and say they are capable of it, and having acted on Greek principles, should have Greek exercises." [33]

As tension mounted between Great Britain and her colonies antiquity seemed to many thoughtful Americans more and more pertinent to their problem. Three or four examples will illustrate this relevancy. In 1766 an anonymous pamphlet published in New York implored the colonists to "animate our Hearts, by calling to our Memories the glorious Examples of Antiquity, and generously risque the Whole to preserve the most *valuable Part.*" [34] More rhetorically still, in *The Farmer's and Monitor's Letters to the Inhabitants of the British Colonies* Arthur and Richard Henry Lee not only raked classical history for examples of glorious resistance to tyrants, but also wrote:

> From the birth of *Roman* liberty, at the expulsion of the Tarquins, to its total extinction by the death of *Brutus,* was little more than 500 years. In this period, how glorious was the empire which freedom established, how firm how happy! What an illustrious train of heroes did this free spirit produce, the *Fabii, Fabricii, Decii, Metelli, Scipiones, Æmelii,* and others without number! The immortal *Cato* has informed us what were the characteristics of this potent republic. . . . Such was the virtue, order, and stability, which liberty produced, such vital energy did it infuse through the whole body of the state, that it baffled every attempt to overthrow it; stood the impetuous assaults of such dreadful foes as *Hannibal* and *Pyrrhus,* firm and unshaken; a battle lost, served but to arouse still greater exertions of that vigour, which animated by a sense of Freedom, was invincible.[35]

What was printed in Virginia was echoed in Massachusetts by Joseph Warren, who, commemorating in 1772 the Boston Massacre of 1770, declared: "It was *this* noble attachment to a free constitution, which raised ancient Rome from the smallest beginnings to that bright summit of happiness and glory to which she arrived; and it was the loss of *this* which plunged her from *that* summit into the black gulph of infamy and slavery." [36] And even that volatile person Charles Lee could write from Charlestown in 1776 to Patrick Henry: "I us'd to regret not being thrown into the World in the glorious third or fourth century of the Romans; but now I am thoroughly reconcil'd to my lot." In his youth, when he read Plutarch for the first time, he became "enthusiastick for liberty" in a republic.[37]

In general, as Charles F. Mullet has shown, the Americans combed two thousand years of history for example and precept. Writers appealed to virtually every classical author likely to be relevant, to principles of political philosophy they found in Greek and Roman historians and orators, to the Roman concept of natural law, to virtuous Roman republicans (concomitantly denouncing despotic Roman emperors, meaning in fact the British monarch), and to the Roman concept of liberty. This was something ordered and philosophical, the values by which Plutarch's heroes lived, or Cicero's "highest reason, instituted in nature, which orders what should be done and prohibits the contrary." The study of Roman colonial policy evident in Livy strengthened the reasoning of the colonials, since Rome eventually gave her colonists the rights of Romans, and the denunciation in Tacitus of Roman decadence, his praise of the ancient Germans was applied to America: the British were decadent, the Americans were not. Incidental to this argument was a denunciation of standing armies and a tendency to find "democracy" vicious and a republic admirable.[38]

But we shall be less confused if, instead of taking up instances piecemeal, we concentrate on two interpreters of the ancient past who profoundly influenced American action— the Frenchman Montesquieu, and John Adams of Braintree. Although American leaders read Voltaire, Rapin, Raynal, Rollin, and eventually Turgot, Condorcet, and others in their efforts to create a viable constitution, it is generally agreed that Montesquieu exerted the most powerful influence among contemporary Frenchmen upon the American mind, particularly in relation to the constitutional problem.[39]

The two books by Montesquieu which immediately concern us are the *Considérations sur les causes de la grandeur et de la décadence des Romains* (Amsterdam, 1734, but available in English translation), and the famous *L'Esprit des loix* (Geneva, 1748), subtitled: "On the relation which laws should have with the constitution of any government, and with the manners, the climate, the religion, the commerce, etc., of any nation." The first is a somber analysis of a past society and an essay in the philosophy of history, the second is in a real sense an outgrowth of the first. Montesquieu's central book became a text by 1787 at Yale, Princeton, and other colleges. In *L'Esprit des loix* the base line of theory is the classic past.

Government, Montesquieu believes, is determined by climate, soil, tradition, manners, trade, and human nature, of which he takes a pessimistic view.[40] Montesquieu was formally a Christian, but he writes: "When a religion adapted to the climate of one country clashes too much with the climate of another, it cannot there be established," and says: "If I could for a moment cease to think that I am a Christian, I should not be able to hinder myself from ranking the destruction of the sect of Zeno among the misfortunes that have befallen the human race." Zeno was the founder of the stoicism to which Cicero, Seneca, Marcus Aurelius, Livy, and Tacitus adhered, with its doctrine that virtue is the highest good. As there is a general popular tendency to think of the leaders of the American revolutionary generation as optimists, it is important to remember not only that there were few followers of the doctrine of human perfectibility, despite a wave of deism, but also that most of the Founding Fathers took a reserved view of human nature and were pessimistic about mankind. Alexander Hamilton and John Adams at once spring to mind, but human folly is also justly estimated by Thomas Jefferson, who was exposed to a good deal of it in his day.

All governments, argues Montesquieu, fall into three general groups: despotic governments, of which the characteristic quality is fear; monarchical, of which the characteristic is honor and ambition; and republican, of which the characteristic is virtue. Virtue in this context means "a love of the republic," it is a "sensation" and not a consequence of acquired knowledge (i.e., something almost instinctual), and may be felt by the meanest as well as the highest person in the state. "I distinguish by the name of virtue, in a republic . . . the love of one's country, that is, the love of equality. It is not a moral, nor a Christian, but a political virtue; and it is the spring which sets the republican government in motion, as honor is the spring which gives motion to monarchy. Hence it is that I have distinguished the love of one's country, and of equality, by the appellation of political virtue." Here virtue is an enlargement of the *amor patriae* which descends to us from antiquity.

"Most of the ancients," we read, "lived under governments that had virtue for their principle; and when this was in full vigour they performed actions unusual in our time, and at which our narrow minds are astonished." *Virtus,* or the special characteristic of republican government, is "conducive to purity of morals," since "the less we are able to satisfy our private passions, the more we abandon ourselves to those of a general nature." And Montesquieu insists that "a love of the democracy is likewise that of frugality. Since every individual ought here to enjoy the same happiness and the same advantages, they should consequently taste the same pleasures, and form the same hopes, which cannot be expected but from a general frugality . . . well-regulated democracies, by establishing domestic frugality, made way at the same time for public expenses, as was the case at Rome and Athens." The classical world enchants him. "It is impossible," he writes, "to be tired of so agreeable a subject as ancient Rome." Livy, says he, points out that no nation remained so long uncorrupted as did republican Rome. How and why did the Romans conquer the world? Because of virtue and through the principle of confederation, the only principle on which republics can expand. Through associative confederations the "Romans attacked the whole globe, and by these [i.e., similar confederacies] the whole globe withstood them; for when Rome had arrived at her highest pitch of grandeur, it was the associations beyond the Danube and the Rhine . . . that enabled the barbarians to resist her." * Thus Montesquieu draws into a single whole the traditions of antiquity and those of the freedom-loving Germanic tribes from which English and American freemen inherited their political rights. The attentive reader has also noted that Montesquieu does not in these passages use "democracy" in a pejorative sense, though he remarks elsewhere that if in democracies people seem to act as they please, political liberty does not consist in an unlimited freedom, but in "tranquillity of mind arising from the opinion each person has of his safety." Legislative power ought, theoretically, to reside "in the whole body of the people," "but since this is impossible in large states, and in small ones is subject to many inconveniences, it is fit the people should transact by their representatives what they cannot transact by themselves." [41]

Montesquieu is of course popularly known as the advocate of the check-and-balance system fundamental to American constitutions. He was, however, not the sole analyst who found checks and balances a central component in the tradition of British liberty, and I suggest that his special importance lies in the comparative view he gives of virtue and government, measured, as I have said, from the base line of the classical past, and in his capacity (confused though the structure of *L'Esprit des loix* may be) to develop from this comparative study general historical concepts that not only fitted in with the eighteenth-century search for universal laws, but also justified a revolutionary break with Britain. For him, as Dedieu points out,[42] the life of a nation is based upon physical and moral principles or causes that assure its existence and its rise. If one of these is corrupted, general corruption and the fall of the *res publica* must follow. This

---

* Eighteenth-century Americans who did not know French presumably read *Considerations on the Cause of the Grandeur and Decline of the Romans* in Volume III of Montesquieu's *Complete Works* in English, published in Dublin in 1777. This great treatise insists upon luxury and grandeur as the ruin of the Roman state, and could be—and was—quoted both against mercenary armies and against an overextension of territory.

in effect is the charge made against Great Britain in the Declaration of Independence. There a form of government has become destructive of its proper ends. There decadence has set in by reason of "a long train of abuses" "having in direct object the establishment of an absolute tyranny over the colonies." The various steps toward this tyranny are carefully documented. In Britain appeals to "native justice and magnanimity" have fallen on ears "deaf to the voice of justice and consanguinity." Let us therefore return upon the example of Rome, where "the legislator had in view the happiness of the citizens at home and their power abroad." To a generation seeking for a sign Montesquieu justified independence by the judgment of cosmic history, just as he assisted the constitution-makers to frame a government that would postpone corruption and the erosion of time through the check-and-balance system as long as possible. In theory the federal Constitution, like republican Rome, is also based upon the principle of confederacy, and Montesquieu is not justly at fault because three-quarters of a century later the nation was to divide over the question whether federalism and confederacy were the same thing.

It is commonplace that most of the participants in the great debate read and cited Montesquieu—such men, for example, as Jonathan Dickinson, James Wilson, Benjamin Rush, Thomas Jefferson, Samuel Adams, and James Madison. Among these is that incorruptible Christian stoic John Adams, who always wrote for the public as if he had a toga on. In him is the tradition of Roman gravity, of *pietas*. He is the Atlas of the American Revolution. He contrasts with his rival, enemy, and friend, Thomas Jefferson, Greek, supple, various, and more volatile. Adams' *Defence of the Constitution of the United States,* three volumes, in 1787, and his *Discourses on Davila,* their sequel, have the right Roman firmness, austerity, and suppressed passion. The first volume of the *Defence* has been elaborately misread into the fallacy that Adams wanted a monarchy, whereas all he wanted was stability and order. The third volume, an elaborate analysis of the political theorizing of Marchamont Nedham (or Needham) of Cromwell's time (who was something of a political turncoat), and the first part of the *Discourses on Davila* particularly illustrate Adams' use of Roman history. A devoted republican, he denies that the multitude have or practice virtue. Of the Roman *plebs* he writes such things as this: "Prejudice, passion, and superstition, appear to have altogether governed the plebians, without the least appearance of their being rational creatures, or moral agents; such was their total ignorance of arts and letters, all the little advantages of education which then existed being monopolized by the patricians." "Every man," he says, "hates an equal; every man desires to be superior to all others." As for democracy, "the word democracy signifies nothing more nor less than a nation of people without any government at all, and before any constitution is instituted." (He wrote the constitution of Massachusetts!) Throughout history, it seemed to him, most republics have "whirled upon their axles or single centers; foamed, raged, and burst, like so many waterspouts upon the ocean. They were all alike ill constituted; all alike miserable; and all ended in similar disgrace and despotism."

But Adams is nevertheless a believer in Roman virtue. Roman virtue will save republics through a balanced constitution, or at least postpone decay—and he passes in review Sparta, Athens, Carthage, Rome, England, and Holland to demonstrate this truth. Though *"sobriety, abstinence,* and *severity* were never remarkable characteristics of democracy, or the democratical branch or mixture in any constitution," a mixture, a balanced government, law, order, control, will, may perhaps work. "While the [Roman] government remained untouched in the various orders, the consuls, senate, and people mutually balancing each other, it might be said, with some truth. that no man could be undone, unless a true and satisfactory reason was rendered to the world for his destruction. But as soon as the senate was destroyed, and the government came untouched into the people's hands, no man lived safe but the triumvirs and their tools." Adams dismissed Augustus, Lepidus, and Antony as demagogues; he admired the few among the elite who "saved the honor, justice, and dignity of the republic," he thinks "Rome never greatly prospered until the people obtained a small mixture of authority upon the senate," but he is not in favor of popular control. Cincinnatus, Curius, Fabius, and other Romans were "examples of virtue which grew up only in a few aristocratical families, were cultivated by emulation between the two orders in the state, and by their struggles to check and balance each other, proved the excellence of the republican principle."

The second section of the *Discourses on Davila* (Davila was an Italian historian of the French civil wars) begins a long exposition of human nature, concerning which Adams is more Roman stoic than Christian. Rivalry, he thinks, "lies at the foundation of our whole moral system in this world." Rightly guided by proper management, emulation, however, can create a proper republic, as it did in Rome:

> Has there ever been a nation who understood the human heart better than the Romans, or made a better use of the passion for consideration, congratulation, and distinction? They considered that, as reason is the guide of life, the senses, the imagination, and affections are the springs of activity. . . . Everything was calculated to attract the attention, to allure the consideration and excite the congratulations of the people; to attach their hearts to individual citizens according to their merit; and to their lawgivers, magistrates, and judges, according to their rank, station, and importance to the state. And this was in the true spirit of republics, in which form of government there is no other consistent method of preserving order, or procuring submission to the laws.

Republics have opportunity to direct emulation toward virtue, but this emulation is possible only in a republic in which formality and status are preserved. By and by comes this passage: "Perhaps a perfect balance, if it ever existed, has not been long maintained in its perfection; yet, such a balance as has been sufficient to liberty, has been supported in some nations for many centuries together; and we must come as near as we can to a perfect equilibrium, or all is lost." [43]

Jefferson was to Adams as Pericles was to Cato, and the continuing elusiveness of the "Jefferson image" [44] in the American mind is evidence of the Athenian suppleness of the Sage of Monticello. To turn, however, from the third to the first president of the United States: without any special literary gift, unusual library, or depth of scholarship, George Washington became Fabius, Cincinnatus, Lycurgus, Solon.[45] The Father of his Country believed in order, status, dignity, and liberty under law; and he had the immense distinction of being the first ruler of the country whose birth and growth he had defended. He was, in Marcus Cunliffe's term, both an English country gentleman and an honorary Roman who quoted Addison's *Cato* and performed like a great consul. *Virtus, gravitas, pietas*—words like these clearly apply to him. Like Romulus he had created a state; and he was, by reason of this fact and by reason of his character, essentially monumental—as American postage stamps have constantly testified. The Marquis de Chastellux wrote of him in terms of statuary:

> If you are presented with medals of Caesar, or Trajan, or Alexander, in examining their features, you will still be led to ask what was their stature, and the form of their persons; but if you discover, in a heap of ruins, the head or the limb of an antique *Apollo*, be not curious about the other parts, but rest assured that they all were conformable to those of a God. Let not this comparison be attributed to enthusiasm! It is not my intention to exaggerate. I wish only to express the impression General Washington has left on my mind; the idea of a perfect whole, that cannot be the product of enthusiasm. . . . Brave without temerity, laborious without ambition, generous without prodigality, noble without pride, virtuous without severity; he seems always to have confined himself within those limits, where the virtues, by cloathing themselves in more lively, but changeable and doubtful colours, may be mistaken for faults. This is the seventh year that he has commanded the army and that he has obeyed the Congress; more need not be said.[46]

After Washington's election as chief magistrate, the intrigues against him during the Revolution having been forgotten and the abuse to be heaped on him not having yet been uttered, a fever of deification ran over the country. On his way from Mount Vernon to New York, for example, he crossed the Schuylkill on a floating bridge decorated with laurel and greenery, all designed by Rembrandt Peale. At either end was a magnificent arch of laurel, emblematic of the triumphal arch of a Roman conqueror, on each side of the bridge was a laurel shrubbery, and as Washington passed over, a lad * ornamented with sprigs of laurel, with the assistance of a piece of machinery, let drop a civic crown upon the hero's head.

When Washington died some 440 funeral elegies were delivered within three months of his death in towns from Maine to Georgia, and always the parallel was antiquity. Thus George Blake in *A Masonic Eulogy* said: "In vain may . . . Plutarch and Polybius vaunt their Alexanders and their Hannibals, their Scipios and Caesars, all their boasted virtues would but serve as an appendix to the biography of our Washington." Josiah Dunham directed his audience to compare Washington with the heroes, patriots, sages, and legislators of antiquity; neither Cromwell, Caesar, nor Alexander had such greatness or virtue. Washington was as shrewd as Fabius, as intrepid as Hannibal, as fortunate as Caesar, as self-effacing as Cincinnatus. Parson Weems, who knew on what side his literary bread was buttered, in his incredible *Life of Washington,* which strewed "the streets of ancient Rome" and "the piney woods of Georgia and South Carolina" with "mangled carcasses," has, in his chapter on the "Character of Washington," rhetorical flourishes like this:

> Did SHAME restrain Alcibiades from a base action in the presence of Socrates? *"Behold,"* says religion, *"a greater than Socrates is here!"* Did the ambition of a civic crown animate Scipio to heroic deeds? Religion holds a crown, at the sight of which

---

* The "lad" was in fact Angelica Peale, the painter's daughter.

the laurels of a Caesar droop to weeds. Did good Aurelius study the happiness of his subjects for this world's glory? Religion displays that world of glory, where those who have laboured to make others happy, shall *"shine like stars for ever and ever."*

Naturally the parson was building up to the famous scene of Washington kneeling in prayer at Valley Forge, thus adroitly fusing the images of Christ and Caesar. And this sort of deification continued. Thus in 1841 Daniel Ullman, speaking in New York, compared Washington's "Farewell Address" to the utterances of the Cumaean Sibyl; and in 1852, in Washington, D. C., John J. Crittenden exclaimed: "The Romans shouted, the Romans exulted when Mark Antony told them that Caesar had left them a few denarii and the privilege of walking in his gardens. That was the imperial bequest. How ignoble, how trifling does the Roman seem to you . . . who exult in the legacy . . . left . . . in the Farewell Address." [47]

In his own lifetime the painters and sculptors took over, with odd results: those who knew Washington were often mediocre, and those who never knew him turned him into all sorts of curious shapes.[48] But even such a painter as Gilbert Stuart, who had competence, seems to have approached Washington with awe, and the results are stately, not human. The Houdon bust, done in Washington's lifetime, is, one feels, less the portrait of a Virginia gentleman than something reclaimed from the Forum. In 1789 Houdon did a Washington more than six feet high, saying he was trying to catch Washington's indignation at being offered a dishonorable advantage. In this statue the Father of his Country strikes a noble pose, his cloak covers the *fasces* of thirteen rods, behind him is the moldboard of a plow, the cane he carries emphasizes an official dignity, and the informing idea is of a wrathful Cincinnatus. The statue was placed in the rotunda of the Richmond capitol in 1796 and bore an inscription by James Madison. Another statue by Canova was commissioned by the state of North Carolina in 1815, explicit instruction being given that the style should be "Roman," and Roman it was. Washington is dressed like a Roman general, sits in a curule chair, has put his sword under his feet, and is reading from stone tablets of the law supported by his left arm and hand. This masterpiece was completed in 1821, brought to Boston in 1824, hauled by twenty-four mules to Raleigh, and there destroyed by fire in 1831, but a smaller replica is still in Italy.

The masterpiece of this school was undoubtedly Greenough's Washington (Pl. IX), which weighs twelve tons and was intended for the national Capitol. It was brought here after incredible difficulties in 1841, removed from the Capitol to East Park, where it long stood under a shed, was later exposed to the elements, and is now in the Smithsonian Museum. Greenough sought grandeur and achieved the grandiose. The proprietor of Mount Vernon, stripped to the waist, appeals to heaven with one arm, across which a fold of his toga is draped, and with the other presents to the spectator a sheathed sword. His left foot, sandaled, is thrust determinedly forward. It looks, wrote the sardonic Philip Hone, as if Washington, "preparing to perform his ablutions is in the act of consigning his sword to the care of the [bath] attendant. . . . Washington . . . was too . . . careful of his health, to expose himself thus in a climate so uncertain as ours." Oliver Larkin, to whom I owe this citation, thinks the statue owes something to the formula for Phidias's seated Zeus.[49] There were of course other statues—Washington riding horseback is a common theme—but the later ones stand outside the oppressive classical tradition of Greenough.

IV

The administration of John Quincy Adams (1825–1829) probably closed the era in which the classical past was a dynamic force in American public life.[50] Adams, unlike Andrew Jackson, had had a severe classical education. Moreover, he had been appointed Boylston Professor of Rhetoric

and Oratory at Harvard in 1806, virtually the only incum-
bent of the chair to devote himself to rhetoric and oratory,
and he had published in 1810 his *Lectures on Rhetoric and
Oratory* in two volumes, which owe much to Isocrates. After
the so-called Jacksonian revolution few presidents were
literary, none was a classicist in the sense that Jefferson was,
and none was portrayed, like Washington, in the character of
a Roman senator nude to the waist. With two great exceptions, architecture and oratory, classicism was given over to
the schools. The great triumphs of American archaeologists
during the nineteenth and twentieth centuries, in the ancient
world were triumphs of professional experts, not of gentleman amateurs like the London Society of the Dilettanti; the
equivalents of Dawkins and Wood on Baalbek, or Stuart on
Athens were, so to speak, E. G. Squier on the Mound Builders
and the antiquities of Nicaragua, and Cyrus Thomas on the
Mound Builders and Mayan Culture. Few statesmen were
convinced, as the Revolutionary and Federal generations
had been, that classical history and the classic philosophers
offered guide lines to the nation. Antiquity of course had
meaning for such writers as Thoreau and Emerson—a whole
book has been written on Emerson's interest in Plutarch;
classical tales were told by poets like Longfellow; Hawthorne
gentled ancient myths for the use of Sunday-school children;
and in the twentieth century classical legend had a powerful
upsurge in *Mourning Becomes Electra* and the narrative and
dramatic tragedies of Robinson Jeffers. But this resurgence
was Freudian, not Sophoclean. The Americans produced no
cis-Atlantic Swinburne, no Landor, no Pater, not even an
American parallel to *A Shropshire Lad* with its dark stoic
overtones. Amiable painting on Greek and Roman themes
was occasionally done by the Americans, who, however, produced no one to rival the glossy Sir Lawrence Alma-Tadema
or even the Wagnerian Nereids of Böcklin. "Greek" statues
and heads there were, in the tradition of Canova and
Thorwaldsen—Hiram Powers' "Greek Slave" (1843) has

passed into American legend—but the innumerable Clyties and the like were more gracile than Greek and smacked of both the schoolroom and the drawing room. The prodigious success of the chariot race in *Ben Hur* (1880) did not turn Lew Wallace into a classicist; the subtitle is "A Tale of the Christ," and the most chauvinistic American could not compare the novel to *Marius the Epicurean* (1885). In truth the creation of the Modern Language Association of America in 1883–1884 marked the passing of the hegemony of classical studies over the field of the humanities.

But the art of oratory, not yet having to compete with newspaper features, columnists, the radio, the moving pictures, television, and the doctrine that the best way to make a public speech is to pretend you are not speaking in public, remained vital long after the Civil War. The great senatorial debates before that conflict, the famous public addresses on ceremonial occasions by Calhoun, Edward Everett, Clay, Webster, and their peers had a full, Ciceronian rhetoric. Speeches followed the theoretical outlines laid down by John Quincy Adams on the basis of classical practice. The most celebrated orator was the godlike Daniel Webster, who looked like a Roman, and who had the pomp and majesty of empire in his voice and in his periods. In his speeches appeals to general principles conceived to be essential to the safety of the country had a classical ring. Webster did not stand alone.

Thus a volume of eulogies occasioned by the simultaneous deaths of John Adams and Thomas Jefferson was published in Hartford in 1826. The towns represented range from Hallowell, Maine, to Richmond, Virginia, and from Charleston, South Carolina, to Nashville, Tennessee. The eulogists all quote Latin, they are all orotund, and the addresses they gave could not be delivered today, but they are nonetheless impressive, because their tacit appeal is to the majesty of the republic. Thus Sheldon Smith of Buffalo begins: "When virtue falls, humanity mourns." The opening paragraph by

William Alexander Duer at Albany speaks of the deceased as if he were lamenting the passing of two great consuls. William Wirt, in Washington, D. C., quotes

> *Praecipitemque Daren, ardens agit aequore toto:*
> *Nunc dextra ingeminans ictus, nunc ille sinistra,*
> *Nec mor, nec requis.*

The stately paragraph near the opening of Webster's famous address in Faneuil Hall has the right Roman ring:

> ADAMS and JEFFERSON are no more; and we are assembled, Fellow Citizens, the aged, the middle aged and the young, by the spontaneous impulse of all, under the authority of the municipal government, with the presence of the Chief Magistrate of the Commonwealth, and others its official representatives, the university, and the learned societies, to bear our part, in those manifestations of respect and gratitude, which universally pervade the land. Adams and Jefferson are no more. On our fiftieth anniversary, the great day of National Jubilee, in the very hour of public rejoicing, in the midst of echoing and re-echoing voices of thanksgiving, while their own names were on all tongues, they took their flight, together, to the world of spirits. If it be true that no man can safely be pronounced happy while he lives; if that event which terminates life, can alone crown its honors and its glory, what felicity is here!

Quam istis felicitas! The paragraph, with its allusion to Herodotus, leads you to expect the orator to address the conscript fathers. Some of Webster's sentences are straight out of the ancient world. Later, Webster introduces a long passage of sonorous Latin into his speech.

Equally impressive is the opening of an oration by him in the House of Representatives (1824) to support a resolution appointing an American agent to Greece. The tone, I suggest, is Senecan:

> We must . . . fly beyond the civilized world; we must pass the dominions of law and the boundaries of knowledge; we must, more especially, withdraw ourselves from this place, and the scenes and objects which here surround us,—if we would sep-

arate ourselves entirely from the influence of all those memorials of herself which ancient Greece has transmitted for the admiration and the benefit of mankind. This free form of government, this popular assembly, the common council held for the common good,—where have we contemplated its earliest models? This practice of free debate and public discussion, the contest of mind with mind, and that popular eloquence, which, if it were now here, on a subject like this, would move the stones of the Capitol,—whose was the language in which all these were first exhibited? Even the edifice in which we assemble, these proportioned columns, this ornamented architecture, all remind us that Greece has existed, and that we, like the rest of mankind, are greatly her debtors.

Nor should one forget the great peroration of his "Reply to Hayne," still too familiar to need quotation, from its somber beginning: "I have not allowed myself, Sir, to look beyond the Union, to see what might lie hidden in the dark recess behind," to the brassy but still magnificent close: "Everywhere, spread all over in characters of living light, blazing on all its ample folds, as they float over the sea and over the land, and in every wind under the whole heavens, that other sentiment, dear to every true American heart,—Liberty *and* Union, now and for ever, one and inseparable!" [51]
The oratorical tradition could not continue at this pitch, yet it lingered long. Schoolboys of my generation used to declaim "Senator Thurston on Cuban Affairs," and oratorical contests were still important school events in the first decades of the present century. But the school readers dropped excerpts in "elocution," the string-tie orator replaced the great artist in public speech, the Chautauqua movement further weakened what the lyceum movement had damaged, and oratory disappeared from American life until at the present hour the very term "Demosthenean" has no meaning for the man on the street.
The second form of long-term classical influence in the nineteenth century was architectural. To sort out the subtle variations among the various colonies of classicism coming

from Great Britain and there domesticated is a task for experts, but if Talbot Hamlin [52] is right in saying that a distinctly new American architecture was born in Washington, D. C., we may infer that while "domestic" Georgian evolved into Greek Revival houses, the young nation had an instinctual feeling that its official expression should begin with the Greek temple style (as in Jefferson's capitol at Richmond) and then slowly develop into the splendors of imperial Rome. Architectural imperialism was, of course, sometimes candied over with strong Renaissance coatings and, by and by, with the stately richness of the Beaux Arts school. To turn over the plates in any competent book on architecture in American history is to reinforce this impression of imperialism. Jefferson, it is commonplace, first used the temple form for an official building, but after him a hundred temples combining Greek, Roman, and Renaissance formulas were found in a hundred places and served for all sorts of public purposes—for a state capitol as at Columbus, Ohio, or Raleigh, North Carolina; for colleges, as in the cases of Girard, Washington and Lee, the University of North Carolina, and Union; for mints, as in Philadelphia and San Francisco; for banks—one has but to look about him; for courthouses, good and bad; for record offices, for churches, for markets, for custom houses, and for much else. Until the rise of the international style classical forms were standard for public buildings.

Housing was another matter. In the deep South and elsewhere where the plantation owner or the local squire required a house that was, as it were, the capitol of a small kingdom, stately pedestal and portico announced dignity and authority within, as in that pathetic ruin in Louisiana which was once the pillared splendor of Belle Grove. But in more domestic architecture and in religion the so-called Greek revival had to contend after the 1830s with a Gothic movement, and pine Gothic churches and "cottages" with a greater or less degree of gingerbread and carpenter's frenzy came into style. The romantics, indeed, were likely to go in for an odd combination of the Gothic and the empirical. In *Home as Found* (1838) Cooper denounces what seems to him a false classicism; [53] and James Jackson Jarves in *The Art Idea* (1864) remarked that "Grecian" buildings are "put . . . to uses foreign to their spirit, and debased by utilitarian details and changes which destroy their true character. . . . Cottages are hid behind wooden porticos, while lean or bisected columns, lank pilasters, triangular masses of framework dubbed pediments, rioted everywhere, upheld by a fervor of admiration because of their origin . . . an invasion of Hellenic forms . . . distorted into positive ugliness by ignorance of their meaning and want of taste in their application." [54]

Whatever its defects as domesticity, classical form on a grand scale achieved two spectacular triumphs. One was the national Capitol, which, conceived in quarreling, nourished in bickering, burned, rebuilt, patched, repatched, blown up into larger size, perpetually under hostile criticism, surmounted by a cast-iron dome beyond the imagination of the emperor Augustus, facing the wrong way, and here and there still housing some of the gaudiest interior decoration of the Gilded Age, yet manages, by clinging to its original symmetry, simplicity, and greatness, to awe the beholder and to symbolize the imperial republic.[55] This stands. But the other great triumph is all but vanished, a dream detested by sound modernists and known to us now only by a few picture books and one great rebuilt structure now housing a museum of technology. I refer, of course, to the World's Columbian Exposition of 1893, put together by one of the greatest groups of architects, designers, and city-planners ever assembled for such a purpose since the Renaissance, as one of them remarked. Here was classicism in the grand manner; here was planning on a prophetically imperial scale; here was power expressed in design, grouping, and form. And contemporaries knew it. Paul Bourget, not usually enthusiastic, exclaimed over "the ecstatic pleasure of that vision." Walter Besant rhapsodized that "never before, in any age, in any country, has there been so wonderful an arrangement of lovely buildings as at Chicago." The electric lighting made him think of the revelation made to Saint John. Sir Henry Trueman Wood, the British representative, wrote: "I find it hopeless to convince my countrymen of the marvelous nature of the spectacle; only those who have seen it can appreciate justly how far this latest of international [expositions] has surpassed all its predecessors in splendor and in greatness, both of conception and of execution." The Court of Honor, the lagoon, the stately symmetry of the principal structures were incomparable; Chicago exhibited, wrote the editor of *Harper's Magazine,* "the noblest and most refined classic art. . . . The artists thus met together were animated by a spirit of concord in a single devotion to art . . . radiant joy and enthusiasm." [56]

The exhibition opened in 1893. Five years later the United States became a world power, reaching for empire as imperial Rome had done. But classicism was now a lesson in history books, and books about ancient history grew fewer and fewer as the twentieth century wore on.

VIII

The Radical Republic

I

I T I S difficult for contemporary Americans, who have abolished the radical left [1] and seem not to know how to manage the radical right, to realize that at its inception and for many years thereafter the United States was viewed abroad (and sometimes at home) with that mingling of hope and horror we later showered upon Soviet Russia. The young nation was an ebullient republic in a world of monarchies (save for two or three minor states). It had a radical federal constitution couched in philosophic terms, and these terms, though they might do for the *philosophes* in the salons, were obviously unfitted for the populace in the streets. The new state was charged with being a democracy when democracy was a term of abuse. It lacked a reigning house and a landed aristocracy but it had (perhaps as a result) a bad record for mob violence, political instability, and defiance of decent custom. Yet this raw people had beaten the mistress of the seas and demonstrated only twenty years after the Seven Years' War that such a powerful European monarchy as Great Britain could not subdue it. What was the world coming to—the intellectual world of Descartes and Newton, the polite world of Chesterfield and Marie Antoinette, the cosmopolitan world of Gibbon and Voltaire, the international world of well-bred society? The Americans were *sauvages*, but they were not, it seemed, *sauvages nobles*. They had had a philosopher named Franklin, but he had gone home to participate in constitution-making. They had had an urbane gentleman named Thomas Jefferson, but he had sided with the radical left.

What the world was coming to was dramatically evident after 1789: it was coming to an explosion that changed the culture of Europe. The French Revolution, clearly, had been triggered by the example of the radical Americans.[2] Had not Lafayette been made an American citizen? Had not Joel Barlow and Tom Paine been made citizens of France? The inauguration of Washington on April 30, 1789, preceded by only five days the fateful meeting of the three estates at Versailles on May 4 and by only about ten weeks the storming of the Bastille on July 14. When John Adams was inaugurated on March 4, 1797, the Directory, that singular mixture of corruption and administrative skill, had been governing France for about two years. When Jefferson was elected in 1800, a military purge had already installed Napoleon as First Consul (1799), and France had sent him across the Alps in May 1800 to win Marengo and in December, by the treaty of Lunéville, to deprive Britain of her last ally. To any right-thinking European this anarchy, this bloodshed, these indecencies had their pattern, if not their origin, from the disorderly Americans. Had not Irish revolutionaries such as Thomas Addis Emmet after 1798 fled to New York? Even Friedrich Gentz, the German echo of Burke, who infinitely preferred the American Revolution (which was distant) to the French Revolution (which was not) quoted the "calm and impartial" historian Ramsay to the effect that though the "*political, military,* and *literary* talents of the people of the United States were improved," "their *moral* qualities were deteriorated." [3] Even Byron, who carried on his own private rebellion against Great Britain, though he praised America at the end of his "Ode to Venice" (1818), wrote John Murray in 1820 that "in future I will compliment nothing but Canada, and desert to the English." [4]

Instability was of the essence of the American nation. The rickety though threatening republic was born in civil war among the members of the British Empire and had tried to conquer or lure other parts of that empire into rebellion. Operating after 1776 under a bad constitution that was not even adopted until 1781, the nation had replaced this by another constitution in 1789. It had been threatened by a monarchical counter-revolution and a military putsch in 1782. It had had to put down treason in 1777, 1780, and 1804–1805. It had, since the treaty of 1789, fought one war in 1798, a second in 1801, a third in 1812, and it carried on incessant excursions over its vague borders into the Indian country. It had confronted insurrection in 1786 and again in 1794, and threats of secession in 1784 (the "State of Franklin"), in 1789, and in 1814. Its currency had been so bad that "not worth a Continental" had passed into the language as a synonym for utter worthlessness. Its armies were citizens who mostly ran away, yet its navy was so excellent that it defeated French and British vessels in spirited single combats. It had had to move its government from one capital on the Delaware lest it be besieged by its own mutinous soldiers, to another capital on the Potomac, whence, a little later, a President had fled so precipitately, the officers of the invading army ate the meal prepared for him in the White House and at their leisure burned the Capitol; but raw frontiersmen had slaughtered Pakenham's veterans before New Orleans in January 1815. What a country! A menace, the product of harebrained theory, a stirrer of dissension, the conqueror of the Barbary pirates, wily in diplomacy, a country that invited the discontented to come to its shores and live while in the same breath it passed the odious Alien and Sedition Acts! A country boiling with odd, revolutionary notions about law, language, loyalty oaths, land-holding, the rights of man, representative government, and the disestablishment of religion!

Who, then, were these Americans? What was this new nation conceived in liberty and dedicated to the proposition that all men are created equal, that dedication having been written by a man who owned slaves?

II

To twentieth-century readers retaining some vague memory of harmless high-school books in history or of such works as *The Courtship of Miles Standish, Evangeline, The Scarlet Letter,* or of a historical romance such as Mary Johnston's *To Have and to Hold,* the colonial period is a simple, peaceful era, once the English have landed and founded Jamestown. *The Courtship of Miles Standish* pictures, not without humor, an orderly little society. *Evangeline* gives us a village of pastoral simplicity ruined by the unseemly British, and though the village is French, we have adopted the Acadian legend. The forces of religion and government in *The Scarlet Letter* are so firmly established as to break Dimmesdale and almost break Hester Prynne. Jamestown in *To Have and to Hold* is the setting for romantic operetta. True, there are Indian massacres and wars against the French, but our side always wins. By and by a shortsighted Parliament and a stubborn King, beginning in 1765, enact a series of measures that violate the principle of no taxation without representation, and after ten years of patient remonstrance we begin a war for independence in 1775. Virginia is settled by gallant gentlemen; Pilgrim and Puritan come to Massachusetts to escape religious tyranny; Lord Baltimore provides a refuge for persecuted Catholics in Maryland; the jolly Dutch, knowing that Irving is going to write about them, found New Amsterdam; William Penn launches a "holy experiment" in Pennsylvania in which any Christian can participate, and the noble Oglethorpe creates Georgia in 1733 as a refuge for oppressed debtors who are not to own slaves.

But the men who were brought to the New World in the

era of English exploration and discovery were, as I have earlier indicated,[5] an unruly lot, obeying orders when they felt like it, disobeying them when they did not, conspiring against their leaders and presenting problems of discipline to their superiors that are, so to speak, handed on to the days of the vigilantes and the lynchers. On shipboard the gentry quarreled among themselves, the crews were as often desperadoes as they were Christians, and the landing forces frequently mutinied or deserted. The return of the remnants of such expeditions led to wild talk in London that alternated, one suspects, between great golden lies and gruesome anecdotes. Therefore, once such an organization as the Plymouth Company or the London Company bestirred itself to found settlements on the Kennebec and the James, it had great difficulty in recruiting settlers, as did Baltimore and Penn. This difficulty increased when a colony utterly vanished, as at Roanoke, or returned, beaten and bedraggled, as did the survivors of the Piscataqua group, or starved and died, as did most of Jamestown. At the end of their first winter only about half of the Pilgrims who landed at Plymouth in December 1620 were still alive, fourteen out of the eighteen wives who came over having died. Of the nine hundred settlers Winthrop led to Massachusetts Bay, two hundred perished during the first season. It took many years for investors and home officials to learn that you could not found a plantation by dumping a few men on a New World shore and that, once these men had painfully built some crude housing, they had still to learn the rudiments of merely keeping alive in an alien climate on alien soil. A high percentage of sickness and death accompanied the process of acclimatization. During the early years of a colony the only resource was, at great cost to the investors, to send annually or semi-annually one or more ships known as the "supply" and stocked with food, clothing, tools, medicine, a new garrison, and so forth. Such a ship was supposed to return laden with products of the new land to be sold for the benefit of the "adventurers." Unfortunately ships did not arrive as planned, or were captured or wrecked or sunk; or, having arrived, served as floating storehouses for peculation by the "cape merchant" or supercargo, who, disregarding the colony, sold food, drink, clothing, arms, bedding, ammunition, and other necessaries to deserters, greedy settlers, passing fishermen, hunters, and Indians. There were good men and women in the straggling settlements—otherwise the colonies would not have survived—but the general performance developed a black legend of lawlessness, so that the seventeenth-century plantations became appropriate places to which to send indentured servants (who often disappeared), women desperate for matrimony, and convicts. Convicts sometimes developed into good subjects, the women were not all like Moll Flanders, and many indentured servants became the founders of sturdy American families. Nevertheless, the colonials in the seventeenth century, like the colonials in nineteenth-century Australia, developed attitudes toward authority, contract, law, and mercantilist economics quite at variance with orthodox views of order, profit, and due obedience to the crown.

From the point of view of the home government, moreover, it was not merely the riffraff who were "radical." The northern colonies, it is commonplace, were a refuge from the tyranny of Laud, and the southern colonies became a refuge from the tyranny of Presbyterianism. Those who fled the mother country were often the bolder and more intransigent spirits no less than the neurotic. Some stayed in the New World, some returned. The actual number of "cavaliers" who came to Virginia has been much disputed, but the number is of less moment than the influence of their legend or the incarnation of royalist vengeance in Governor William Berkeley. The actual slowing down or returning home of Puritan migration during the English Civil Wars and the Parliamentary and Cromwellian regimes is important, but not so important as the tradition of iron-handed rule that grew up in Massachusetts Bay. Even if the seventeenth-century colonial had been more obedient than he commonly was, he sometimes found it difficult to know to whom he owed allegiance. Less than a quarter of a century after the founding of Jamestown, Charles I embarked on his fateful policy of personal rule. Twelve years after the founding of Boston he fled from Whitehall to York. The year that Roger Williams got his act of incorporation from the Long Parliament, the Roundheads seemed to have lost, but the year Claiborne landed an armed force on Kent Island in Chesapeake Bay, the Battle of Naseby showed that they had won. The year Peter Stuyvesant became a Dutch despot in New Amsterdam, Charles was executed for having been an English despot in London. When was one a radical and when was one not a radical?

Radicalism is a term the meaning of which everybody thinks he knows, and the definition of which nobody can give. In public life, certainly, radicalism usually means the assertion of dogma more or less basically opposed to the mores, opinions, traditions, and values of an elite that has been long enough in power to accumulate against itself a great deal of active dislike. The assertion of radical dogma may begin peacefully enough, but by and by it is often transmogrified into a belligerent claim to self-evident virtue and a bellicose assertion that one's opponents are evil men. Thus at the opening of *The Rights of Man* Paine solemnly asserts that Burke's "unprovoked attack" on the French National Assembly contains "everything which rancour, prejudice, ignorance or knowledge could suggest"; and if Burke handled French and English radicals with equal linguistic violence in his *Reflections on the Late Revolution in France,* let us remember that he then represented the radical right, as Paine and the Americans represented the radical left.

The original owners of plantations promised great things to the settlers, and the original creators of refugee colonies held out great hopes for immediate purification of the human race. Settlers were disappointed in both types of colonies. Propaganda for the joint-stock enterprise and for the proprietary colonies anticipates modern propaganda for the prairie farm, real estate in Florida, and garden suburbs within commuting distance of your business. The come-on was of the own-your-own-home variety, including equability of climate, ease of "manuring," the promise of rich harvests, no taxes or light ones, and an indulgent landlord. In the rush among "adventurers," noblemen, and colonial officials to acquire vast holdings in the wilderness, however, the little man was often overlooked. He was likely to turn sullen. He came to resent his dependent state and the unfulfillment of his roseate dream, and departed between the dark and the daylight for any convenient wilderness, where he took to squatting, hunting, the fur trade, scalping, or some other individualistic occupation, and turned by and by into that familiar type, the man who is "ag'in the guv'ment" and whose values Leatherstocking is, despite Cooper's love for the landed gentry, going to voice eloquently in the nineteenth century.

Such colonies as Plymouth, Massachusetts Bay, the Connecticut River towns, Rhode Island, and Pennsylvania were founded to improve humanity by building Zion in the woods. By definition, however, Zion could not be all things to all men, not even in Rhode Island and Pennsylvania, and antinomians, Quakers, Catholics, Baptists, Germans, fur traders, and other nonorthodox types were either cast out or forbidden to vote. In 1701, for example, William Penn wrote Governor Hamilton of West Jersey that the conduct in that colony of "rioters" * was "dishonorable and licentious . . . I know not what punishment those rioters do not deserve, and I had rather live alone than not have such people corrigible." [6] The "rioters" remained incorrigible.

Exiling the heterodox or correcting the incorrigible did not *ipso facto* turn such people into law-loving subjects of the king or the proprietor or the company. Indeed, one did not even have to possess odd views to dislike a theologically directed magistracy in New England or the threat of a transplanted episcopate in New York. Discontent could run

---

* As early as 1782 in Pennsylvania rioting was defined as the assembling of at least three persons armed with weapons designing to terrorize peaceable persons or injure property or person.

rampant for all sorts of reasons from rent to religion. But how protest? The little man then as now sought leaders, and clever leaders sought out the little man. The result was the creation of a strain of radicalism in American history that is often inconsistent but always interesting. It was both populist and philosophic.

It is difficult to know when the populace becomes the crowd, the crowd turns into a mob, the mob turns into somebody's semi-private army, and the semi-private army becomes the semi-official militia of an outraged people, but these things happened in the colonial seventeenth century. If we pass over early mutinies, disorders among fishermen along the coast, defiant groups such as the gang of vagabonds Thomas Weston gathered about him at Wessagussett on Boston Bay, quarrels over the power of proprietary governments to impose their will on renters, or the refusal of Quakers in New Jersey, Pennsylvania, or North Carolina to do anything about defense, we may cite three significant early instances of American crowd "radicalism" taking shape in some sense as populist action. The first, which led to anarchy and civil war in Chesapeake Bay, is associated with William Claiborne. Claiborne held, or claimed to hold, various official titles from Virginia (and perhaps from the crown), and, under cover of a Scotch license to trade with the Indians, he seized Kent Island, which, when it was made part of Lord Baltimore's patent, he refused to yield in tenancy. There followed a kind of tragi-comic civil war. Claiborne's private navy took to seizing Maryland boats; two boats from Maryland shot Claiborne's naval commander (this was in 1634–1635); Claiborne went to England; Maryland sent an armed force to occupy the island; Claiborne came back and in conjunction with Richard Ingle attacked Maryland, forcing the proprietary governor to flee; the "insurgents" plundered the plantation of Thomas Cornwallis, the finest in Maryland, and instituted a "Puritan" assembly; the assembly's men were attacked by forces under Governor Stone which were defeated; lives were lost, hangings were threatened, and Claiborne and a supporter set off for England to justify their actions and to overthrow the Baltimore family. In this they were unsuccessful, though as late as 1677 Claiborne was still petitioning for the right to retain Kent Island. Every point in this brief narrative is under dispute,[7] but it seems evident that the wily Claiborne cloaked his designs in the highest legal terms, and that a great deal of extreme language was exchanged—"felony," "murderers," "sedition," "pride, rage, and insolency of enemies," "a popish Anti-Christian Government," "traitors to our country, fighters against God, and covenant breakers." Here we have a fusion of propaganda, the vague shadow of a charismatic leadership, and an odd fusion of mob and militia that does not endure.

Claiborne clothed his case in high-sounding terms and appeared as the champion of the little men he employed or who traded with him, as against the tyranny of the establishment. Possibly he was somewhat bewildered when his movement got out of hand and he found himself associated with Ingle and others who really wanted to overthrow the government. The insurrection headed by Nathaniel Bacon in 1676 in Virginia against the tyranny of Governor Berkeley was also criss-crossed by problems of trading rights, Indian massacres, land tenure, the rights of the common man, and "democracy" against "oligarchy." Here, too, a charismatic leader, this time more clearly defined, raises a semi-private army (and even a quasi-private navy), conducts war, drives a governor out, besieges Jamestown, burns it, and is unable to control pillaging by his men. The death of this popular leader is mysterious and his burial place unknown. Two royal commissioners, sent to investigate, described Bacon as "of ominous, pensive, melancholly Aspect, of a pestilent and prevalent Logical discourse tending to atheisme . . . of a most imperious and dangerous hidden Pride of heart . . . very ambitious and arrogant," [8] but it was not thus that Bacon appeared to his passionate followers, a large fraction of whom were illiterate.[9] Despite this latter fact, Bacon used his legal training to draft a "Declaration of the People" which contains phrases about "Oppressions," "the Caball and mistery" with which Berkeley and his friends have been running Virginia, "spounges" that "have suckt up the Publique Treasure" which had been "privately contrived away by unworthy Favourites and juggling Parasites," and so on. Since with Bacon's death this movement passed into nothingness, Berkeley was able to hang thirty-seven of the rebels, compelled others, kneeling before him with halters around their necks, to acknowledge "treason," and distributed fines, imprisonment, and sentences of banishment with a prodigal hand. Bacon's rebellion was a far more serious affair than Claiborne's intransigence, but the pattern is like it—alleged tyranny, the assertion of "rights," the unpredictable behavior of an armed crowd (or mob), and the collapse of the whole movement.

Differing in detail but like in its general dynamics was the Leisler rebellion in New York against the colonial government. The leader had something of Bacon's temperament, an armed militia seized the fort and ousted customary authority, the movement got out of hand and took the form of civil war, and rebellion collapsed upon the execution of Leisler and a companion in 1691, both of whom died protesting that they meant only to maintain the best interests of the crown and of the "reformed protestant Churches" "against popery or any Schism or heresy." [10]

If one puts aside the action of the Bostonians in seizing Governor Andros and all the officials of the "Dominion of New England" in 1688, no crowd or mob action between the accession of William and Mary and the passage of the Stamp Act is quite of the stature of Bacon's or Leisler's rebellion. Since no British army was regularly stationed in the colonies until 1768, this looks like a tribute to the royal governor's capacity to maintain order. But the reasons for this lull are to be sought elsewhere. For one thing, the wars known as King William's War, Queen Anne's War, King George's War, and the French and Indian War not only occupied public attention but seemed also to threaten the colonies with invasion, as, indeed, they sometimes did. For another thing, despite the paper-money problem, postwar prosperity commonly followed one of these conflicts. For a third, this was the period during which the imperial government treated the colonies with intermittent attention and salutary neglect. Nevertheless the Americans continued to be unruly. In East Jersey various uprisings involved the destruction of property, the closing of courts, the release of prisoners, and the appearance of an unauthorized "militia" under arms.[11] During the War of Jenkins' Ear (1739–1742), when the crown enlisted an American expeditionary force for service in the Caribbean, the colonials and the regulars almost came to blows and exchanged a good deal of high language.[12] In 1747 the Bostonians rioted for three days against a press gang. In New York City in 1766 a theater was mobbed, various persons were injured, the building was wrecked and part of it burned in a bonfire because the populace, suffering from unemployment, wished to express its resentment against the wealthy class. In Newport there were various encounters between the customs officials or the crews of ships and Rhode Islanders determined to protect their pigs, or profits gained from smuggling or piracy.[13] When in his "Speech on Conciliation with the American Colonies" Burke in 1775 described the Americans as a "fierce people" who "became suspicious, restive and untractable, whenever they see the least attempt to wrest from them by force, or shuffle from them by chicane, what they think the only advantages worth living for," he had a long history to look back upon.

Determination to resist the Stamp Act quickly developed a pattern of violence that ran from New Hampshire to South Carolina. In Boston, long an unruly town, the mob was controlled at the center by a group known as The Loyal Nine (parents of the Sons of Liberty) and had for its generalissimo one Ebenezer Mackintosh, a shoemaker.[14] There Andrew Oliver, the stamp distributor, and Lord Bute were hanged in effigy; Oliver's warehouse was wrecked and his home was gutted; Governor Hutchinson's house was first besieged and afterward wrecked, paintings, furniture, library, and silver were carried off, the interior was ruined, and £900 in cash was stolen. The home of William Story and his office were sacked, and so was the residence of Benjamin Hallowell. This "mob" included "forty substantial citizens thinly disguised in the trousers and jackets of mechanics," and a like transparent "disguising" was to be employed again at the Boston Tea Party. In Newport a mob wrecked the houses of Dr. Thomas Moffat and Martin Howard, Jr., including Moffat's fine collection of scientific instruments and his collection of paintings. In Maryland a mob forced the local stamp distributor, Zachary Hood, to flee for his life, and the same thing happened in Charleston, South Carolina. In Connecticut another mob offered Jared Ingersoll the choice of being lynched or resigning his post as stamp distributor; and the stamp distributor for New Hampshire faced a similar dilemma.

All this was occasioned by the Stamp Act. But in 1768 in Boston there was a riot over the seizure by the customs officials of John Hancock's ship, Liberty; in 1770 a clash between the Sons of Liberty and British troops in New York on Golden Hill resulted in a pitched battle; and in Boston that same year the so-called Boston Massacre was the climax of a series of affrays. In 1771 the "Battle of Alamance" between Governor Tryon and the "Regulators" resulted in the execution of James Few, leader of the Regulators, and of six others, in 1772 the customs schooner Gaspee was set afire by Rhode Islanders led by the merchant John Brown, the commander of the schooner being wounded; and, as in the case of the Stamp Act, the landing of tea in 1773–1774 was stopped by crowd or mob action in Philadelphia, New York, Boston, Annapolis, and Charleston, the mobs being often "disguised" as Indians. We do not customarily think of New Hampshire as an especially "revolutionary" colony, since the last royal governor, John Wentworth, was a judicious and tactful man; yet a modern historian compares the mobs and the actions of the committees of public safety in that colony to the actions of the French Committee of Public Safety.[15]

Violent mob or crowd action was accompanied, instigated, or followed by the violent language of propaganda, carefully studied by Philip Davidson; and we who usually think of the American Revolution in the stately words of Jefferson and John Adams forget the verbal hysteria of otherwise cultured men. Samuel Adams, who wrote under some twenty-five pseudonyms, was capable of: "I will oppose this tyranny at the threshold, though the fabric of liberty fall, and I perish in its ruins." In 1768 Josiah Quincy described the British government in terms scarcely true of Oriental despotism: "Are not pensioners, stipendiaries, and salary-men (unknown before,) hourly multiplying on us, to riot in the spoils of miserable America? . . . Is not the bread taken out of the childrens mouths and given unto the Dogs? Are not our estates given to corrupt sycophants, without a design, or even a pretence, of solliciting our assent, and our lives put into the hands of those whose tender mercies are cruelties?" Most historians agree that the British troops behaved rather well and that the Boston mob that occasioned the so-called massacre of 1770 was deeply at fault. Not so, however, Dr. Joseph Warren, who was capable of this incredible prose:

> Hither let me lead the tender mother to weep over her beloved son—come widowed mourner, here satiate thy grief; behold thy murdered husband gasping on the ground, and to complete the pompous show of wretchedness bring in each hand thy infant children to bewail their father's fate—take heed, ye infant babes, lest, whilst your streaming eyes are fixed on the ghastly corpse, *your feet slide on the stones bespattered with your father's brains* . . . does some fiend, fierce from the depths of hell, with all the rancorous malice which the apostate damned can feel, twang her deadly arrows at our breast? No . . . it is the hand of Britain that inflicts the wound.

He was no worse than the Reverend Jonas Clark, celebrating the anniversary of Lexington:

> With a *cruelty* and barbarity, which would have made the most hardened savage blush, they shed INNOCENT BLOOD!— But, O *my* GOD!—! How shall I speak!—or how describe the

distress, the *horror* of that *awful morn,* that *gloomy day!* . . .
There the tender father bled, and there the beloved son! There
the hoary head, and there the blooming youth! . . . *They*
bleed—they die, not by the sword of an open enemy . . . in
the field of battle, but by the hand of those that delight in spoil,
and *lurk privily that they may shed innocent blood!*

Inasmuch as the British marched openly down the road to
Lexington and Concord and were later picked off by minute-
men lurking privily behind stone walls, one has here an interesting glimpse into the relation of truth to propaganda.
But as John Cleaveland addressed to General Gage in the
Essex Gazette in 1775 language of this sort: "Without speedy
repentance, you will have an aggravated damnation in hell
. . . you are not only a robber, a murderer and a usurper,
but a wicked Rebel: A rebel against the authority of truth, law,
equity, the English constitution of government, these colony
states, and humanity itself," [16] the argument was clear: the
British could do no right and the Americans could do no
wrong.

In an environment of violent words, violent change, and
violent action giving birth to self-constituted leaders, secret
intercolonial committees, such organizations of terror as the
Sons of Liberty, and eventually revolutionary assemblies that
take over the functions of traditional governments, fair treatment of the opposition is not to be expected. Some attempt
to deal fairly with the Loyalists, who were, after all, in theory
as much entitled to express their views as were the patriots,
can be seen in the beginning, but the attempt did not eventu-
ate into policy. The revolution was not only a rebellion
against crown and Parliament, it was also an internecine civil
war in which Americans fought against Americans. The
crown raised at least ten corps of American Loyalists, some
of whom secured supplies for the British Army or destroyed
supplies for the Americans, some of whom garrisoned posts
from Passamaquoddy southward, some of whom fought under
Tarleton in the Carolinas, some of whom waged guerrilla
warfare in areas such as Westchester County, New York,

some of whom were allied to the Indians, and all of whom seemed to encourage desertions like that of Arnold and the temporary treason of Charles Lee. But even before the start of major hostilities Loyalists were boycotted, insulted, tarred and feathered, forced off their estates and out of their homes, and suffered the ruin of business or occupation. Inevitably they concentrated in the port towns, where they might have the protection of the British Navy and Army. Eleven hundred exiles sailed from Boston for Nova Scotia when that city was evacuated, and in July 1775 Judge Samuel Curwen already reported "an army of New Englanders" in London. When Philadelphia was evacuated by the British, three times as many Loyalists are supposed to have fled as those who left Boston. Probably the heaviest concentration of Loyalists was in New York, a colony that is supposed to have supplied more soldiers to George III than to George Washington; when the British finally evacuated New York at least thirty thousand civilians had left for Nova Scotia. Five thousand Loyalists went to East Florida, six or seven thousand to the Bahamas, an unknown number to Jamaica, lower Canada, and other places within the empire. The reports spread abroad by this diaspora of cultivated families inevitably pictured the Americans as lawless radicals rebelling against mild and benevolent rule.

Tory estates were confiscated by the revolutionary legislatures, and these estates were sometimes princely. In New York much of Hudson Valley, Westchester, Staten Island, and Long Island real estate was held by Tories, and there were of course enormous holdings in Pennsylvania, Virginia, the Carolinas, and elsewhere. The final disposition of this land and of its income offers a fascinating problem to the historian, the economist, and the psychologist; in general, though after the cessation of hostilities compensation was supposed to be made, the financial bankruptcy of the Confederation and the primitive emotions aroused by what was in effect looting prevented the sixty or seventy thousand who fled from receiving what they felt was their due. Nor could the exiled Tory easily forget the village mob and the village demagogue who had threatened his life and the security of his family and his property, ransacked his buildings, charged him with harboring profiteers, and generally misbehaved. But it would be tedious to rehearse still more such violence as the so-called doctors' riot in New York in 1788, occasioned by charges of grave-robbing, or Shays's rebellion in western Massachusetts, which terrorized the courts, besieged Springfield, and was put down by General Lincoln at the head of 4400 men, the Know-Ye party in Rhode Island, or the Whisky Rebellion under Bradford in 1791 in western Pennsylvania, to subdue which Washington called out 15,000 militia. Let me conclude this picture of the eighteenth-century America as a radical nation of violence with an episode in New Hampshire. There, in 1786, two hundred men who wanted cheap money assembled six miles from Exeter, where the legislature was meeting, chose leaders, armed themselves with muskets, swords, and clubs, and, like the Parisian mob during the French Revolution, invaded the chamber where the assembly was meeting. The assembly refused to yield, whereupon "the drum beat to arms; as many as had guns were ordered to load them with balls, sentries were placed at the doors, and the whole Legislature were held prisoners; the mob threatening death to any person who should attempt to escape." The assembly attempted to adjourn, but the mob demanded the issuance of paper money, equal distribution of property, and the cancellation of all debts. Only the threat of Exeter citizens to "bring up the artillery" dispersed the gathering. The ringleaders were seized by the militia but were never punished.[17]

American mobs were amenable to cunning leadership, sometimes disguised, sometimes demagogic; they pillaged, robbed, destroyed property, defied law, interfered with the normal course of justice, legislation, and administration, occasionally inflicted physical injuries, and were now and then the cause, direct or indirect, of deaths in their own number or among those they attacked. They came by and by to be resented by Americans; for example, in *The Anarchiad* in 1786:

> In visions fair the scenes of fate unroll,
> And Massachusetts opens on my soul;
> There Chaos, Anarch old, asserts his sway,
> And mobs in myriads blacken all the way:
> See Day's stern port—behold the martial frame
> Of Shays' and Shattuck's mob-compelling name:
> See the bold Hampshirites on Springfield pour,
> The fierce Tauntonians crowd the alewife shore.
> O'er *Concord* fields the bands of *discord* spread,
> And Wor'ster trembles at their thundering tread:
> See from proud Egremont the woodchuck train,
> Sweep their dark files, and shade with rags the plain.
> Lo, THE COURT FALLS; th'affrighted judges run,
> Clerks, Lawyers, Sheriffs, every mother's son.
> The stocks, the gallows lose th'expected prize,
> See the jails open, and the thieves arise.
> Thy constitution, Chaos, is restor'd;
> Law sinks before thy uncreating word.

This, to be sure, is a parody of Pope and of the *Rolliad,* but the sentiments are genuine; the authors, probably David Humphreys and Lemuel Hopkins, are supposed to be battling for "the majesty of law, and for the federal government." [18]

On the other hand American mobs were curiously lacking in furious, deep-seated, and bloodthirsty resentment. No royal governor was hanged or shot by a drumhead court martial. No stamp collector or customs official was summarily executed, though some of them suffered physical injury. No "tyrant" was decapitated as the unfortunate governor of the Bastille was decapitated, and nobody's head was borne about the streets of Philadelphia or Boston on a pole. There was no American parallel to the Jacquerie, the Noyades, the September massacres, or the Reign of Terror. No one was castrated; though charges of rape made good propaganda, it is hard to authenticate cases of rape through mob action; and there was no American equivalent to the Black Hole of Calcutta, even if wandering bands of Skinners sometimes whipped suspects and occasional patriots tarred and feathered a Tory. Deep as American feelings might be, the Revolution was nothing like the Thirty Years' War and erupted in nothing remotely resembling the massacre of Saint Bartholomew. Nevertheless, in the eyes of all right-thinking men the illegalities, the violences, the breakdown in due processes of law, the populist insistence that the crowd was the whole people were the result of the absence in the United States of traditional modes of control and of the presence of radical "philosophical" theories of government and society.

Mob action became a kind of tradition, powerfully coloring the image of the American in foreign countries. It was always easy to assemble indignant men on the frontier, where the "Arkansas toothpick" (knife or dagger) and the pistol became standard equipment and where, whatever treaties or territorial laws might say, settlers and hunters could be quickly assembled to attack Indians, Mexicans, cattle thieves, and horse rustlers. The lower Mississippi became the homeland of desperadoes, of whom Murrell's gang (supposed to number a thousand) was typical. When rivermen were ordered to leave Vicksburg and Natchez in 1835, they defied the order, and a mob of respectable citizens hanged five of them in the name of justice. A wave of violence swept the South in the thirties; in the summer of 1835 a mob led by former Senator Robert Y. Hayne attacked the federal post office in Charleston and destroyed sacks of mail, and the lower South in the same decade was swept by unreasoning fear of a Negro insurrection, as a result of which a number of white persons and a few Negroes were lynched. By the 1850s immediate action by the crowd in defense of "constitutional rights" made the life of antislavery advocates intolerable, vigilante committees were appointed, the split in the Methodist Church over slavery occasioned crowd violence, and the election of 1856, like the John Brown raid at Harpers Ferry three years later, set off another round of extralegal actions.[19] An exploration of the British consular reports for the 1850s shows the amount of attention paid to American lawlessness; [20] and of course after the Civil War the invention of the Ku Klux Klan, lynch mobs, agrarian disturbances in the West, the Haymarket riot, and the riots connected with the Homestead strike of 1892 and the Pullman strike of 1894 continued the pattern. It is scarcely necessary to add that sit-ins, "marches" (on the pattern of Coxey's Army or the Bonus March), and other forms of mass action on behalf of desegregation follow the pattern established in seventeenth-century America—a great cause, a more or less charismatic leadership, the assertion of fundamental rights, and resulting imprisonment, violence, injury, and on occasion death.

III

Mob action was not an American invention, nor did European life run smoothly during these same centuries. For example, the Lord George Gordon riot in 1780, in which 450 persons were killed and infinite damage was done to both public and private buildings in London, was far more savage and destructive than any demonstration here. But crowd action in América seemed to be a form of direct political action, an exercise of the will of the people in the name of popular sovereignty, the assertion of fundamental law or social principle ("this is a white man's country"), or an expression of impatience with legislative or executive delay. The doctrine that the crowd may from time to time take public action into its own hands is not only extralegal but also becomes in a sense definitely non-European. Potential immigrants had to be assured that the United States was neither as violent nor as radical as legend made it out to be; and British novelists, many of whom had never visited the United States, invented "Yankee" characters who were illiterate, lacked culture, were full of swagger, expressed contempt for traditional government, chewed tobacco, wore coffee-colored clothing, and formed a mixture of "melancholy and intrepidity." [21]

Mob action need not be *per se* "radical," and American mob action could perhaps be excused or explained by saying that one could not expect the refinements of royal capitals in the wilderness or in remote provincial towns. But a difficulty immediately arose. The Americans did not think of themselves as crude or barbarous but as the heirs of all the ages in the foremost files of time. They were not merely populist, they were, it presently appeared, positively progressive. They believed they were opening a new epoch in the history of mankind. They took literally Bishop Berkeley's famous poem:

> Westward the course of empire takes its way;
> The four first acts already past,
> A fifth shall end the drama with the day;
> Time's noblest offspring is the last.

The last act was not merely to be nobler than the first four, it was to be "different"—anti-monarchical, anti-aristocratic, anti-feudal, and anti-privilege. In vain did such philosophers as Buffon, Raynal, and the Abbé de Pauw argue that plants, animals, and men degenerated in the New World; in vain did experienced statesmen shake their heads at a republic stretching twelve hundred miles from Maine to Georgia and a thousand miles from Boston to the Mississippi; in vain did such a thinker as Condorcet write the American Philosophical Society to inquire by what possible arithmetic the Americans could form a representative government. Franklin at a famous dinner party and Jefferson in a famous book refuted Buffon and de Pauw; and American leaders counterattacked by announcing that Europe was degenerate because the entire European system was false.

Such an assertion, one imagines, came as a shock to any eighteenth-century observer who had been following the development of ideas in the future United States. Only four years before the Stamp Act riots the Reverend Henry Caner, preaching in King's Chapel, Boston, to the royal governor, had, in describing George III, spoken of "the Goodness of his Heart" and said that "the Administration had been conducted by a Patriot of as much Wisdom and Integrity, and of as great Abilities, as ever blest the Nation or adorn'd the Court." [22] Only a year before the Boston Tea Party, the Reverend Moses Parsons, delivering the election sermon, declared: "There is not, I suppose, a native of this Province, who does not bear unfeigned loyalty to King George *the third*." [23] Yet by 1774 Edmund Burke roundly declared in Parliament that the Americans "have questioned all the parts of your legislative power, and by the battery of such questions have shaken the solid structure of this empire to its deepest foundations"; [24] and that same year in (of all places!) the *Royal American Magazine* somebody in New Haven had poetized:

> Fair freedom now her ensigns bright displays,
> And peace and plenty bless the golden days.
> In mighty pomp America shall rise,
> Her glories spreading to the boundless skies;
> Of ev'ry fair she boasts th'assembled charms,
> The queen of empires and the nurse of arms.[25]

Two years afterward the history of the same king of Great Britain was described in the most important state paper of the Revolution as "a history of repeated injuries and usurpations . . . having in direct object the establishment of an absolute Tyranny over these States"; and Tom Paine, who was to exercise an international influence, in his *Common Sense* characterized monarchy as "the most prosperous invention the devil ever set on foot for the promotion of idolatry," traced the origin of all royal houses to the "principal ruffian of some restless gang," and declared that the only king in America was God, who "doth not make havoc of mankind like the royal brute of Great Britain." [26] In retrospect it appeared that the Europeans should have paid more attention to Lord Dunmore, governor of Virginia, when he wrote in 1772:

I have learnt from experience that the established Authority of any government in America, and the policy of Government at home, are both insufficient to restrain the Americans; and that they do and will remove as their avidity and restlessness incite them. They acquire no attachment to Place; but wandering about seems engrafted in their Nature . . . impressed from their earliest infancy with Sentiments and habits, very different from those acquired by persons of a Similar condition in England, they do not conceive that Government has any right to forbid their taking possession of a Vast tract of Country, either uninhabited, or which Serves only as a Shelter to a few Scattered Tribes of Indians. Nor can they be easily brought to entertain any belief of the permanent obligation of Treaties made with those People.[27]

European liberals such as Turgot,* experienced colonial administrators such as Thomas Pownall, libertarians such as Lafayette, enthusiastic young men such as Southey and Coleridge, stormy Germans such as Klinger, and English radicals of the caliber of Horne Tooke and Joseph Priestley hailed the new state as something that was to set Europe right, and some of them took refuge here.[28] Naturally the sovereigns, especially after 1789, were less enthusiastic. In vain did such American conservatives as John Adams try to ward off the implication that the United States was a mere populist democracy;[29] in vain did the authors of *The Federalist,* ostensibly addressing New York but really addressing mankind, argue that the new Constitution was a grave measure intended to check popular ebullience; in vain did Hamilton insist that "Europe is at a great distance from us," which could only mean that the United States was also at a great distance from Europe.[30] The stigma of radicalism was fixed upon the Americans. Aside from the fact that the United States had no monarch, no hereditary aristocracy, no tradition of culture, no landed gentry enjoying the right of

* Turgot wrote Dr. Price in 1778: "This people is the hope of the human race. It may become the model. It ought to show the world by facts, that men can be free and yet peaceful, and may dispense with the chains in which tyrants and knaves of every colour have presumed to bind them. . . ."

primogeniture, no established church, no secret police, no royal council of state, no house of peers, no "society," and no feudal tenure (at least in theory); aside from the naval prowess of the republic and the marksmanship of the Western militia of Carroll and Coffee at New Orleans; aside from the danger that popular institutions, successful in the United States and momentarily successful in France, might spread by infection and overthrow the existing order, America presented four threats to European governments: it kept up a steady pro-republican and anti-monarchical propaganda; it had plenty of land obtainable on a freehold basis; it offered alluring prospects to European emigrants weary of war, taxes, and royal or aristocratic tyranny; and it seemed to be creating the perfect agrarian society of which poets and philosophers had dreamed.

The propaganda was incessant from the days of Tom Paine and Jefferson through Emerson's injunction to flee the courtly muses of Europe and Whitman's fear of feudalism to the humor of Mark Twain and Will Rogers. A catena of passages will illustrate its character. Here is Tom Paine:

> Man has no property in man; neither has any generation a property in the generations which are to follow. The Parliament or the people of 1688, or of any other period, had no more right to dispose of the people of the present day, or to bind or control them *in any shape whatever,* than the Parliament or the people of the present day have to dispose of, bind, or control those who are to live a hundred or a thousand years hence.

> . . . Mr. Burke represents England as wanting capacity to take care of itself, and that its liberties must be taken care of by a king, holding it in "contempt." . . . besides the folly of the declaration, it happens that the facts are all against Mr. Burke. It was by the government *being hereditary,* that the liberties of the people were endangered.

> I consider a King in England as something which the military keep to cheat with, in the same manner that wooden gods and

conjuror's wands were kept in time of idolatry and superstition . . .

The history of France is chiefly concerned with the misfortunes of the nation, and we find that the vices of kings have been the root and origin of these misfortunes. . . .[31]

Here is Jefferson, who, if he did not publish as extensively as Paine, was nevertheless an influential figure:

Of all the errors which can possibly be committed in the education of youth, that of sending them to Europe is the most fatal . . . no American should come to Europe under 30 years of age: and [he who] does, will lose in science, in virtue, in health and in happiness, for which manners are a poor compensation, were we even to admit the hollow, unmeaning manners of Europe to be preferable to the simplicity and sincerity of our own country. . . .

Behold me at length on the vaunted scene of Europe! . . . I find the general fate of humanity here most deplorable. The truth of Voltaire's observation offers itself perpetually, that every man here must be either the hammer or the anvil . . . the great mass of the people are . . . suffering under physical and moral oppression. . . . Intrigues of love occupy the younger, and those of ambition the more elderly of the great. . . . Much, very much inferior this to the tranquil permanent felicity with which domestic society in America blesses most of it's inhabitants, leaving them to follow steadily those pursuits which health and reason approve, and rendering truly delicious the intervals of these pursuits.

Let us view the disadvantages of sending a youth to Europe. . . . If he goes to England he learns drinking, horse-racing and boxing. . . . He acquires a fondness for European luxury and dissipation and a contempt for the simplicity of his own country; he is fascinated with the privileges of the European aristocrats, and sees with abhorrence the lovely equality which the poor enjoys with the rich in his own country. . . . It appears to me . . . that an American coming to Europe for education loses in his knowledge, in his morals, in his health, in his habits, and in his happiness.[32]

Jefferson advised young men, if they went to Europe, to study kings as they would animals in a menagerie. And here are some representative passages from the Connecticut Wits:

> Look not to Europe, for examples just
> Of order, manners, customs, doctrines, laws,
> Of happiness, or virtue. Cast around
> The eye of searching reason, and declare
> What Europe offers, but a patchwork sway;
> The garment Gothic, worn to fritter'd shreds,
>
> .   .   .   .
>
> Such as the sway, the system shows entire,
> Of silly pomp, and meanness train'd t' adore;
> Of wealth enormous, and enormous want;
> Of lazy sinecures, and suffering toil;
>
> .   .   .   .
>
> Rites farsical, and phrenzied unbelief.
>
>   Shun the lures
> Of Europe. Cherish still, watch, hold,
> And hold through every trial, every snare,
> All that is thine.
>
> Thou seest proud grandeur wheel her sunny car;
> While kings, and nobles, roll bespangled by,
> And the tall palace lessens in the sky;
>
> .   .   .   .
>
> Ah, yonder turn thy wealth-inchanted eyes,
> Where the poor, friendless wretch expiring lies!
>
> .   .   .   .
>
> See half a realm one tyrant scarce sustain,
> While meagre thousands round him glean the plain!
> See, for his mistress' robe, a village sold,
> Whose matrons shrink from nakedness and cold!
>
> .   .   .   .
>
> . . . Wives, and daughters, plead, and weep, in vain;
> Or yield to infamy themselves, to save
> Their sire from prison, famine, and the grave.[33]

It is scarcely necessary to quote from Joel Barlow's *The Conspiracy of Kings* (1792) and his *Advice to the Privileged Orders* (1791). If the eighteenth-century men were vigorous in their language, the nineteenth-century Americans merely repeated it in gentler terms. The naïve American of Henry James and William Dean Howells, puzzled by the corruption or the sophistication of Europe, is the heir of a long tradition. The feudal system survives in England, wrote Emerson in *English Traits* (1856), "in the steep inequality of property and privilege, in the limited franchise, in the social barriers which confine patronage and promotion to a caste, and still more in the submissive ideas pervading these people," but if the "courage of England" should fail, he would go back to Massachusetts and "say to my countrymen, the old race are all gone, and the elasticity and hope of mankind must henceforth remain on the Alleghany ranges, or nowhere." [34] It was a forecast of a new, "radical," and American century.

In the Old World land was held by feudal tenure or a watered-down version of it, and the peasant was bound to the soil by serfdom, as in Russia, by communal ties, or by some other legal or traditional formula. After the French Revolution introduced the idea of a nation in arms, enforced military service drove many to seek a new life, and so did overcrowding, displacement because of the nascent industrial revolution, the enclosure movements, and successive economic depressions. The prospect of unlimited freehold tenure became an irresistible argument for removing to America and so getting out from under "griping landlords" and acquiring full political membership in an agrarian democracy; and, as Eisinger points out, the nostalgia for a return to the land that marks much European writing in the seventeenth and eighteenth century (as in Wordsworth, *Hermann und Dorothea,* and the last act of *Faust*) took practical form in the allure of a farming paradise in the United States. It must not be forgotten in this connection that the issues of independence and republicanism were debated in this country by the Westchester Farmer, the Pennsylvania Farmer, and the Amer-

ican Farmer of Crèvecœur. American theorists assumed, even
if tacitly, that in an ideal state everyone had some right to the
soil, as the arguments of Paine, Jefferson, Tench Coxe,
George Logan, and others testify, and assumed also that the
farmer is the ideal political unit in a republic—a manly, independent citizen who can be trusted to vote intelligently
because the soil somehow fulfills his personality.[35] Consider
as expressing average opinion in the early decades a passage
like this from Timothy Dwight's *Greenfield Hill* (1794):

> In little farms
> They measur'd all thy realms, to every child
> In equal shares descending; no entail
> The first-born lifting into bloated pomp,
> Tainting with lust, and sloth, and pride, and rage,
> The world around him: all the race beside,
> Like brood of ostrich, left for chance to rear,
> And every foot to trample.
>
> .   .   .   .
>
>   Beneath their eye,
> And forming hand, in every hamlet, rose
> The nurturing school: in every village, smil'd
> The heav'n-inviting church, and every town
> A world within itself, with order, peace,
> And harmony, adjusted all its weal.[36]

Not only did literary figures from Dwight, Irving, Bryant,
Whittier, and Longfellow to Henry Ward Beecher, Will
Carleton, and James Whitcomb Riley celebrate the self-
reliance, industry, domestic virtues, and religious faith nur-
tured on the farm and in the near-by village, but the school
readers of the nineteenth century dramatized alike the barefoot boy with cheek of tan and Mary, whose little lamb followed her to school. In such books the children of the honest
farmer are preferred to the offspring of the half-Europeanized
village squire, and in fiction the American farm, until the
rise of realism, improves the lot of the English tenant, the
continental peasant, and the Russian serf. *My Ántonia,* the
story of the Shimerda family, is but a late instance of a con-

tinuing tradition now overlooked by "sophisticated" literary critics.

Guides and inducements to emigrate multiplied in Europe during the eighteenth century and after the Napoleonic wars. The earlier ones combine the appeal of easy agriculture and economic independence with an appeal to "liberty"—that is, the desirability of supporting a new country that was obviously the last, best hope of man.[37] Thus a pamphlet published in London as early as 1710, entitled *A Letter from South Carolina . . . written by a Swiss Gentleman, to his Friend at Bern,* which ran to three editions, declares:

> How much better is it for those who have but a small Subsistence at home, to retire to a Place where they may with moderate industry be supplied with all the Necessaries of Life, than to follow the miserable Trade of Destroying for a Shilling a Day? How much better for Men to improve their own Lands, for the use of themselves, and Posterity; to sit under their own Vine, and eat the Fruits of their Labour; than to be Instruments in the Hands of Tyrants, to ravage and depopulate the Earth.[38]

After the Seven Years' War this sort of thing increased.

Crèvecœur's *Letters from an American Farmer,* published in London in 1782, in Paris in 1783, in Philadelphia in 1794, with its picture of the good fortunes of Andrew the Hebridean and its famous essay "What Is an American?" preached a like doctrine: "Can a wretch, who wanders about, who works and starves, whose life is a continual scene of sore affliction or pinching penury; can that man call England or any other kingdom his country?" America here appears as a sort of premature Statue of Liberty welcoming the poor and the oppressed:

> Welcome to my shores, distressed European; bless the hour in which thou didst see my verdant fields, my fair navigable rivers, and my green mountains!—If thou wilt work, I have bread for thee; if thou wilt be honest, sober, and industrious, I have greater rewards to confer on thee—ease and independence. . . . I shall endow thee beside with the immunities of a freeman, if

thou wilt carefully educate thy children, teach them gratitude
to God, and reverence to that government, that philanthropic
government, which has collected here so many men and made
them happy.[39]

An anonymous pamphlet, *Thoughts on Emigration, To
Which are Added, Miscellaneous Observations Relating to
the United States of America, and a Short Account of the
State of Kentucky* (1792) bears for its motto: "Where liberty
is, there is our country," and stresses lower taxes, simpler
laws, love of independence, religious equality, better education, and the urge to come out of the land of Egypt. In
Europe even "men of principle . . . have taken a part in
suppressing the spirit of liberty . . . in carrying devastation
and death to the Indies. They may remonstrate:—but what
avail their remonstrances? They have no voice in the legislature: or if they had; the clamours of those who fatten upon
the spoil, would drown their voice." In contrast: "If in casting our eyes over a country, we behold fertility of soil, simplicity of manners, equality of rights;—upon these we fix
our attention." [40] In other words, migrate to the United
States.

Thomas Cooper, in answering the question: "You ask
what appear to me the general inducements to people to quit
England for America?" replied: *"The total absence of anxiety
respecting the future success of a family,"* and he went on
to add:

The government is the government *of* the people, and *for* the
people. There are no tythes nor game laws. . . . There are no
men of great rank, nor many of great riches. Nor have the rich
there the power of oppressing the less rich, for poverty, such
as in Great Britain, is almost unknown. Nor are their streets
crouded with beggars. . . . You see no where in America the
disgusting and melancholy contrast, so common in Europe, of
vice, and filth, and rags, and wretchedness in the immediate
neighbourhood of the most wanton extravagance, and the most
useless and luxurious parade. Nor are the common people so
depraved as in Great Britain.[41]

Alas for republics! Cooper was jailed, suffered many times from the tyranny of majority opinion, and lost his pristine enthusiasm for "democracy."

Matthew Carey's "Reflections on the Subject of Emigration from Europe," a pamphlet that stresses unemployment and overcrowding in the British Isles, says that the United States needs laborers, and adds: "The facility of acquiring landed property in this country, has been uniformly so great, and the inducements to take an independent grade in society, are such powerful incentives to the purchase of that species of property, that labourers and hired people of all descriptions . . . have been, at all times . . . scarce and in demand." Cooper also emphasizes the "endearing relation" possible in America between parents and children, the rationality of American marriages, security of the person, lightness of taxation, freedom of religion, and, curiously enough, not only the absence of game laws but the right of everyone to carry arms.[42] After 1815, and particularly after 1830, the romantic attractions of "liberty" are less apparent in the emigrants' manuals, which more and more turn into handbooks of practical advice. Nevertheless the American republic remains a "radical" mirage on the horizon of the oppressed of other countries into our own time.[43] All this was as subversive as the mob.

IV

In Boston on July 4, 1825, Charles Sprague made an address neither better nor worse than many others of its kind.

The achievement of American Independence was not merely the separation of a few obscure colonies from their parent realm; it was the practical annunciation to created man, that he was created *free!* and it will stand in history, the epoch from which to compute the real duration of political liberty. Intolerance and tyranny had for ages leagued to keep their victim down.[44]

In Philadelphia five years later Zelotes Fuller delivered an oration on Washington's birthday, in which he said:

> Here, talent is not frowned into silence or trampled in the dust, for the want of gold to support its dignity, nor for the want of noble parentage; but commands the respectful atten- tions, of all the truly wise and candid, however obscure the corner from whence it emanates, and receives that encourage- ment and support from a generous government, to which it is justly and lawfully entitled. . . . No country could possibly possess greater advantages and facilities, for continuing free and independent, than what is possessed by America. . . . Such is the state of our country, such the state of our agricul- tural and manufacturing departments, that it is not necessary, in order to obtain all the needed blessings, and most of the luxuries of life, that we should leave our own native shores.[45]

Here were large and radical claims, a doctrine that mankind had opened a new chapter in its history, that the real dura- tion of political liberty was to be marked from 1776, that in this land of democratic equality merit was instantly rec- ognized. Was the contention true? A hundred travelers came from Europe to find out and report. Commonly they came prepared to be astonished or to condemn; not until Tocque- ville did anybody come with an open mind. They were struck by the disparity between the golden dream and the vulgar reality; if they were liberals, they took the dream as earnest of future growth; if they were reactionaries, their general at- titude was one of "I told you so."

Perhaps the contrast between the two modes of interpre- tation cannot be more clearly shown than by Tom Moore, who published in 1806 a book called *Epistles, Odes, and Other Poems,* much of it written in America during the sec- ond administration of Thomas Jefferson. Moore had been a young Irish liberal; he was now a British Tory; he was to become once more a liberal, but the book appeared during his Tory phase. Here is Moore's picture of the golden dream:

> Here shall religion's pure and balmy draught
> In form no more from cups of state be quaff'd

But flow for all, through nation, rank, and sect,
Free as that heaven its tranquil waves reflect.
Around the columns of the public shrine
Shall growing arts their gradual wreath intwine,
Nor breathe corruption from the flowering braid,
Nor mine that fabric which they bloom to shade.
No longer here shall Justice bound her view,
Or wrong the many, while she rights the few;
But take her range through all the social frame,
Pure and pervading as that vital flame
Which warms at once our best and meanest part,
And thrills a hair while it expands a heart!
Oh golden dream!

But what were the facts?

Who can, with patience, for a moment see
The medley mass of pride and misery,
Of whips and charters, manacles and rights,
Of slaving blacks and democratic whites,
And all the piebald polity that reigns
In free confusion o'er Columbia's plains?

.   .   .   .

I'd rather hold my neck
By doubtful tenure from a sultan's beck,
In climes, where liberty has scarce been nam'd,
Nor any right, but that of ruling claim'd,
Than thus to live, where bastard Freedom waves
Her fustian flag in mockery over slaves.

And again:

Take Christians, Mohawks, democrats, and all
From the rude wigwam to the congress-hall,
From man the savage, whether slav'd or free,
To man the civiliz'd, less tame than he,—
'Tis one dull chaos, one unfertile strife
Betwixt half-polish'd and half-barbarous life;
Where every ill the ancient world could brew
Is mix'd with every grossness of the new.[46]

The polarities in Moore's verse—the golden dream and the
disturbing reality—can also be represented by examining

travel books written by two Frenchmen, the one sympathetic to "liberty" and believing that America was a radical step forward, the other taking exactly the opposite point of view. The first was the Girondin who called himself Brissot de Warville, a disciple of Voltaire and Rousseau guillotined in 1793, who visited the United States in 1788, determined, he said, to study the operations of liberty in order to instruct his countrymen. The secret of preserving liberty lies in the morals of the people, which the Americans have and which the French have not yet acquired. The basis of a happy nation is agriculture. "I assure you that the Americans are and will be for a long time free; it is because nine tenths of them live by agriculture; and when there shall be five hundred millions of men in America, all may be proprietors." In France this would be impossible: to divide the fifty million acres of arable land there would result in an allotment of only two acres to each man. The index of republican happiness is simplicity. "The leaders of the revolution in Holland, in the sixteenth century, seated on the grass at a repast of herrings and onions, received, with a stern simplicity, the deputies of the haughty Spaniard. This is the portrait of men who feel their dignity, and know the superiority of freemen over the slaves of kings." This simplicity the Americans have recovered or achieved:

> Nothing is more charming than an inside view of a church on Sunday. The good cloth coat covers the man; callicoes and chintzes dress the women and children, without being spoiled by those gewgaws which whim and caprice have added to them among our women. Powder and pomatum never sully the heads of infants and children: I see them, with pain, however, on the heads of men. . . . The member of Congress is placed by the side of the shoemaker who elected him; they fraternize together, and converse with familiarity. You see no person here taking upon himself those important airs which you too often meet with in France.

America, which contemplates "no other limits but those of the universe, no other restraint but the laws made by her representatives," is the radical hope of humanity—"that regeneration of the physical and moral man, which must be an infallible consequence of their constitutions." Here "the general good is the common end of every individual,—the end cherished, implanted, so to speak, by the constitution in every heart. . . . O Frenchmen! who wish this valuable instruction, study the Americans of the present day. Open this book: you will here see to what degree of prosperity the blessings of freedom can elevate the industry of man." But Brissot consciously or unconsciously frightened conservatives with his "idea of a *king-people* and an *elective chief*" and his disturbing picture of American expansiveness:

> You will see them attempting all sorts of speculations; opening the fertile bosom of the soil, lately covered by forests; tracing unknown seas; establishing new communications, new markets; naturalizing, in their own country, those precious manufactures which England had reserved to herself; and, by this accumulation of the means of industry, they change the balance that was formerly against America, and turn it to their own advantage.[47]

Among those who were disturbed was the chevalier Félix de Beaujour, who in the next decade delivered a quite different report. He was here from 1800 to 1810. His book was translated and published in London in 1814, and the translator was quite frank in saying why he had put it into English —it was to expose the Americans for what they were:

> North America became the seat of French diplomatic intrigue, and by the hold the French Revolution had taken on the people of America, a degree of turbulent and party spirit was engendered, that, in many instances, implicated the honour and sovereignty of the federal government. . . . Unfortunately . . . there has been a fund of uniform hostility in the American government, a spirit of aggrandizement, and a wish to extend the acknowledged rights of neutrals, beyond former example; which . . . has at length, terminated in open warfare.

In exact contradiction to Brissot, Beaujour looked for the balkanization of the United States. The American government, he wrote, "has scarcely evinced any thing else but proofs of weakness; and, in future, greater vigour cannot be expected from it, as long as it is conducted by lawyers, a species of men the least proper to govern others, because they have nearly all a false judgment and dull character . . . they think they can govern empires, in the same manner as they would govern a club." Beaujour is forced to acknowledge some admirable things in the United States—better diet, children so handsome they "deck the American streets like flowers," the absence of beggary, and the lighter burden of military service (the most famous American generals "were no more than partisans"); nevertheless "the American has a crudity in his manners," and though virtue is the chief spring of a republic, "that of the American republic seems to be an unbounded love of money." Although the Americans know "that same happiness of which the people of old Europe seem for ever deprived," it is because they are "only thinly scattered over a vast territory," and the time must come when they, too, will "experience that fatal inquietude which torments the numerous habitants of our cities, and which arises out of the daily agitation of the human passions, out of the pride of some, the envy of others, and the corruption of all." He spends a good deal of time demonstrating that the United States must fall apart, and declares it is not a great power and can never be one, and that "like the ship-owners of the Barbary coast, the Americans conceive they can only prosper but when the whole of Europe is on fire." [48]

When travelers write books they are justified in describing what they have seen and need not rise to generalization. Nevertheless, no department of travel literature is richer in social and philosophic generalizations than is that written by European travelers visiting the United States, especially before 1870, as they struggle to understand the republican experiment. An examination of a group of these accounts written between 1777 and 1842 (the date of Dickens' *American*

Notes) reveals the eagerness of authors to predict the future success or failure of the radical republic.[49] Some, like Thomas Brothers, frankly announce their partisan purpose: the title of his book is *The United States of North America As They Are; Not As They Are Generally Described. Being a Cure for Radicalism.*[50] Some like Isaac Weld, Jr., declare they went out without prejudice and reached negative judgments: Weld's book ends: "I shall speedily take my departure from this continent, well pleased at having seen as much of it as I have done; but I shall leave it without a sigh, and without entertaining the slightest wish to revisit it." [51] The authors of the more notorious titles in this library—Captain Basil Hall, Mrs. Trollope, Captain Marryat, and Charles Dickens —complain of vulgarity, lawlessness, mobs, vanity, the love of money-getting, lack of cultivation, and provincialism, qualities they invariably impute to the social and political experimentalism of the United States.[52] The form of the American government may be republican, said Basil Hall, but American life is democratic, and democracy has "a direct tendency to lower the standard of talents, of knowledge, and of public spirit, besides putting public virtue in great danger." Democracy, he wrote, "when once let loose, is exactly like any other inundation—it is sure to find its level,—and whatever it cannot reach, it undermines and finally subverts." [53] Captain Marryat was even more emphatic:

A democratic form of government is productive of . . . demoralizing effects. Its rewards are few. Honours of every description, which stir up the soul of man to noble deeds—worthy incitements, they have none. The only compensation they can offer for services is money; and the only distinction—the only means of raising himself above his fellows left to the American —is wealth; consequently, the acquisition of wealth has become the great spring of action.

The American government has steadily degenerated since the administrations of Washington and must do so because "as men increase and multiply so do they deteriorate; the closer they are packed the more vicious they become." [54]

Perhaps the most amusing anecdote supposed to illustrate the viciousness of egalitarianism is by Richard Parkinson "late of Orange Hill, near Baltimore," who complained in 1805: "I have been obliged to clean my own boots and shoes when I have had four servants in the house; and myself, wife, and family, have risen in a morning to milk the cows when our servants were in bed. I should term such very bad management in England; but the idea of liberty and equality . . . destroys all the rights of the master, and every man does as he likes. Even taking fruit from your garden, or orchard, is not looked upon as a theft." [55] And possibly the profoundest remark in this library is one by Alexander Mackay: "Liberty in England has been wrung from power—power in America has arisen out of liberty. In the one case, power has been fettered that freedom might expand; in the other, freedom has been restricted that power might exist." [56]

These passages are from "anti-American" books. Many British commentators—for example, Birkbeck, Hodgson, the cantankerous William Cobbett, and Andrew Melish— were more sympathetic, and Continental travelers as a whole probably tended to be less negative in their attitudes: after all, they had not lost a colonial empire. Characteristic of the enthusiasts are the Marquis de Chastellux and perhaps Volney. Such is the present happiness of America, wrote Chastellux of the 1780s, "that she has no poor, that every man in it enjoys a certain ease and independence, and that if some have been able to obtain a smaller portion of them than others, they are so surrounded by resources, that the future is more looked to, than their present situation. Such is the general tendency to a state of equality; that the same enjoyments which would be doomed superfluous in every other part of the world, are here considered necessaries." [57] Volney, though he had grave doubts about the Americans after he ran into the anti-French fever of 1798, wrote nevertheless: "France, and indeed Europe in general, presented to my view nothing but a gloomy and tempestuous prospect. . . . Here I beheld nothing but a splendid prospect of future peace and happiness, flowing from the wide extent of improveable territory; from the facility of procuring property in land; from the necessity and the profits of labour; from the liberty of action and industry; and from the equity of the government, a virtue to which it owes its very weakness." [58] There were other speculative Frenchmen and some Germans, but the appearance of Alexis de Tocqueville's *Democracy in America* in 1835 threw all other Continental interpreters of the radical republic in the shade. This great book was quickly made available in a translation (not altogether adequate) by Henry Reeve, and Tocqueville, together with his great successor, Lord Bryce, may be said to have put the philosophic interpretation of the American experiment on a permanent basis. The Civil War raised grave doubts about the permanence of the American federal union, but, the war being won, few there were to doubt that the United States of America was here to stay.[59] The gradual fading out of the reputation of the Americans for being a radical people is a phenomenon of the late nineteenth and the twentieth centuries—perhaps Woodrow Wilson's "New Freedom," perhaps F. D. R.'s "New Deal" marks the twilight of our radical repute, but as long as that reputation lingered, though we might not be a world power, we were a power and a puzzle in the worlds of ideas, politics, and social history.

Republican Culture

I

IN COMPARISON with the modern genius for disaster the damage, dislocation, and death resulting from the tumults and the wars in America between the agitation of 1765 against the Stamp Act and the Whisky Rebellion of 1794 are puny stuff. Even if the time span be extended to include the War of 1812, the total amount of destruction from our point of view remains small. Neither the Revolutionary War nor the Naval War against France, nor the War of 1812, nor the various Indian wars of this period, nor all of them together, accumulated casualties comparable to those of the Peninsular Campaigns of Wellington, Grant's battles in the Wilderness, or any major conflict in World War I or World War II. British and Americans burned each other's towns and houses—Falmouth, Fairfield, Norwalk, Norfolk are examples; the damage done by the War of 1812 included the burning of the public buildings in Washington (and some of the private ones), various conflagrations along the Niagara frontier, and a forgotten amount of suffering and destruction along the western borders of the United States; [1] there were massacres, murders and cases of arson by Indians; but there was no saturation bombing. Civilians were killed, and there were grisly doings in the Wyoming and Cherry Valleys, but the total of civilian deaths was nothing like those incurred during the Battle of London or the wiping out of Hiroshima.

But destruction and dislocation are relative. A population of four million thinly scattered over an enormous area can be as much disturbed by the loss of one hundred thousand and what may seem minor property damage as a population of forty million is by the deaths of hundreds of thousands and the destruction of the central areas of its great cities. It must not be forgotten, moreover, that the American Revolution altered a whole way of life, established a new axis not merely for politics but for culture, and raised an ultimate question: how much of the traditional was to be retained, perhaps in modified form, and how much must be invented? The disappearance of the old regime created a real, if temporary, vacuum which eager theorists wished to fill with a new order of the ages. Sound American doctrine required a turning away from decayed, corrupt, and feudal Europe and the substitution of a republican culture for its outworn traditions. This substitution was the more necessary since, from the resistance to the Stamp Act, the non-importation agreements, and the Revolution through the era of the Napoleonic Wars, normal traffic with Europe was either cut off, rerouted, or disguised.

Nor should it be forgotten that the steady depreciation of colonial currency in the absence of hard money, and the even greater depreciation of continental paper money increased the difficulties of exchange. During the Revolution, Boston, New York, Newport, Philadelphia, Charleston, and Savannah were besieged, beleaguered, or occupied alternately by mutually hostile armies, the officers of which were anxious to ferret out supporters of the other side, while private soldiers looted in the best manner of eighteenth-century pillage. In such a center as New York, while it was occupied by the British, there was a feverish prosperity which included the importation of luxury goods and printed books, but generally in these port towns, centers of cultural activity as they were, normal business was strangely altered, education

lagged (and in some cases virtually vanished), religion suffered because churches were destroyed, subjected to vandal-
ism, or used for stables, hospitals, or other secular purpose,
and the ordinary practice of law, medicine, and the fine arts
was either stopped or made difficult. Libraries were scattered,
paintings ripped up, and buildings were burned or suffered
injury. Immediately after the close of the Revolution there
was the usual postwar boom, but the middle eighties saw a
depression, and the country did not fully recover until Hamilton's financial measures put the republic on a sound money
basis and established a sound national credit. All this does not
mean that those activities we sum up as cultural lay dormant
through these years but it does mean that their ordinary development was deflected.

History being a one-way process, one cannot tell what
would have been true of American growth had the country
not been born in turmoil and had it not had to struggle for
existence during the convulsions of the French Revolution
and the Napoleonic Era. But it is at least illuminating to see
what happened in the lives of certain men of talent who, in
other circumstances, might have developed professional careers, so to speak, in a direct American line. Non-importation agreements and a measure such as the closing of the
port of Boston stopped lawyers like John Adams in mid-
career as rising members of the bar—in Adams' case, to the
benefit of the country. Dr. Joseph Warren, apparently an
excellent physician, neglected medicine to attend to politics
and was killed on Breed's Hill. Timothy Ruggles, the op-
ponent of James Otis and president of the Stamp Act Congress, who practiced law in Sandwich, removed to Hardwick
(near Worcester), supported the royal government, was driven
from Hardwick to Boston, became commander of the Loyal
American Association, lost his estates, and removed to Nova
Scotia in 1783. Benjamin Thompson, born in Woburn, Massachusetts, in 1753, became a country gentleman in Concord,
New Hampshire, was threatened by a mob, turned into a
Tory spy, fled to London in the summer of 1776, and en-

tered upon the scientific career that made him Count Rumford of the Holy Roman Empire and influenced American science only from a distance. Benjamin West went to London at the end of the Seven Years' War, found it comfortable, remained there, and helped young American painters only as they came to him. John Singleton Copley fled from Massachusetts in 1774 when his life had been threatened by a mob in search of a concealed Tory. Thomas Hutchinson, in 1763 "the most influential man in Massachusetts politics," victim of mob violence, went to England in 1774 and never returned. Joseph Galloway, a leading legal luminary in the middle colonies, once associated with Franklin, went to London in 1778, took up religion in his old age, and died in exile. Jonathan Boucher, who thought Annapolis "the genteelest town in North America" and who preached with a pair of pistols on the lectern, was nevertheless driven out of Maryland, spending his later years in philological pursuits in Europe. John Trumbull left the country in 1779, apparently fearing exposure of a doubtful deal in military stores, and in his effort to keep alive engaged in other dubious enterprises made possible by a revolutionary epoch; if he counts in the annals of American art, his career was nevertheless checkered. Charles Willson Peale virtually ceased painting when he accepted a succession of military and civil posts; after the peace, he engraved mezzotints to keep alive.

After writing eight satires against the British, Freneau, returning from the West Indies, was captured by them and almost died on a prison ship in New York harbor. Francis Hopkinson, like Freneau, wrote on the patriot side; the British plundered his house at Bordenton. Timothy Dwight resigned from Yale in 1777 because of the war. Royall Tyler, dramatist and fiction-writer, served intermittently in the American forces and helped to suppress Shays's rebellion; he got around to producing *The Contrast* (1787) only after the liquidation of that uprising. The correspondence of William Bartram the naturalist with his British patron, Dr. John Fothergill, was sadly broken into by hostilities. Dr.

Benjamin Rush, leading medical man, was unhappily involved in a series of quarrels over the management of the American Army and even tried to rid the country of Washington, events that did not stop, but that certainly delayed, his work as a scientist. Jonathan Odell, poet and propagandist, a go-between in the André affair, was compelled to flee to England and eventually settled in New Brunswick. His fellow poet, the engaging Joseph Stansbury, acted as Arnold's agent in opening a treasonable correspondence with the British, tried after the peace to resume life in Philadelphia, was imprisoned, went to New York, then to Nova Scotia, thence to Philadelphia, and in 1793 removed to New York, a loss to imaginative literature. These are representative instances, minor calamities in comparison with the guillotining of Chénier, the suicides of Condillac and Kleist, the duel that killed Pushkin, or the embittered exiles of Byron and Madame de Staël, but such dislocations as these among a small and scattered elite did not make for steady cultural growth, even though some returned; for example, Samuel Seabury, who became the first bishop of the Episcopal Church in the United States, and Thomas Robinson, who, after fleeing to Nova Scotia, came back to spend the rest of his life in Delaware.

These are individual losses or disruptions of what might have been lives of steady growth. But a whole class of the American elite disappeared with the withdrawal of the Loyalists, whose lives were indeed unhappy. I have in the preceding chapter noted characteristic incidents of mob violence directed against the Tories. These could be indefinitely multiplied. In his classic *The Loyalists of the American Revolution*, C. H. Van Tyne devotes a whole chapter entitled "The Inquisition" to the increasing harassment of the Loyalists; equally revealing is Alexander C. Flick's definitive *Loyalism in New York During the American Revolution:* [2] the parallels between American action, legal and illegal, against the Tories, and the actions of the mob and of Committees of Public Safety during the French Revolution against aristocrats are embarrassing to any generous heart. In New York City at one time Tories were tarred and feathered or ridden naked through the streets; for example, Theophilus Hardenbrook, architect and builder, "was taken from his house by a desperate mob, who tore all his clothes from his body, rode him round the city in a cart, pelted and beat him with sticks in so cruel and barbarous a manner that he . . . very nearly had lost his life." [3] In Virginia, after the capture of Norfolk by the militia, when William Donaldson refused to take an oath of allegiance to the state, he was put in jail and his property was plundered; and another Loyalist, who hid his effects in a blacksmith shop, when the fact was discovered, saw his kindly blacksmith tarred and feathered. When General Charles Lee went to Portsmouth, finding that town a "hotbed of Toryism," he forced the inhabitants to abandon it, burned the houses of the more prominent Loyalists, and made one Tory look on while his house went up in smoke. "This step," wrote Lee, "was not quite consistent with the regular mode of proceeding." [4] Loyalists, when opportunity came, retaliated on the rebels, but the rebels had the last word and the several states passed legislation forbidding Tories to practice their professions, teach school, engage in business, collect rent, and so on; and most states banished them and confiscated their real estate and their property; nor, such was the bitterness of feeling, did it prove easy to carry out the terms of the treaty of peace by which the Americans engaged to compensate Loyalists for their losses.

Loyalists, unable to live except under the protection of the British Army and Navy, collected in the ports when these were occupied by the royal forces, but when the troops left, the Loyalists departed also. Thus 1100 Loyalists sailed out of Boston when Howe evacuated that city in March 1776; 3000 left Charleston and 7000 left Savannah (this number included about 5000 Negroes) with the departing British. When the royal forces evacuated Philadelphia, somewhere between 3000 and 3500 Loyalists left with them. The greatest exodus came when the British finally gave up New York City: something over 29,000 Tories sailed away. Statistical accuracy is impossible; many later returned to take up their lives and professions as best they could, and a considerable number of concealed Tories acquiesced in the new order of things and remained. But it is a fair guess that about 75,000 Loyalists were lost to the country. If not all of them belonged to the elite, it is probable that a majority of them were from the upper class, as is evidenced by their successful new careers in the Maritime Provinces, Ontario, the West Indies, and Great Britain. Thus a study of the Loyalists of Massachusetts and their claims shows that the exiles numbered about 200 Harvard graduates, including 28 Harvard lawyers, and leading physicians, surgeons, apothecaries, teachers, merchants, printers, and military men. Examination of the 38 portraits reproduced in the monograph suggests that the originals were persons of culture. Some fifty women were included, and 200 merchant families went into exile.[5] Besides the Tory families in Philadelphia proper, some two-thirds of those "attainted" by Pennsylvania legislation were land-owners in the eastern counties, their families being connected with Philadelphia merchants.[6] At the beginning of the war there were about 300 Anglican parishes in America; though complaint was made of the laziness and indifference of some Anglican clergymen, the group as a whole was an educated clerisy, many of whose members fled the country. One analysis of New York Tories distinguishes seven classes: royal officials; landed proprietors and their tenants; professional men; wealthy merchants; wealthy conservative farmers; colonial politicians; and conservatives of various grades. Another, stipulating that the aristocracy of culture in that state was largely Tory, sets up categories of office-holding Tories; persons whose friends were among the official class; the Anglican clergy; the dynastic Tory (comparable to the Jacobite); "legality" Tories, who held that parliament had a perfect right to tax the colonies; religious Tories of the "fear God and honor the king" persuasion; and factional Tories—in New York, likely to be members of the De Lancey party.[7] In any event the departure of so many of the elite * altered the course of American cultural development.

The Loyalist diaspora was not, however, the sole setback to a developing nation; there was in addition the loss of the physical instruments of culture. Tory printing presses were destroyed by mob action. Tory libraries were scattered. † Furniture, clothing, tableware, and pictures were destroyed or disappeared. Even the gardens of Newport were not safe, for they were plundered by British soldiers, whose wives sold their products, since the British regulars held all Americans in contempt.[8] And of course Loyalists were not the sole sufferers. In November 1777, the British, in occupation of Philadelphia, burned a number of fine houses north of the city on the excuse that they sheltered Americans: Deborah Logan counted seventeen such fires from the roof of her house in Chestnut Street. When the Americans re-entered the city after the British evacuated it,

> What sights met their eyes! The trees were destroyed on all sides; churches and public buildings defiled—they had been used as stables for the horses; camp litter and filth everywhere; fences broken; houses quite down or robbed of their doors, windows, roofs and floors; gardens and orchards trampled up and ruined. All kinds of movable property such as furniture, machinery, books, clothing and tools were destroyed or stolen, if they had been left behind by their Whig owners. The State House was in such a "filthy and sordid situation" that Congress, when it returned, was obliged to meet in the College hall. The country northward for several miles, particularly by reason of the depredations of the Hessians, was "one common waste." The "dirt, filth, stench and flies in and about the town," said Christopher Marshall upon re-entering it, on June 24, were "scarcely credible." [9]

---

* In this discussion I have used the terms "Tory" and "Loyalist" interchangeably, though I am aware that some scholars make a technical distinction between them.

† Joseph Hooper of Marblehead lost five hundred volumes when he was forced to flee from his "elegant mansion" built only eighteen months earlier; Charles Paxton, James Putnam, and William Latta, all of Massachusetts, mourned the loss of libraries, as did, of course, Governor Hutchinson.

Tory estates and houses were promptly confiscated or sold, if this had not already been done, and flirtatious young ladies who had perhaps danced at the Mischianza were severely condemned by a society which put prominent Quakers under guard.

New York suffered even more severely. In April 1775, the British warship *Asia* fired some random shots into the town; two weeks afterward at least one-third of the citizens had fled with their household goods; and when General Charles Lee arrived with the vanguard of the American Army in 1776, he met scores of refugees hastening north. The city heard nothing but the rumbling of carts over the pavements, the shouts of men, and the sounds of flight. New York was nearly deserted, most of the houses empty and locked. By and by the British moved in; despite orders, the soldiers broke into the houses of the rich, and as one reporter wrote: "Oh, the houses in New York, if you could but see the insides of them, occupied by the dirtiest people on the continent! If the owners ever get possession again, I am sure they must be years in cleaning them." In that year a fire broke out that destroyed one-quarter of the city—the estimate is 500 houses—and could not be controlled because there were no fire brigades; and in 1778 another fire destroyed 64 houses and £250,000 worth of property. Trinity Church burned, so did others; most of the remaining churches, the college, and the public buildings were occupied by cavalry horses or served as hospitals or as prisons.[10]

British soldiers broke into the New York City Hall, where the books and apparatus of King's College (Columbia) had been stored, and plundered it; the president, Myles Cooper, had fled in May 1775, before the Sons of Liberty. The last colonial commencement at Harvard was held in 1771. There was not another public ceremony for ten years, and during the siege of Boston the buildings were commandeered for military purposes and, when classes were resumed, remained in a forlorn condition for a long time; there were constant shortages of textbooks and frequent enforced "vacations."

Yale was in difficulties throughout the revolution. At Princeton, Nassau Hall was severely damaged during the Trenton-Princeton fights and served for a barracks and a hospital. Loyalist trustees of the College of Philadelphia were dismissed and the charter of the institution revoked. William and Mary suffered on several occasions, especially when it was occupied by the soldiers of Cornwallis and when it served as a military hospital. Libraries were also damaged. Thus the Redwood Library in Newport lost half its books, and in New York, besides the loss of the college library, the collections of the Corporation Library, the New York Society Library, and the Union Library were scattered. One severe handicap now too often forgotten was the paper shortage. Papermills had been scarce, the importation of paper difficult and expensive, papermakers had enlisted in the Continental forces or run off with the Loyalists, and paper was so scarce as to handicap military operations because written orders could not always be sent as they should be and also because of the lack of paper for cartridges. Small wonder that the number of American imprints decreased from 1775 to 1782, that John Adams sent a few sheets of writing paper from Philadelphia to Abigail in Braintree as a rare gift, or that as late as 1783 the journals of the assembly of North Carolina could not be published because there was nothing to print them on.[11]

It was hard to get into focus Turgot's statement to Dr. Price in 1778 that the American people were the hope of the human race, and the brute fact of an outbreak in New York on July 4, 1788, between the Federalists and the anti-Federalists over ratifying the new Constitution, in which men fought one another with swords, bayonets, clubs, and stones, killing one rioter and wounding eighteen others; or the enthusiastic reception of the news of ratification July 24, 1788, when the Federalists went to the home of the editor of the *Journal,* the organ of Governor Clinton, smashed the windows, carried off the type, surrounded the governor's home (he was absent) and beat the rogue's march to indicate their republicanism.[12] Something had to intervene.

II

What intervened was a negative force and a positive theory.

When the British finally departed, taking the Hessians with them (excepting those in both armies, deserters, prisoners, or soldiers, their enlistments having expired, who elected to remain), they left behind them an emotional legacy developed during ten years of quarreling with the mother country and seven years of civil war. The French enjoyed their day of popularity, particularly the gallant young officers who were so polite and so "republican," but their going relieved the Americans of the burden of feeding and quartering the troops, not to speak of the eternal sexual problems associated with armies. The bitterness between Whig and Tory did not cease with the peace, but on the contrary seemed momentarily to increase; and household after household could tell of brothers divided, of hostile allegiances, of quarrels over property and inheritance made the more distasteful by the peace treaty and by the fact that some of the "traitors" returned to regain what they had lost. The popularity of France, moreover, except among a hard core of enthusiasts, rapidly diminished with the execution of Louis XVI and Marie Antoinette, the horrors of the September massacres and the Reign of Terror, the arrogance of Citizen Genêt, the XYZ affair, the Naval War with France, and the unpredictable demands of a nation that changed its form of government fourteen times in twenty-six years. Nor were American emotions altogether soothed by the commercial depression of the mid-eighties, which was blamed on Europe and concerning which Tench Coxe wrote in 1787:

The commercial citizens of America have for some time felt the deepest distress. Among the principal causes of their unhappy situation were the inconsiderate spirit of adventure in this country, which pervaded almost every kingdom in Europe, and the prodigious credits from thence given to our merchants on the return of peace. To these may be added the high spirits and the golden dreams, which naturally followed such a war, closed with so much honor and peace.—Triumphant over a great enemy, courted by the most powerful nations in the world, it was not in human nature that America should immediately comprehend her new situation. Really possessed of the means of future greatness, she anticipated the most distant benefits of the revolution, and considered them as already in her hands.[13]

Tormented by rebellion, Indian warfare, the refusal of the British to evacuate posts on the frontier, the ingratitude and instability of France, and the indifference or helplessness of Holland and Spain, the Americans had somehow to canalize their bitterness and disillusion, and it is not surprising that a hatred of monarchy, a distrust of Europe, a kind of vague, yet powerful xenophobia, overran not only the country but its leaders as well.

It was perhaps to be expected that the great propagandist of the Revolution, Tom Paine, should view monarchy as founded in delusion and call it accursed of God, and declare that since the Norman Conquest thirty kings and two minors had reigned in England, during which time there had been no less than eight civil wars and nineteen rebellions, whereas the republics of Europe were always at peace. The argument, if it be one, stuck; it was reinforced by the vehement rhetoric of *The Rights of Man*—"It was not against Louis XVI, but against the despotic principles of the government, that the nation revolted"; "the idea of hereditary legislators is as inconsistent as that of hereditary judges, or hereditary juries"; "by engendering the church with the state, a sort of mule-animal, capable only of destroying, and not of breeding up, is produced"; "the difference between a republican and a courtier with respect to monarchy, is, that the one opposes monarchy, believing it to be something, and the other laughs at it, knowing it to be nothing"; "Mr. Burke talks about what he calls an hereditary crown, as if it were some production of nature"; "when we survey the wretched condition of man under the monarchical and hereditary system of government, dragged from his home by one power, or driven by another, and impoverished by taxes more than by enemies, it becomes evident that those systems are bad, and that a general revolution in the principle and construction of governments is necessary." [14] Paine was not sole and singular in his opinions.

Thomas Jefferson, who came to understand France more thoroughly than Paine ever did, declared that the European nations "seemed . . . to know little about us, but as rebels," lamented that the French theory of limited monarchy eventuated in "thirty years of war, foreign and domestic, the loss of millions of lives, the prostration of private happiness, and foreign subjugation of their own country"—an "atrocious conspiracy of Kings against their people"—dismissed monarchies as "a government of wolves over sheep," and advised young Americans to stay at home, or if they must visit European courts, see them "as you would see the tower of London or menagerie of Versailles with their lions, tigers, hyenas, and other beasts of prey, standing in the same relation to their fellows." The French, he thought, were essentially good, but "of twenty millions of people supposed to be in France, I am of opinion there are nineteen millions more wretched, more accursed in every circumstance of human existence than the most conspicuously wretched individual of the whole United States." He was equally denunciatory in another passage written that same year (1785), already quoted; and in a solemn letter written in his old age to the President of the United States (James Monroe) Jefferson insisted that the United States should stay away from all things European.[15] Yet he was one of the most cosmopolitan-minded geniuses of his age.

John Adams was of like opinion. Recording in his diary a long conversation between Mr. Whitefoord, secretary to Oswald, one of the peace commissioners, and himself, he wrote:

> For my own part, I thought America had been long enough involved in the wars of Europe. She had been a foot-ball between contending nations from the beginning, and it was very easy to foresee that France and England both would endeavor

to involve us in their future wars. . . . That my thoughts had been from the beginning constantly employed to arrange all our European connections to this end [i.e., of independence] and that they would continue to be so employed.

A week later he had a conversation with Oswald, who asked him if he was afraid of being the tool of the powers of Europe.

"Indeed I am," says I. "What powers?" said he. "All of them," said I. "It is obvious that all the powers of Europe will be continually manoeuvring with us, to work us into their real or imaginary balance of power. They will all wish to make of us a make-weight candle, when they are weighing out their pounds. Indeed, it is not surprising; for we shall very often, if not always, be able to turn the scale. But I think it ought to be our rule not to meddle; and that of all the powers of Europe, not to desire us, or, perhaps, even permit us, to interfere, if they can help it." [16]

Abigail Adams' disgust with the manners of the French ladies is one of the most notable things in her correspondence.

One did not have to live in Europe, however, to distrust Europeans. Alexander Hamilton, who never set foot in Europe, in a debate in the New York Assembly about the taxing powers of the Confederation, warned that body: "Wars with each other would beget standing armies—a source of more real danger to our liberties than all the power that could be conferred upon the representatives of the union. And wars with each other would lead to opposite alliances with foreign powers, and plunge us into all the labyrinths of European politics." This argument he repeated in a speech in the Constitutional Convention on June 29, 1787, and in his contributions to *The Federalist* based his plea for a strong central government on his profound distrust of Europe. The world, he said, is divided into four parts.

Unhappily for the other three, Europe by her arms and her negociations, by force and by fraud, has, in different degrees extended her dominion over them all. Africa, Asia, and America have successively felt her domination. The superiority, she has long maintained, has tempted her to plume herself as the Mistress of the World, and to consider the rest of mankind as created for her benefit. Men admired as profound philosophers have, in direct terms, attributed to her inhabitants a physical superiority; and have gravely asserted that all animals, and with them, the human species, degenerate in America—that even dogs cease to bark after having breathed a while in our atmosphere. . . . It belongs to us to vindicate the honor of the human race, and to teach that assuming brother moderation. . . . Let Americans disdain to be the instruments of European greatness! [17]

And James Madison held a similar opinion, for he wrote in *The Federalist,* No. 46, January 29, 1788:

But were the people to possess the additional advantages of local government chosen by themselves, who could collect the national will, and direct the national force; and of officers appointed out of the militia, by these governments and attached both to them and to the militia, it may be affirmed with the greatest assurance, that the throne of every tyranny in Europe would be speedily overturned, in spite of the legions which surround it.[18]

The classic final statement of anti-Europeanism was Washington's Farewell Address:

Against the insidious wiles of foreign influence, (I conjure you to believe me, fellow citizens) the jealousy of a free people ought to be *constantly* awake; since history and experience prove that foreign influence is one of the most baneful foes of Republican Government. But that jealousy to be useful must be impartial. . . . The Great rule of conduct for us, in regard to foreign Nations is in extending our commercial relations to have with them as little *political* connection as possible. . . . Europe has a set of primary interests, which to us have none, or a very remote relation. . . . Hence therefore it must be unwise in us to implicate ourselves, by artificial ties, in the ordinary vicissitudes of her politics, or the ordinary combinations and collisions of her friendships, or enmities: Our detached and distant situation invites and enables us to pursue a

different course. . . . Why forego the advantages of so peculiar a situation? Why quit our own to stand upon foreign
ground? Why, by interweaving our destiny with that of any
part of Europe, entangle our peace and prosperity to the toils
of European Ambition, Rivalship, Interest, Humour or Ca-
price? [19]

III

What the Americans attempted to substitute in place of
the vanished Loyalist elite and the Europe they repudiated
was a doctrine of republican culture that rested upon a group
of confused and confusing ideas, three of which were, certainly, that, the United States being a republic, it must
cherish frugality and simplicity, that the healthiest basis of
life was agrarianism, and that the country was as a matter of
course the hope of the human race. Much had vanished besides the Loyalists—the crown, royal and proprietary governments, feudal (manorial) holdings (some were to linger in
New York), a system of quitrents that implied tenure, the
legality of entail and primogeniture, and an established
church.[20] Aristocratic or minority control of public life,
though it lingered in some of the Southern states and for a
time in Massachusetts, New York, Rhode Island, and Connecticut, weakened and disappeared with the adoption of
popular constitutions which, despite some property qualifications for the franchise, became more and more democratic as
these were amended or replaced. But the control of culture by
the common man, though it seemed to have a kind of triumph
in the Jacksonian period,[21] ran into a good many difficulties,
and during the years from 1775 to 1837 (the end of Jackson's
second term), the doctrine of republican culture collided with
two fundamental components of Western civilization: culture
requires a leisure class for its development, yet a leisure class
was not necessarily produced by the American farming system
(except in the South); and the Americans, despite brave pro-

nouncements that they had repudiated Europe, could not escape history. They were part of the Western world. Kicked out of the door, Europe crept back through the window. The Americans might avoid entangling alliances with monarchies; they might under John Quincy Adams and James Monroe, his Secretary of State, insist after the Congress of Vienna that American political institutions were unique and non-European, and demand the end of further "imperialism" in the New World, but they could not invent a new language, a new system of laws, new educational institutions, a new philosophy, and new forms of literature and the arts that would not be tainted with the profligacy and politics they were pleased to attribute to the Old World. But they tried.

Scores of theorists laid down philosophical principles, but because he was part European, part American, Crèvecœur, who called himself J. Hector St. John, is characteristic and revealing. His *Letters from an American Farmer* is a classic in this category. He admits that life on the frontier does not produce the best Americans—for that you had better go to Nantucket, where a barren waste has been turned into a prosperous community—but when he comes to define the American as "a new man, who acts upon new principles" and must therefore "entertain new ideas and form new opinions," he insists that though "good and evil . . . are to be found in all societies," he can thank God that his lot is to be an American farmer instead of a Russian boor or a Hungarian peasant. On American agriculture "is founded our rank, our freedom, our power, as citizens; our importance, as inhabitants." Among other blessings the plentifulness of land cools the flame of sectarianism: "if the sectaries are not settled close together, if they are mixed with other denominations, their zeal will cool for want of fuel, and will be extinguished in a little while." Look now upon this picture, then on this:

> Europe contains hardly any other distinctions but lords and tenants; this fair country alone is settled by freeholders, the

possessors of the soil they cultivate, members of the government they obey, and the framers of their own laws, by means of their representatives . . . our distance from Europe, far from diminishing, rather adds to, our usefulness and consequence as men and subjects. Had our forefathers remained there, they would only have crouded it, and perhaps prolonged those convulsions which had shaken it so long. Ye poor Europeans, ye, who sweat, and work for the great; ye, who are obliged to give so many sheaves to the church, so many to your government, and have hardly any left for yourselves; ye, who are held in less estimation than favourite hunters or useless lap-dogs; ye, who only breathe the air of nature, because it cannot be withholden from you; it is here that ye can conceive the possibility of those feelings I have been describing; it is here the laws of naturalization invite every one to partake of our great labours and felicity, to till unrented, untaxed lands!

And finally, the European

sees the industry of his native country displayed in a new manner, and traces, in their works, the embryos of all the arts, sciences, and ingenuity, which flourish in Europe. Here he beholds fair cities, substantial villages, extensive fields, an immense country filled with decent houses, good roads, orchards, meadows, and bridges, where, a hundred years ago, all was wild, woody, and uncultivated. . . . He is arrived on a new continent: a modern society offers itself to his contemplation, different from what he had hitherto seen. It is not composed, as in Europe, of great lords who possess every thing, and of a herd of people who have nothing. Here are no aristocratical families, no courts, no kings, no bishops, no ecclesiastical dominions, no invisible power giving to a few a very visible one, no great manufactures employing thousands, no great refinements of luxury. . . . Lawyer or merchant are the fairest titles our towns afford: that of a farmer is the only appellation of the rural inhabitants of our country. . . . Here man is free as he ought to be. . . . Many ages will not see the shores of our great lakes replenished with inland nations, nor the unknown bounds of North America entirely peopled. . . . Every thing has tended to regenerate them, New laws, a new mode of living, a new social system.[22]

I add from Tench Coxe an important component of this theory, which is implicit in Crèvecœur but not as directly expressed. Coxe protests against the "extravagant and wasteful use of foreign manufactures [since the close of the Revolution]. They have been so cheap, so plenty, and so easily obtained on credit, that the consumption of them has been absolutely wanton. . . . [But] our dresses, furniture and carriages would be fashionable, because they were American and proper in our situation, not because they were foreign, shewy or expensive," if home manufactures were more generally used. It is chiefly in the towns, not on the farms that this "madness for foreign finery rages and destroys"; wherefore "it behoves us to consider our untimely passion for European luxuries as a malignant and alarming symptom, threatening convulsions and dissolution to the political body." [23] The revolt from the village—and the farm—is still many decades in the future. Typical of average opinion was Estwick Evans, who took "a pedestrious tour" through the Western states and territories in 1818. From his account I select three characteristic statements:

> The United States is the place, above all others, for correct opinions, upon questions involved in the great science of morals, as far as it respects the natural rights of individuals, the necessary modification of those rights in civil society, and the rights of nations as collective moral agents. Europe has been, and still is a school of wrong; and those who are instructed by her participate in the sophistry of her reasoning, the tyranny of her views, and the inconsistency of her practice.

> Agriculture is the most natural, necessary, and honourable employment of man. Ignorant pride and vain folly may represent it as derogatory; but in so doing they show how very far they are from true greatness. Agriculture furnishes for vigorous constitutions the most salutary exercise; and here the brightest geniuses may find ample employment.—An unlimited field for experiment in many branches of natural philosophy is here presented, and there is no sphere of life so well calculated as this to practice individual virtue and public advantage.

How wonderfully impressive is the prospect, which this country represents to the politician, during his cogitation upon our remote destinies! Every thing is conspiring to render the United States far more populous than Europe. In the course of a few hundred years all that is great, and splendid will characterize us.—The arts of Greece, the arms of Rome, the pride of England will be ours. May God avert the rest! [24]

But how begin establishing the arts of Greece, the arms of Rome, and the pride of England? One obvious place was the national language, which was, unfortunately, also the language of George III. Absurd stories circulated about the desirability of doing away with English and substituting a language compounded from the Indian tongues, or of using Hebrew, or Greek, or Latin. These seem to have been mainly gossip, but the problem of English was taken seriously—as it still is, if the hot debate over the most recent edition of *Webster's International Dictionary* is evidence. If the Americans continued to accept English models, would they not be influenced by corrupt monarchical ideas? Among those who thought so was Noah Webster, in many respects the heir of Benjamin Franklin. He wrote John Canfield from Goshen, New York, January 6, 1783, that a reformation of the language was absolutely necessary, since "an attention to literature [by which the age meant any formal composition] must be the principal bulwark against the encroachments of civil and ecclesiastical tyrants, and American Liberty can die only with her *Maecenases*." He wrote Jedidiah Morse from New Haven, March 6, 1806, that "the time will come when our citizens will not think themselves obliged to receive English opinions, right or wrong; when that time shall arrive, I know not; but perhaps it is time to make a stand on the subject of language." And he wrote Joel Barlow from the same town on November 12, 1807, that he had it in view "to detach this country as much as possible from its dependence on the parent country . . . I consider this species of dependence as extremely prejudicial as it regards our political interest in a variety of ways," since if you make English books the standard of truth on all subjects, this *"checks improvement,"* this "puts an *end to inquiry."* Others—for example, an un-known correspondent of Governor Wentworth of New Hamp-shire in 1772/4, and John Adams in 1780—proposed an academy to control the language, since it is "impossible for us to form an idea of the perfection, the beauty, the grandeur, and the sublimity, to which our language may arrive in the progress of time, passing through the improving tongues of our rising posterity." Still others—for example, a contributor to the *Royal American Magazine* in January 1774—felt that though the English language had "greatly improved" in Britain, yet "its highest perfection with every other branch of human knowledge is perhaps reserved for the land of light and freedom," meaning America.

Franklin apparently thought the Americans should insti-tute spelling reform, an experiment that Webster tried for a time, succeeding so far as to take the *u* out of such words as *honour* and in fixing certain other changes, and Noah Web-ster agreed that a new country under a new government "will produce, in the course of time, a language in North America as different from the future language of England as the mod-ern Dutch, Spanish, and Swedish are from the German or from one another." "I have too much pride," he said, "to stand indebted to Great Britain for books to learn [*sic!*] our children the letters of the alphabet." His life became a battle and a march for an American language. He published in 1783 his famous blueback speller, from which all un-Americanisms had been carefully removed (his model was Dilworth the Briton) and which, aided by that especially American institu-tion the spelling-bee, as late as 1875 in its newest version was selling more than a million copies a year; he got out his *Dis-sertations on the English Language* (1789), intended, among other aims, "to draw the outlines of a system better adapted to our forms of government; and to detach Americans from the dependence on foreign opinions and manners, which is fatal to the efforts of genius in this country"; and he pub-lished in two volumes in 1828 *An American Dictionary of the*

English Language (which, by an odd irony, he finished in Cambridge, England) because, as he said, "the differences in the language of the two countries will continue to multiply, and render it necessary that we should have *Dictionaries of the American language*."

Why were not Franklin and Irving as good "authorities" as any British writers? Was not style, at least among the educated classes, purer in the United States than it was abroad? Webster also printed an *American Selection of Lessons in Reading and Speaking* (1785), but schoolteachers preferred such books as Caleb Bingham's *The American Preceptor* (1795), which exhibited an even greater predilection for the "productions of American genius." Noah Webster and his generation inaugurated arguments over the national language that have never died out; and Henry James's *The Question of Our Speech* (1905) and Mencken's *The American Language* (1919 *et seq.*) are merely the heirs of the argument.[25] Characteristic of its earlier stage was the epigraph from Mirabeau which Webster prefixed to his reader: "Begin with the Infant in his Cradle: Let the first Word he Lisps be Washington." The search for an American language seems less absurd when one remembers that in the Western world at that time the relation of language to reason and to nationality was a leading problem: witness Herder's *Ueber den Ursprung der Sprache* (1772), Bentham's campaign for a reform of legal language (1789–1802), Horne Tooke's odd book, *The Diversions of Purley* (1786–1805), and the first researches of Jacob Grimm (1811) and Franz Bopp (1816).

The problem of an American language was complex; the problem of American law was even more complicated. The colonials had imported English common law, statutory law, royal charters, and ecclesiastical law, or turned hostile to one or more of these concepts, and in New England the concept of human law was made subordinate for a while to divine legislation based on biblical precepts. Seventeenth-century development offered innumerable opportunities to ignore, evade, reinterpret, or supersede charter and statute. There were few lawyers and few law books, and the law in any formal sense was virtually a monopoly of the governing elite in most colonies. Colonial judges were more likely to be laymen than learned jurists. By the middle of the eighteenth century, however, the legal profession was relatively established. There was a short-lived legal association in New York after 1748, an increasing number of American members of the Inns of Court after 1750, and a Massachusetts Bar Association after 1761.

This history should not be interpreted to mean that the earlier colonials were naïve about the law.[26] But by the third quarter of the eighteenth century American legal needs had developed sufficiently to make the nature of law a central issue, as increased wealth, questionable land titles, problems of inheritance and contract, the entailing of estates, and other issues developed, the solution of which must be either referred to England or worked out in North America. Consequently one finds such men as James Otis, John Adams, and George Wythe embarking upon professional legal careers. But law books and professional treatises remained scarce or amateurish, despite Burke's affirmation that in no country, perhaps, elsewhere in the world was the law so generally studied; and the extraordinary vogue of Blackstone's *Commentaries* (scarcely sympathetic to American revolutionary theory), the first American edition of which was printed in Philadelphia in 1771–1772, is probably due to the necessity of filling a vacuum. In the profoundest sense the Revolution was not merely a quarrel over the legal powers of king, Parliament, and colonies, it was an attempt to institute in the New World a fresh doctrine of the law, as James Wilson pointed out in his lectures on law (1790–1791) before the College of Pennsylvania. He said:

> But law and liberty cannot rationally become the objects of our love, unless they first become the objects of our knowledge. . . . Indeed, neither of them can be known, because neither of them can exist, without the other. Without liberty, law loses its nature and its name, and becomes oppression. Without law,

liberty also loses its nature and its name, and becomes licentiousness. . . .

And he continued:

For the western world, new and rich discoveries in jurisprudence have been reserved. We have found that, in order to arrive, in this first of human sciences, at a point of perfection hitherto unattained, it is not necessary to intermix the different species of government. We have discovered, that one of them —the best and purest—that, in which the supreme power remains with the people at large, is capable of being formed, arranged, proportioned, and organized in such a manner, as to exclude the inconveniences, and to secure the advantages of all the three (monarchical, aristocratical, and democratical forms). On the basis of goodness, we erect the pillars of wisdom and strength.[27]

This was all very well as theory which later political scientists were to endorse,[28] but the actual situation, complicated by the depreciation of the currency, the increase in the debtor class, and the disappearance of British credits, involved the closing of courts, the abolition of customary legal procedures, and, among the unthinking, the populist attitude that laws, lawyers, and courts were a nuisance left over from royal servitude or that law was something for the legislature to enact at the dictate of the sovereign people. Enthusiasts wanted to repudiate English law; other enthusiasts wanted to know why a republic should fall back upon legal precedents emanating from a tyrannical monarchy. Distrust of lawyers was endemic in the western counties of the several states and on the frontiers; on the other hand the frontiersman admired "smartness," new states required new constitutions and new statutes, and the lawyer-politician type rose to great influence. Meanwhile, in the general tohu-bohu, judges during the Revolution and after, since they had to turn somewhere, turned to English law to justify their decisions; the result was that curious mixture of English precedent [29] and republican innovation we now take for granted. By and by John Marshall was to take advantage of a novel form of republican government to inaugurate or fortify the doctrine of federal judicial review.

Americans, or at any rate some Americans, were loath to believe that the common law could be integrated into a republican system. In Connecticut, when Joel Barlow came up for examination before a group of lawyers in 1786, though he admitted that the English law had once been common sense, he argued that new conditions meant a new theory of legality.[30] In Pennsylvania a legislative statute of 1807 prohibited attorneys from reading in court any precedent or case decided outside the United States; and when this was vetoed by the governor, a second legislative act (1810) made it unlawful to quote in any court any British precedent or adjudication since the Declaration of Independence—a concept that did not endure. In Philadelphia Joseph Hopkins had published in 1809 his *Considerations on the Abolition of the Common Law in the United States*. Virginia in 1792, New Jersey in 1799, and Kentucky in 1808 voted that no parliamentary statute should have force, though they seem to have accepted the precedency of the common law; whether the two ideas might be in conflict was something for lawyers and judges to work out. By authority of the Northwest Ordinance, Ohio in 1795 accepted the common law, and reaffirmed this action in 1802 and again in 1805, but in 1806 the legislature repealed the statute, and much was said about "tyranny." The upshot of the whole controversy was a pragmatic compromise: English common law was accepted in the new republic where its acceptance, by and large, made sense and could be fused with a doctrine of republican virtue. By 1807 the *American Register* could declare that "the law is a very prosperous and gainful occupation in the United States. It has probably a greater number of votaries, in proportion to the whole community, than in any other country," and lawyers, legislatures, judges, and the more intelligent part of the community had accepted that illogical but working compromise between English precedents and the American system that we have with us to this hour.[31]

In the area of religion the innovations of republican culture can be quickly summarized: the federal Constitution forced the separation of church and state, and such established churches as there had been in the several states disappeared one by one after 1776. Disestablishment was made easier by the growing secularism of the later eighteenth century, by the deliquescence of hard-core Calvinism, despite the Great Awakening of 1726–1756, by the obvious fact that the Anglican Church could not continue as such after independence, by the losses suffered by church property during the period of warfare, and by the probability that the majority of Americans in 1776 were not members of any organized church, though not therefore necessarily hostile to religion. To some patriots "free thought" seemed a necessary component of republican theory in view of the "tyranny" of established churches in Europe, and for a time deism seemed to offer brilliant promise of a new belief for the New World. Despite the deistic outlook of a good many American leaders, deism weakened and virtually vanished in the reaction against the excesses of the French Revolution—what G. Adolf Koch has called the triumph of fidelity.[32] Despite the heroic past of the Catholic missionary movement, Roman Catholicism remained a negligible factor in the first shaping of American religious life.

But if there was no formal republican "church," the profound alteration of the church-state relationship helped create a special national religious life. The churches—until the 1840s overwhelmingly Protestant—had to support themselves and any theological schools, academies, colleges, and publishing ventures they might care to create; what they secured from government was mainly freedom from taxation, charters for religious establishments, schools, and so on, preferential treatment in minor matters connected with the tariff, and of course the right to hold property, a right commonly exercised by the laity. The Roman Catholic hierarchy insisted that parochial trusteeism would not do, and Bishop England's invention of a diocesan board as a kind of working compro-

O STRANGE NEW WORLD

mise between democracy and the hierarchy did not survive him.[33] Of more immediate importance is the American insistence upon religion as an individual experience: the Americans changed their church memberships, invented new religions,* set up standards for theological training (or denied that any standards were necessary), and formed national associations for religious purposes (such as the American Bible Society in 1816, and the American Sunday-School Union in 1817) in an astonishing degree. Since the nation was Protestant, despite the constitutional separation of church and state, trustees of state universities, especially in the South, gave these institutions a Protestant religious coloring, dropping "unbelievers" from the faculty and requiring a sound Christian moralism in the classroom. The same thing was true of academies supported at public expense and of the public schools, nor has the puzzle been solved to everybody's satisfaction in our own time. Atheists apparently cannot be elected to public office in the United States, no President of which has failed to belong to some religious denomination; and if there is a half-truth in Henry James's observation that "the field of American life is as bare of the Church as a billiard table of a centerpiece," the counter balancing half-truth is that mass revivalism as practiced by Charles G. Finney, Moody and Sankey, Billy Sunday, and the Reverend William Graham is virtually an American invention.[34] But I can here merely suggest some of the consequences of the separation of church and state in the United States, adjuring the interested

---

* One curious aspect of the doctrine that in America religion could be started all over again was the arrival in New York in 1774 of Ann Lee and twenty followers calling themselves the United Society of Believers in Christ's Second Appearing. Ann Lee made converts, set up several communities, including one at Harvard, Massachusetts, and induced her followers to take up sacred dancing and abandon sex. These were the Shakers. But Shaker harmony was destroyed by the appearance of one Jemima Wilkinson, known as the Public Universal Friend. The Public Universal Friend got involved with a wealthy judge, founded a community called Jerusalem on Seneca Lake, helped herself to anything she wanted, saying "The Friend hath need of these things," and died in 1819, after which her colony disintegrated.

reader to consult a vast literature on the history of religion in America.[35]

The problem of republican education was also baffling. The United States is supposed to be the original home of the public-school system and to have developed that equally peculiar institution the state university, and the origins of the first of these have been traced back to the "Old Deluder" law in Massachusetts Bay, whereby every town was required to establish a school (1647).[36] But the law was evaded as often as possible,[37] and in any real sense the obligation of the state to make education accessible to all had to await the nineteenth century for fulfillment.[38] The colonial colleges did a good deal to prepare the way for the Revolution: a historian of higher education in America declares that out of about 2500 college graduates alive in 1775 about one-quarter entered military service,[39] and an analysis of 50 leaders of thought and action (on both sides) shows that only 17 had no higher education and that out of 43 with some chance for it, 26 (or more than half) were products of the colonial colleges, and most of the others were probably tutored by college personnel. William and Mary and Princeton were notable for the graduates they contributed to the revolutionary cause. We smile at the high-sounding phraseology common to academic charters; that for Brown University (as it became), granted in 1764, reads, for example: "Institutions of liberal education are highly beneficial to society, by forming the rising generation to virtue, knowledge and useful literature; and thus preserving in the community a succession of men duly qualified for discharging the offices of life with usefulness and reputation." But the glittering generalities were justified by the event; and it is probable that retaining the *disputatio* in the college curriculum helped the discussion of republican principles. Superior minds among the students were likely to respond to the demand for linguistic acuity possible in construing Greek, Latin, and Hebrew, and to the opportunities for debate in their pursuit of logic, metaphysics, and theology, so that Meriwether, though over-rhetorical in his claim, is justified in writing:

> The contest with England hinged upon the construing of language, the meaning of statutes, the essence of practice and customs. It was a great debate as to the rights of each side in which ultimate decision rested upon the deep foundation stones of human conduct. The two Adamses, Madison, Jefferson, and their brethren were at home in this field. . . . They knew how to build an argument, to construct a logical fortress; that had been their pastime since youth. They could marshal words, they could explore the past, they could clinch with quotation or with reference to an overshadowing name; they had been doing that for years.[40]

We continue the practice in panel discussions—rather badly.

If there be some merit in this claim, it is a little surprising that the federal Constitution does not mention education, but if education was left to the states as a primary responsibility, that did not mean there was a lack of discussion about the relation between education and republican virtue. The Northwest Ordinance of 1783, product of the Confederation, set aside section sixteen in every township for the support of schools, and the Ordinance of 1787 declared that "Religion, morality, and knowledge being necessary to good government and the happiness of mankind, schools and the means of education shall be forever encouraged"—an instruction affixed to the wall of the Regents' Room at the University of Michigan to remind them of their responsibility. Revolutionary state constitutions accepted, at least on paper, public responsibility for education, and the University of North Carolina was created legally in December 1789, though it was not opened to students until 1795; the University of Georgia, though the first to be chartered (1785), was not established until 1801. The University of Vermont dates from 1800, the University of South Carolina from 1801. If the federal government was generous in granting land for the support of such institutions when new states were formed, the number grew but slowly, for there were only seventeen state universities at the outbreak of the Civil War. The University of Virginia, famous as the creation of Thomas Jefferson, dates from 1819 but its earlier years scarcely fulfilled the dream of its great founder.

This, however, is to get ahead of the problem of theory. Since from 1775 to 1815 it is probable that the churches had less influence on American culture than in any subsequent forty-year period, secularism vitalized, and for a time controlled, the forces of education in the new nation. Secularism, or, if one prefers, the "later enlightenment," accepted a simple and uniform theory of human nature, as Merle Curti has pointed out.[41] Human nature is plastic; therefore man may by suitable education develop his own rational and moral capacities. Human nature, furthermore, is motivated by great and understandable laws—reason and morality, the doctrine of the prevailing school of Scotch Common Sense philosophy. Man is dual; the body is the seat of base impulses, but the mind is made up of capacities (faculties) classified as understanding, feeling, and will. Through proper education man can will to control his baser impulses and translate his innate moral promptings into affirmative social action. Sound early training will discipline the reason and the will for a sound republican society. The doctrine was buttressed by a classical theory of economics, in which the individual acts rationally for the good of the whole; could be married to Christian theology; and was taught in such books as Thomas C. Upham's *Moral Philosophy* (1831) and Francis Wayland's *Elements of Moral Science* (1835).

Meanwhile an important literature on republican education developed, the central date of which was that of a prize offered in 1797 by the American Philosophical Society for the "best system of liberal education and literary instruction, adapted to the genius of the Government of the United States." The award was divided between Samuel Knox and Samuel Harrison Smith, each of whom published his essay. But the eighties and nineties were prolific in these conjectural pamphlets,[42] none of which had the coverage of Jefferson's bill in 1779 to set up a complete system of public education in Virginia culminating in the state university. Frenchmen such as Pierre Du Pont de Nemours, François Quesnay, and Lafitte du Courteil contributed to the discussion.

What all these statements stress is the new social responsibility for education developing out of republican institutions. This education, everybody argues, cannot be strongly influenced by European ideas, since it must support republican principles—hence the emphasis upon virtue. If classical literature is a repository of such principles, well and good, but more important is the grounding of young persons in the principles of morality and democracy. Yet education must likewise be useful, so that the monographs throw considerable weight on science and on history teaching by philosophic example. Finally American education must not be class-bound, it must open a career to talent (nothing was said about the slaves). Representative is this passage from Benjamin Rush to the effect that

> While we inculcate these republican duties upon our pupil, we must not neglect, at the same time, to inspire him with republican principles. He must be taught that there can be no durable liberty but in a republic, and that government, like all other sciences, is of a progressive nature. The chains which have bound this science in Europe are happily unloosed in America. Here it is open to investigation and improvement. While philosophy has protected us by its discoveries from a thousand natural evils, government has unhappily not followed with an equal pace. . . . I conceive, that it is possible to combine power in such a way as not only to encrease the happiness but to promote the duration of republican forms of government far beyond the terms limited for them by history, or the common opinions of mankind . . . our business is to make them men, citizens and Christians. . . . Above all, let our youth be instructed in the history of the ancient republics, and the progress of liberty and tyranny in the different states of Europe.

One problem was the relation of the Bible (Protestant, of course) to republican education: the deists wanted to throw it out, but did not this "divine book" favor above all others "that equality among mankind, that respect for just laws, and all those sober and frugal virtues, which constitute the soul of republicanism"? [43] All did not agree, but the immediate future lay with Rush. All these essays were curiously vague about the specific nature of elementary and secondary schooling, but there was a general tendency to argue for a national university as the crown of republicanism. It seemed to occur to nobody that an educational system built around propaganda for a republic merely paralleled educational systems built around propaganda for a church or for a monarchy.

I V

In the arts and sciences the innovations of republican culture are more generally known than in some other fields, though in painting and literature they are sometimes disguised as "nationalism" or "romanticism." [44] It was a period in the Western world when the natural philosopher thought God's thoughts after him, and as, from the point of view of developing science, it made little difference whether the deity was the God of the Christians or the God of the deists, most scientists got along well enough until the religious reaction roused emotions against such "infidels" as Joseph Priestley and Thomas Cooper. Fortunately for his happiness Benjamin Franklin died in 1790, before the religious revival had set in; and fortunately for *his* happiness Benjamin Rush, furiously assailed by William Cobbett for depopulating the earth, managed to remain within the fold of one or another Christian denomination. As for Jefferson, the fury of the assaults upon his infidelity is part of American history; pioneer that he was in many scientific areas, he was in a sense saved by the authorship of the Declaration of Independence, the Presidency, the success of the Lewis and Clark expedition, useful inventions, and the truth that, though his church allegiance was doubtful, he claimed to be a Christian and in 1803 began selecting passages from the New Testament that he thought illustrated the "Morals of Jesus."

The more immediate aims of science in the epoch seem to have been four: to demonstrate the goodness and wisdom of God as these were manifest in nature, particularly in American nature; to import and domesticate in a republic European scientific knowledge; through American genius to achieve for the United States its proper place in the sun; and, above all, to be guided toward utility, which included everything from the control of yellow fever to the invention of the mold-board plow. The Constitution empowered Congress to "promote the progress of science and the useful arts by securing for limited times to authors and inventors the exclusive rights to their respective writings and discoveries," and on April 10, 1790, a federal enactment placed the granting of patents in the hands of the Secretary of State, the Secretary of War, and the Attorney General. A patent office was not opened until 1836. The colleges were relatively backward in supporting scientific research, though there were professorships of "natural philosophy" galore, but science in our sense was for a long while thought to be (as in England) an occupation for gentlemen with plenty of leisure and curiosity. The American Philosophical Society was such an organization of gentlemen, which dated from 1743; the first learned society after independence had been virtually achieved was the American Academy of Arts and Sciences, organized in Boston in 1780 by John Adams, Samuel Adams, John Hancock, James Bowdoin, and others. Various medical societies were established in the eighties and nineties (a few preceded the war), various other state societies were created for promoting chemistry, or the useful arts, or history, or the arts and sciences—one great advantage of the early years of this republic was that the split between two cultures was nowhere evident—and in 1812 there was created an Academy of Natural Sciences. The Columbian Institute of 1816 eventually turned into the National Institution, and that in time cradled the Smithsonian Institution, incorporated after endless Congressional debates in 1846.

In the flush times of getting a brand-new nation under way words became surcharged with emotion rather than with meaning, so much so that Noah Webster is almost alone in his insistence on defining terms. During the decades before, say, 1830, science meant, vaguely, any form of organized learning, the "sciences" slid easily into the penumbra of the "arts," and the arts included everything from invention and manufacture to epic poetry and historical painting. The word "literature" itself, it is too often forgotten, meant virtually anything that took shape as the printed word, a fact that vitiates a good deal of airy theorizing about American literary development—meaning the development of imaginative writing. The curiosity of antiquarian musicology has rummaged out a few pleasant eighteenth-century musical composers in America such as William Billings and Francis Hopkinson, whose work is even reproduced nowadays on phonograph records, or occasions such recordings, but we have to wait long for the full-blooded "Americanism" of a Sousa march.

American sculpture was mainly born and nourished in Italy, though the historian of American art can speak with appropriate enthusiasm about American carvings in wood, including domestic furniture and ships' figureheads; and there were a few sculptors who, as one of them hinted, began their careers among gravestones. But American painting received a powerful impetus from American literature and from the heroical in the immediate American past; and the decoration of steamboat interiors, the rage for panoramas, the providing of the national Capitol with historical scenes, the recording of naval victories, illustrating the increasing number of American magazines, and demands for portraits among the wealthy offered a practical support for the graphic arts. Peale's attempt at an art museum in Philadelphia, followed by his struggle to establish an art school there, eventuated in the Pennsylvania Academy of Fine Arts, the noble purpose of which was nothing less than the elevation of the national taste:

> To promote the cultivation of the Fine Arts in the U.S.A., by introducing correct and elegant copies from the works of the first Masters in Sculpture and Painting, and by thus facilitating the access to such standards, and also by occasionally conferring moderate but honorable premiums, and otherwise assisting the Studies and exciting the efforts of the Artists, gradually to unfold, enlighten and invigorate the talents of our Countrymen.[45]

By and by this grew into the National Academy of the Arts of Design, and, as usual, a conflict between the older and the younger generations developed. By 1834 there had been sufficient work done in American art for William Dunlap to publish his *History of the Rise and Progress of the Arts of Design in the United States* in two volumes. It was formerly proper to look down one's nose at American painting (with few exceptions) before the Civil War, but, not to speak of the really great achievements of the Hudson River School, to which I shall come in the next chapter, the great Karolik collections in the Boston Museum of Fine Arts prove how wrong this attitude has been. In truth the thesis could be defended that the art of painting in America approached maturity before the art of literature. As for architecture, the need for great public buildings and the necessity of housing a continuously expanding population gave a remarkable impetus to American builders and designers, among other things producing in the 1830s that characteristic American invention (possible only in a country with seemingly inexhaustible timber resources), the balloon frame.[46]

But the great battle was fought in literature, a contest that has been recorded over and over again. The central point was put with great acuteness by Longfellow in a forgotten romance of his, *Kavanagh* (1849), in Chapter XX of which Mr. Churchill, the schoolmaster of Fairmeadow, has to deal with Mr. Hathaway, who, like a hundred actual persons, wants to establish a new magazine in order to "raise the character of American literature." Omitting Mr. Churchill's interruptions, one finds Mr. Hathaway arguing:

> I think, Mr. Churchill, that we want a national literature commensurate with our mountains and rivers,—commensurate with Niagara, and the Alleghanies, and the Great Lakes. We want a national epic that shall correspond to the size of the country; that shall be to all other epics what Banvard's Panorama of the Mississippi is to all other paintings,—the largest in the world! We want a national drama in which scope enough shall be given to our gigantic ideas, and to the unparalleled activity and progress of our people! In a word, we want a national literature altogether shaggy and unshorn, that shall shake the earth, like a herd of buffaloes thundering over the prairies!

To which the schoolmaster replies (and I again omit conversational interruptions):

> Great has a very different meaning when applied to a river, and when applied to a literature. Large and shallow may perhaps be applied to both. Literature is rather an image of the spiritual world than of the physical, is it not?—of the internal, rather than the external. Mountains, lakes, and rivers, are, after all, only its scenery and decorations, not its substance and essence. A man will not necessarily be a great poet because he lives near a great mountain. . . . Nationality is a good thing to a certain extent, but universality is better. All that is best in the great poets of all countries is not what is national in them, but what is universal. Their roots are in their native soil; but their branches wave in the unpatriotic air, that speaks the same language unto all men, and their leaves shine with the illimitable light that pervades all lands.

Few passages in American literature sum up so succinctly the two sides of a great cultural debate.

A thousand orators, essayists, magazine writers, editors, and men of talent and genius in public life or from the privacy of their libraries issued manifestoes on the subject. Most of the magazines founded between 1794 and 1825 regarded themselves as torchbearers of republican virtue; the bitterness of the literary debate was increased by sneers from England or by English travelers, at the provincialities of the American muse. Teachers were drawn into the great debate; for example, Edward Tyrrel Channing, about to become Boylston Professor of Rhetoric and Oratory at Harvard College, who adjured the local chapter of Phi Beta Kappa:

> Cultivate domestic literature as a source of national dignity, a foundation of respect from foreigners. Would you be feared for your power on land and ocean?—would you be envied for your fertile soil and free institutions?—and will you not secure gratitude and veneration by your additions to the intellectual wealth of the world?—will you not value the mild but enduring power which the cultivated mind is sure to possess? Are you trying the great experiment of republican influences upon the security, the domestic happiness of man, his elevation of character, his love of country; and will you not prove that letters may flourish in the Commonwealth,—that we need not wait for the luxuries, the patronage, the glitter of despotism, before the age of our philosophers and poets shall dawn? [47]

The utterance is characteristic. On the other side, Federalist critics, contributors to the *Boston Anthology and Boston Review* (1803–1811), insisted that the United States was *not* self-sufficient, that all cultivated men participated in a universal republic of letters, and that chauvinism, democracy, and decline were interchangeable terms, a view in which they were supported by the dominant critical theory of their time.[48] Would not cosmic history culminating in the creation of the United States be a great point? Timothy Dwight's *The Conquest of Canaan* (1785) and Joel Barlow's *The Columbiad* (1807), both unreadable, obediently appeared. Would not the Indian be a unique "American" subject? J. W. Eastburn and Robert Sands produced *Yamoyden* in 1820—and where is *Yamoyden* today? Would not the American past, including the Mound Builders, be helpful? Bryant filled his volume with such poems as "An Indian at the Burial-Place of his Fathers," "The Prairies," and "The Fountain." [49] Were not warlike American exploits on land and sea proper tribute to the American muse? Cooper produced *The Spy* in 1821 and *The Pilot* in 1823, William Gilmore Simms *The Yemassee* in 1835. Was there not something characteristic and "republican" in American humor? Irving and Paulding made fun of the Dutch from this point of view, and Royall Tyler in *The Contrast* (1787) displayed the comic advantage possessed by republican virtue over urban sophistication, just as Mrs. Mowatt in *Fashion* (1845) was to demonstrate the superior acuteness of a simple farmer from Catteraugus County over the pretensions of city folk.

There is nothing original in the theme of Emerson's "The American Scholar" of 1837; the greatness of the address is that it intelligently compromised these extremes. Let us have done, he said, with the courtly muses of Europe, let us, indeed, sit at the feet of the familiar and the low and think about the meal in the firkin, the milk in the pan, but only on this condition: "Give me insight into to-day, and you may have the antique and future worlds." By the 1850s, the first wonderful decade in American literature, the dispute was not so much settled as outmoded; the ten years that produced, among other things, *The Scarlet Letter, Representative Men, The Conspiracy of Pontiac, Uncle Tom's Cabin, Walden, Hiawatha, The Autocrat of the Breakfast Table, Moby Dick,* and *Leaves of Grass* were paying very little attention to the courtly muses of Europe, the judgments of the *Edinburgh Review,* or the delicate question whether court patronage was necessary to maintain literature. Republican culture had come into its own, if not on the theoretical lines laid down in the eighteenth century, then on other lines, possibly less well defined, that nevertheless led the arts, or at least some of them, into maturity. Yet less than twenty years before "The American Scholar," Richard Flower, visiting the Illinois country, had written:

> Here are few public buildings worthy of notice. No kings going to open Parliament with gilded coaches and cream-coloured horses, with a train of dragoons at their heels.—No Lord Mayor's show.—No Towers filled with royal tigers and lions.— No old castles which beautify the rural scenes of the country,

whose melancholy history informs the curious traveller that their foundation was bedded in tyranny, and their superstructure the retainers of weeping prisoners, often of rank, as well as oppressed plebians. No cathedrals or old churches to ornament the cities as well as the counties of England,—monuments of superstition when erected, and of injustice and oppression even to this day, having for their support tithe-proctors, and surveyors, continually obstructing the progress of agriculture, and exciting contentions and law suits to an extent for which all the preaching of the clergy of England cannot represent an equivalent, or balance the evil produced by a worldly and avaricious priesthood. America has none of these costly ornaments or beautiful monuments of oppression. I thank God she has not; and hope she may be exempt from them, although strange to tell, I have found amongst both clergy and laity some few who wish for these degradations.[50]

The incongruity between this embattled "radicalism" of 1819 and the judicious Emerson of 1837 seems to indicate that republican culture had come of age.

American Landscape[1]

I

ROBERT FROST has made two phrases memorable, one to the effect that the land was ours before we were the land's and the other something about realizing westward. Both point to the simplest basic fact about the New World and to one of the most difficult problems in cultural explication. The basic fact is that the New World was physically new to European man; the problems arise out of the fantastic number of inferences that have been drawn from this truth. Figures on the increasing tallness of Americans, generation after generation, the imputation of a causal relation between the "mom" complex supposed to be characteristic of American males and the huge consumption of milk in this country, the increasing expectation that in any international athletic contest the Americans will come out on top, the inference (once held) that American writing cannot be rich and full because the American landscape lacks historical, feudal, medieval, human, classical, or family associations, the opposite argument (once appealed to) that American literature must be great because the American landscape is grand—these and other generalizations arise from the feeling that the physical newness of America must in the long run affect the American character, American art, American values, or something else. And one does not have to go in for complex theories of economic determinism or physiological shaping or climatology to believe that the dynamics of American development must include the relation of man to earth. Indeed, the thesis could be defended that from the landing of Columbus to the latest rise in the cost of houses American history can be "explained" by the scramble for real estate. Consider the assumption by monarchs of ownership of countries they never saw, the granting to chartered companies, proprietors, and royal favorites of vast domains, the tensions over quitrents and land claims in the colonial and revolutionary eras, the grabbing of Tory estates, the perennial problem of the public domain, the acquisition of millions of acres by railroads, the preservation of public parks and public forests against encroachment, the zoning-law problem, the legal or illegal codes that exclude Jews or Negroes or some other group from a "nice" bit of exurbia—the list is endless. The freehold concept has its importance in American literature,[2] but the notion of individual ownership is in flat contradiction to the emotional appeal of the uncharted forest, the unfenced range, the trackless mountains, and the open sky. Illuminating it is to reflect how important the theme of land proves to be in Cooper, Thoreau, Whittier, Whitman, Howells, Harold Frederick; in the "farm novel"; in the novels of the frontier, of the mining town, of the cowboy, of the slum (the slum landlord is a standard fictional villain); and in muckraking fiction concerning street-railway franchises, railroad grants, and all the rest. Think of *The Gilded Age* by Twain and Warner—what would it be without the Tennessee lands? Or *The Octopus* without its endless ocean of wheat? Bucolic themes such as the ol' swimmin' hole, the courtin', the barefoot boy with cheek of tan, the snowbound farmstead, and sentimental tales about friendship village, the "local color" farm, the mountain cove, and the Maine fishing village concern the American land in another way and are, in their values, different from, say, Turgenev's *A Sportsman's Sketches*, German *Dorfromanen*, the *Heidi* of Johanna Spyri, and stories of the landed gentry and shopkeepers of the shire town in Trollope and of peasants in Zola, Hardy, or Bjørnson, though parallels of course exist. But modern criticism is so bent on finding Freudianism and frustration in American writing past and present, it will not observe how profoundly the American landscape and land ownership have conditioned American literature.

Our present inquiry, however, concerns neither historical generalizations nor economic questions nor another tentative answer to that ancient riddle: what makes for nationalism in American writing? To become imaginatively potent, American landscape had, indeed, to be realized westward— must, that is, be expressed in words or pictures. A convention of values had to be set up or derived from it, as Henry Nash Smith has shown in *Virgin Land,* concerning our Western terrain. To articulate this concept, modes of expression, as I have already hinted,[3] had to be discovered or invented; and the struggles of the Americans to formulate for themselves the meaning of the landscape is an absorbing chapter in the history of American sensibility.

The incapacity of the earliest explorers to articulate with precision what they had seen was, I have suggested, a function of the primitive state of landscape description and of topographical painting in the fifteenth and early sixteenth centuries. That incapacity was gradually overcome, and by the time Hakluyt's great collection appeared, it was possible for writers (though seldom for painters) to be specific rather than general in their descriptions. First settlers in a wilderness were inevitably more concerned with keeping alive than with aesthetic response, so that, despite occasional patches of excellent descriptive writing in the American seventeenth century, most of the detailed work is social, economic, political, religious, and military. For example, William Bradford was an admirable man and a good writer, but the best he can do with the first landing of the Pilgrims is this:

. . . but they soone lost both them [the Indians] and them selves, falling into shuch [*sic*] thickets as were ready to tear their cloaths and armore in peeces, but were most distressed for wante of drinke. But at length they found water, and refreshed them selves, being the first New-England water they drunke of, and was now in thir great thirste as pleasante unto them as wine or bear had been in for-times. Afterwards they directed their course to come to the other shore, for they knew it was a necke of land they were to crosse over, and so at length gott to the sea-side, and marched to this supposed river, and by the way found a pond of clear fresh water, and shortly after a good quantitie of clear ground wher the Indeans had formerly set corne, and some of their graves.[4]

Bradford continues in this plain, direct way for some pages, but what he tells us is scarcely more specific than was Columbus's report.

Unfortunately for the expression of American sensibility, about the time that colonial writers were in a position to do better—contrast, for example, almost any topographical passage in Byrd's *History of the Dividing Line* with the quotation from Bradford—the literary world of England passed out of the vigor of Restoration prose and verse into the neoclassicism of the age of Walpole. Stylistic ideals did not thereafter include the specific, the colorful, the vulgar and picturesque phrase, "low" words of ungenteel occupations, or the verbal equivalent of the vivid colloquialism of Hogarth's cartoons; on the contrary, genteel stylistic ideals were those of James Thomson of *The Seasons* (1726–1730), of the Reverend Edward Young's *Night Thoughts* (1742–1745), of Dr. Johnson (who made little fishes talk like whales) and, by and by, of Henry Mackenzie's *Man of the World* (1773) and Mrs. Chapone's *Letters on the Improvement of the Mind* (1773). I do not speak, of course, of figures like Fielding or Gibbon who each in his own way created an individual or idiosyncratic style, but of the general level of writing, which, one fears, was quite as accessible to the Americans as were Smollett or Goldsmith or Burke. Here, for example, is James Thomson talking about the sun:

> At thee the ruby lights its deeping glow,
> And with a waving radiance inward flames.
> From thee the sapphire, solid ether, takes
> Its hue cerulean; and, of evening tinct,
> The purple-streaming amethyst is thine.
> With thy own smile the yellow topaz burns;
> Nor deeper verdure dyes the robe of Spring,
> When first she gives it to the southern gale,
> Than the green emerald shows.
>
> —"Summer"

And here is Thomson trying to describe a particular scene:

> Should I my steps turn to the rural seat,
> Whose lofty elms and venerable oaks
> Invite the rook, who high amid the boughs,
> In early Spring, his airy city builds,
> And ceaseless caws amusive; there, well-pleased,
> I might the various polity survey
> Of the mix'd household kind.
>
> —"Spring"

The various polity include "the careful hen," "the fearless cock," "the finely-checquer'd duck," "the stately-sailing swan" who "gives out his snowy plumage to the gale," and other birds, all "gentle tenants of the shade." Doubtless *The Seasons* did something for sensibility, but this is bad writing now and was, I think, bad writing then. The great Americans, commonly working in political or scientific prose, surmounted the handicaps of a genteel style; ordinary writers did not, and the result, so far as American landscape is concerned, was complete disaster.

Here, for instance, is William Dawson, later to be president of William and Mary, in *Poems on Several Occasions* (Williamsburg, 1736) struggling to be poetical about a morning in Virginia:

> Awake my Soul, with the constant Morn
> Carol th'ALMIGHTY's Praise; awake and tune
> The vocal Shell to sympathetic Sounds,

And heav'nly Confort [*sic*]. See! the radiant Sun
Stains with etherial Gold the varied *East,*
And vast Expanse; behold! with Giant stride
He' advances ruddy, and with him returns
The sweet Vicissitude of Day, and all
Th'obsequious Train of filial Colours. Now
The vivid Green extends her welcome Sway
O'er the Sequester'd Lawns, and smiling Meads:
And now the purpled *Violet* resumes
Its costly Dye; and all th' extended Plains
Confess th'ALMIGHTY's Hand, of Ornament
Profuse. Behold! with fleshy *Pink* they smile
Enamel'd, and the *Daisy's* dwarfy Bloom
Of pallid Hue, and gorgeous *Marygold.*

Comment on the inadequacies of this is superfluous.[5]

The celebrated Thomas Godfrey, whose *Juvenile Poems* were published in Philadelphia in 1765, tried to combine warfare and gentility in a poem from Fort Henry, dated August 10, 1758:

From where his lofty head TALHEO rears,
And o'er the wild in majesty appears,
What shall I write that *————* won't disdain,
Or worth, from Thee one moment's space to gain?
The Muse, in vain, I court the lovely maid,
Views with contempt the rude unpolish'd shade,
Not only this, she flies fierce war's alarms,
And seeks where peace invites with softer charms
.   .   .   .

Where the glad Swain sings on th' enamel'd green,
And views unaw'd by fears the pleasing scene.
Here no enchanting prospects yield delight,
But darksome forests intercept the sight;
Here fill'd with dread the trembling peasants go,
And start with terror at each nodding bough. . . .

There is much more of it, including this remarkable couplet:

She shews the fatal field, all drench'd in gore,
And in sad accents cries, my *Howe's* no more! [6]

There were no peasants in America, and, one suspects, no swains singing o'er the enameled green.

As it may be argued that poets are like that, here is an excerpt from the admired Mather Byles (1707–1788), whose sermons, according to Tyler, were marked "by neatness of phrase, and expertness in the manipulation of his materials," no less than by "fresh and striking views of things." [7] The learned preacher is struggling with springtime:

> *The Time of the Singing of Birds is come,* and our *Ears* are regaled by all the Harmony of the Groves and Forests. The idle Musicians of the Spring fill the Fields and the Skies with their artless Melody. A thousand Odours are thrown from every Bough; and scatter through the Air, to gratify our *Smell. The Flowers appear on the Earth;* and the opening Buds, and rising Grass dress the rich Landscape, and paint the Scene to delight and charm our *Eyes.*[8]

This was published in Boston in 1741, republished in 1769. Evidently it appealed to the genteel.

It is a relief to turn back from this sort of thing to honest John Lederer, who was apparently the first European to explore the Piedmont and the Blue Ridge and who wrote:

> The eighteenth of *March,* after I had in vain assayed to ride up, I alighted, and left my horse with one of the Indians, whilst with the other two I climbed up the Rocks, which were so incumbered with bushes and brambles, that the ascent proved very difficult: besides, the first precipice was so steep, that if I lookt down, I was immediately taken with a swimming in my head; though afterwards the way was more easie. The height of this Mountain was very extraordinary: for notwithstanding I set out with the first appearence of light, it was late in the evening before I gained the top, from whence the next morning I had a beautiful prospect of the *Atlantick*-Ocean washing the *Virginian*-shore; but to the North and West, my sight was suddenly bounded by Mountains higher than that I stood upon. Here did I wander in Snow, for the most part, till the Four and twentieth day of *March,* hoping to finde some passage through the Mountains; but the coldness of the Air and Earth together,

seizing my Hands and Feet with numbness, put me to a *ne plus ultra. . . .*[9]

This is as plain as Defoe, but it is also panoramic, and it was precisely panoramic technique that was necessary in dealing with American scenery.

The full panoramic landscape organized in aesthetic principles was, however, the special creation of Thomas Jefferson in his *Notes on Virginia.* In this book he did it twice: once in describing the Natural Bridge, and once in describing the confluence of the Shenandoah and the Potomac. Let us look at one of these famous set pieces:

The passage of the Potomac through the Blue Ridge is, perhaps, one of the most stupendous scenes in nature. You stand on a very high point of land. On your right comes up the Shenandoah, having ranged along the foot of the mountain an hundred miles to seek a vent. On your left approaches the Potomac, in quest of a passage also. In the moment of their junction, they rush together against the mountain, rend it asunder, and pass off to the sea. The first glance of this scene hurries our senses into the opinion, that this earth has been created in time, that the mountains were formed first, that the rivers began to flow afterwards, that in this place, particularly, they have been dammed up by the Blue Ridge of mountains, and have formed an ocean which filled the whole valley; that continuing to rise they have at length broken over at this spot, and have torn the mountain down from its summit to its base. The piles of rock on each hand, particularly on the Shenandoah, the evident marks of their disrupture and avulsion from their beds by the most powerful agents of nature, corroborate the impression. But the distant finishing which nature has given to the picture, is of a very different character. It is a true contrast to the foreground. It is as placid and delightful as that is wild and tremendous. For the mountain being cloven asunder, she presents to your eye, through the cleft, a small catch of smooth blue horizon, at an infinite distance in the plain country, inviting you, as it were, from the riot and tumult roaring around, to pass through the breach and participate of the calm below. Here the eye ultimately composes itself; and that way, too, the road happens actually to lead. You cross the Potomac above the junction, pass along its side through the base of the mountain for three miles, its terrible precipices hanging in fragments over you, and within about twenty miles reach Fredericktown, and the fine country round that. This scene is worth a voyage across the Atlantic.[10]

I quote this description *in extenso* because of the important elements of which it is composed. It is in the first place both panoramic and painterly, and its general pattern is that of a good many landscapes of the future Hudson River School. In the second place Jefferson insists upon vastness and upon the allure of the distant, that "small catch of smooth blue horizon" which invites one to pass through the breach of the mountains, though "at an infinite distance in the plain country," and find eventual peace. In the third place the vastness of space leads him to meditate upon vastness in time: his imagination goes back to the beginning of the New World when the Blue Ridge dammed up an ocean. Finally there are artfully inwoven suggestions of gigantic force that has left awe-inspiring evidence behind—the mountains have been rent asunder, the rivers have torn them from summit to base, in this wild and tremendous scene the rocks are evidence of "disrupture and avulsion," the waters (and the winds?) give forth riot and tumult "roaring around," and terrible precipices hang over one in fragments as one seeks the "fine country" beyond the wilderness. The accuracy of Jefferson's geology is not here in question, but only the cunning of his pen and his sense of the vast and powerful in landscape, the melodramatic history of the empty New World over endless stretches of time.

II

I do not know whether members of the Hudson River School read the *Notes on Virginia,* but the first important group of American painters, representative members of which are Thomas Cole, Asher B. Durand, Thomas Doughty, Thomas Moran, Frederick E. Church (he built a weird palace near Hudson, New York, in the 1870s), J. W. Casilaer, J. F. Kensett, Worthington Whittredge, and Albert Bierstadt, painted landscapes, so to say, on the Jefferson principle of panorama, even when the artists were following such European painters as Ruisdael, Claude Lorrain, and Salvator Rosa. They began in the Hudson valley, spread along the Mohawk to Niagara Falls or else into the Catskills and the Adirondacks, turned sometimes to the Housatonic and the Connecticut or invaded the White Mountains (they seldom got south of the Blue Ridge),* some eventually were captivated by the Great Plains, the Rockies, and the Yosemite, and one of them (Church) became noted for his grandiose Andean landscapes. Others preceded or joined or were influenced by them; for example, Washington Allston, some of whose canvases, such as "The Deluge" (1804) and "Elijah Fed by Ravens" (1818), are melodramatic and, for the period, high-keyed. (The dead tree in Allston's foregrounds becomes almost a sign-manual of wild landscapes by the Hudson River School.) In 1824 or 1825 William G. Wall, having painted twenty water colors of scenes along the Hudson, had them engraved and published in New York by I. Megarey. The engravings descend the stream, ending at New York Harbor, but pausing at falls, rapids, dams, mountains, highlands, "pallisadoes" and, more rarely, domestic scenes. † The publication of this elephant folio [11] may be said to inaugurate the Hudson River School, which was influential into the seventies.

Painting in the full tide of the romantic movement (they read Byron, Alison on taste, books on the picturesque, Coo-

---

* If they can be counted among the Hudson River School (which is doubtful), exceptions are Martin J. Heade and Joseph R. Meeker.

† The text accompanying a "View near Sandy Hill" says in part: "To the eye accustomed to dwell on the calm and cultivated beauty of a European landscape, if the scenery of the annexed engraving appear defective, it affords . . . a cheerful and striking contrast to the rude and solitary grandeur of the Highlands." In general the "note" of the series is one of the "rude and solitary grandeur" of the American scene.

per, Irving, Walter Scott, and so on), contemporaries of Delacroix, Géricault, Turner, Waldmüller, and Friedrich, they sought to depict the poetry—sometimes the allegory—of nature in their domestic landscapes, and the sublimity of wild nature and the majesty of God in other canvases. Hence their delight in mighty rivers winding across the canvas, in leading the eye up shimmering lakes into an endless sky, in great waterfalls (John Trumbull, William Dunlap, Victor de Grailly, Frederick Church, John Vanderlyn, J. F. Kensett and others "did" Niagara), in wild mountain passes, stunning clouds, Wagnerian rainbows, gigantic storms, and melodramatic events such as a prairie fire, a wagon train attacked by Indians, drifting icebergs, or a volcano in eruption. Interpreting nature on this grand scale created the necessity for a cosmic moralism, an intent of relation among the majesty of deity, the wildness of nature, the littleness of man, and the future of the republic. Aside from Allston, the most philosophical of these painters was Thomas Cole, who created such enormous allegorical canvases as "The Course of Empire" (expressing Volney's cyclical theory of power) and "The Titan's Goblet," in which the tree of life turns into a goblet containing the ocean. Cole believed that "religious fellowship with nature ever fills the bosom with incommunicable happiness" and wanted to sing a "sublime song" rather than paint. When Bryant delivered a funeral oration over him he sublimed into a single interpretation of the American landscape Cole's fusion of poetry and painting: in Cole's maturer productions, he said, there was

the delight which was expressed at the opportunity of contemplating pictures which carried the eye over scenes of wild grandeur peculiar to our country, over our ariel [sic] mountain-tops with their mighty growth of forest never touched by the axe, along the banks of streams never deformed by culture, and into the depth of skies bright with the hues of our own climate; skies such as few but Cole could ever paint, and through the transparent abysses of which it seemed that you might send an arrow out of sight.[12]

How was pygmy man not merely to subdue the wilderness but also found an enduring republic? Landscape could teach him that he might be, and frequently was, at the mercy of great natural forces, yet if he would but penetrate into the beauty and harmony of the whole, if he would set himself to understand the dynamism of the world, all, under God, might go well. The doctrine was curiously parallel to that of Goethe's *Faust*. Symbolical is Durand's "Kindred Spirits" (Pl. XI), in which Bryant and Cole, standing on a rocky ledge in the Catskills, overlook a mountain brook that emanates from a distant winding gorge. They are surrounded by wild nature, the glories of which they are earnestly discussing; a single bird flies over the chasm both to emphasize its depth and perhaps to suggest the doctrine of Bryant's poem "To a Waterfowl," that bird whose certain flight God sustains from zone to zone through the boundless sky.

Domestic landscapes painted by the Hudson River School (and its allies) commonly show diminutive figures in the foreground working at outdoor tasks, departing for church, fishing, or, as in Durand's "Mohawk Valley," contemplating nature. But beyond the farm, or the village, or the church, or the meadow, or the fishing pool, or the picnic spot, or the park, there lies vast, extended nature—shimmering skies, a mysterious mist, mountains that block the view, vistas that compel the eye to climb upward through the picture and lose itself in a vague and immense distance. When their theme is wild nature man shrinks to even smaller size, a tiny being in the foreground whose back may be turned to the viewer while he contemplates the grandeur of God; or man disappears altogether, as he does from Kensett's "Rocky Pool," Johnson's "Mount Marcy," and Cole's "The Ox-bow." * Along the Eastern Seaboard wildness, sublimity, and picturesque evidence of the work of an almighty hand were more easily pictured in mountain scenery, once Niagara

---

* The painting in the Metropolitan Museum of Art is Cole's; the much more domesticated replica in the Cleveland Museum of Art is apparently by an imitator.

Falls commenced to lose its pristine appeal; and landscapes such as Alvin Fisher's "Mountain Stream," Doughty's "In Nature's Wonderland" (imagined or topographical?), and Cole's "The Pass Called 'The Notch of the White Mountains,'" and his "Mountain Sunrise," most of them equipped with the inevitable dead treetrunk, emphasized the doctrine. I shall come in a moment to the more melodramatic treatment of the Far West. Meanwhile this interpretation of the American land was reinforced by literary men and scientists.

Close friend of the artists and sculptors of his period, James Fenimore Cooper, the prose poet of the American wilderness, composed his descriptions as carefully as if he were outlining a Hudson River School canvas. Thus in *The Last of the Mohicans* (Chapter xix) he wants the reader to know how rugged and majestic was the setting for the massacre at Fort William Henry, and he writes:

The mountain on which they stood, elevated, perhaps, a thousand feet in the air, was a high cone that rose a little in advance of that range which stretches for miles along the western shores of the lake, until meeting its sister piles, beyond the water, it ran off toward the Canadas, in confused and broken masses of rock thinly sprinkled with evergreens. Immediately at the feet of the party, the southern shore of the Horicon [Lake George] swept in a broad semicircle, from mountain to mountain, marking a wide strand, that soon rose into an uneven and somewhat elevated plain. To the north, stretched the limpid, and, as it appeared from that dizzy height, the narrow sheet of the "holy lake," indented with numberless bays, embellished by fantastic headlands, and dotted with countless islands. At the distance of a few leagues, the bed of the waters became lost among mountains, or was wrapped in the masses of vapor that came slowly rolling along their bosom, before a light morning air. But a narrow opening beneath the crests of the hills pointed out the passage by which they found their way still further north, to spread their pure and ample sheets again, before pouring their tribute into the distant Champlain. To the south stretched the defile, or broken plain. . . . For several miles in this direction, the mountains appeared reluctant to yield their dominion, but within reach of the eye they diverged, and finally melted into the level and sandy lands, across which we have accompanied our adventurers in their . . . journey. Along both ranges of hills, which bounded the opposite sides of the lake and valley, clouds of light vapor were rising in spiral wreaths from the uninhabited woods, looking like the smokes of hidden cottages; or rolled lazily down the declivities, to mingle with the fogs of the lower land. A single, solitary, snow-white cloud floated above the valley, and marked the spot beneath which lay the silent pool of the "bloody pond."

Cooper has managed to mingle Jefferson's "cleft" inviting one to go on ("a narrow opening beneath the crests of the hills pointed out the passage") and Jefferson's sense of height and space, with most of the attributes of a Hudson River School landscape: the mountains, the endless stretch of water, fantastic headlands, piles of rock, curling vapors and—a concentration point for the picture—the single, solitary, snow-white cloud dramatically placed above the bloody pond.

As it may be objected that this spatial composition is, after all, out of a historical novel, let us note what the eye of William Cullen Bryant, poet of forest and prairie and also a friend of the Hudson River painters, could make of the White Mountains in 1847:

The scenery of these mountains has not been sufficiently praised. But for the glaciers, but for the peaks white with perpetual snow, it would be scarcely worth while to see Switzerland. . . . The depth of the valleys, the steepness of the mountain-sides, the variety of aspect shown by their summits, the deep gulfs of forest below, seamed with the open courses of rivers, the vast extent of the mountain region seen north and south of us, gleaming with many lakes, filled me with surprise and astonishment. . . . I have been told . . . that the While Mountains in autumn present an aspect more glorious than even the splendors of the perpetual ice of the Alps. All this mighty multitude of mountains, rising from valleys filled with dense forests, have then put on their hues of gold and scarlet, and, seen more distinctly on account of their brightness of color, seem to tower higher in the clear blue of the sky. At that season of the year they are little visited, and only awaken the wonder of the occasional traveller.[13]

Here are space and wildness, but what about deity? In this same region God was sufficiently looked after by Christian geologists such as Edward Hitchcock, who was not only anxious to retain the Mosaic account of creation, but desired to find in American geology proofs of divine benevolence, particularly in landscape. God has arranged the surface of the earth so "as to gratify a taste for fine scenery"—and where more appealingly than in the White Mountains? In order that even the blind may see, Hitchcock asks the reader to accompany him in imagination on a tour up the Connecticut into the "White Hills," "where his soul will swell with new and strong emotions, if his natural sensibilities to the grand and beautiful have not become thoroughly dead with him." As the observer approaches the mountains,

the sides of the valley will gradually close in upon him, and rise higher and higher, until he will find their naked granitic summits almost jutting over his path, to the height of several thousand feet, seeming to form the very battlements of heaven. Now and then will he see the cataract leaping hundreds of feet down their sides, and the naked path of some recent landslip, which carried death and desolation in its track. From this deep and wild chasm he will at length emerge, and climb the vast ridge, until he has seen the forest trees dwindle, and at length disappear; and standing upon the naked summit, immensity seems stretched out before him.

The climax comes on the top of Mount Washington

when the vast panorama is completed, and the world seems spread out at his feet. Yet it does not seem to be a peopled world, for no mighty city lies beneath him. For why should he regard so small an object as a city, when the world is before him?—a world of mountains, bearing the impress of God's own hand, standing in solitary grandeur, just as he piled them up in primeval ages, and stretching away on every side as far as the eye can reach. On that pinnacle of the northern regions no sound of man or beast breaks in upon the awful stillness which reigns there, and which seems to bring the soul into near community with the Deity.

And as this quondam president of Amherst College was persuaded that the principal aim of government, at least in Massachusetts, was to lift up men "into the sunshine of Christianity, civilization, and freedom," there seemed to him to exist a working connection between the grandeur of God on Mount Washington and the theory of republican society.[14]

III

It would be interesting to follow the reporter and the painter across the Alleghenies and into the Ohio country— the Alleghenies from whose summit Thaddeus Mason Harris in 1803 saw a "view still more diversified and magnificent, crowded with mountains upon mountains in every direction; between and beyond which were seen the blue tops of others more distant, mellowed down to the softest shades, till all was lost in unison with the clouds," which by and by developed "a gliding radiance to the opening scene"; [15] the Ohio, which

> rolls his amber tide
> And nature blossoms in her virgin pride,

where cities are to rise and "spiry towns increase. With gilded domes and every art of peace." [16] But we cannot pause for everything, though some travelers making the endless journey through the Erie Canal admired the fusion of American utilitarianism and "romantic" scenery,* and almost everybody paused to be overwhelmed by the naked energy of Niagara Falls.[17] Western Pennsylvania, Kentucky's dark and bloody ground, the Cherokee-Chickasaw country, and southwestern America this side of the lower Mississippi occasioned

---

* A typical scene is George Harvey's painting "Pittsford on the Erie Canal" (1837).

on the whole few excursions into panoramic landscape, whatever the interest awakened by cougars and Indians, panthers and bears might do for such melodramatic fiction as Robert Montgomery Bird's *Nick of the Woods* (1837). An exception is in a slight way Alexander Wilson and in a somewhat larger way John James Audubon.[18] The Ohio River was described as beautiful, though terrifying in flood time, and when the traveler reached the rolling country north of it or the flat land of central Ohio and the prairies of Indiana and Illinois, he commented on the fertility of the soil, the fecundity of life, and the possibility of settlement. But all this has been worked out by Dorothy Anne Dondore in her *The Prairie and the Making of Middle America* and needs no recapitulation here.

A point of special emotional focus appeared, however. What about the Mound Builders, whose tumuli extended from central New York westward? Conjecture derived them from the lost tribes of Israel, the Phoenicians, the Egyptians, and even the companions of Madoc, Prince of Wales. In 1817 De Witt Clinton, speaking before the Literary and Philosophical Society of New York, thought the subject should be investigated, and in 1829 James Macauley, in his formless three-volume *History of the State of New York,* inferred a kind of vanished imperial race which had built these tumuli. Presumably that rising young New York editor, William Cullen Bryant, read these and other like works, for when he visited two brothers of his in the Illinois country in 1832, he rode over the prairie on horseback, and his *Poems* of 1832 included "The Prairies," a fusion of personal observation, conjectures about the Mound Builders, and a theory of history. If the prairie gave his eye an endless field of sight, brooding on the past gave his imagination an endless field in time. He addressed himself to these "Gardens of the Desert," this vast and gently swelling ocean whose "surface rolls and fluctuates to the eye." It was the work of beneficent deity. But the Mound Builders, who were doubtless a "disciplined and populous race," among whom

> lovers walked, and wooed
> In a forgotten language, and old tunes,
> From instruments of unremembered form,
> Gave the soft winds a voice

—what had happened to them? The Indians had destroyed them, save here and there some solitary fugitive who surrendered and married into the tribe of his conquerors. And the melancholy lesson?

> Thus arise
> Races of living things, glorious in strength,
> And perish, as the quickening breath of God
> Fills them or is withdrawn.

The great solitude was nevertheless quick with present life:

> Myriads of insects, gaudy as the flowers
> They flutter over, gentle quadrupeds,
> And birds, that scarce have learned the fear of man,
> Are here, and sliding reptiles of the ground,
> Startlingly beautiful. The graceful deer
> Bounds to the wood at my approach. The bee
> .   .   .   .
> Fills the savannas with his murmurings.
> .   .   .   .
> I listen long
> To his domestic hum and think I hear
> The sound of that advancing multitude
> Which soon shall fill these deserts.

The majesty of Bryant's blank verse introduces or reinforces a fresh component in the imaginative response to American landscape—cosmic melancholy resulting from the cyclic theory of history:

> Are they here—
> The dead of other days?—and did the dust
> Of these fair solitudes once stir with life
> And burn with passion?

It was a note he had sounded in "Thanatopsis"—

> lose thyself in the continuous woods
> Where rolls the Oregon, and hears no sound,
> Save his own dashings—yet—the dead are there,[19]

a note reiterated in other characteristic poems such as "The Ages," "Inscription for the Entrance to a Wood," "A Forest Hymn," and various Indian legends. The more Bryant learned about time and landscape, the more insignificant man became. In *The Prairie* (1827) Cooper had placed in the mouths of the aged Leatherstocking and Dr. Obed Battius a discussion of time, history, and the prairie that anticipated Bryant's imaginative response to the cyclical theory suggested by American landscapes.

Parkman knew something about the West at first hand, and though he admired the beauty of the prairie and the variety and fecundity of its flora and fauna, he did not find it an Earthly Paradise. In *The Conspiracy of Pontiac* he put his knowledge and his imagination to effective use. After expatiating on the countless elk, deer, bison, wildcats, raccoons, and oppossums, and the beauty of the prairie spring, he went on:

> Yet this western paradise is not free from the primal curse. The beneficent sun, which kindles into life so many forms of loveliness and beauty, fails not to engender venom and death from the rank slime of pestilential swamp and marsh. In some stagnant pool, buried in the jungle-like depths of the forest, where the hot and lifeless water reeks with exhalations, the watersnake basks by the margin, or winds his checkered length of loathsome beauty across the sleepy surface. From beneath the rotten carcass of some fallen tree, the moccason [*sic*] thrusts out his broad flat head, ready to dart on the intruder. On the dry, sun-scorched prairie, the rattlesnake, a more generous enemy, reposes in his spiral coil. He scorns to shun the eye of day, as if conscious of the honor accorded to his name by the warlike [i.e., Indian] race, who, jointly with him, claim lordship over the land. But some intrusive footstep awakes him from his slumbers. His neck is arched; the white fangs gleam in his distended jaws; his small eyes dart rays of unutterable fierceness;

and his rattles, invisible with their quick vibration, ring the
sharp warning which no man will dare to contemn.

The land [is] thus prodigal of good and evil, so remote from
the sea, so primitive in its aspect. . . .

As for the panoramic sense, nothing is more impressive than
Parkman's conjuring up the grandeur of the Mississippi
river basin when La Salle takes possession of Louisiana in the
name of the king of France:

> . . . the broad bosom of the great Gulf opened on his sight,
> tossing its restless billows, limitless, voiceless, lonely as when
> born of chaos, without a sail, without a sign of life. . . . On
> that day, the realm of France received on parchment a stupen-
> dous accession. The fertile plains of Texas; the vast basin of the
> Mississippi, from its frozen northern springs to the sultry bor-
> ders of the Gulf; from the woody ridges of the Alleghanies to
> the bare peaks of the Rocky mountains,—a region of savannas
> and forests, sun-cracked deserts, and grassy prairies, watered by
> a thousand rivers, ranged by a thousand warlike tribes, passed
> beneath the sceptre of the Sultan of Versailles; and all by virtue
> of a feeble human voice, inaudible at half a mile.[20]

Parkman achieved a like rhetorical splendor in his imaginative description of the mighty forces of the Mississippi and
Missouri Rivers tearing at the heart of a continent. He was
awed, as was virtually everybody else who described the ill-
named Father of Waters and its tributaries:

> The Mississippi descended from the distant north; while from
> its fountains in the west, three thousand miles away, the Mis-
> souri poured its torrent towards the same common centre. Born
> among mountains, trackless even now [1870], except by the
> adventurous footstep of the trapper,—nurtured amid the howl-
> ing of beasts and the war-cries of savages, never silent in that
> wilderness,—it holds its angry course through sun-scorched des-
> erts, among towers and palaces, the architecture of no human
> hand, among lodges of barbarian hordes, and herds of bison
> blackening the prairie to the horizon. Fierce, reckless, head-
> strong, exulting in its tumultuous force, it plays a thousand
> freaks of wanton power; bearing away forests from its shores,

and planting them, with roots uppermost, in its quicksands; sweeping off islands, and rebuilding them; frothing and raging in foam and whirlpool, and, again, gliding, with dwindled current along its sandy channel. At length, dark with uncurbed fury, it pours its muddy tide into the reluctant Mississippi. That majestic river, drawing life from the pure fountains of the north, wandering among emerald prairies and wood-crowned bluffs, loses all its earlier charm with this unhallowed union. At first, it shrinks as with repugnance; and along the same channel the two streams flow side by side, with unmingled waters. But the disturbing power prevails at length; and the united torrent bears onward in its might, boiling up from the bottom, whirling in many a vortex, flooding its shores with a malign deluge fraught with pestilence and fever, and burying forests in its depths, to ensnare the heedless voyager. Mightiest among rivers, it is the connecting link of adverse climates and contrasted races; and while at its northern source the fur-clad Indian shivers in the cold, where it mingles with the ocean, the growth of the tropics springs along its banks, and the panting negro cools his limbs in its refreshing waters.[21]

Parkman merely put into striking form the impressions of innumerable travelers—Audubon, Edmund Flagg, Basil Hall, Mrs. Trollope, Thomas Nuttall, Charles A. Murray, Captain Marryat, Alexander Mackay, a hundred more. To tourists from abroad, accustomed to well-watered western Europe, glimpses of the Missouri-Mississippi system were like glimpses into the wild anarchy of chaos; and even to Americans, used though they might be to floods on the Susquehannah, the Connecticut, or the Delaware, the savagery, desolation, and wild, destructive force of the central river system of the continent came as rude shock. The lower Mississippi seemed also to engender a savage culture on its banks, recorded with a mixture of delight and disgust in Twain's *Life on the Mississippi*. This savagery echoed the savage actions of the waters. Thomas Nuttall, who became a botanist at Harvard, descended the Mississippi in 1819. He and his companions tried to steer their bark by consulting the only rudimentary guide to the river then in print, *The*

Pittsburgh Navigator, but this proved of small help. Somewhere in the Chickasaw Bluffs region fog set in, it rained perpetually, they heard for two miles the sound of water breaking on some obstacle, like the cascade of a mill-race, and at two in the afternoon they were being swept toward one hundred tall trees fixed in all postures nearly across the river. The only channel appeared to be a labyrinth horribly filled with black and gigantic trunks of trees, along which the current foamed with terrific velocity. They were able to get ashore and from their desolate landing place saw the wrecks of two large flatboats lost during a recent earthquake. "Nothing . . . appeared on every hand but houseless solitude, and gloomy silence, the inundation precluding the possibility of settlement."

> The river, as it sweeps along the curve, according to its force and magnitude, produces excavations in the banks; which, consisting of friable materials, are perpetually washing away and leaving broken and perpendicular ledges, often lined with fallen trees, so as to be very dangerous to the approach of boats which would be dashed to pieces by the velocity of the current. These slips in the banks are almost perpetual, and by the undermining of eddies often remarkable in their extent. To-day we witnessed two horrid sinkings of the bank, by each of which not less than an acre of land had fallen in a day or two ago, with all the trees and cane upon them, down to the present level of the river, a depth of 30 or 40 feet perpendicular.

And beyond the river system was the great silence. Thus across the Arkansas, which Nuttall explored, "It is truly remarkable how greatly the sound of objects becomes absorbed in these extensive woodless plains. No echo answers the voice, and its tones die away in boundless and enfeebled undulations." [22] Niagara Falls was primeval; this was primitive. Niagara awakened feelings of the sublime; this lawless rage for destruction feelings of terror only. And across the river there were new dimensions of terrain and climate that reduced even American man to increasing insignificance. To survive amid this epic loneliness, these conflagrations on the prairie, these cruel snows and savage winds, this treeless plain and waterless desert, new human types had to be developed or old types modified, and soon the only persons who could cope with this solitude appeared—the Western guide like Kit Carson, the mountain man, the trapper, the plainsman, and by and by the cowboy, the Western woman leading her vigorous, irregular, and dominating life, like Calamity Jane in fact and Ma Pettingill in fiction, and at the end the Western humorists, such as Mark Twain and Will Rogers.

IV

For the trans-Mississippi country north of the Arkansas and west of the Mississippi proper, though it seemed at first like the Illinois prairie or the forest lands of western Tennessee except that everything was more spacious, got queerer and queerer, especially after explorers pushed past the hundredth meridian. The tall grass of the prairie gave way to the short grass of the Great Plains and that, by and by, to sagebrush and greasewood; the dark brown soils of eastern Nebraska melted into the gray soil of the arid regions as the plain continued to tilt imperceptibly upward to the mountains; the water courses grew fewer, vegetation seemed to confine itself to their unpredictable meanderings as they cut their way downward into the subsoil. The sky was expanded and oppressive; the pitiless sun seemed determined to keep the Americans out. Somewhere in the distance were the Rockies that Lewis and Clark had penetrated, but they too at times seemed illusory. Thus when the Long expedition first sighted them, Edwin James, a chronicler of that heroic effort, wrote: "for some time we were unable to decide whether what we saw were mountains, or banks of cumulus clouds skirting the horizon, and glittering in the reflected rays of the sun. . . . They became visible by detaching themselves from the sky beyond, and not by emerging from beneath the sensible horizon." [23] Were they not perhaps the ultimate boundary of

the American empire? Indeed, could republican culture be
made to exist on these sandy wastes under this pitiless sky?
Josiah Gregg thought the lack of trees was due to prairie
fires and was hopeful that "these sterile regions might yet
be . . . revived and fertilized, and their surface covered one
day by flourishing settlements to the Rocky Mountains," but
Edwin James, who claimed that even the eastern prairies
were unhealthy by reason of a flatness that keeps the water
stagnant and the atmosphere humid, was pessimistic. "In
regard to this extensive section of country, I do not hesitate
in giving the opinion, that it is almost wholly unfit for cultivation, and of course uninhabitable by a people depending
upon agriculture for their subsistence . . . the scarcity of
wood and water, almost uniformly prevalent, will prove an
insuperable obstacle." The one sure value in everything up
to the forty-ninth parallel was that this endless waste would
"serve as a barrier to prevent too great an extension of our
population westward, and secure us against the machinations
or incursions of an enemy." [24] Thus the concept of the Great
American Desert was formed. After reading the record of
the struggles of the Long expedition over "one thousand
miles of dreary and monotonous plain," the "showers of
burning sand," and the lack of water for man and beast, one
has a certain sympathy with the concept.

But the desert idea began to lose force. The picturesque-
ness of existence along the great Western rivers, the romantic
life of the horse Indians of the plains (the wild horses were
another Spanish legacy), not to speak of other Indians, the
millions of bison, the uncountable flights of pigeons, the
colorful flora and fauna of plain and mountain, unknown in
the east, the weird rock formations along incredible rivers,
the strangeness of light and sky and storm and heat and cold,
and, above all, the fact that before the general use of the
camera one or more artists had to be attached to any scientific
survey or exploring expedition to record visual images of the
West—these and other considerations, not forgetting the at-

tractions of adventure in the last great open spaces of the Occidental world, drew artists there, no less than adventurers, miners, explorers, fur-traders, and military men. With George Caleb Bingham they pictured the carefree flatboat-men on the Mississippi, or with George Catlin they painted scenes along the upper Missouri—buffalo herds crossing a river, the prairie bluffs a thousand miles above Saint Louis, the odd landscape about Le Grand Détour. Or, like Charles Bodmer, they were fascinated by weird cliffs and preposterous rock formations. Or with Frank Buchser they painted people fording the Platte River, or pictured sunrise over the plains at Laramie. Catlin made careful portraits of Indian chiefs. Charles Bodmer was attached to the Western expedition of Prince Maximilian of Wied-Neuwied, and Alfred Jacob Miller was hired by the Scot Captain William Drummond Stewart to paint for him four years later in 1837. Miller, by the by, though he sentimentalized his Indian "females," was interested in space and speed, melodrama and wonder: his "action pictures," like those of Delacroix, are studies in the threat of death, and his "Rock Formations," "Distant View of Lake by the Mountain of Winds," "Lake Scene," and other canvases have perhaps some of the qualities of Turner and certainly those of the Hudson River School. John Mix Stanley, Seth Eastman, William Ranney, Friedrich Kurz (who painted the Minnatarees on the upper Missouri as if they were Homeric horse-tamers), Charles Wimar, Paul Kane, Charles Deas, and others—we who have until lately identified "Western art" with the work of Frederic Remington and Charles Russell now know how many men of pictorial talent preceded these late sketches and statuettes of cowboys and cavalrymen. The watercolors, drawings, and oils of the older generation have been lost, burned, scattered, damaged, and neglected until recently, but we are beginning to understand how they influenced the national imagination by revealing a world far more dramatic than anything in agrarian or urban middle-class America, landscapes as full of colors as a box of jewels and shaped like the settings for romantic Italian operas, spaces and horizons and skies beyond the experience of the settled East.[25]

Long before the cowboy and the sheriff commenced to haunt the movies, the West was having its influence. Lithographs, Currier & Ives pictures, steel engravings in the magazines and in the publicity pamphlets of the railroads as these pushed westward, copies of favorite pictures—a late example is almost any one of the paintings of Custer's defeat at the Little Big Horn—these became the Great West in the popular mind. "Ned Buntline" in 1869 published *Buffalo Bill, The King of the Border Men,* "the wildest, truest story I ever wrote," the first of a series of such fictions or dramatizations, and Buffalo Bill himself appeared on the stage in 1878.[26] Little boys defended Fort Bridger in the backyard, went scouting down the alleys in the character of Kit Carson, or conducted thrilling buffalo hunts, interrupted by hostile Indians, in the vacant lot. But this is to get ahead of the story and away from the landscape problem.

In this pictorialization of the West two dominant themes emerge and intertwine at midcentury: the theme of grandeur and the theme of science. In 1857 Albert Bierstadt, then twenty-seven years old, returned from Europe; the next year he joined one of the successive surveying parties led by General F. W. Lander to map out the best overland trail. The party was attacked by Indians, but Bierstadt, excited by the grandeur of Wyoming, seems to have left the expedition in time to sketch the Wind River country, and returned to New York to exhibit a series of canvases in 1859. His "Thunderstorm in the Rocky Mountains" brought him instant fame; when his vast "The Rocky Mountains" was exhibited in 1863 great advertising streamers announced the event to New Yorkers. He went from vastness to vastness—"Laramie Peak" (1861), "Lander's Peak" (1863), "Looking down the Yosemite Valley" (1865), "El Capitan, Merced River" (1866), "The Valley of the Yosemite" (1866) (Pl. XII). Until the eighties he was the best-paid painter in America; when the tide turned, he died poor in 1902. Bierstadt's immense panoramas, striving to record the grandeur of the West, sometimes end by being grandiose; yet anyone who has driven from northern Colorado into Wyoming while a thunderstorm was gathering in the mountains back of Cheyenne and the skies were still blue over the vast plain eastward and the front range of the Rockies began to cut off the westering sun, knows that the West can be as gaudy as a picture postcard. Bierstadt could also do small subjects well, as some of the paintings in the Karolik collection testify, but his immense and popular panoramic views revealed a gigantism, a theatricality, a sense of incredible, shimmering light and melodramatic darkness that belonged only to an inhuman wilderness. It is interesting to contrast his "Ascutney Mountain from Claremont, New Hampshire" (1862), a standard Hudson River domestic landscape, with the vast depth and height of his "The Rocky Mountains" a year later, in which the remote and snowy peaks that close the picture seem to be part of some tremendous other world.

His contemporary, Thomas Moran, an admirer of Turner and in consequence admired by Ruskin, returned from Europe in 1871 and shortly thereafter joined one of the innumerable expeditions into the Wyoming country led by Ferdinand Vandiver Hayden, reconnaissance geologist and naturalist. The result in Moran was utter enthusiasm: in 1871 he painted his memorable "The Grand Canyon of the Yellowstone," and in 1873 he tried the Grand Canyon of the Colorado ("The Chasm of the Colorado"). They were instant successes; and Louis Prang of Boston commissioned Moran to make a set of watercolors of the Yellowstone that were greatly admired. His "The Mountain of the Holy Cross" (1874) was equally impressive, and so was his "Hot Springs near the Yellowstone" with its Turneresque coloring and light. Moran avoided the theatricality which was the chief weakness of Bierstadt, but his pictures were built on the same grand scale and impressed the beholder with the same sense of illimitable space and elemental power.

Bierstadt and Moran, though they attached themselves to expeditions, had no scientific interest and were content to register an aesthetic response of awe and amazement. But the intent of the so-called *Pacific Railroad Reports,* possibly the most magnificent production of its kind ever published by the United States government, surveys of the West made by five different exploring parties during the years 1853–1855, was scientific, though science in this case also produced some of the finest art work having to do with the wilderness.[27] Artists of the standing of John Mix Stanley and H. B. Möllhausen were attached to various branches of the survey, and in addition some of the engineers, Army officers, and other scientific men attached, drew and painted acceptably. These large, leisurely reports in twelve huge volumes are a neglected source of information about the West, partly by reason of their formidable size, partly because of their eccentric indexing. The illustrations are of four kinds: inferior black-and-white woodcuts or engravings introduced into the text; scores of superb drawings illustrating the conchology, paleontology, botany, and zoology of the regions surveyed; wonderful colored pictures of birds and animals that still retain their brilliance and that suggest the exquisite work of Audubon; and scores of colored lithographs intended not merely to visualize railroad rights of way but also to charm the eye and acquaint the reader with the strange and wonderful country through which railroads might be built. Seven out of the twelve volumes are illustrated with such lithographs, the colors of which have faded with time but the charm of which is inexhaustible.

Unlike Bierstadt and Moran, who wished to increase the wildness of Western scenes by omitting humanity, these lithographs usually pose some understandable human activity in the foreground and compel the eye to pass over this to canyon or mountain, stream or plain beyond. The sense of space, the sense of strangeness, the sense of the exotic are strikingly conveyed. An unsigned lithograph in Volume VI (opposite page 80) entitled "Three Sisters and Canyon of McKenzie's

Fork of Willamette River from Camp P" (the Williamson
expedition) shows two Indians staring into an immense vista
—range on range of rugged mountains culminating in three
snowy peaks on the far horizon. Möllhausen's lithograph
"Zuni" in Volume III (opposite page 67) introduces the eye
to something as fantastic as the craters on the moon. A lithograph by Stanley based on a sketch by R. H. Kern in Volume
II (opposite page 63), "Rock Hills between Green and White
Rivers," with the "Wahsatch" Mountains in the distance, is
as striking as any of the "endless landscapes" beloved by
German romanticism, and equally imaginative, though of a
slightly different construction, is "Summit of the Nearest
Ridges South of Grand River" (opposite page 48) in the
same volume. It is tantalizing to have to resort thus to speci-
men and listing in dealing with material so rich and varied;
I can but entreat the reader, if he be near a library that contains a set, to go to look through them. The government spent
over a million dollars printing these volumes (1855–1861)—
more, indeed, than it spent on the expeditions themselves;
and Congressmen and Senators distributed them widely,
partly to satisfy local pressures. The narrative text is full and
discursive.

If one tried to isolate significant components in the deline-
ation of Western landscape in paint or words, one would
find, I think, at least five leading elements: (1) astonishment;
(2) plenitude; (3) vastness; (4) incongruity; and (5) melancholy.

The amazement which Europeans first experienced on
coming to the New World in the early centuries was dupli-
cated by Americans (and Europeans) coming to the Great
West in later centuries, though the amazement was occasioned by other objects * and felt by a later generation or

---

* Some of the elements in the situation were, however, identical. The problem of a leader's retaining effective control over men habitually unrestrained
by customary law and of dealing effectively with a cunning or superior enemy
(Mexican or Indian) on the Great Plains or in the mountain regions was
quite like that I have discussed in the chapter on Renaissance man in America. The treatment of the "vagabond hero" Rose by Captain Bonneville or

generations. Any casual reading in the vast library of Western travels [28] will discover passage after passage of this sort.
This is how Frémont records a view from the central chain
of the Rocky Mountains (1843):

> We were now approaching the loftiest part of the Wind River
> chain; and I left the valley a few miles from our encampment,
> intending to penetrate the mountains as far as possible with
> the whole party. We were soon involved in very broken ground,
> among long ridges covered with fragments of granite. Winding
> our way up a long ravine, we came unexpectedly in view of a
> most beautiful lake, set like a gem in the mountains. The sheet
> of water lay transversely across the direction we had been pur-
> suing; and, descending the steep, rocky ridge, where it was nec-
> essary to lead our horses, we followed its banks to the southern
> extremity. Here a view of the utmost magnificence and gran-
> deur burst upon our eyes. With nothing between us and their
> feet to lessen the effect of the whole height, a grand bed of
> snow-capped mountains rose before us, pile upon pile, glowing
> in the bright light of an August day. Immediately below them
> lay the lake, between two ridges covered with dark pines which
> swept down from the main chain to the spot where we stood.
> Here, where the lake glittered in the open sunlight, its banks
> of yellow sand and the light foliage of aspen groves contrasted
> well with the gloomy pines. "Never before," said Preuss,* "in
> this country or in Europe, have I seen such magnificent, grand
> rocks." [29]

The first explorers of Yellowstone Park rubbed their eyes,
incredulous. Joseph L. Meek records an expedition of 1829
into a region "like Pittsburgh on a winter morning" with the
vapor from boiling springs, haunted by whistling steam vents,
dotted with cone-shaped mounds surmounted by craters

Irving's *The Adventures of Captain Bonneville,* and Frémont's conduct in
California in 1846 vis-à-vis Sutter and Castro are cases in point. When one
member of the "California Battalion" declined to attack the "peaceful Cali-
fornians," Frémont "quickly converted him by clapping him for one night
in a hot, ill-ventilated dungeon of Sutter's Fort which was swarming with
fleas." (Allan Nevins, *Frémont,* 2 vols., New York, 1928, I:315.)

* Charles Preuss was the cartographer of the party.

from which issue blue flames and molten brimstone, and devoid of living creatures.[30]

So much for amazement. What of plenitude? Here is Washington Irving writing in that neglected masterpiece, *Astoria* (1836), of the wild pigeons (now extinct) on the Nodowa (Nodoway) River, a confluent of the Missouri:

> The pigeons, too, were filling the woods in vast migratory flocks. It is almost incredible to describe the prodigious flight of these birds in the western wildernesses. They appear absolutely in clouds, and move with astonishing velocity, their wings making a whistling sound as they fly. The rapid evolutions of these flocks, wheeling and shifting suddenly as if with one mind and one impulse; the flashing changes of color they present, as their backs, their breasts, or the under part of their wings are turned to the spectator, are singularly pleasant. When they alight, if on the ground, they cover whole acres at a time; if upon trees, the branches often break beneath their weight. If suddenly startled while feeding in the midst of a forest, the noise they make in getting on the wing is like the roar of a cataract or the sound of distant thunder.
>
> A flight of this kind, like an Egyptian flight of locusts, devours everything that serves for its food as it passes along. . . . [There is a] discipline observed in these immense flocks, so that each may have a chance of picking up food. As the front ranks must meet with the greatest abundance, and the rear ranks must have scanty pickings, the instant a rank finds itself the hindmost, it rises in the air, flies over the whole flock and takes its place in the advance. The next rank follows in its course, and thus the last is continually becoming the first and all by turns have a front place at the banquet.[31]

I need not expatiate on the accounts in these travel narratives of endless herds of bison, the sense that the Western forests were inexhaustible and that the Western waters were filled with fish, or the assumption that trapping could go on forever.

The vastness of the West is evident in the canvases of Bierstadt and Moran. Here is the way it impressed Isabella L.

Bird, who in 1879 merely repeats the emotions of a hundred predecessors:

> I usually dislike bird's-eye and panoramic views, but though from a mountain, this was not one. Serrated ridges, not much lower than that on which we stood, rose, one beyond another, far as that pure atmosphere could carry the vision, broken into awful chasms deep with ice and snow, rising into pinnacles piercing the heavenly blue with their cold, barren grey, on, on for ever, till the most distant range upbore unsullied snow alone. There were fair lakes mirroring the dark pine woods, canyons dark and blue-black with unbroken expanses of pines, snow-slashed pinnacles, wintry heights frowning upon lovely parks, watered and wooded, lying in the lap of summer. . . . It was something at last to stand upon the storm-rent crown of this lonely sentinel of the Rocky Range, on one of the mightiest vertebrae of the backbone of the North American continent, and to see the waters start for both oceans. Uplifted above love and hate and storms of passion, calm amidst the eternal silences, fanned by zephyrs and bathed in living blue, peace rested for that one bright day on the Peak, as if it were some region
>
> "Where falls not rain, or hail, or any snow,
> Or ever wind blows loudly." [32]

The sense of incongruity was fed from many sources: the difference between the well-regulated seasons of the year in the East and the unpredictability of Western climate; the contrast between some lush river-bottom and the arid plain out of which it had been carved; the impression of an empty land and the "ramparts, terraces, domes, towers, citadels and castles . . . cupolas, and magnificent porticoes, and here and there a solitary column and crumbling pedestal" as of "some ancient and boundless city in ruins" that Catlin found on the upper Missouri; [33] the melodramatic opposition of snowy peaks and green plains, of immense waterfalls and placid lakes, and, above all, the disappointing difference between the grandeur and sublimity of the world and the filth, dirt, squalor, and meanness of the Indian tribes, who were emphatically not haunted by the sounding cataract, the tall rock, the deep and gloomy wood and experienced no feeling and no love for the still, sad music of humanity. Nor, despite the dashing Frémont, the spectacular Buffalo Bill, Kit Carson, the celebrated Slade, and other picturesque figures, did the white man initially live in consonance with the grandeur and beauty of his environment, or display those chivalric qualities that seemed congruous with the Pyrenees or the Alpine story of William Tell. The incongruity between a landscape fit for gods and the pettiness of man serves, indeed, as the basis of much Western humor: *Roughing It* is the classic statement in our literature of this sense of incongruity. Mono Lake, wrote Twain, eight thousand feet above sea level, a "solemn, silent, sailless sea," an expanse of gray water a hundred miles in circumference, two pumice islands in its center, "the winding sheet of the dead volcano, whose vast crater the lake has seized upon and occupied" is sufficiently impressive. But Mark Twain and his companions are principally interested in it as a washtub—"we tied the week's washing astern of our boat, and sailed a quarter of a mile, and the job was complete." The next episode concerns a dog with raw places on him, who jumped overboard into the alkali water, and finally got ashore, struck out over the mountains, and ran away "at a gait which we estimated at about two hundred and fifty miles an hour." After these comic episodes Twain turns back to describe the lake as the abomination of desolation, but he ends with a funny passage about snow on the Fourth of July.[34]

As for the melancholy induced by this enormous wilderness, it was almost Biblical, for it seemed indeed a wilderness and a desert where the mountains were made desolate, even though some observers looked happily to peopling the great plains and the mountain states with stalwart Americans. No part of the United States more clearly demonstrated the terrible ineluctable quality of primal nature. Wrote John Wesley Powell in the nineties:

It has been the dream of mankind to control the clouds. Savage men dance for rain, and beat drums, and deck altars with the plumes of birds, and smoke pipes to create mimic clouds, and make offerings of meal to the wind gods, and perform long dramatic ceremonies as they pray for rain. All savage tribes thus seek to govern the clouds with terpsichorean worship. . . . But terpsichorean, sacrificial and fiducial graces fail to change the desert into the garden, or transform the flood-storm into a refreshing shower. Years of drought and famine come and years of flood and famine go, and the climate is not changed for dance, libation or prayer.[35]

Against this vastness, against the inexorability of nature, man, even at his proudest, was reduced to something like the ephemera of Franklin's apologue; thus, the state capitol at Helena, Montana, a goodly building in itself, viewed against the mountains or from some far peak looks like a toy bank. And the melancholy of the West was increased by the sense of human transience. All races, all occupations, all emotions seemed fugitive against the sweep of the plains and the eternal, snow-capped peaks. How many unknown races had perished! The story of the Indian is a story of weakness and defeat. The mountain men, the trappers, the fur-traders, the buffalo-hunters strutted their little hour upon the stage and then were gone. Melancholy envelops the story of the open range and the cowboy, vanished now except from Hollywood.[36]

> I'm a poor lonesome cowboy,
> I'm a poor lonesome cowboy,
> I'm a poor lonesome cowboy,
> And a long ways from home.

Nothing was more transient than mining, nothing more melancholy than the abandoned mining camps the miners left behind:

The camp was played out. Those who had tents folded them and left. The cabins were abandoned and fell down piecemeal to be converted into fuel by the few who lingered. Why any lingered they could not tell, unless from habit. The prospect was barren as the Silurian limestone and the place as valueless as the wreck of the old arastra clinging to its bed on the bank of the river—too rotten to burn. Bits of neglected flumes had become so warped that they turned over, stood on end or reclined against decayed trestle-work; broken wheelbarrows, old shovels without handles, and blunted picks, eaten with rust, reposed upon or protruded from abandoned dumps or prospect holes. The river bank had been washed down leaving great gaps, and cobble stones and big boulders piled up in midstream made a sterile island, around which the crystal waters surged as if angry at the intrusion. The Genius of Desolation would be lonesome in such a place, and, but for the ford close at hand and consequently an occasional traveler, would commit suicide.[37]

However small boys may delight in gunsmoke, however Owen Wister's Virginian may carry on in Wyoming his code of transplanted Southern chivalry, an elegiac note characterizes much Western literature. The preposterous Joaquin Miller is of no consequence in American literary development, and he is best known for his imitative Byronism. Nevertheless, a characteristic melancholy haunts his verses, as in "Joaquin Murietta":

> The brown hawk swoops low to the ground,
> And nimble chipmunks, small and still,
> Dart striped lines across the sill
> That manly feet shall press no more.
> The flume lies warping in the sun,
> The pan sits empty by the door,
> The pickax on its bedrock floor,
> Lies rusting in the silent mine.
> There comes no single sound nor sign
> Of life, beside yon monks in brown
> That dart their dim shapes up and down
> The rocks that swelter in the sun.
>
> .   .   .   .
>
> A lonely stillness, so like death,
> So touches, terrifies all things,
> That even rooks that fly o'erhead
> Are hush'd, and seem to hold their breath,
> To fly with muffled wings,

And heavy as if made of lead.
Some skulls that crumble to the touch,
Some joints of thin and chalk-like bone,
A tall black chimney, all alone,
That leans as if upon a crutch,
Alone are left to mark or tell,
Instead of cross or cryptic stone,
Where Joaquin stood and brave men fell.[38]

One feels that this setting, these events, this total obliteration
of humanity are not possible on the Atlantic seaboard; and
I think it illuminating that the "note" of *Westering* (1934) by
Thomas Hornsby Ferril of Colorado is one of melancholy and
that the most austerely anti-human poet in American literature is Robinson Jeffers of California, in whose work the
cold, clean, silent fury of rock and sea defeats the passions of
men.[39]

V

I do not pretend that the five qualities I have ascribed to
the impact of the West upon imagination are found only
in this context, but only that their combination has made
its special impression upon American culture. We have
always had westwardness. It seems to me therefore of less
importance that the city proletariat or the bankrupt farmers
did not drift westward at the time and in the masses
that some theories of American development require than
that westwardness has been a constant in American development until, and even beyond, the official closing of the frontier in 1890. We have not only had, or thought we had, plenty
of natural resources, we have had, or thought we had, plenty
of space into which to run. The effects of this grand and simple assumption upon American development have been enormous. The American family is more often rootless than not
because the younger generation could—and can—always go
somewhere else. Compare three European family novels—

George Eliot's *Middlemarch,* Thomas Mann's *Buddenbrooks,* and John Galsworthy's *The Forsyte Saga*—with three characteristic treatments of the family before the Civil War by Americans: Cooper's *Afloat and Ashore* and *Miles Wallingford,* his "anti-rent" trilogy (*Satanstoe, The Chainbearer,* and *The Redskins*), and Mrs. Stowe's *Uncle Tom's Cabin.* In the first three the novels are centripetal, the family idea like a lodestone pulls even rebels to the center, the continuity of generations in a particular area is assumed as the major *donnée* of the tale. But in the second the family seat is mainly, so to speak, a point of departure for immense adventures by sea or land. *Uncle Tom's Cabin,* for example, which begins in Kentucky, ends in Louisiana, and the breaking-up rather than the continuity of generations is the theme that haunts the book no less than the theme of slavery. Even though the Littlepage people in the anti-rent novels do not leave New York state, one does not feel in Cooper the solid continuity in family living that characterizes *Middlemarch,* and though Miles Wallingford wants to get back his estate, the idea does not enclose and envelop him as the idea of succession in a single place encloses and envelops the family of Buddenbrooks. It was impossible in France or Germany for a local Horace Greeley to advise the young, "Go West, young man, go West," but this was natural, indeed, inevitable in the United States.

Space has had its profound effect upon American religion. Not only was it impossible to hold sects long together, but it was difficult to hold the generations together in a given church locality. In America it has always been relatively easy to escape from social ties; and as Crèvecœur early observed, zeal in Europe is confined but in America it evaporates in the great distance it has to travel. Space in North America developed a great "free market" in souls, whom traveling evangelists, like cow-herders on the open plains, tried to keep together in some continuing and coherent mass. Not only does the American freely change from church to church, but, as one shrewd religious commentator has observed, a genuine passion for souls among ministers overwhelmed an equally important passion for truth; the result is, perhaps, the weakness of theological thought by native Americans. We have had, says this same commentator, both geographical and social space, or escape from the proximity of ties; inevitably, since there was no other general direction in which to move, the escape was westward into a landscape constantly increasing in scale, one that made our connections with the past of the Atlantic community more and more tenuous.[40]

We have become, largely as a result of our spread westward in the American landscape, a people of speed. It is symbolical that the emotional climax of our railroad-building was the completion of a line from East to West at Promontory Point, Utah, on May 10, 1869, although North and South had just been split apart by a gigantic civil war. Few principal railway lines run from Canada to the Gulf of Mexico; and our smart trains, even today, are mainly on the Western runs, not those going south to Richmond, Atlanta, Nashville, or Houston. Our great throughways likewise run more often east and west than they do north and south: consider the Massachusetts Turnpike, the New York Thruway, the Pennsylvania Turnpike, those in Ohio, Indiana, and Illinois, and so on westward. The airlines likewise play up connections between the East Coast cities and San Francisco, Los Angeles, or Honolulu, boasting that they are steadily reducing the time it takes to fly across the continent; one hears much less of the time it takes to fly from Canada to New Orleans. The Western landscape dims (or did until recently) our eastward vision; the immigrant coming hither came to escape history, despite the injunction that escape from history is impossible. He put the past behind him, with the result over decades, whether radicalism or conservatism reign, that the American people are a people in space rather than a people in time. Westward, indeed, the star of empire has made its way until the great republic has annexed as its forty-ninth state Alaska, the eastern boundary of which is virtually the 140th meridian, and, as its fiftieth, the Hawaiian Islands, which lie 2100 nautical miles west of the Golden Gate. The American landscape has widened from the little sandspit of Cape Cod and the tiny rocky peninsula of Cape Ann to the vastness of California and the immensity of the Pacific. The star of empire has gone realizing westward into a strange new land and a strange new sea.

Afterword

A DISTINGUISHED Hispanic-American scholar has recently published a study mainly concerned with Amerigo Vespucci, which he entitled *The Invention of America*. This phrase, with its charming ambiguity hovering between the concept of discovery and the concept of creativity, is perhaps the special meaning of this book. For America has been neither discovery nor creation but something of both. We are neither as unique as the siege psychology of the radical right asseverates nor as featureless as denouncers of American monotony and propagandists for the wave of the future declare we are. We are Europe at one remove or two, but we are part of Europe still. Once a remote outpost of the later Middle Ages, we have become the bulwark of the Western world. We began as a dream in the sunset; we are now seriously talking about men in the moon. We operate under the oldest written constitution in the world, product of a system of psychology long since discarded, but we continue to believe in our own novelty, we continue to find something fresh and marvelous in our gadgetry, our know-how, our adaptability, our pragmatism, which owes its aim to Emerson, its technology to Franklin, each of whom was both a European and an American mind.

The republic has seen four of its Presidents assassinated in less than a century; yet we somehow flatter ourselves we are an improvement upon a Europe that assassinated a czar of Russia in 1881, a president of France in 1894, a king of Italy in 1900, and the entire Serbian royal family in 1903. Nor, when the assassination of an Austrian archduke in 1914 brought American armies to Europe for the first time, did we admit that we, too, are Western men—Cummings, Hemingway, Dos Passos, Faulkner insisted it was all an idle crusade. It took uglier villains than the Renaissance despots, bloodier massacres than that of Saint Bartholomew to reunite us with our ancestors. We no longer read Lowell; yet his line about a strange new world that never yet was young is a more penetrating paradox than modern phrases about America as Eden, America as Darkness, America as Violence, perhaps because Lowell tried to be what Goethe was, a good European. Of course we have had our Utopian dreams; so did Europe, especially after 1492, 1789, 1830, 1848, and 1917. We have had our tragic and our gloomy hours—the Civil War, the Great Depression are two such experiences—but so did Europe in the fifteenth century, in the sixteenth, the seventeenth, the eighteenth, the nineteenth, and the twentieth. We have had our violent moments and our violent men. So has Europe from Cesare Borgia to Hitler, from the Thirty Years' War to the Berlin Wall. If we were once separated (or so we thought) from the corruptions of the Old World by the broad Atlantic, our own inventiveness reunited us to our ancestors by way of the airplane and the atom bomb.

America is, then, related to Europe by alternations of attraction and repulsion. These chapters, principally concerned with the earlier decades of the American story, are attempts to trace the history of certain aspects of Lowell's governing paradox.

The first finding of an actual world in the West seemed for a moment to validate a thousand dreams of plenitude and peace, but along with Paradise history, alas! devised the snake. A clash of cultures, a battle of religions begot, revealed, or increased cruelty and death, disease and treachery, torture and starvation in lands so incredibly filled with unpredictables, one wonders how the Europeans survived. Men of the Old World, whether Protestant or Catholic, could not make

the Indian understand that fertility rites and ritualistic cannibalism were improper ingredients of true religion; and the
Indian, naïvely welcoming the white men as, conceivably,
gods and certainly as guests, was baffled by concepts of
sovereignty, property, boundary lines, treaties, and "civilized" warfare. Striking back in the only way he could, he
ended by destroying himself.

Meanwhile the vast, expansive power of Renaissance culture, at once anarchic and authoritarian, demanding subordi-
nation, yet nourishing individuality, rolled across the enormous empires of Portugal and Spain, touched the colonial
holdings of France, and tinctured even the English colonies
with its fusion of pageantry and rebellion, the serious consideration of existence and the cunning manipulation of
personal relationships. Most important in point of continuing influence was the absolute necessity of re-establishing in
the New World the Renaissance concept of leadership (or
the superior man), by which, and by which alone, the Spanish
captain, the French explorer, and the English colonizer could
control the energy, ebullient or sullen, of men a thousand
miles away from any permanent seat of authority. The place
of fraud and cunning is as great in the New World story as it
is in the Old. American dreamers do not yet understand that
the adoption of a constitution for rational man did not *ipso
facto* eradicate a tradition of Machiavellian survival values
older than Jamestown, Plymouth, and Massachusetts Bay.
American life to this day bears the mark of this traditional
technology of control, a regrettable but necessary duplicity.
Fortunately this is not the total story.

For the colonial enterprise not only imported, it also reshaped, conduct. Men are never wholly products of their
environment, but they must forever reckon with it. Men
were presumably neither baser nor better in the Catholic
colonies to the south than they were in the English Protestant
colonies in North America, but by and by it appeared that
the typical North American genius was to be Benjamin
Franklin, child of the Protestant ethic and of self-regarding

virtue, benevolent, shrewd, and worldly wise, hypocritical, energetic, a great new incarnation of human energy. He became for better or worse the spiritual father of that most characteristic expression of nineteenth-century American life, the businessman, who, however, in proportion as he gained millions, tended to look backward and form himself on the great merchant princes of the Renaissance.[1] The evolution of the Protestant ethic into the philanthropic foundation endowed by millionaires is one of the most astonishing transformations of European ideas into American techniques to be found in history.

Colonists became colonials, colonials became provincials— but provincials in what provinces? Provinces of what empire? Behind the familiar story of the rise, decline, and fall of the old British Empire there is another story, shadowy yet important; namely, the rediscovery of the classical past by the Enlightenment, in which leading Americans participated. For there was a period between the Seven Years' War and the French Directorate when, despite national clashes and the devolution of empires, it really seemed that intelligent men were about to embrace a cosmopolitan culture. The provinces of that culture were not political but cultural, and enlightened men regarded themselves not merely as Frenchmen or Americans, Spaniards or Dutchmen, but as members of a world order descending from Athens and Rome, or at least from Greece and Rome as these were understood by the eighteenth-century mind. The American Revolution dissolved American ties with the House of Hanover, but its leaders reaffirmed our ties with Brutus and Cato—with thinkers, that is, who really believed in virtue and with patriots who really believed in a republic. Montesquieu's affirmation that virtue is the necessary quality of a republic was also in a way an affirmation of a belief that republican virtue was cosmopolitan virtue, for he took a dim view of kings. The Americans, who were never part of either Greece or Rome, conducted the first modern revolution under a Cincinnatus of the West, whose successors in the curule chair were John Adams, the American equivalent of Cato, and Thomas Jefferson, an American Hellene. If the return of the American millionaire upon the Renaissance concept of the merchant prince is remarkable, equally remarkable is the return in American history of the new republic upon the old.[2]

But the new republic was in the New World; and if, like nations in the Old, it was subjected to the nationalistic fervors released by the Revolution which created it, by the French Revolution, and by the Europe of Napoleon and the Holy Alliance, it displayed its nationalism in a special way. The calm of eighteenth-century rationality was broken by various doctrines of race, nationality, destiny, and experiment throughout the Western world; and the American, this new man, inhabitant of the only important republic in a world of hostile monarchies, felt called upon to instruct the universe not only in political truth but in cultural development. He was, in this endeavor, handicapped by an ancient tension between authority and the individual; and the assertion of individuality against authority, often taking shape as violence, was by him sometimes confused with the defeat of legality and order by individuality—a defeat manifest upon an ever-shifting frontier but by no means absent from older and more settled areas in the United States. Moreover, the radicalism of an experimental republic was manifest even to republicans, who were sometimes embarrassed by their own logic. Although the party of conservatism might deprecate or denounce the excesses of revolution in Europe, it could not with decency stop the results of revolution here. A radically new republic, it was held, must produce a radically new culture—hence those manifold experiments in our earlier decades, some of them funny, some of them of profound importance, directed toward the creation of novel ideas of law, of language, of religion, of education, of the arts, of literature.

Who was this new man, this American? We do not yet know. But finding an answer to Crèvecœur's famous query dominates our cultural history for decades. Whatever he was or might become, he lived in a brave new world; and the widening imaginative acceptance of the expansive qualities of American space and sky plays a leading role in American consciousness during the nineteenth century, a period when cosmology was still linked with science and with art. When one pauses to consider the implication of this basic interest upon American imaginative development in painting, poetry, prose, and religion, one realizes that in the physiographic sense there were two discoveries of the New World—one beginning with Columbus, the other beginning, so to speak, with the discovery that the voice of God spoke in the thunder of Niagara, on the heights of American mountain ranges, in the elemental power of American rivers, the endless sweep of prairie, desert, and Great Plains. And so this study comes full circle, returning upon the land itself. Other elements were to show their influence, particularly in the nineteenth century.

Reference Notes

Chapter I: The Image of the New World

1. For the text of this poem (by Giuliano Dati), together with all that can be learned about its authorship, see *La storia della inventione delle nuove insule de Channaria Indiane,* Introduzione e note di Mario Ruffini, Torino, 1958 (?). The poem embroiders on the letter; the second stanza, for example, makes an appeal to the greatness of antique virtue.
2. The bibliography is even more complicated than my text indicates. See for an introduction to the problem Cecil Jane, ed., *Select Documents Illustrating the Four Voyages of Columbus,* 2 vols., London, Printed for the Hakluyt Society, 1930–1933, Vol. I, pp. cxiii–clv. On the vexed question of what language (or languages) Columbus used see the introductory essay in Ramón Menéndez Pidal, *La lengua de Cristóbal Colón, el estilo de Santa Teresa y otros estudios sobre el siglo XVI,* Buenos Aires and Mexico, 1944. Still useful is William Eleroy Curtis, "The Existing Autographs of Christopher Columbus," *Annual Report of the American Historical Association for 1894,* pp. 445–518. And see also Samuel Eliot Morison, *Portuguese Voyages to America in the Fifteenth Century,* Cambridge (Mass.), 1940.
3. Samuel Purchas, *Hakluytus Posthumus or Purchas His Pilgrimes,* 20 vols., Glasgow, Printed for the Hakluyt Society, 1905–1907, Vol. XIII, pp. 414, 415. For the Italian text, a modern translation, and a learned discussion of the problem, see Richard Henry Major, *The Voyages of the Venetian Brothers, Nicolò and Antonio Zeno to the Northern Seas in the XIV Century,* London, Printed for the Hakluyt Society, 1873.
4. Still excellent is Paul Gaffarel, *Étude sur les rapports de l'Amérique et de l'ancien continent avant Christophe Colomb,* Paris, 1869.
5. Convenient is *The Norse Discovery of America: A Compilation in Extenso of all the Sagas, Manuscripts, and Inscriptive Memorials Relating to the Finding and Settlement of the New World in the Eleventh Century,* Norroena Society, London, Stockholm, etc., 1907. The editorial work is by a number of hands. In saying that the principle of plenitude is important in the Norse accounts I do not mean there were no other elements. Professor Walter B. Rideout calls my attention to Machiavel-

lian tactics and the slaughter by Freydis, Eric's daughter. See pp. 96f. of *The Norse Discovery of America*.

6. Richard Hakluyt, *The Principal Navigations Voyages Traffiques & Discoveries of the English Nation*, 12 vols., Glasgow, Printed for the Hakluyt Society, 1903–1905, Vol. VII, p. 134.

7. *The Dialogues of Plato Translated into English by Benjamin Jowett*, 4 vols., Oxford, 1871, Vol. II, *Timaeus*, pp. 518–21; *Critias*, pp. 599–612.

8. Ignatius Donnelly, *Atlantis: The Antediluvian World*, New York, 1882 (although Donnelly died in 1901 a revised edition was published as late as 1949!); Edwin Björkman, *The Search for Atlantis: Excursions by a Layman among Old Legends and New Discoveries*, New York, 1927.

9. There is a vast literature in many languages on Atlantis. In English the most sensible treatment by one who thinks the lost continent existed and possibly laid the foundations for Western civilization is probably Lewis Spence, *The Problem of Atlantis*, 2d ed., New York and London, 1925. In many respects Spence follows Paul Gaffarel, "L'Atlantide," *Revue de Géographie*, 6: 241–59, 331–45, 421–30 (April–June 1880), and 7: 21–29 (July 1880), an article that seems to exhaust the original sources and all opinions on the topic.

10. On this fascinating topic there is again a rich literature. The discussion of the maps in Vol. I of Justin Winsor, ed., *The Narrative and Critical History of America*, 8 vols., Boston, 1884–1889, and of course the maps themselves have charm and value. Also excellent is Gonzalo Menéndez Pidal, *Imagen del mundo hacia 1570, sugún noticias del Consejo de Indias y los tratadistas españoles*, Madrid, 1944. An invaluable article by E. Beauvois, "L'Élysée transatlantique et l'éden occidental," *Revue de l'Histoire des Religions*, 7(3): 273–318 (May, June 1883) argues for a Celtic origin of Greek and Latin myths about the Fortunate Islands, the Earthly Paradise, and like legends. See also William Henry Babcock, *Legendary Islands of the Atlantic: A Study in Medieval Geography*, New York, 1922; Arthur Percival Newton, *Travels and Travellers of the Middle Ages* (in *The History of Civilization* series), New York, 1926; Enrique de Gandía, *Historia crítica de los mitos de la conquista americana*, Madrid, 1929; Howard Rollin Patch, *The Other World according to Descriptions in Medieval Literature*, Cambridge (Mass.), 1950, especially Chapter v, a magisterial study. Some of these discussions go back to Vols. II and III of Alexandre de Humboldt, *Examen critique de l'histoire de la géographie du nouveau continent et des progrès de l'astronomie nautique aux quinzième et seizième siècles*, 5 vols., Paris, 1836–1839. Two recent studies are Richard Hennig, "Atlantische Fabelinseln und Entdeckung Amerikas," *Historische Zeitschrift*, 153 (3) : 461–500; and Loren Baritz, "The Idea of the West," *American Historical Review*, 46 (3): 617–40 (April 1941). For a complete account of both myth and history concerning El Dorado see Constantino Bayle, S.J., *El Dorado Fantasma*, 2d ed., with an introduction by José Joaquín Casas, Madrid, 1943; and for an account of the legend of the seven cities, Costa Baretto, *A lenda das Sete-Cidades*, Porto, 1949, and Stephen Clissold, *The Seven Cities of Cibola*, New York, 1961.

11. See Edmond Buron, *Ymago Mundi de Pierre d'Ailly,* 3 vols., Paris, 1930–1931, Vol. I, pp. 234–35, 241. Two classical equivalents of this felicity are the life of the Meropians, Aelian, *Varia Historia,* Lib. III, xviii, a parallel to the Atlantis story; and the pleasures of living on the island of Ogygia, Plutarch, *Moralia,* "Concerning the Face Which Appears in the Orb of the Moon."

12. Jane, *Select Documents,* Vol. II, pp. 30–46.

13. In this connection see the amazing collection of passages in Chapter v of Patch, *The Other World.*

14. J. Huizinga, *The Waning of the Middle Ages* (Anchor Books), Garden City, 1954, pp. 31, 29. See also Chapter xi, "The Vision of Death," for the obsession of the fourteenth and fifteenth centuries with mortality. He says in another place: ". . . always and everywhere in the literature of the age we find a confessed pessimism" (p. 37). On the vogue of the Dance of Death in literature and the graphic arts there is considerable literature. See Leonard Kurtz, *The Dance of Death and the Macabre Spirit in European Literature,* New York, 1934. Possibly the renunciation of the world in Thomas à Kempis's *Imitation of Christ,* written between 1417 and 1421, owes much to the disorder of the century.

15. Charles Edward Trinkaus, Jr., in *Adversity's Noblemen: The Italian Humanists on Happiness,* New York, 1940, argues with force and shrewdness that the concept of the happy humanist is a modern fiction.

16. A good edition of Politian is Poliziano, *Rime* (Raccolta Nazionale dei Classici della Società Editrice Rinascimento del Libro), Florence, 1929. But there are others.

17. Quoted in Julius Böheim, *Das Landschaftsgefühl des Ausgehenden Mittelalters,* Leipzig and Berlin, 1934, p. 99. Sir Kenneth Clark, in *Landscape into Art* (Beacon Paperbooks), Boston, 1961, p. 19, says the first indisputable piece of topography in art is that of the Swiss painter Konrad Witz, "The Miraculous Draught of Fishes" (1444), which remains exceptional for fifty years.

18. Eleanor Prescott Hammond, *English Verse between Chaucer and Surrey,* Durham (N.C.), 1927, p. 105; Janet Ross and Edward Hutton, *Poesie volgari di Lorenzo de' Medici,* 2 vols., Edinburgh, 1912, Vol. I, p. 68; Aimé Champollion-Figeac, *Les Poésies du Duc Charles d'Orléans,* Paris, 1842, p. 102.

19. The classic discussion is that by John Addington Symonds, *Renaissance in Italy: Italian Literature,* London, 1881, Part II, Chapter xii, pp. 194f. See also Part I, p. 170.

20. James Harvey Robinson and Henry Winchester Rolfe, *Petrarch: The First Modern Scholar and Man of Letters,* New York, 1898, p. 319. But see also Ernest Hatch Wilkins, *Life of Petrarch,* Chicago, 1961, pp. 12–13.

21. See, for example, Pedro Henríquez-Ureña, *Literary Currents in Hispanic America,* Cambridge (Mass.), 1945; Leonardo Olschki, *Storia letteraria delle scoperte geografiche: studi e ricerche,* Florence, 1937, Ramón Menéndez Pidal, *La lengua de Cristóbal Colón.* Contrast the rich specificity of Cabeça de Vaca in enumerating the flora and fauna

of Florida in 1542. F. W. Hodge and T. H. Lewis, eds., *Spanish Explorers in the Southern United States, 1528–1543,* New York, 1907, pp. 29–30.

22. I have used the translation by Jane, *Select Documents,* Vol. I, pp. 4–10. The Spanish and the English are on facing pages.

23. The slowness with which Columbus was elevated by the European imagination to heroic stature is made evident in the extraordinary and thoughtful article by Leicester Bradner, "Columbus in Sixteenth-Century Poetry," *Essays Honoring Lawrence C. Wroth,* Portland (Maine), 1951, pp. 15–30. He points out that Peter Martyr gives only brief space to Columbus's life and character in the *Decades* (1511–1530), that only in 1535 did Oviedo in his *Historia general y natural de las Indias* give him something like adequate space, and that, aside from some relatively casual treatments (for example that of Frascatoro in his *Syphilis,* 1530), it was not until 1581, in Rome, that Columbus became the hero of a major poem, *De nauigatione C. Columbi libri quattuor* by Lorenzo Gambara of Brescia (1506–1596).

24. In "Richard Eden's Copy of the 1533 *Decades of Peter Martyr*" (*Essays Honoring Lawrence C. Wroth*), Elizabeth Baer argues that "the entrance of Queen Mary and King Philip into London in 1554 inspired [Eden] to translate Peter Martyr and produce his book, *The Decades of the Newe Worlde,* to flatter the new monarchs by glorifying the deeds of the Spaniards and to rouse the English people to a realization of the value to the nation of the new discoveries." Perhaps. Philip was not one to brook a rival near the throne.

25. Book I of the *Metamorphoses,* translated by Horace Gregory, New York, 1958, pp. 5–6. The passages from Peter Martyr are from *De Orbe Novo: The Eight Decades of Peter Martyr d'Anghera,* translated from the Latin with notes and introduction by Francis Augustus MacNutt, 2 vols., New York, 1912, Vol. I, pp. 79, 104.

26. Peter Martyr, *De Orbe Novo,* Vol. I, pp. 119–20.

27. *The Letters of Amerigo Vespucci and Other Documents Illustrative of his Career,* translated with notes and introduction by Clements R. Markham, London, Printed for the Hakluyt Society, 1894, pp. 7f. The best study in English of Vespucci seems to be Frederick J. Pohl, *Amerigo Vespucci, Pilot Major,* New York, 1944. For present purposes it is more important to know what Europe read "by Vespucci" than how much of it was forgery.

28. Hakluyt, *Principal Navigations,* Vol. VIII, pp. 298, 304–305. Even as late as Father Andrew White's *Brief Relation* (ca. 1634) the Indians were still admirable. See *A Relation of the Colony of the Lord Baron of Baltimore . . .* translated by N. C. Brooks, Baltimore, 1847. Peter Force, ed., *Tracts and Other Papers relating principally to the . . . Colonies in North America . . . ,* 4 vols., Washington, 1836–1846, Vol. IV, no. 12.

29. For the miniature see Leonardo Olschki, *Storia Letteraria,* p. 37, and see also the long note on pp. 223–24. Olschki has also discussed that matter in "Ponce de León's Fountain of Youth: History of a Geographic

Myth," *The Hispanic American Historical Review*, 21(3): 361–85 (August 1941). The quotation from Peter Martyr is from Book VII of Decade VII, *De Orbe Novo*, Vol. II, pp. 292–95.

30. Woodbury Lowery, *The Spanish Settlements within the Present Limits of the United States, 1513–1561*, 2 vols., New York, 1901, Vol. I, p. 135.

31. Edmund Spenser, *The Faerie Queene*, Book II, "Proem," stanzas i–iv.

32. For the quotation see the chapter by Antonio Pastor, "Spanish Civilization in the Great Age of Discovery" in Arthur Percival Newton, *The Great Age of Discovery*, London, 1932, pp. 41–42. I have simplified Pastor's analysis but I hope without damage. On Charles V see Roger Bigelow Merriman, *The Rise of the Spanish Empire in the Old World and the New*, 4 vols., New York, 1918–1934, especially Vol. III.

33. Hakluyt, *Principal Navigations*, Vol. VII, p. 150.

34. My passages are from the admirable translation by John Grier Varner and Jeanette Johnson Varner, *The Florida of the Inca*, Austin (Texas), 1951, the opening chapters of Book II, part i, pp. 62–98. A soberer account is found in Chapter 9 of the "Narrative of the Expedition of Hernando de Soto, by the Gentleman of Elvas," for which see Hodge and Lewis, *Spanish Explorers*.

35. See M. J. Schretlen, *Dutch and Flemish Woodcuts of the 15th Century*, London, 1925. See also in this connection Böheim, *Das Landschaftsgefühl des Ausgehenden Mittelalters*.

36. For a strange pictorial treatment of "Indians" in costumes and with accouterments suggesting a Renaissance carnival see Josef Benzing, "Die Indianerbordüre und ihre Nachschnitte, 1518–1521," *Archiv für Geschichte des Buchwesens*, 2: 742–48 (1960).

37. See *The New World: The First Pictures of America made by John White and Jacques Le Moyne and Engraved by Theodore De Bry*, edited and annotated by Stefan Lorant, New York, 1946.

Chapter II: The Anti-Image

1. Sir Thomas More's *Utopia* was written in 1515–1516 and published in Latin at Louvain in 1516, at Paris in 1517, and at Basle in 1518. The English translation by Ralph Robinson was printed in 1551. A good modern edition is that by J. H. Lupton, Oxford, 1895.

2. See Silvio A. Zavala, *La "Utopia" de Tomas Moro en la Nueva España y otros estudios (Biblioteca historica mexicana de obras ineditas, No. 4)*, Mexico, 1937, pp. 3–29.

3. François Rabelais, *Gargantua and Pantagruel*, translated by J. M. Cohen (Penguin Books), Baltimore, 1955, p. 709.

4. Nicolas Monardes, *Primera y segunda y tercera partes de la historia medicinal de las cosas que se traen de nuestras Indias occidentales que siruen en medicina*, Seville, 1574.

5. *Joyfull Newes out of the Newe Founde World written in Spanish by*

Nicholas Monardes Physician of Seville and Englished by John Frampton, Anno 1577, with an introduction by Stephen Gaselee, 2 vols., London, 1925. Monardes was also translated into Italian and French. The quoted phrases are to be found in Vol. I, pp. 3, 99, 106, 107, 109, 110, 114.

6. See in this connection Bernard Cohen, "The New World as a Source of Science for Europe," *Actes du IXᵉ Congrès International d'Histoire des Sciences,* Barcelona and Madrid, 1959, pp. 95–130.

7. The text of the essays varies from edition to edition. I have followed the translation of Montaigne by Donald M. Frame, Stanford, 1957. "Of Cannibals" is on pp. 150–59. The paragraph I cite from "Of Coaches" is on p. 693. This essay is in Book III and was written in 1585–1588.

8. Chinard turns up a book (which I have not seen) by Le R. P. Claude d'Abeville, *Histoire de la mission des Pères Capucins en l'Isle de Maragnon et terres circonvoysines,* Paris, 1614, in which Father Claude finds nothing monstrous in the New World, only happiness and fecundity. "Happy Brazil, sweet abbey of Thélème, where Panurge . . . would have loved to take refuge after his travels and peregrinations" is Chinard's ironic comment. Gilbert Chinard, *L'Amérique et le rêve exotique dans la littérature française au xvii et au xviii siècles,* Paris, 1913, p. 18.

9. I have depended as before on Jane, *Select Documents,* Vol. II, p. 104. But as showing the conflict in the European mind between the Edenic image and the discovery of New World cruelty see the excellent translation, with notes, by Fernandez de Ybarra of "The Letter of Dr. Diego Alvarez Chanca, Dated 1494, Relating to the Second Voyage of Columbus to America," *Smithsonian Miscellaneous Collections,* 48: 428–57 (1907).

10. Peter Martyr, *De Orbe Novo,* Vol. I, p. 103.

11. Hakluyt, *Principal Navigations,* Vol. VII, pp. 227–28, 283.

12. Ibid., Vol. VIII, p. 116.

13. Ibid., Vol. VIII, p. 357.

14. Ibid., Hakluyt's translation, Vol. VIII, p. 452.

15. From "The Voyage made by M. John Hawkins Esquire . . . begun in An. Dom. 1564," ibid., Vol. X, p. 57.

16. William H. Prescott, *History of the Conquest of Mexico,* ed. John Foster Kirk, Philadelphia, 1873, Vol. III, pp. 217–18. Cortés' own report on the discovery of treasure and on the fighting can be conveniently read in *Letters of Cortés: The Five Letters of Relation from Fernando Cortés to the Emperor Charles V,* translated and edited by Francis Augustus MacNutt, 2 vols., New York, 1908.

17. William H. Prescott, *History of the Conquest of Peru,* 2 vols., New York, 1847, Vol. I, p. 418.

18. Hakluyt, *Principal Navigations,* Vol. X, pp. 338–431.

19. Ibid., Vol. XI, pp. 114–15. The fullest study I have seen of the El Dorado legend is Constantino Bayle, S.J., *El Dorado Fantasma.*

20. See in this connection Lewis Hanke, *Aristotle and the American Indians,* London, 1959. Hanke points out that the issues involved in Indian slavery were available to Elizabethan readers inasmuch as, following a long extract from Las Casas on Spanish cruelty, Purchas prints "The

summe of the disputation betweene Fryer Bartholomew de las Casas or Casaus, and Doctor Sepuleda." See Purchas, *Hakluytus Posthumus*, Vol. XVIII, pp. 176–80. See also on the whole subject Luciano Pereña Vicente, *Mision de España en America, 1540–1560*, Madrid, 1956. Documents by Bartolomé Carranza, Melchor Cano, Diego Covarrubias, and Juan de la Peña support the thesis of Francisco de Vitoria against Sepúlveda, and are important as showing that Las Casas was not alone in his belief that all men are born free.

21. See for a graphic account of the hardships of the Atlantic passage in the mid-eighteenth century Gottlieb Mittelberger, *Journey to Pennsylvania*, trans. and ed. by Oscar Handlin and John Clive, Cambridge (Mass.), 1960.

22. The quotation is from the revised translation of the Italian appearing in George Parker Winship, ed., *Sailors' Narratives of Voyages along the New England Coast, 1524–1624*, Boston, 1905, pp. 5–7, 21–22. The sentence quoted from Peter Martyr is in the *De Orbe Novo*, Vol. I, p. 217.

23. Jane, *Select Documents*, Vol. I, pp. 30, 32. See also Edward Arber, ed., *The First Three English Books on America*, Birmingham, 1885, "A Treatyse of the Newe India," pp. 29–30.

24. Markham, *Letters of Amerigo Vespucci*, pp. 37–47.

25. Hakluyt, *Principal Navigations*, Vol. VII, p. 227.

26. Arber, *First Three English Books*, p. 70.

27. Clements R. Markham, ed., *The Hawkins' Voyages during the Reigns of Henry VIII, Queen Elizabeth, and James I*, London, Printed for the Hakluyt Society, 1878, p. 323.

28. At Porto Bello on Darien the wretched group of Spaniards led by Nicuesa ate their dogs, toads, the dead bodies of Indians they had massacred, and buried corpses already putrefying. Out of 700 men only 40 survived. Peter Martyr, *De Orbe Novo*, Vol. I, pp. 275–76. On cannibalism among the wretched members of Narváez's men see the narrative of Alvar Núñez Cabeça de Vaca in Hodge, *Spanish Explorers in the Southern United States*, p. 63. Dried human flesh preserved Esquivel.

29. Francisco López de Gómara, *The Pleasant Historie of the Conquest of the VVeast India, now called new Spayne*, translated by Thomas Nichols, New York (Scholars' Facsimiles & Reprints), 1940, pp. 203, 393.

30. The first quotation is from Father Le Jeune's "Brief Relation of the Journey to New France," *The Jesuit Relations and Allied Documents*, 73 vols., Cleveland, 1896–1901, Vol. V, pp. 29–31. The original is in Latin. For more horrors see pp. 51–55. The letter of the Reverend John Corbley can be read in Samuel G. Drake, ed., *Indian Captivities or Life in the Wigwam*, New York, 1857, pp. 336–37. The Drake collection comprises 31 narratives running from the captivity of Juan Ortiz in 1528 to that of J. W. B. Thompson in 1836.

31. Peter Martyr, *De Orbe Novo*, Vol. II, p. 261.

32. Hakluyt, *Principal Navigations*, Vol. VII, p. 220.

33. Ibid., pp. 220, 282, 305.

34. Ibid., p. 373.

35. Ibid., p. 400.

36. Ibid., Vol. IX, p. 382.

37. Ibid., Vol. X, p. 29.

38. Ibid., Vol. XI, p. 107.

39. Edward Arber and A. G. Bradley, eds., *Travels and Works of Captain John Smith,* 2 vols., Edinburgh, 1910, Vol. I, p. 75. A new edition of Smith's writings is promised.

40. "An Account of the Canadian Mission," *Jesuit Relations,* Vol. I, p. 287.

41. Ibid., Vol. III, p. 33. And compare p. 131.

42. Ibid., Vol. I, p. 173.

43. There is of course an enormous literature. For an extensive bibliography on the theory that the Indians were descended from the ten lost tribes of Israel see Appendix A of Lewis Hanke, *The First Social Experiments in America,* Cambridge (Mass.), 1935. On some of the novel problems in theology, ethics, and law created by the discovery of "savages" in the New World see Rosario Romeo, "Le Scoperte Americane nella Conscienza Italiana del Cinquecento," *Revista Storica Italiana,* 65(2): 222–57; (3): 326–79 (Naples, 1953). Still excellent on the problem of Indian origins is Justin Winsor's great *Narrative and Critical History,* Vol. I in general and Chapter V of Volume II, though of course the anthropological lore has to be updated. The pioneer study of the treatment of the Indian in American literature (still a good one) is Herman F. C. ten Kate, "The Indian in Literature," *Annual Report of the Smithsonian Institution, 1921,* Washington, 1922, pp. 507–28; writing as an ethnologist, ten Kate found most of the literary treatments of limited value. His essay is a condensation of work published in Dutch in 1919 and 1920. A full-length "literary" treatment is that of Albert Keiser, *The Indian in American Literature,* New York, 1933. A far more penetrating analysis of the problem of the conflict of cultures is Roy Harvey Pearce, *The Savages of America: A Study of the Indian and the Idea of Civilization,* Baltimore, 1953.

44. Varner, *The Florida of the Inca,* p. 281.

45. George Alsop, *A Character of the Province of Maryland* (1666), Chapter II, *passim.* There are various editions.

46. Johnson, *Wonder-Working Providence,* p. 263.

47. Cabeça de Vaca, narrative, in Hodge and Lewis, *Spanish Explorers,* pp. 64–65.

48. Varner, *The Florida of the Inca,* pp. 493–94.

49. Charles H. Lincoln, ed., *Narratives of the Indian Wars, 1675–1699,* New York, 1913, p. 86.

50. I draw my incidents from the two standard accounts: Varner, *The Florida of the Inca, passim,* and the "Narrative of the Expedition of Hernando De Soto, By the Gentleman of Elvas," translated by Buckingham Smith (rev.), in Hodge and Lewis, *Spanish Explorers.*

51. For the observation by "R. H.," see Lincoln, *Narratives of the Indian Wars,* p. 105; for Johnson's, see *Wonder-Working Providence,* p. 169. On the Indian wars, see also John Underhill, *Neuues from America* (1638), John Mason, *A Brief History of the Pequot War* (1670?),

Samuel Penhallow, *The History of the Wars of New-England, With the Eastern Indians,* Boston, 1726, and (more favorable to the Indians) Daniel Gookin, *Historical Collections of the Indians in New England* (1677), in which Gookin, not unaware of Indian wiliness, nevertheless stoutly defends the Christian Indians. The praying Indians were sometimes treacherous, and the whites massacred thirty of them on one occasion.

52. See Roy Harvey Pearce, "The Significance of the Captivity Narratives," *American Literature,* 19 (I): 1–20 (March 1947), and "The 'Ruines of Mankind': The Indian and the Puritan Mind," *Journal of the History of Ideas,* XIII(2): 200–217 (January 1952).

53. Arber, *First Three English Books,* pp. 131ff., Eden's translation of Peter Martyr.

54. Jane, *Select Documents,* Vol. II, pp. 16–18.

55. *Jesuit Relations,* Vol. II, pp. 27–29.

56. Hakluyt, *Principal Navigations,* Vol. VII, p. 152. For an orderly survey of English voyages into the Arctic see George Born Manhart, *The English Search for a Northwest Passage in the Time of Queen Elizabeth,* Philadelphia, 1924.

57. Hakluyt, *Principal Navigations,* Vol. VII, pp. 208, 214, 232–33.

58. Ibid., pp. 234–35. For a "horrible snow: that fell on July 26" see p. 238.

59. Ibid., p. 334.

60. Ibid., p. 228.

61. *Jesuit Relations,* Vol. III, p. 61.

62. Peter Martyr, *De Orbe Novo,* Vol. I, p. 354.

63. Ibid., pp. 247, 261.

64. Hakluyt, *Principal Navigations,* Vol. X, pp. 345, 409, 418.

65. Purchas, *Hakluytus Posthumus,* Vol. XV, pp. 65–66.

66. Ibid., pp. 215, 228.

67. Ibid., pp. 38–39.

68. Peter Martyr, *De Orbe Novo,* Vol. II, p. 374.

69. Hakluyt, *Principal Navigations,* Vol. VIII, p. 70.

70. "The Narrative of the Expedition of Coronado. By Pedro De Castañeda," translated by George Parker Winship, in Hodge and Lewis, *Spanish Explorers,* pp. 325, 333.

71. "Narrative of Alvar Núñez de Vaca" in ibid., pp. 16, 17, 41. See also the account of the hurricane off Cuba, p. 4.

72. "Narrative of the Gentleman of Elvas" in ibid., pp. 204, 263. Ponce de León encountered ocean currents that drove him backward (the Gulf Stream), and that puzzled and terrified him. See Lloyd A. Brown, "The River in the Ocean," *Essays Honoring Lawrence C. Wroth,* p. 69.

Chapter III: Renaissance Culture and America

1. See W. Bennet Munro, "The Droit de Banalité during the French Regime in Canada," *Annual Report of the American Historical Association* for 1899, Vol. I, pp. 207f. The home government insisted upon

the adoption in Canada of the Coûtume de Paris as "modernized" in 1580, though most of the French immigrants came from agricultural Normandy. And see in this general context Walter Alexander Riddell, *Rise of Ecclesiastical Control in Quebec, Columbia University Studies in History, Economics, and Public Law,* No. 174, 1916.

2. Sigmund Diamond, "From Organization to Society: Virginia in the Seventeenth Century," *American Journal of Sociology,* 63(5): 457–75 (March 1958); and "An Experiment in 'Feudalism': French Canada in the Seventeenth Century," *William and Mary Quarterly,* 3d ser., 18(1): 3–32 (January 1961).

3. R. B. Cunningham Grahame, *A Vanished Arcadia,* New York, 1901, p. 188.

4. E. A. J. Johnson, *American Economic Thought in the Seventeenth Century,* London, 1932, Chapter VII, "The Morality of the Marketplace" and Chapter XII, "The Condemnation of Communism"; and Joseph Dorfman, *The Economic Mind in American Civilization,* 5 vols., New York, 1946–1959, Vol. I, Book i, Chapter III, "The New England Way." Surely "communalism" rather than "communism" is the better term.

5. Américo Castro, *España en su historia: cristianos, moros y judios,* Buenos Aires, 1948, especially Chapters II–VII. There is a translation by Edmund L. King, *The Structure of Spanish History,* Princeton, 1954, the text of which is somewhat more extensive.

6. Hakluyt, *Principal Navigations,* Vol. IX, pp. 398–465; and Robert Tomson's narrative in G. R. G. Conway, *An Englishman and the Mexican Inquisition, 1556–1560,* Mexico, privately printed, 1927.

7. For an admirable study showing the strength and weakness of centralized control from a distance see John Tate Lanning, *The University in the Kingdom of Guatemala,* Ithaca (N.Y.), 1955. There are of course innumerable studies in the political, diplomatic, and economic spheres.

8. See, *inter alia,* Don E. Smith, "The Viceroy of New Spain in the Eighteenth Century," *Annual Report of the American Historical Association for 1908,* 1: 169–81; and Herbert I. Priestley, *José de Gálvez, Visitor-General of New Spain, 1765–1771,* Berkeley (Calif.), 1916.

9. See John Tate Lanning, *The Spanish Missions of Georgia,* Chapel Hill (N.C.), 1935.

10. In the West, of course, the great problem was the control of Alta California. On the Spanish in California, Charles Edward Chapman, *The Founding of Spanish California: the Northwestward Expansion of New Spain, 1687–1783,* New York, 1916, though old, is still excellent. But there is a vast literature on California and on the Southwest: thus the quarto-centennial of Coronado's expedition produced a small library, of which George P. Hammond and Agaouti Rey, *Narratives of the Coronado Expedition, 1540–1542,* Albuquerque, 1940, and A. Grove Day, *Coronado's Quest: The Discovery of the Southwestern States,* Berkeley and Los Angeles, 1940, are excellent instances. Finally, as Arthur P. Whitaker reminds us, "For a century and a half after the discovery of America, the Gulf of Mexico remained a Spanish lake, and for another

half century the gulf coast from Florida to Texas remained a no-man's land. [Only] in the second half of the seventeenth century this splendid isolation was broken down. . . ." *Mississippi Valley Historical Review,** 27 (1): 91 (June 1940). Nor did Spain always give up easily. See, e.g., Philip C. Brooks, "Spain's Farewell to Louisiana, 1803–1821," *MVHR,* 27(1): 29–42 (June 1940).

11. On the linguistic influence see Harold W. Bentley, *A Dictionary of Spanish Terms in English with Special Reference to the American Southwest,* New York, 1932. More popular but valid is Ramon F. Adams, *Western Words: A Dictionary of the Range, Cow Camp and Trail,* Norman (Okla.), 1944. With reference to the larger question of Spanish influence upon the British colonies and the United States I am aware that no historical question has been more characteristically moot. The two extremes are represented by two articles or summaries of papers in the *MVHR.* Alfred B. Thomas, as reported in that magazine (23: 230–31 [September 1936]), in a paper entitled "Permanency of the Influence of Spanish Culture in the United States," delivered at a meeting, makes very wide claims for cereals, orchards, viniculture, the cattle industry, jurisprudence, architecture, folklore, and much else. In the same magazine for March 1955 (41: 579–600) Earl Pomeroy, in an article "Toward a Reorientation of Western History: Continuity and Environment," minimizes virtually every claim made by Thomas, concluding that "the role of Spanish culture in the Southwest has been exaggerated from the day of . . . the Ramona legend to the day of the latest real estate speculator who manufactures Spanish-sounding place names." But are not "Spanish-sounding place names" themselves an example of influence? For general surveys see Herbert E. Bolton, *The Spanish Borderlands: A Chronicle of Old Florida and the Southwest,* New Haven, 1921, and his *Wider Horizons in American History,* New York, 1939. David R. Moore, *A History of Latin America,* New York, 1938, is still excellent, and more recent studies include two by Harry Bernstein, *Origins of Inter-American Interest, 1700–1812,* New York, 1945, and *Making an Inter-American Mind,* Gainesville (Fla.), 1961. Without prejudice to any book it may be justly remarked that propaganda sometimes overcomes scholarship in this field. For a view that seems to me both just and sympathetic see the preface to Bolton's *Spanish Borderlands.* This scholar observes that "from Sacramento to St. Augustine nearly everybody holds his land by a title going back to Mexico or Madrid." See also Silvio Zavala, "A General View of the Colonial History of the New World," *The American Historical Review,* 66(4): 913–29 (July 1961). For a charming account of the Inca see Julia Fitzmaurice-Kelly, *El Inca Garcilasso de la Vega,* Oxford, 1921, and on the existence of an Incan "nobility," *The Inca Concept of Sovereignty and the Spanish Administration in Peru, The University of Texas Institute of Latin-American Studies: Latin-American Studies,* No. 4, Austin, 1948.

12. Two excellent accounts of the viceregal system and Spanish colonial

---

* Hereinafter cited as *MVHR.*

administration generally are Bernard Moses, *The Spanish Dependencies in South America: An Introduction to the History of their Civilisation*, 2 vols., New York and London, 1914, Vol. I, Chapter XIV, "The Council of the Indies and the India House," Chapter XV, "The Audiencia and the Viceroy"; Vol. II, Chapter XII, "The Church in Relation to the Civil Government"; and Clarence H. Haring, *The Spanish Empire in America*, New York, 1947, Chapters IV–X.

13. See J. Vicena Vives, ed., *Historia social y económica de España y América*, 5 vols., Barcelona, 1957–1959, Vol. III, *Imperio, aristocracia, absolutismo* by Juan Regla and Guillermo Cespedes, p. 400; and see Charles S. Bruden, *Religious Aspects of the Conquest of Mexico*, Durham (N.C.), 1930, *passim*.

14. Irving A. Leonard, *Romances of Chivalry in the Spanish Indies: With Some Registros of Shipments of Books to the Spanish Colonies*, Berkeley (Calif.), 1933. He finds, for example, that in 1584 112 cases of books were shipped to Vera Cruz alone, and that from October 15 to December 16, 1585, 75 cases of books were carried on muleback from Vera Cruz to Mexico City (p. 27). But see also Mr. Leonard's more extensive, *Books of the Brave*, Cambridge (Mass.), 1949.

15. John Van Horne, "The Attitude toward the Enemy in Sixteenth Century Spanish Narrative Poetry," *Romanic Review*, 16(4): 341–61 (October–December 1925). Among the authors he examines are Ercilla, Lasso de la Vega, and Saavedra Guzman, and the anonymous writer of the *Conquista de la Nueva Castilla*.

16. A translation of *La Araucana* was begun by Walter Owen in 1945 (Buenos Aires) and a complete translation was published by Charles Maxwell Lancaster and Paul Thomas Manchester (*The Araucaniad*) by the Vanderbilt University Press, also in 1945. The Owen version has both the Spanish and the English texts.

17. I quote from the not too accurate translation of 1772, *A Voyage to South America . . . by Don George Juan and Don Antonio de Ulloa*, 2 vols., London, 1772, Vol. II, pp. 41–52. The original passages may be found in *Relación histórica del viage a la América meridional hecho de orden de S. Mag . . . por Don Jorge Juan . . . y Don Antonio de Ulloa*, 2 vols., Madrid, 1748, Vol. II, pp. 59–66. This report is said to have occasioned a modernization of the viceregal system. For a Mexican parallel see Chapter I of Irving A. Leonard, *Baroque Times in Old Mexico*, Ann Arbor (Mich.), 1959; and for the splendid review by the viceroy of the Coronado expedition before it set out from Compostela, Bolton, *The Spanish Borderlands*, pp. 88–89. Bolton also describes the accouterment of Luis de Velasco when he joined the expedition of Juan de Oñata for the conquest of New Mexico in 1598, pp. 171–72. The original of the Coronado account is in Pedro de Castañeda. And see Chapter IV of Herbert I. Priestley, *Tristán de Luna, Conquistador of the Old South: A Study of Spanish Imperial Strategy*, Glendale (Calif.), 1936, for still more ceremonial.

18. Gabriel Méndez Plancarte, ed., *Humanismo méxicano del siglo XVI*, Mexico, 1946, pp. 3–25, speaks of the education of the Indians. The best

study in English on university education in the period is John Tate Lanning, *Academic Culture in the Spanish Colonies,* London and New York, 1940, who points out (p. 39) the difficulty Indians experienced in receiving higher education, a difficulty not experienced in the sixteenth century, apparently, by *mestizos.* Bernardino de Sahagún has had several editions, the best being that in five volumes published in Mexico in 1938. Mauricio Magdalena has extracted some choice pages from Sahagún in *Suma Indiana,* Mexico, 1943 (Biblioteca del Estudiante Universario). Among various editions of Balbuena's *Grandeza Mexicana* one in the same series (Mexico, 1941) is excellent.

19. Consult Clarence H. Haring, *The Buccaneers of the West Indies in the XVII Century,* New York, 1910. The challenge written in English and Spanish and nailed on a tree in Jamaica by Manuel Rivero Pardal in 1670 has all the style of a chivalric challenge. See pp. 161f., especially the account of Spanish resistance to the buccaneers, 30 men remaining out of 314 in the original garrison.

20. John Spencer Bassett, *The Life of Andrew Jackson,* 2 vols. in one, 2d ed., New York, 1928, Vol. I, p. 243. For yet another area of ignorance consult John P. Bloom, "New Mexico Viewed by Anglo-Americans, 1846–1849," *New Mexico Historical Review,* 34: 165–98 (July 1959).

21. *Mexico, 1825–1828: The Journal and Correspondence of Edward Thornton Tayloe,* ed. C. Harvey Gardiner, Chapel Hill (N.C.), 1959, pp. 46, 50–53, 67, 112, 181.

22. Albert M. Gilliam, *Travels over the Table Lands and Cordilleras of Mexico during the Years 1843 and 44; including a Description of California* . . . , Philadelphia, 1846, pp. 42–43, 48, 165, 453. Gilliam was much moved by the siege of the Alamo.

23. Brantz Mayer, *Mexico As It Was and As It Is,* New York, 1844, pp. v, 3, 17, 41, 71f., 79, 81, 166, 284–85, 328, 351–53. The book is dedicated to Powhatan Ellis, minister plenipotentiary to Mexico.

24. William W. Carpenter, *Travels and Adventures in Mexico,* New York, 1851; *To Mexico with Scott: Letters of Captain E. Kirby Smith to his Wife,* Cambridge (Mass.), 1917, p. 142. All these writers admire the romantic grandeur of Mexican scenery.

25. Thomas B. Thorpe, *Our Army at Monterey,* Philadelphia, 1847, p. 114.

26. Richard M'Sherry, *El Pulchero: or, A Mixed Dish from Mexico,* Philadelphia, pp. 84–85. His letter XVIII described Mexico City in glowing terms.

27. For the continuing validity of Renaissance culture in Mexico consult Julio Jiménez Rueda, *Historia de la cultura en México: el virreinato,* Mexico, 1950, with its excellent bibliography. On American condescension toward Mexican culture see Cecil Robinson, *With the Ears of Strangers: The Mexican in American Literature,* Tucson, 1963.

28. Alfonso Reyes, *Obras Completas,* 12 vols., Mexico, 1955–1960, are, I think, not complete. My quotations are from the excellent translation by Harriet de Onís of some of Reyes' essays, *The Position of America and Other Essays,* New York, 1950.

29. See Mary Austin, *The American Rhythm*, New York, 1923; Waldo Frank, *The Re-Discovery of America*, New York, 1929, *America Hispana*, New York, 1931, and *In the American Jungle*, New York, 1937. Possibly D. H. Lawrence should here be cited. I do not mean that these authors take over the ideas of Alfonso Reyes but only that they understand them.

30. An excellent general architectural guide is George Kubler and Martin Soria, *Art and Architecture in Spain and Portugal and their American Dominions, 1500 to 1800*, London, 1959. Though the main emphasis is Hispanic, this book analyzes the Portuguese-Brazilian tradition, ancestor of the exciting contemporary architecture of Brasilia and Rio de Janeiro, for which I have not space.

31. See Rexford Newcomb, *The Franciscan Mission Architecture of Alta California*, New York, 1916; Cleve Hallenbeck, *Spanish Missions of the Old Southwest*, Garden City, 1926; Frank C. Lockwood, *Story of the Spanish Missions of the Middle Southwest*, Santa Ana, 1934 (the author's real name is Francis Cummins Lockwood). A special study of great interest is Manuel Toussaint, *Arte Mudéjar en América*, Mexico, 1946; and an excellent general account is Pál Kelemen, *Baroque and Rococo in Latin America*, New York, 1951, which contains a fine bibliography.

32. The great standard work by an American scholar is Chandler Rathfon Post's magisterial *History of Spanish Painting*, 12 vols., Cambridge (Mass.), 1930–1958, alas! never to be finished.

33. On Gottschalk's relation to Latin American and Negro music see the excellent discussion by Gilbert Chase, *America's Music: from the Pilgrims to the Present*, New York, 1955, Chapter 15, "The Exotic Periphery." Gottschalk's own *Notes of a Pianist*, edited by his sister Clara and translated from the French by Robert E. Peterson, Philadelphia, 1881, is lively and amusing, but contains very little about music. On the general musical problem see Gilbert Chase, "The Foundations of Musical Culture in Latin America," *Intellectual Trends in Latin America, The University of Texas Institute of Latin-American Studies; Latin-American Studies*, No. 1, Austin, 1945, pp. 35–43.

34. See Julian Juderías, *La Leyenda negra*, Barcelona, 1943 (originally published in 1914).

35. The standard study is Stanley T. Williams, *The Spanish Background of American Literature*, 2 vols., New Haven, 1955.

36. William Robertson, *The History of the Reign of the Emperor Charles V* (1769); *The History of America* (1777). Joel Barlow, *The Vision of Columbus*, was printed in 1787.

37. Leading Columbus scholars include Henri Harrisse, who once taught at the University of North Carolina, where students (according to legend) threw chalk at him, Justin Winsor, and the living Samuel Eliot Morison.

38. Washington Irving, *Works*, Kinderhook Edition (Author's Revised Edition), New York, 1865, Vol. IV, pp. 131–32.

39. The leading documents are George Bancroft, *History of the United States*, 10 vols., Boston, 1834–1874; William H. Prescott, *The History*

of Ferdinand and Isabella, 3 vols., Boston, 1838, *The Conquest of Mexico,* New York, 1843, *The Conquest of Peru,* New York, 1847, and (unfinished) *Philip II,* Boston, 1855–1858; John L. Motley, *The History of the United Netherlands,* 4 vols., London, 1861–1868, *The Life and Death of John of Barneveld,* 2 vols., New York, 1875.

40. David Levin, *History as Romantic Art,* Stanford, 1959.

41. William Bennet Munro, *Crusaders of New France* (Chronicles of America), New Haven, 1918, p. 11.

42. Each of the two monarchs, Henry VIII and Francis I, sought to impress the ministers and officials of the other with his splendor as an index of power. For a French account see Robert Goubaux and P.-André Lemoisne, eds., *Mémoires du Maréchal de Florange dit le Jeune Adventureux,* 2 vols., Paris, Société de l'Histoire de France, 1913, Vol. I, pp. 262–73; for an English one, Edward Hall, *Chronicle, Containing the History of England during the Reign of Henry Fourth . . . to the End of the Reign of Henry the Eighth,* London, 1809, pp. 604–20. But see also the account of the coronation ceremony of 1509, or for that matter the ceremony accompanying the entrance of Louis XI into Paris, *Memoirs of Philip de Commines* [sic], translated, 2 vols., London, 1823, Vol. II, pp. 418f. A growing ceremonial, writes G. R. Elton in the *New Cambridge Modern History,* Vol. II, p. 439, most gorgeous in France, but most formal in England, set monarchs apart from lesser men.

43. J. Lucas-Dubreton, *La Renaissance italienne: vie et mœurs au xvᵉ siècle,* Paris, Le Club du Livre d'Historie (Présence de l'Historic), 1959.

44. Alfred S. West, ed., *Bacon's Essays,* Cambridge, 1926, p. 155.

45. Prescott, *The Conquest of Mexico,* Kirk edition, Vol. I, p. 331.

46. Ibid., Vol. III, p. 289 and reference.

47. *The True History of the Conquest of Mexico . . . by Bernal Diaz del Castillo,* translated by Maurice Keating, London, 1800, p. 480.

48. Purchas, *Hakluytus Posthumus,* Vol. XIX, pp. 59–60, 56–57.

49. Amusingly described by Morris Bishop, *Champlain: The Life of Fortitude,* New York, 1948, pp. 104–105; and see "Les Muses de la Novvelle France," nine pieces bound at the end of Marc Lescarbot, *Histoire de la Novvelle France,* M DC IX in the Houghton Library, Harvard College.

50. The standard work seems to be Alan Gowans, *Church Architecture in New France,* New Brunswick (N.J.), 1955, on which I depend.

51. See the first two chapters in Chase, *America's Music.*

52. Howard Mumford Jones, *The Literature of Virginia in the Seventeenth Century. Memoirs of the American Academy of Arts and Sciences,* Boston, 1946.

53. Ibid., pp. 14, 15.

54. Moses Coit Tyler, *A History of American Literature 1607–1765,* 2 vols., New York, 1878. There is a useful one-volume edition published at Ithaca (N.Y.) in 1949. Tyler's admirable analysis of the motives for writing is found in Section II of Chapter I.

55. Ibid., Ithaca edition, p. 157.

56. The standard studies are Esther Cloudman Dunn, *Shakespeare in*

America, New York, 1939, and Henry W. Simon, *The Reading of Shake-speare in American Schools,* New York, 1932. On the Bible in the United States see P. Marion Simms, *The Bible in America,* New York, 1936.

57. Dr. Paul Baker has in preparation a book on Americans in Italy.

58. The innumerable American editions of Mrs. Jameson can be traced in the Library of Congress catalogue. The tenth edition of the *Memoires* was republished in Boston in 1859, for example. She was also the author of *Shakespeare's Heroines.* Miss Helen Northup of the University of Wisconsin Library turned up at least seven makers of sepia "art" prints, mostly Renaissance; and there was of course the famous Prang series as well.

59. Charles Eliot Norton, *Notes of Travel and Study in Italy,* Boston, 1859, pp. vi, 312. The following Ruskinian interpretation of Fra Angelico is characteristic: "The air of heaven is fanned by the bright wings of his angels; the peace of heaven is in their countenances. No spot of earth dims the shining colors of their robes . . . But Fra Angelico had preserved his piety only by withdrawal from the world" (p. 312).

60. Bernard Berenson's studies include *The Central Italian Painters of the Renaissance* (1897), and the three books entitled *The Study and Criticism of Italian Art* (1901–1916), *The North Italian Painters of the Renaissance* (1907), and *Venetian Painting in America: The Fifteenth Century* (1916).

61. See Henry Francis Taylor, *Pierpont Morgan,* New York, 1957.

62. Paul Bourget, *Outre-Mer: Notes sur l'Amérique,* 2 vols., Paris, 1894, Vol. I, pp. 32, 34, 64–65.

63. Consult, *inter alia,* John Burchard and Albert Bush-Brown, *The Architecture of America: A Social and Cultural History,* Boston, 1961; Wayne Andrews, *Architecture, Ambition and Americans,* New York, 1947; Frederick Gutheim, *1857–1957: One Hundred Years of Architecture in America,* New York, 1957; Edith Wharton and Ogden Codman, *The Decoration of Houses,* New York, 1902; and biographies of the architects chiefly concerned. And see in this connection Daniel M. Fox, *Engines of Culture: Philanthropy and Art Museums,* Madison, State Historical Society of Wisconsin for the Department of History, University of Wisconsin, 1963.

Chapter IV: Renaissance Man in America

1. There are many studies. Two typical ones are John E. Mason, *Gentle Folk in the Making: Studies in the History of English Courtesy Literature and Related Topics from 1531 to 1774,* Philadelphia, 1935; and Edward Harrison Cady, *The Gentleman in America,* Syracuse, 1949. Each contains an extensive bibliography.

2. For an excellent example see Louis B. Wright, *The First Gentlemen of Virginia: Intellectual Qualities of the Early Colonial Ruling Class,* San Marino (Calif.), 1940.

3. Arber, *Travels and Works of Captain John Smith,* Vol. II, p. 809.

4. Cotton Mather, *Edulcorator. A brief Essay on the Waters of Marah*

Sweetened, With a Remarkable Relation of the Deporable [sic] *Occasion for it, In the Praemature Death of Captain Josiah Winslow* . . . Boston, 1725, pp. 28–29.

5. Jonathan Edwards, *True Saints, When Absent from the Body, are present with the Lord,* Boston, 1747, p. 27.

6. *Travels in North-America, in the years 1780, 1781, and 1782. By the Marquis de Chastellux . . . Tr. . . . by an English Gentleman,* 2 vols., London, 1787, Vol. II, pp. 42–43. See also in this connection Louis B. Wright, "Richard Lee II. A Belated Elizabethan in Virginia," *Huntington Library Quarterly,* II(1): 1–35 (October 1938).

7. Castiglione, *The Book of the Courtier* (Hoby's translation), Everyman Library edition, pp. 19, 37, 95–96. There are other passages of such advice.

8. In Arber, *First Three English Books,* pp. 5–6. See also the lengthy preface to Eden's translation of Peter Martyr, pp. 49–60, in the same collection.

9. See *Cambridge History of English Literature,* Cambridge, 1949, Vol. III, pp. 370, 372; and on the whole subject of the glorification of Elizabeth see Elkin Calhoun Wilson, *England's Eliza,* Cambridge (Mass.), 1939.

10. Hakluyt, *Principal Navigations,* Vol. VII, p. 150; Vol. VIII, pp. 36–39; Vol. X, pp. 346, 351, 443, 446.

11. Ibid., Vol. VII, p. 190.

12. Ibid., Vol. VII, pp. 342, 417; Vol. XI, p. 213; Vol. VIII, p. 65.

13. Peter Martyr, *De Orbe Novo,* Vol. II, p. 340; but see also Vol. I, p. 217.

14. Lewis Einstein, *Tudor Ideals,* New York, 1921, p. 174.

15. *The Literary History of the United States* (rev. ed. in 1 vol.), New York, 1953, p. 27. The chapter is by Randolph G. Adams.

16. On Commynes see the illuminating study by Wilfred B. Neff, *The "Moral" Language of Philippe de Commynes,* n.p., 1937.

17. My bloody tale is compounded out of such familiar sources as J. A. Symonds, *The Renaissance in Italy: The Age of the Despots;* Jacob Burckhardt, *The Civilization of the Renaissance in Italy;* Machiavelli; and Lewis Einstein, *Tudor Ideals.*

18. Hakluyt, *Principal Navigations,* Vol. VII, pp. 322–25.

19. Ibid., p. 355.

20. Jane, *Select Documents,* Vol. II, pp. 50–54.

21. For more details of these and other stories of indiscipline see Boies Penrose, *Travel and Discovery in the Renaissance, 1420–1620,* Cambridge (Mass.), 1952, and references.

22. Hakluyt, *Principal Navigations,* Vol. VII, p. 279.

23. Ibid., p. 415.

24. Ibid., p. 444.

25. Ibid., Vol. VIII, pp. 43, 47, 61.

26. Ibid., pp. 166–80.

27. Ibid., Vol. X, pp. 82–88.

28. Ibid., Vol. XI, pp. 381–89.

29. Machiavelli, *Discourses on the First Decade of Titus Livius,* translated by Ninian Hill Thomson, London, 1883, pp. 15–17, 42, 95–96, 336.

30. All this is of course in Prescott, Bernal Díaz, and others.

31. "Narrative of Alvar Nuñez de Vaca," translated by Buckingham Smith, in Hodge and Lewis, *Spanish Explorers,* pp. 14, 33–34, 39, 41–42; "Narrative of the Gentleman of Elvas" in same, pp. 175, 233; Varner, *The Florida of the Inca,* pp. 36, 195, 204, 245, 288, 500–501. De Soto was quite able to put down a mutiny (p. 386), and the Inca contrasts him with Vasco Porcallo, of whom he says: "But always when a man makes decisions in serious matters without considering the wise advice of friends, he is likely to end in violent and even desperate repentance, the victim of much infamy and harm" (p. 100).

32. I have analyzed some of the source material about Virginia in my *The Literature of Virginia in the Seventeenth Century.* The opening chapters of Mary Newton Stanard's narrative account, *The Story of Virginia's First Century,* Philadelphia, 1928, give most of the facts, few of which are in dispute. For more scholarly treatment see Wesley Frank Craven, *The Southern Colonies in the Seventeenth Century, 1607–1689,* Baton Rouge (La.), 1949. The quoted matter is from William Stith, *History of the First Discovery and Settlement of Virginia: Being an Essay toward a General History of this Colony,* Williamsburg, 1747, p. 103. In the *Annual Report of the American Historical Association* for 1899, Vol. V, pp. 311–63, Walter F. Prince in an article entitled "The First Criminal Code of Virginia" gives a judicious interpretation of the facts and of the general tenor of criminal law in the century.

33. *Archives of Maryland,* Baltimore, 1883——, Vol. III, p. 30; Vol. V, pp. 134–35 ("Complaint from Heaven with a Hue and crye and a petition out of Virginia and Maryland," 1676); Vol. VIII, pp. 125, 126.

34. John Hammond, *Leah and Rachel,* in C. C. Hall, *Narratives of Early Maryland,* New York, 1910, pp. 285, 300. Hammond was first published in London in 1656. Of course other comments by him are far more favorable.

35. Quoted from the *Calendar of State Papers, Colonial America and West Indies, 1661–68,* by Basil Soller in his "Transported Convict Laborers in Maryland During the Colonial Period," *Maryland Historical Magazine,* 2: 17–47 (1907).

36. "The Relation of Mr Garrott Vansweeringen of the City of St Maries concerning his knowledge of the Seating of Delaware Bay and River to the Southward of the 40th Degree Northern Latitude by the Dutch and Sweedes . . . ," *Archives of Maryland,* Vol. V, pp. 411–17.

37. John Esquemeling, *The Buccaneers of America,* ed. H. Powell, London, 1909, pp. 82–94. On the complex bibliography of Esquemeling (whose name is spelled in a variety of ways) see pp. 277–82 of the book by Haring cited in Chapter III, note 19. *The Memoirs of a Buccaneer; Being a Wondrous and Unrepentant Account of the Prodigious Adventures and Amours of King Louis XIV's Servant Louis Adhémar Timothée Le Golif . . . Told by Himself,* Alaux and t'Serstevens, eds., translated by Malcom Barnes, London, 1954, despite its *ad captandum*

title, seems to be authentic and throws light on the life of a buccaneer.
38. My account of the buccaneers is based on Esquemeling, Haring's admirable *Buccaneers of the West Indies* and Chapter VI of J. H. Parry and P. M. Sherlock, *A Short History of the West Indies*, London, 1960.
39. Cyrus H. Karraker, *Piracy Was a Business*, Rindge (N.H.), 1953.
40. Henry F. Thompson, "A Pirate in Chesapeake Bay," *Maryland Historical Magazine*, 1: 15–27 (1906).
41. Kidd is gallantly defended in Harold T. Wilkins, *Captain Kidd and his Skeleton Island*, New York, 1937. See also Willard H. Bonner, "The Reputation of Captain Kidd," *New England Quarterly*, 17(2): 179–208 (June 1944).
42. Philip Gosse, the English historian of piracy, has compiled *The Pirates' Who's Who*, London, 1924, which, though not carefully checked, rests upon considerable reading. The standard history of piracy is of course Charles Johnson, *General History of the Pyrates*, London, 1724. A second volume (1726) deals mainly with the Madagascar pirates. Of more immediate American interest are George Francis Dow and John Henry Edmonds, *The Pirates of the New England Coast, 1630–1730*, Salem, Marine Research Society, 1923; and Francis B. C. Bradlee, *Piracy in the West Indies and its Suppression*, Salem, The Essex Institute, 1923. The official record of a piracy trial in Boston in 1834 (the brig *Mexican*, of Salem) and accompanying pamphlets involving protests, confessions, and demands for a new trial; and the *Trial of the Officers and Crew of the Privateer Savannah, on the Charge of Piracy . . .* , New York, 1862, are authentic for the nineteenth century; and, at the other end of the temporal spectrum, James A. Williamson, "Piracy and Honest Trade," *Blackwood's Magazine*, 1374: 546–56 (April 1930), which discusses some off-color work by Frobisher, shows how hard it was in Tudor England to distinguish between piracy and honest trade. I have not, in this whole discussion, labored to distinguish the filibusters from the pirates or the buccaneers.
43. Thus Johnson in his *Wonder-Working Providence* uses "Machiavellian" not to describe Indian cunning but to characterize heresy. See the heading of Chapter XL of Book I: "Of the cunning policy of Satan in that machevillian Principle, divide and overcome . . ."
44. Penhallow, *History of the Wars of New-England*, pp. ii, v. For a characteristic account see pp. 21–22.
45. On Jamaica see Parry and Sherlock, *Short History* and Frank Cundall, *The Governors of Jamaica in the Seventeenth Century*, London, 1936, and *The Governors of Jamaica in the First Half of the Eighteenth Century*, London, 1937. See also Lowell Joseph Ragatz, *The Fall of the Planter Class in the British Caribbean, 1763–1833; A Study in Social and Economic History*, New York and London, 1928.
46. Philip Alexander Bruce, *Institutional History of Virginia in the Seventeenth Century*, 2 vols., New York and London, 1910, Vol. II, pp. 360–61. See also William E. Dodd, "The Emergence of the First Social Order in the United States," *American Historical Review*, 40(2): 217–31 (January 1935); Richard Croom Beatty, *William Byrd of Westover*, Bos-

ton, 1912; Wright, *First Gentlemen of Virginia;* and Philip Alexander
Bruce, *The Virginia Plutarch,* 2 vols., Chapel Hill (N.C.), 1929, appropriate chapters in the first volume. In *Mother Earth: Land Grants in
Virginia, 1607–1699, Jamestown 350th Anniversary Historical Booklets,*
No. 12, Richmond, 1957, W. Stitt Robinson, Jr., gives a sympathetic account of the grantees, but notes the "light regard for the spirit of the
law" only too evident, cites evidence of "many false certificates of rights,"
and points out that in 1649 all the Northern Neck was granted to seven
supporters of Charles II.

47. See David John Mays, *Edmund Pendleton, 1721–1803,* 2 vols., Cambridge (Mass.), 1952, Vol. I, Chapter 11.

48. Herbert L. Osgood, *American Colonies in the Eighteenth Century,*
4 vols., New York, 1924–1925, Vol. IV, Chapter VIII.

49. Archibald Henderson, "A Pre-Revolutionary Revolt in the Old
Southwest," *MVHR,* 17(2): 191–212 (September 1930).

50. Thomas Perkins Abernethy, "Social Relations and Political Control
in the Old Southwest," *MVHR,* 16(4): 529–37 (March 1930).

51. Page Smith, *John Adams,* 2 vols., Garden City, 1962, Vol. I, p. 231
and ref.

52. Alfred N. Chandler, *Land Title Origins: A Tale of Force and Fraud,*
New York, 1945, finds most such titles originating in illegality, but his
is a *Tendenzschrift.*

53. Virginia D. Harrington, *The New York Merchant on the Eve of
the Revolution,* New York, 1935, pp. 14–15, 37, 127.

54. My references are to the so-called Collier edition of Cooper, 1891–
1893. The passage about the proprietors is from *The Chainbearer* in
this set, p. 191, and is accompanied by a footnote of Cooper's in which
he says that the Rensselaer family got virtually nothing out of their
estates until a generation or two before 1844. The definition of the
gentleman is found on p. 172. *The Crater* has recently been edited by
Thomas Philbrick, with an admirable introduction, Cambridge (Mass.),
The John Harvard Library, 1962.

55. A stout defense of the validity of the railroad land grants is that by
Robert S. Henry, "The Railroad Land Grant Legend in American History Texts," *MVHR,* 32(2): 171–94 (September 1945). This set off a
considerable discussion running through volumes 32 and 33 of this
magazine.

56. The quotation from *The Octopus,* New York, 1901, is from p. 634.
The best edition of *Memoirs of an American Citizen* is that edited by
Daniel Aaron, Cambridge (Mass.), The John Harvard Library, 1963.

Chapter V: The Colonial Idea in England

1. A characteristic reference, though not the earliest, is found in Sir
William Alexander, *The Mapp and Description of New-England* (1630):
"The *Romanes* comming to command a well peopled World, had no vse
of Colonies, but only thereby to reward such old deseruing Souldiers as

(age and merit pleading an immunitie from any further constrained trauell) had brauely exceeded the ordinary course of time appointed for military service . . ." Again: "The *Romanes* did build some Townes which they did plant with their owne people by all rigour to curbe the Natiues next adjacent . . ." David Laing, ed., *Royal Letters, Charters, and Tracts, relating to the Colonization of New Scotland,* Edinburgh, Bannatyne Club Publications, 1867, pp. 3–4. Clarence Haring, however, finds considerable Roman likeness in Spanish theory. See his *The Spanish Empire in America,* New York, 1947, pp. 28–29.

2. The original is without pagination, but this is on signature F4.

3. *The Historie of Travaile into Virginia Britannia* remained in manuscript until it was edited by R. H. Major and published in London for the Hakluyt Society, 1849. My quotation is from p. 18. A new edition from another text, Louis B. Wright and Virginia Freund, eds., was published by the Hakluyt Society in 1953.

4. For a representative passage on the conflict between the communal character of settlement-making and private initiative see Ralph Hamor's account of Virginia under Dale and Gates in Purchas, *Hakluytus Posthumus,* Vol. XIX, p. 95. On the relation between American settlements and English cities see Alexander Brown, *The Genesis of the United States,* 2 vols., Boston, 1890, Vol. I, pp. 250f.; and Edward D. Neill, *Virginia Vetusta,* Albany, 1885, pp. 68–74, the last being an appeal to the "major and jurats" for municipal support.

5. See George Hill, *The MacDonnells of Antrim,* Belfast, 1873, p. 407; Edmund Spenser, *View of the Present State of Ireland,* edited by W. L. Renwick, London, 1934, pp. 157–58; Richard Bagwell, *Ireland under the Tudors,* 3 vols., London, 1885–1900, Vol. II, p. 211; and Constantia Maxwell, *Irish History from Contemporary Sources, 1509–1610,* London, 1923, *passim.*

6. See Maxwell, *Irish History,* p. 219 and *passim* for more material of this kind. And see also the characteristic letter from H. Heath to Sir Ferdinando Gorges, October 6, 1600 (?) in J. P. Baxter, ed., *Sir Ferdinando Gorges and His Province of Maine,* 3 vols., Boston, The Prince Society, 1890, Vol. III, pp. 84–86.

7. Maxwell, *Irish History,* pp. 234, 212, 220, 198.

8. Ibid., p. 117.

9. Bagwell, *Ireland under the Tudors,* Vol. II, p. 113.

10. Spenser, *View of the Present State of Ireland,* pp. 72, 73–75, 81. But for a far more favorable view see Edmund Curtis, *A History of Ireland,* London, 1936. A sixth edition of this book appeared in 1950.

11. The second edition, retitled *The Discovery and Conquest of Terra Florida* (1611), edited by William B. Rye, London, printed for the Hakluyt Society, 1851, pp. 27–28 and 6–7.

12. Arber and Bradley, *Travels and Works of Captain John Smith,* Vol. I, pp. 66, 72; Edward Arber, *The Story of the Pilgrim Fathers,* London, 1897, p. 453; Thomas Morton, *New English Canaan,* edited by C. F. Adams, Jr., Boston, The Prince Society, 1883, p. 134; *Collections Massa-*

chusetts Historical Society, Boston, Series I, Vol. I, p. 135; Series IV, Vol. VI, pp. 194–95; *Publications of the Narragansett Club,* Providence, Vol. VI, pp. 32–34.

13. See W. G. Gosling, *The Life of Sir Humphrey Gilbert,* London, 1911, pp. 46–47, 48.

14. "A Trewe Relacyon of the p'cedeinges and occurentes of momente wch have happened in Virginia," in Neill, *Virginia Vetusta,* p. viii. But in *A Relation of Maryland* (1635) the Indians are treated with respect, possibly out of propaganda purposes. See Chapter V of this account as reprinted in Hall, *Narratives of Early Maryland.*

15. The account of Carew's life in the *Dictionary of National Biography* states there are 42 manuscript volumes by Carew on Irish affairs in the Lambeth Library and four more in the Bodleian.

16. *British Calendar of State Papers, Domestic, 1591–1594,* p. 181; and *Archaeologia Americana: Transactions and Collections of the American Antiquarian Society,* 4: 27–28.

17. Francis Bacon, *Works,* edited by Basil Montagu, London, 1826, Vol. V, pp. 169f. On English distaste for the Brehon laws see the passage quoted in Maxwell, *Irish History,* pp. 351–52; on the charge of Irish sloth, ibid., pp. 90–91; and on the idea of a military establishment, Spenser, *View of the Present State of Ireland,* pp. 161f.

18. For the documents concerning Nova Scotia see Laing, *Royal Letters . . . ;* on Lord Baltimore see Bernard C. Steiner, "The First Lord Baltimore and His Colonial Projects," *Annual Report of the American Historical Association* for 1905, Vol. I, pp. 111–22.

19. "A Brife description of Ireland: Made in this yeere. 1589. by Robert Payne. vnto xxv. of his partners from whom he is vndertaker there. Truely published verbatim, according to his letters, by Nich, Gorsan one of the said partners, for that he would his countrymen should be partakers of the many good Notes therein conteined. With diuers Notes taken out of others the Authoures letters written to his said partners, sithenes the first Impression, well worth the reading," London, 1590, in Aquilla Smith, ed., *Tracts Relating to Ireland printed for the Irish Archaeological Society,* Dublin, 1841, Vol. I, *passim.*

20. The most thorough study of the whole problem is probably Moritz Julius Bonn, *Die Englische Kolonisation in Irland,* 2 vols., Stuttgart and Berlin, 1906. But see also George Hill, *An Historical Account of the Plantation in Ulster at the Commencement of the Seventeenth Century, 1608–1620,* Belfast, 1877. John White in his *The Planters Plea* (1630) had to combat the notion that Ireland was a better place than New England. See Force, *Tracts,* Vol. II, No. 3.

21. See *Correspondence of the Family of Hatton, being chiefly Letters addressed to Christopher, first Viscount Hatton,* edited by E. M. Thompson, 2 vols., London, The Camden Society, 1878, *passim.*

22. Quoted in Maxwell, *Irish History,* p. 248 note. See also the accompanying passage from the Calendar of State Papers, Ireland, to the effect that though there are some wise and virtuous settlers, there are too many

"traitors, murderers, thieves, coseners, cony-catchers, shifting mates, runners away with other men's wives, some having two or three wives, persons divorced living loosely, bankrupts, carnall gospellers, Papists, Puritans, and Brownists" (1598).

23. C. C. Hall, *Narratives of Early Maryland*, p. 200.

24. Stith, *History of the First Discovery*, pp. 103, 168.

25. Hall, *Narratives of Early Maryland*, p. 285.

26. "The Relation of Mr Garrott Vansweeringen of the City of St Maries concerning his knowledge of the Seating of Delaware Bay and River to the Southward of the 40th Degree Northern Latitude by the Dutch and Sweedes . . . ," *Archives of Maryland*, Vol. V, pp. 411f.

27. Some idea of the extent of this literature can be gleaned by consulting P. Lee Phillips, "A List of Books Relating to America, in the Register of the London Company of Stationers from 1562 to 1638," *Annual Report of the American Historical Association* for 1896, Vol. I, pp. 1251f.

28. Hall, *Narratives of Early Maryland*, pp. 16–23.

29. The "Coppie of a letter . . . 1607" is in Edward D. Neill, *Early Settlement of Virginia and Virginiola . . .* , Minneapolis, 1878, pp. 10–11; Johnson's *Nova Britannia* is reprinted in Force, *Tracts,* Vol. I, No. 6; and the *Trve Declaration* in ibid., Vol. III, No. 1.

30. In Force, *Tracts,* Vol. III, No. 2.

31. Ibid., Vol. I, No. 6, pp. 27–28. Cf. *A Trve Declaration* (1610) in ibid., Vol. III, No. 1, p. 24.

32. *The Planters Plea* (1630), Force, *Tracts,* Vol. II, No. 3, p. 31.

33. William Strachey, *Historie of Travaile into Virginia Britannia,* edited by H. Major, London, Printed for the Hakluyt Society, 1849, p. 14. For the Crashaw reference see his *A Sermon Preached in London before . . . his Maiesties Counsell . . . for Virginea,* London, 1610, sig. E3 verso.

34. See Robert Gordon, *Encovragements* (1625), reprinted in Laing, *Royal Letters . . .* , the dedicatory epistle.

35. Robert Gray, *A Good Speed to Virginia,* London, 1609, the dedication.

36. *A Description of New England* (1616) in Arber, *Travels and Works of Captain John Smith,* Vol. I, p. 208.

37. Force, *Tracts,* Vol. I, No. 6, p. 26.

38. "A true Report," in Hakluyt, *Principal Navigations,* Vol. VIII, pp. 126–27.

39. Ralph Lane to Sir Philip Sidney, writing from Roanoke in 1585. See *Archaeologia Americana,* 4 (1860): 17.

40. From the "Epistle Dedicatorie" of the first edition of Hakluyt, *Principal Navigations,* Vol. I, p. xx.

41. On this whole subject see James A. Williamson, *Short History of British Expansion,* London, 1927; his *Hawkins of Plymouth,* London, 1949; and his *The Age of Drake,* 2d ed., London, 1946; also "A Discourse of the Commoditie of the Taking of the Straight of Magellans,"

in R. H. Tawney and Ellen Powers, eds., *Tudor Economic Documents,* 3 vols., London, 1924, Vol. III, pp. 224–32; and Arthur Percival Newton, *The Colonising Activities of the English Puritans: The Last Phase of the Elizabethan Struggle with Spain,* New Haven, 1914.

42. Hakluyt, *Principal Navigations,* Vol. VII, p. 186, and see Vol. VIII, p. 112.

43. Richard Hakluyt, *Divers Voyages,* London, Printed for the Hakluyt Society, 1850, p. 8.

44. Charles Dean, ed., *A Discourse of Western Planting,* Vol. II of *Documentary History of the State of Maine,* Cambridge (Mass.), 1877. See especially sections iv and xx.

45. Quoted from Symonds' sermon at Whitechapel, April 25, 1609, in Edward D. Neill, *The English Colonization of America During the Seventeenth Century,* London, 1871, pp. 29–31.

46. "A Sermon vpon The Eight Ver(s)e of the First Chapter of the Acts of The Apostles. Preached To the Honourable Company of the Virginian Plantation, 13. Nouemb. 1622" in Geoffrey Keynes, ed., *X Sermons Preached by . . . John Donne,* London, 1923, p. 52.

47. Patrick Copland, *Virginia's God be Thanked, or A Sermon Of Thanksgiving For The Happie Successe of the affayres in Virginia this last yeare . . . ,* London, 1622, p. 31.

48. I have listed a catena of passages of complaint about criminals and idle vagabonds in the colonies in my "The Colonial Impulse," *Proceedings of the American Philosophical Society,* 90(2): 148 (1946).

49. Hall, *Narratives of Early Maryland,* pp. 294–95.

50. Thomas Wentworth Higginson, *Life of Francis Higginson,* New York, 1891, pp. 72, 75.

51. Brown, *Genesis,* Vol. I, pp. 252–53.

52. Force, *Tracts,* Vol. II, No. 8, pp. 7–8.

53. Hall, *Narratives of Early Maryland,* p. 295. But see Basil Sollers, "Transported Convict Laborers in Maryland during the Colonial Period," *Maryland Historical Magazine,* 2(1): 17–47 (March 1907).

54. For the quotation from Gorges see Baxter, *Sir Ferdinando Gorges . . . ,* Vol. III, p. 161. For that from Winslow see *Good News from New England: or a true Relation of things very remarkable at the Plantation of Plymouth in New England* (London, 1624) in E. Arber, *Story of the Pilgrim Fathers,* London and Boston, 1897, pp. 514, 515.

55. Said to be the earliest narrative of the wreck of the *Sea Venture,* this ballad may be found in Neill, *Early Settlement,* pp. 29–35.

56. "Reasons and Considerations" appended to Robert Cushman's *Relation . . . of the . . . Proceedings of the English Plantation settled at Plymouth* (1622) in Arber, *Story of the Pilgrim Fathers,* pp. 499–500.

57. John Winthrop, *General Considerations for the Plantation in New England,* in *Winthrop Papers,* 5 vols., Boston, Massachusetts Historical Society, 1929–1947, Vol. III, p. 118.

58. John White, *The Planters Plea* (1630) in Force, *Tracts,* Vol. II, No. 3, pp. 2–3.

59. Thomas Morton, *New English Canaan . . . ,* p. 120.

60. Hakluyt, *Principal Navigations,* Vol. VIII, pp. 9–10.
61. *A True Declaration . . . of Virginia* (1610), Force, *Tracts,* Vol. III, No. 1, pp. 5–6.
62. *Gods Promise to His Plantations . . .* (1630), *Old South Leaflets,* Vol. III, No. 53, Boston, n.d., p. 7.
63. Crashaw, sig F3 and verso.
64. *Winthrop Papers,* Vol. II, p. 120. There is a considerable and repetitious literature on this ethical problem.
65. Hakluyt, *Divers Voyages,* p. 8.
66. Robert Gordon, *Encouragements, For such as shall have intention to bee Vndertakers in the new plantation of Cape Briton . . .* (Edinburgh, 1625), sig. C., verso, in Laing, *Royal Letters. . . .*
67. *A true Relation of a Sea Fight betweene two great and well appointed Spanish Ships, or Men of Warre; and an English Ship . . .* , in Purchas, *Hakluytus Posthumus,* Vol. XIX, p. 142.
68. In Force, *Tracts,* Vol. II, No. 3, p. 45.

Chapter VI: The Useful and the Good

1. Beginning with Werner Sombart, *Der Moderne Kapitalismus,* Leipzig, 1902 (unless one wants to begin with Karl Marx), leading documents are: Max Weber, *The Protestant Ethic and the Spirit of Capitalism,* translated by Talcott Parsons, New York and London, 1930 (the original German essays were published in 1904–1905); R. H. Tawney, *Religion and the Rise of Capitalism: A Historical Study,* New York, 1926; E. Troeltsch, *Die Soziallehren der Christlichen Kirchen und Gruppen,* Tübingen, 1912, translated by Olive Wyon as *The Social Teaching of the Christian Churches,* 2 vols., New York and London, 1931; Henri Hauser, *Les Débuts du Capitalisme,* Paris, 1927; H. M. Robertson, *Aspects of the Rise of Economic Individualism,* Cambridge, 1933; A. Fanfani, *Le Origini dello Spirito Capitalistico in Italia,* Milan, 1933, and *Cattolicesmo e Protestantesimo nella Formazione Storica del Capitalismo,* Milan, 1934; Albert Hyma, *Christianity, Capitalism and Communism: A Historical Analysis,* Ann Arbor (Mich.), 1937. Two illuminating articles are Frank H. Knight, "Historical and Theoretical Issues in the Problem of Modern Capitalism," *Journal of Economic and Business History,* 1(1): 118–36 (November 1928); and Carl F. Taeusch, "The Concept of 'Usury,'" *Journal of the History of Ideas,* 3(3): 291–318 (June 1942). For a clear statement of the Protestant ethic as this was understood in seventeenth-century New England see Perry Miller, *The New England Mind: From Colony to Province,* Cambridge (Mass.), 1953. By and large Lutheranism was not involved.
2. Van Wyck Brooks, *The Wine of the Puritans,* New York, 1909, and *America's Coming-of-Age,* New York, 1915; Charles A. Beard, *An Economic Interpretation of the Constitution,* New York, 1913; Charles A. and Mary Beard, *The Rise of American Civilization,* 2 vols., rev. ed., New York, 1947, and *America in Mid-Passage,* New York, 1939; Vernon Louis Parrington, *Main Currents in American Thought,* 3 vols., New

York, 1927–1930 (Vol. III was left unfinished at his death); Frederick Jackson Turner, *The Frontier in American History*, New York, 1920 (this expands the famous essay of 1893, "The Significance of the Frontier in American History"). Turner was less content with economic motivation as a "cause" than my necessarily simplified statement allows.

3. See in this connection "The Hebraic Background of Puritanism" by Clifford K. Shipton, *Publications of the American Jewish Historical Society*, 47(3): 140–53 (March 1958).

4. Writing in 1700, the Reverend Thomas Bray estimated the "Papists" as one-twelfth the number of the inhabitants of Maryland. *A Memorial Representing the Present State of Religion on the Continent of North America*, London, 1700, *Thomas Bray Publications*, No. 5, p. 9.

5. "Business and Religion" by James W. Culliton, in *Business and Religion: A New Depth Dimension in Management*, edited by Edward C. Bursk, New York, 1959, p. 6.

6. William Ames, *Conscience with the Power and Cases Thereof, Divided into Five Bookes*, London, 1643, pp. 248–64 *passim*. An interesting light on the Puritan sense for business is shed by Chapters 42–45 on contracts.

7. See Chapter III, p. 73.

8. Cotton Mather, *A Christian at His Calling. Two brief Discourses. One Directing A Christian in his General Calling; Another Directing him in his Personal Calling*, Boston, 1701.

9. John Danforth, *The Right Christian Temper in every Condition*, Boston, 1702, p. 3.

10. William Cooper, *Jabez's Character and Prayer A Little Consider'd and Improv'd, in a Sermon to a Society of Young Men in Boston*, Boston, 1716, pp. 7, 11.

11. Benjamin Colman, *The Blessing of Zebulun & Issachar, a Sermon Preached Before the Great and General court . . . in Boston, November 19, 1719*, Boston, 1719, pp. 8, 13.

12. "An Addition to the Present Melancholy Circumstances of the Province Considered," Boston, 1719, in *Publications of the Prince Society*, Vol. 32, *Colonial Currency Reprints*, 1: 368–69, 370.

13. Thomas Symmes, *Good Soldiers Described and Animated*, Boston, 1720, p. 2.

14. Moses Dickinson, *A Sermon Delivered at the Funeral, of the Honorable Thomas Fitch, Esq; Late Governor of the Colony of Connecticut*, New Haven, 1774, pp. 5, 6.

15. ". . . under the secular influence of mercantilism the ordering of the economy in the interest of a heavenly kingdom or the salvation of the individual's soul was replaced by considerations of the welfare of the British Kingdom and the salvation of the nation's favorable balance of trade." C. Robert Haywood, "The Influence of Mercantilism on Social Attitudes in the South, 1700–1763," *Journal of the History of Ideas*, 20(4): 578 (October–December 1959). In this general connection see Curtis P. Nettels, "The Money Supply of the American Colonies before 1720," *University of Wisconsin Studies in the Social Sciences and History*, No. 20, Madison, 1934, and in another connection E. A. Johnson,

"Some Evidence of Mercantilism in the Massachusetts-Bay," *New England Quarterly*, 1(3): 371–95 (July 1928).

16. Richard Wells, *A Few Political Reflections submitted To the Consideration of the British Colonies, by a Citizen of Philadelphia*, Philadelphia, 1774, pp. 11, 23. I follow Hildeburn in attributing this to Wells.

17. Cotton Mather, *Bonifacius. An Essay Upon the Good, that is to be Devised and Designed, by those Who Desire to Answer the Great End of Life, and to do Good While they Live*, Boston, 1710.

18. Cotton Mather, *A Christian at His Calling*.

19. It does not commit the Quakers to secularity to point out with Dr. Frederick B. Tolles that the Matherian concept of man's calling was taken for granted by the Quaker merchants of Philadelphia, who helped shape the credit-making virtues in Benjamin Franklin's theory. See his "Benjamin Franklin's Business Mentors: the Philadelphia Quaker Merchants," *The William and Mary Quarterly*, 3d ser., 4(1): 60–69 (January 1947).

20. Cotton Mather, *Agricola. Or, The Religious Husbandman: The Main Intentions of Religion, Served in the Business and Language of Husbandry*, Boston, 1727, p. 63.

21. I do not give bibliographical references for these Franklin items, which can be found in any good anthology of his writings, such as Frank Luther Mott and Chester E. Jorgenson, eds., *Benjamin Franklin: Representative Selections*, New York, 1936. There are at least four "layers" of composition in the *Autobiography*. See for the best critical edition Max Farrand, ed., *Benjamin Franklin's Memoirs, Parallel Text Edition*, Berkeley and Los Angeles, 1949. Meanwhile one awaits the completion of the new edition of Franklin. The best brief study of the vogue of Franklin's doctrine is Louis B. Wright, "Franklin's Legacy to the Gilded Age," *Virginia Quarterly Review*, 22(2): 268–79 (spring 1946).

22. Samuel Cooper, *A Sermon Preached in Boston, New-England, Before the Society for Encouraging Industry, and Employing the Poor, August 8, 1753*, Boston, 1753, pp. 2, 12–13, 26.

23. Ebenezer Pemberton, *A Sermon Preached in the Audience of the Honourable His Majesty's Council, And the Honourable House of Representatives Of the Province of the Massachusetts-Bay . . .* , Boston, 1757, pp. 15, 18.

24. George Duffield, *A Sermon Preached in the Third Presbyterian Church in the City of Philadelphia, On Thursday December 11, 1783 . . .* , Philadelphia, 1784, p. 17.

25. John M'Knight, *The Divine Goodness to the United States of America, Particularly in the Course of the Last Year. A Thanksgiving Sermon, Preached in New-York, February 19, 1795*, New York, 1795, p. 20.

26. Joseph Lathrop, *God's Challenge to Infidels to defend their cause, illustrated and applied in a Sermon, delivered in West Springfield, May 4, 1797 . . .* , 2d ed., Cambridge (Mass.), 1807, p. 6.

27. Virginia D. Harrington, *The New York Merchant on the Eve of the Revolution*, New York, 1935, pp. 93–94. I do not know whether it is significant that a parallel study by Leila Seelers, *Charleston Business*

on the Eve of the American Revolution, Chapel Hill (N.C.), 1934, reports no such practices.

28. *Royal American Magazine,* 1(1): 10 (January 1774).

29. Tench Coxe, *An Address to an Assembly of the Friends of American Manufacturers, Convened for the Purpose of establishing a Society for the Encouragement of Manufacturers and the Useful Arts, read to the University of Pennsylvania, on Thursday the 9th. of August 1787,* Philadelphia, 1787, pp. 29–30.

30. Morgan J. Rhees, *The Good Samaritan. An Oration Delivered on Sunday Evening, May 22d, 1796, in Behalf of the Philadelphia Society for the Information and Assistance of persons Emigrating From Foreign Countries,* Philadelphia, 1796, p. 12.

31. I depend upon Samuel Rezneck, "The Rise and Early Development of Industrial Consciousness in the United States, 1750–1830," *Journal of Economic and Business History,* 4 (4-Supplement): 784–811 (August 1932).

32. Quoted in C. Robert Haywood, "The Influence of Mercantilism on Social Attitudes in the South, 1700–1763," *Journal of the History of Ideas,* 20(4): 577–86 (October–December 1959). Haywood is especially illuminating about the relation between social controls in the South and secular mercantile ethics as contrasted with the ethics of heaven.

33. Clifford S. Griffin has uncovered this gem (and a great many more) in his "Religious Benevolence as Social Control, 1815–1860," *MVHR,* 44: 423–44 (December 1957). Anti-Catholic bias distinguishes much of this "literature."

34. Henry Wheaton, *An Address pronounced at the opening of The New-York Athenaeum, December 14, 1824,* New York, 1824, p. 34.

35. O. L. Holley, *An Address delivered before the mechanics of Troy . . . on the 4th. of July, 1825,* Troy (N.Y.), 1825, p. 10.

36. Solomon Lincoln, Jr., *An Oration Delivered before the Citizens of Hingham on the Fourth of July, 1826,* Hingham (Mass.), 1826, pp. 13–14, 15.

37. Francis Wayland, *The Elements of Moral Science,* revised and improved ed., Boston and New York, 1872, pp. 103, 109, 193, 194, 240, 245, 248, 250, 253, 257, 351. See Edward H. Madden, "Francis Wayland and the Limits of Moral Responsibility," *Proceedings of the American Philosophical Society,* 100(4): 348–59 (August 22, 1962).

38. Henry Ward Beecher, *Lectures to Young Men on Various Important Subjects,* Boston, 1851. See pp. 24, 30–31. On the folly of denouncing wealth read Lecture III. There is a vast continuing library addressed to the rising generation. Here are some representative examples: Charles Butler, *The American Gentleman,* Philadelphia, 1836; John Frost, *The Young Merchant,* New York, 1841; Frank Ferguson, *The Young Man,* Boston, 1848; Timothy Shay Arthur (the author of *Ten Nights in a Barroom*), *Advice to Young Men on their Duties and Conduct in Life,* Boston, 1848; William Van Doren, *Mercantile Morals,* New York, 1852; Daniel Wise, *The Young Man's Counsellor,* New York, 1854; Francis E. Clark, *Our Business Boys,* Boston, 1884; Charles Reynolds Brown, *The*

Young Man's Affairs, New York, 1909. Russell H. Conwell's astonishing *Acres of Diamonds* stands a little apart from this library; a limited edition was published in Philadelphia for Temple University in 1959. It was also reprinted in 1960 in a series of "Inspirational Classics."

39. *North American Review*, 73: 271 (July 1851); 81: 517 (October 1855); 83: 217–218, 231 (July 1856).

40. Andrew Carnegie, *The Gospel of Wealth*, ed. Edward C. Kirkland, Cambridge (Mass.), 1962, pp. viii, xvi, 55, 71–72.

41. Orison Swett Marden, *Success*, Boston and Chicago, 1897, *passim*; *He Can Who Thinks He Can*, New York, 1908, p. 240.

42. Albert Shaw, *The Outlook for the Average Man*, New York, 1907, pp. 11, 46, 65.

43. Theodore Roosevelt, *American Ideals*, New York, 1926. (This is Volume XIII of the so-called National Edition of the *Works*.) William Allen White contributes an introduction, "Saith the Preacher," which I cite. The long paragraph from Roosevelt himself is found on p. 331 of *The Strenuous Life*, in the same volume. See also p. 323.

44. G. W. Steevens, *The Land of the Dollar*, New York, 1897, p. 271.

45. Nathaniel Hawthorne, *The Marble Faun*, in *Works*, 1883, p. 276. A standard study (and an admirable one it is) is Irvin G. Wyllie, *The Self-Made Man in America: The Myth of Rags to Riches*, New Brunswick (N.J.), 1954. Note especially Chapters 4, 6, 7 and the excellent bibliography.

46. See in this connection Kenneth Wiggins Porter, "Trends in American Business Biography," *Journal of Economic and Business History*, 4(4): 583–610 (August 1932).

47. Freeman Hunt, *Lives of American Merchants*, 2 vols., New York, Vol. I, 1855; Vol. II, 1857. The quoted matter is in Vol. II, pp. 445 and 388. On Hunt consult Jerome Thomases, "Freeman Hunt's America," *MVHR*, 30(3): 395–407 (December 1943). Thomases quotes a number of passages from clergymen and others writing in the magazine on the doctrine of Christian stewardship.

48. Carlos Martyn, *William E. Dodge: The Christian Merchant*, New York, 1890, p. 171. The book is a classic example of the later development (and diffusion) of the Protestant ethic in business.

49. Ellis Paxon Oberholtzer, *Jay Cooke, The Financier of the Civil War*, 2 vols., Philadelphia, 1907, Vol. II, p. 463.

50. Henrietta M. Larson, *Jay Cooke, Private Banker*, Cambridge (Mass.), 1936, pp. 192–93, and Oberholtzer, *Jay Cooke*, Vol. II, pp. 501 and 168.

51. William T. Hutchinson, *Cyrus Hall McCormick*: Vol. I, *Seed-Time, 1809–1856;* Vol. II, *Harvest, 1856–1884*, New York, 1930–1935. See Vol. I, pp. 461–62, 463.

52. Wheaton Joshua Lane, *Commodore Vanderbilt: An Epic of the Steam Age*, New York, 1942, pp. 309–10, 320.

53. George B. McC. Harvey, *Henry Clay Frick, The Man*, New York, 1928, p. 364.

54. See *The Autobiography of Andrew Carnegie*, Boston, 1920. Other characteristic business biographies of the period include *The Americani-*

zation of Edward Bok, New York, 1920; Burton J. Hendrick, *The Life of Andrew Carnegie,* 2 vols., New York, 1932; Henry Ford, *My Life and Work* (in collaboration with Samuel Crowther), New York, 1922; Herbert D. Croly, *Marcus Alonza Hanna: His Life and Work.* New York, 1912; John Kennedy Winkler, *Morgan the Magnificent,* New York, 1930; and Albert Bigelow Paine, *In One Man's Life: Being Chapters from the Personal and Business Career of Theodore Vail,* New York, 1921. For a summary view of this generation from a hostile standpoint see Matthew Josephson, *The Robber Barons,* New York, 1934.

55. I have depended almost wholly on Allan Nevins' definitive *John D. Rockefeller,* 2 vols., New York, 1940.

56. Sigmund Diamond, *The Reputation of the American Business Man,* Cambridge (Mass.), 1955. The passage from Horace Mann is on p. 47.

57. This is curiously evidenced in two more recent studies. In his *Economic Virtues in the United States,* New York, 1930, Donald McConnell gives a superficial survey of the history of business ethos, but seems to be committed to the proposition that "money-making in the West was without the pale of virtuous behavior" (p. 40). And despite a chapter on "The Ideology and the Cultural Heritage," *The American Business Creed* by Francis X. Sutton and others, Cambridge (Mass.), 1956, displays little or no interest in the ethical heritage of the business world.

Chapter VII: Roman Virtue

1. *Senator* appears as early as 1766. "Most noble senators, our bosoms glow with the warmth of affection, and heighth of gratitude!" David S. Rowland, *Divine Providence illustrated and improved . . .* Providence, 1766, p. v. This was a sermon on the royal birthday, rejoicing in the repeal of the Stamp Act. But there are, I am sure, earlier instances.

2. On the classic origins of a connection between *Virtus* and the safety of the state see two admirable articles: Harold Mattingly, "The Roman 'Virtues,'" *Harvard Theological Review,* 30(2): 103–17 (April 1937); and M. P. Charlesworth, *"Pietas* and *Victoria:* The Emperor and the Citizen," *The Journal of Roman Studies,* 33(1–2): 1–10 (1943). Christianity eventually turned the imperial virtues into forms of polite address such as Vestra Pietas, Vestra Mansuetudo, and Vestra Tranquillitas.

3. I draw my illustrations *passim* from John Addington Symonds, *Renaissance in Italy: The Revival of Learning,* London, 1877, which, despite the need for corrections, still seems to me the scholarly work that best conveys the excitement of humanism. As his final chapter shows, Symonds was by no means blind to the defects of the humanists. The standard literary and intellectual survey is that dull masterpiece, Henry Hallam, *Introduction to the Literature of Europe in the Fifteenth, Sixteenth, and Seventeenth Centuries,* originally published in 1837–1839. The most accessible edition in the United States is one in 2 vols., New York, 1891.

4. Julian Boyd *et al.*, eds., *The Papers of Thomas Jefferson*, Princeton, 1948——, Vol. IX, p. 240, Vol. XI, pp. 226–28. I follow the intelligent reconstruction in this edition of the letter to Madame Tessé.

5. The standard study is William Ellery Leonard, *Byron and Byronism in America*, Boston, 1905.

6. For Hawthorne's curious and contradictory responses to the remains of antiquity consult his *French and Italian Notebooks, passim*. The *locus classicus* in Mark Twain is of course *Innocents Abroad* (1869). One of the most curious books to deal with the theme is Charles Eliot Norton, *Travel and Study in Italy* (1860), in which a violent anti-Catholicism colors interpretation; yet Norton became a chief proponent of a general American neoclassical movement. Paul H. Baker has in preparation a careful study of American visitors to Italy in the nineteenth century.

7. Robert Ralston Cawley, *Unpathed Waters: Studies in the Influence of the Voyagers on Elizabethan Literature*, Princeton, 1940.

8. Hakluyt, *Principal Navigations*, Vol. I, pp. lxv–lxvi.

9. Powhatan's speech is in the Arber-Bradley edition of Smith, *Travels and Works*, Vol. I, pp. 135–36. Compare with it the two speeches by Calgacus ("they make a solitude and call it peace") and by Agricola in *Agricola*, ccs. 30–34. One is also reminded of some of the speeches in Sallust's history of the Jugurthan war.

10. *Publications of the Colonial Society of Massachusetts, Collections*, 15: 24–25 (1925).

11. Samuel E. Morison, *Three Centuries of Harvard, 1636–1936*, Cambridge (Mass.), 1936, p. 22.

12. For a representative list see Samuel E. Morison, "Old School and College Books in the Prince Library," *More Books: The Bulletin of the Boston Public Library*, 11(3): 77–93 (March 1936). In "Private Libraries in Colonial Virginia," *American Literature*, 10(1): 24–52 (March 1938) George K. Smart examines titles in about 100 libraries from 1650 to 1787. Some libraries listed books by bulk only, or by shape. About a quarter of the identifiable titles were in languages and the classics, Greek works often appearing in Latin translations, and Greek and Latin authors often in modern translations. Ovid was popular; after him, Cicero, Virgil, and Caesar, Horace, Seneca, Plautus, Terence, and Sallust. Plutarch's *Lives* is listed 22 times. Xenophon and Homer predominate among the Greeks. Smart concludes that classical learning was less extensive than interest in a few more obvious classical authors. Louis B. Wright, on the other hand, "The Classical Tradition in Colonial Virginia," *Papers of the Bibliographical Society of America*, 33: 85–97 (1939) stresses the classical interest of Virginia gentlemen, but seems to generalize from too few instances and to confine himself to large libraries, whereas about half of those examined by Smart contained only from 25 to 50 titles. It is interesting that in *The Revolutionary Movement in Pennsylvania, 1760–1776, University of Pennsylvania Publications in History*, No. 1, Philadelphia, 1901, Charles H. Lincoln, though advancing the sound proposition that history was a favorite study in that colony,

speaks of Locke, Hooker, Sidney, Coke, Bacon, Montesquieu, Burlamaqui, Hume, and Sir Thomas More, but mentions no antique historian.

The whole problem is difficult. If one assumes that the present holdings of the Library of Congress are a rough index of American interest in books, what is to be inferred from the following statistical list? Editions of leading classical writers dating from 1800 or earlier in that library are in number: Cicero, 44; Horace, 33; Ovid, 27; Sallust, 19; Tacitus, 15; Suetonius, 15; Plutarch, 11; Livy, 6; Thucydides, 5. Was Cicero therefore five times as influential before 1800 as Tacitus? *The Charter, Laws, Catalogue of Books . . . of the Juliana Library in Lancaster,* published in Philadelphia in 1766, lists about 212 titles. Of these only the following can fairly be called "classical": Josephus in Whiston's translation, Longinus in Smith's translation, Middleton's Cicero, the orations of Demosthenes, Pope's Homer, and Dryden's Plutarch—6 out of more than 200. Yet the library had Puffendorf, an Aldine Greek Bible, Hooker, Brown's *Estimate,* Locke, Newton's *Opticks,* Bolingbroke, Fenélon, Voltaire, Rollin, Fontenelle, Rabelais, and Montesquieu. The preface praises ancient Greece and Rome for their learning! If one wishes to be further confused let him consult Arthur O. Norton, "Harvard Text-Books and Reference Books of the Seventeenth Century," *Publications of the Colonial Society of Massachusetts, Transactions, 1930–33,* 28: 361–438; Samuel Eliot Morison, "The Library of George Alcocke, Medical Student, 1676," in the same, 350–57; and Charles F. Robinson and Robin Robinson, "Three Early Massachusetts Libraries," in the same, 107–75. This article lists about 565 titles, but Plutarch, Aristophanes, Isocrates, Cicero, Homer, and one or two others make pretty slim pickings among classical authors.

13. Morison, *Three Centuries,* p. 35; Wright, "The Classical Tradition," 86.

14. Cotton Mather, *Manuductio ad Ministerium,* Boston, 1726, pp. 28–29. But in fairness the reader should note the discussion of style, pp. 43f.

15. Michael Kraus, *The Atlantic Civilization: Eighteenth-Century Origins,* Ithaca (N.Y.), 1949, pp. 217, 218, 219. The quotation from the *Gentleman's Magazine* is from 15: 422.

16. For studies in this transition see Kenneth B. Murdock, "William Hubbard and the Providential Interpretation of History," *Proceedings of the American Antiquarian Society,* n.s., 52(1): 15–37 (April 1942), and Stow Persons, "The Cyclical Theory of History in Eighteenth Century America," *American Quarterly,* 6(2): 147–63 (summer 1954).

17. All the histories of architecture in America touch on this theme. A particular study is Harold Donaldson Eberlein, *The Architecture of Colonial America,* Boston, 1915. John Burchard and Albert Bush-Brown, *The Architecture of America: A Social and Cultural History,* Boston, 1961, is heavily weighted on the side of modernism. On the social contexts of colonial Georgian see also Thomas J. Wertenbaker, *The Golden Age of Colonial Culture,* New York, 1942, *passim.*

18. James Logan, *M. T. Cicero's Cato Major, or his Discourse of Old-*

Age: With Explanatory Notes, Philadelphia, 1744. The quoted phrase is on p. v, and the book is one of the best specimens of Franklin's typography.

19. Richard Peters, *A Sermon on Education. Wherein Some Account is given of the Academy, Established in the City of Philadelphia. Preach'd at the Opening thereof, on the Seventh Day of January, 1750–1,* Philadelphia, 1751, pp. 4, 21. This too was printed by Franklin.

20. *The Independent Reflector: or, Weekly Essays on Sundry Important Subjects, More particularly adapted to the Province of New-York,* No. XVII, March 22, 1753, pp. 67, 68. It is amusing to note that the paper carries a motto from Cicero: *"Ne quid falsi dicere audeat, ne quid veri non audeat."* A modern edition edited by Milton M. Klein has appeared in the John Harvard Library, Cambridge (Mass.), 1963.

21. David John Mays, *Edmund Pendleton, 1721–1803: A Biography,* 2 vols., Cambridge (Mass.), 1952, Vol. I, p. 23.

22. I borrow from my discussion of this theme in *The Pursuit of Happiness,* Cambridge (Mass.), 1953, pp. 74–80, to which the reader is referred for the sources of these and other quotations. Perhaps I ought to add as another example of the Horatian ideal this passage from Nathaniel Evans' "Epistolary Ode to a Friend," *Poems on Several Occasions,* Philadelphia, 1722:

> He who contented spends his days—
> Calm as the clear unruffled stream,
> His life in gentle current strays,
> Mild as the maiden's silver dream,
> Be he born to till the field,
> Or in war the sword to wield;
> If he o'er the midnight oil,
> Wastes his life in learned toil (p. 10).

Evans also wrote an "Ode . . . in the Manner of Horace," and Schuylkill winds his solitary way through a number of his poems.

23. J. B. Brissot de Warville, *New Travels in the United States of America Performed in M. DCC.LXXXVIII,* 2d ed., corrected, 2 vols., London, 1794, Vol. I, p. 91. As late as 1819 Francis Hall makes a parallel comment on Jefferson at Monticello in *Travels in Canada, and the United States, in 1816 and 1817,* 2d ed., London, 1819, pp. 297–98.

24. It is of course not argued that the drive against luxury derives solely from classical education. On the contrary it is as old as the colonies, as is evidenced in what Perry Miller has taught us to call the jeremiad sermon preached on fast days and other penitential or ceremonial occasions. See his *The New England Mind: The Seventeenth Century,* New York, 1954; *The New England Mind: From Colony to Province,* Cambridge, 1953; and "From Covenant to Revival" in James Ward Smith and J. Leland Jamison, eds., *Religion in American Life: The Shaping of American Religion,* Princeton, 1961, pp. 322–68.

25. See, for example, *John Hancock, An Oration; delivered March 5, 1774, at the Request of the Inhabitants of the Town of Boston: to Commemorate the Bloody Tragedy of the Fifth of March 1770,* Boston, 1774:

"Hence, all the arts which idleness and luxury could invent, were used, to betray our youth of one sex into extravagance and effeminacy, and of the other to infamy and ruin; and did they [the British] not succeed but too well?" (p. 8).

26. For the quoted passages see the *Antigallican*, No. II (December 1757). See also Nos. III (January 1758), IV (February 1758) and V (April 1758), on industry, frugality, luxury, the age of the Antonines, Solon, Peisistratus, Justin, Cicero, and Thrasybulus. East Apthorp, *The Felicity of the Times, A Sermon Preached at Christ Church, Cambridge . . .*, Boston, 1753, pp. 9, 11; John Adams, *Works*, 10 vols., Boston, 1850–1856, Vol. III, p. 489; Jonathan Mayhew, *The Snare broken. A thanksgiving-Discourse*, Boston, 1766, p. 18; Fred Lewis Pattee, ed., *The Poems of Philip Freneau*, 3 vols., Princeton, 1902–1907, Vol. I, pp. 69–70; Vol. III, p. 387; *The Royal American Magazine*, I(1) (January 1774): 10, 34; Benjamin Rush, *An Oration, Delivered February 4, 1774, before the American Philosophical Society . . . Containing, An Enquiry into the Natural History of Medicine among the Indians*, Philadelphia, 1774, especially pp. 66–69.

27. Andrew Burnaby, *Travels through North America*, 3d ed., 1798, rptd., New York, 1904, p. 53 note.

28. *An Historical Review and Directory of North America . . .*, 2 vols., Cork, 1801, Vol. I: pp. 30–31.

29. In *The Cult of Antiquity and the French Revolutionaries: A Study of the Development of the Revolutionary Spirit*, Chicago, 1937, Harold T. Parker distinguishes three interpretations of antiquity among the French: one held that the society of republican Greece and Rome was too uncouth and backward for imitation; one read their history as a golden age too perfect for return, and one saw in them something practicable for modernity. Plutarch and Plato aside, emphasis was on the Latin writers. The three interpretations have their parallels in the American eighteenth century, but not to the same degree; for example, the American vogue of Volney seems not to have led the Americans, like him, to condemn the ancient past out of hand. Mr. Parker makes an important observation when he notes that Cicero, Sallust, Tacitus, and Plutarch, among others, each lived in a period of recurring violence and therefore praised the virtues of past time.

30. John C. Fitzpatrick, ed., *The Writings of George Washington*, 39 vols., Washington, 1931–1944, Vol. XXXV, p. 432, Letter to Dr. James Anderson, April 3, 1797. Washington's notion of his age is curious. The phrase about vine and fig tree rings through all of his correspondence for 1797–1798.

31. Jeremy Belknap, *History of New Hampshire*, 2d ed., 3 vols., Boston, 1813, Vol. III, p. 251. In this context, Albert Gallatin once dreamed of a Rousseau-like Eden in the Kanawha Valley. See Henry M. Dater, "Albert Gallatin—Land Speculator," *MVHR*, 26(1): 21–38 (June 1939).

32. I follow Richard Mott Gummere, "A Scottish Classicist in Colonial America," *Publications of the Colonial Society of Massachusetts*, 35, *Transactions*, 1942–1946, pp. 146f.

33. *Massachusetts Historical Society Proceedings,* 43, 1909–1910, p. 629.
I owe this citation to Michael Kraus, *The Atlantic Civilization,* p. 219.
34. *Considerations upon the Rights of the Colonists in the Privileges
of British Subjects,* New York, 1766, p. 24.
35. *The Farmer's and Monitor's Letters to the Inhabitants of the British
Colonies,* Williamsburg, 1769. I call these by Richard and Henry Lee,
but the bibliography is confused. The publication consists of a reprint
of Dickinson's *Letters from a Farmer in Pennsylvania,* "The Monitor,"
Nos. 1–10, by Arthur Lee, "The Liberty Song" by Dickinson and Arthur
Lee, and a preface by Richard Henry Lee.
36. Joseph Warren, *An Oration delivered March 5th, 1772, At the Request of the Inhabitants of the Town of Boston,* 2d ed., Boston, 1772,
pp. 6, 7. Warren, like the Lees, laments the decline of Rome into
despotism.
37. The Charles Lee Papers in *New York Historical Society Collections,*
1871–1874, 4 vols., Vol. II, p. 177, Vol. IV, p. 26.
38. I summarize, I hope without falsifying, the findings by Charles F.
Mullet, "Classical Influences on the American Revolution," *Classical
Journal,* 35(2): 92–104 (November 1939). See also Alice M. Baldwin, *The
New England Clergy and the American Revolution,* Durham (N.C.),
1928, *passim;* Richard Mott Gummere, "John Dickinson, the Classical
Penman of the Revolution," *Classical Journal,* 52(2): 81–88 (November
1956), his "Thomas Hutchinson and Samuel Adams: A Controversy in
the Classical Tradition," *Boston Public Library Quarterly,* 10(3): 119–
130 (July 1958); "Classical Precedents in the Writings of James Wilson,"
Publications of the Colonial Society of Massachusetts, 32, *Transactions,*
1933–1937, pp. 525f.; "The Classical Ancestry of the United States Constitution," *American Quarterly,* 14(1): 3–18 (summer 1962). By the time
this book appears Mr. Gummere will have cumulated his many studies
into a published volume, *The American Colonial Mind and the Classical
Tradition.*
39. See Fernand Cattelain, *Étude sur l'influence de Montesquieu dans
les constitutions américaines,* Besançon, 1927; and Paul Merrill Spurlin,
Montesquieu in America, 1760–1801, Baton Rouge (La.), 1940, apparently reprinted from the Louisiana State University Romance Language
Series No. IV. Although no work by Montesquieu was published in this
country during the eighteenth century, English translations multiplied
after 1750, an American edition of the *Spirit of the Laws* was proposed
in Boston in 1772, Madison's notes on the Constitutional Convention
show that Montesquieu was cited oftener than Locke, and the *Spirit of
the Laws,* whether in French or English, became invaluable for its analysis of the British constitution. As I hope not to be indulging in the
"single source" fallacy, let me add that many colonial leaders read the
kind of books analyzed in Zera S. Fink, *The Classical Republicans: An
Essay in the Recovery of a Pattern of Thought in Seventeenth Century
England,* Evanston (Ill.), 1948, and that a writer such as Harrington,
himself dependent upon classical historians and philosophers for testimony, would lead them to reconsider the meaning of classical experience.

40. See Joseph Dedieu, *Montesquieu: L'Homme et l'Oeuvre*, Paris, 1943, for a summary view; and the excellent monograph by Henry Vyverberg, *Historical Pessimism in the French Enlightenment*, Cambridge (Mass.), 1958.

41. Any good edition of Montesquieu will offer these and like passages, but I have used the Nugent translation, with its admirable introduction by Franz Neumann, 2 vols., New York, 1949. For Montesquieu's definition of virtue as a republican characteristic see Vol. I, pp. lxxi and 40. Most of the rest of what I quote or summarize is to be found in Vol. I.

42. Dedieu refers to Chapter XVIII of the *Considérations des causes de la grandeur et de la décadence des Romains*. His own discussion is on pp. 127f. I do not see that the importance of Montesquieu is in any way negated by Gilbert Chinard's argument that Montesquieu simply codified a tradition going back to Polybius. See his "Polybius and the American Constitution," *Journal of the History of Ideas*, 1(1): 38–58 (January 1940); and also Richard M. Gummere, "The Classical Ancestry of the United States Constitution," *American Quarterly*, 14(1): 3–18 (spring 1962).

43. John Adams, *Works*, 10 vols., ed. C. F. Adams, Boston, 1850–1856, Vol. VI, pp. 12, 43, 86–87, 209, 217, 243. Adams agreed with Montesquieu on the principle of virtue in a republic (Vol. VI, p. 207). The serious student should read the *Dissertation on the Canon and Feudal Law* (1763) in Vol. III, *Novanglus* and *Thoughts on Government Applicable to the Present State of the American Colonies* (1774) in Vol. IV, and the two earlier portions of the *Defence* in Vol. V if he wishes to gain some sense of the wide influence of classical reading upon Adams. In Chapter II of his *John Adams and the Prophets of Progress*, Cambridge (Mass.), 1962, Zoltan Háraszti has a study of "John Adams among his books" that shows, among other matters, how rich was his library in Greek and Latin writers. Greek was "one of the flames" of his youth, and his earliest preserved book is a textbook edition of Cicero's orations inscribed 1749/50. Adams once tried to establish an academy of Latin and Greek in Quincy and succeeded in having a temple erected there in 1828.

44. See Merrill D. Peterson's remarkable study, *The Jefferson Image in the American Mind*, New York, 1960. To Francis Hall (*Travels in Canada and the United States in 1818 and 1819*, 2d ed., London, 1819, pp. 297–98) Jefferson was a Greek philosopher: "I slept a night at Monticello, and left it in the morning, with such a feeling as the traveller quits the mouldering remains of a Grecian temple, or the pilgrim a fountain in the desert. It would indeed argue great torpor, both of understanding and heart, to have looked without veneration and interest, on the man who drew up the declaration of American independence . . . and who, while he dedicates the evening of his glorious days to the pursuits of science and literature, shuns none of the humbler duties of private life. . . . What monarch would venture thus to exhibit himself in the nakedness of his humanity? On what royal brow would the laurel replace the diadem? But they who are born and educated to be kings, are not expected to be philosophers."

45. Thomas Minns, "Some Sobriquets Applied to Washington," *Publications of the Colonial Society of Massachusetts,* 8, *Transactions,* 1902–1904, pp. 275–86. Fabius was not always used as a compliment, and Minns suggests that "Father of his Country" is a phrase that owes much to conferences with the Indians ("Great White Father").

46. Marquis de Chastellux, *Travels in North America* (trans.), 2 vols., London, 1787, Vol. I, pp. 137–38.

47. Margaret B. Stillwell, "Checklist of Eulogies and Funeral Orations on the Death of George Washington, December 1799—February, 1800," *Bulletin of the New York Public Library,* 20(5): 403–41 (May 1916); George Blake, *A Masonic Eulogy on the Life of the Illustrious Brother George Washington,* Boston, 1800 (5800!); Josiah Dunham, *A Funeral Oration on George Washington,* Boston, 1800, p. 10; Marcus Cunliffe, ed., *The Life of Washington by Mason L. Weems,* Cambridge (Mass.), 1962, pp. 173, 181, 220–21; Daniel Ullmann, *An Address delivered in the Tabernacle, before the Tippecanoe and Other Harrison Associations,* New York, 1841, p. 8; *Congressional Banquet at Washington in Honor of George Washington and the Principles of Washington, February 22, 1852,* Boston, 1852, pp. 3f. There is an enormous literature on the reputation of Washington. Marcus Cunliffe, *George Washington, Man and Monument,* Boston, 1958, Chapter V, gives a good summary view. My description of the crossing of the Schuylkill comes from Joseph Jackson, "Washington in Philadelphia," *Pennsylvania Magazine of History and Biography,* 56(2): 110–55 (April 1932).

48. See Gustav Eisen, *Portraits of Washington,* 3 vols., New York, 1932; and John Hill Morgan and Mantle Fielding, *Life Portraits of Washington,* Philadelphia, 1931.

49. Oliver W. Larkin, *Art and Life in America,* New York, 1949, pp. 182–83.

50. Evidences of the continuity of the classical tradition into the nineteenth century are common enough. According to *The Literary Magazine and American Register* (Philadelphia), 2(14): 598 (November 1804), a press was being established in that city to republish the Greek and Roman classics. In *The Monthly Anthology* for that same year (1: 109) we read how "the high order of families in Rome gained their importance from the great exploits of their ancestors . . . exploits . . . perpetuated by statues," and in this spirit the Americans should exploit the fine arts. And during J. Q. Adams' administration David L. Child, in *An Oration Pronounced before the Republicans of Boston, July 4, 1826,* Boston, 1826, found in Cincinnatus the image of the perfect republican and declared with pride that America has avoided the errors of ancient republics and imitated the records of glorious Greece and majestic Rome.

51. *The Writings and Speeches of Daniel Webster,* 18 vols., Boston, 1903, Vol. I, p. 289; Vol. V, p. 61; Vol. VI, p. 75. All biographers comment on Webster's interest in classical letters. For further evidence of the relation between oratory and classicism see Edward G. Parker, *The Golden Age of American Oratory,* Boston, 1857, which is dedicated to

Yale College; and the chapter on Yancey, "The Orator of Secession," in William Garrott Brown, *The Lower South in American History,* New York, 1902.

52. Talbot Hamlin, *Greek Revival Architecture in America,* New York, 1944. See especially Chapters 2 and 3.

53. See Chapters VIII and IX of *Home as Found;* and also Chapter X of *The Pioneers* (1823).

54. James Jackson Jarves, *The Art-Idea,* ed. Benjamin Rowland, Cambridge (Mass.), 1960, pp. 231–32.

55. The standard work is Glenn Brown, *History of the United States Capitol,* 2 vols., Washington, 1900, 1903.

56. My quotations come from Harvey M. Watts, "The White City," *The T Square Club Journal of Philadelphia,* 1(16): 24–27, 41–46 (May 1931), a vigorous refutation of modern attacks on the Exposition. There is a rich, if vanishing, literature on the Chicago World's Fair, of which the *History of the World's Columbian Exposition,* 4 vols., New York, 1898, is the chief exhibit. One can still pick up excellent volumes of "views" of the Columbian Exposition in second-hand bookshops. A great deal of information can be gleaned from the columns of the *American Architect and Building News,* Vols. 39–44. One writer (40: 181.) called the fair "a creation . . . nearly allied in beauty to festal and imperial Rome."

Chapter VIII: The Radical Republic

1. See Henry F. May, "The End of American Radicalism," *American Quarterly,* 2(4): 291–302 (winter 1950).

2. On the stirring effect of the American Revolution upon revolutionary impulses in Ireland, Great Britain, the Low Countries, Switzerland, and of course France consult Jacques Godechot, *Les Révolutions (1770–1799),* Paris, 1963, especially Chapter III. The best study of the French response to America through the Napoleonic regime is Durand Echeverria, *Mirage in the West: A History of the French Image of American Society to 1815,* Princeton, 1957.

3. Frederick (*sic*) Gentz, *The French and American Revolutions Compared,* translated by John Quincy Adams, Chicago, 1955, p. 83.

4. Ernest Hartley Coleridge, ed., *The Works of Lord Byron: Poetry. A New, Revised and Enlarged Edition,* 7 vols., London, 1901, Vol. IV, p. 198 and note.

5. See Chapter IV.

6. Quoted from the Penn manuscripts by Edward Corbyn Obert Beatty, *William Penn as Social Philosopher,* New York, 1939, p. 78. Penn came to have a low opinion of the crowd. See the quoted matter on pp. 69–72.

7. Claiborne seems to have "gone along" with Inge rather than seriously rebelling against Lord Baltimore. See Bernard C. Steiner, *Beginnings of Maryland, 1631–1639, Johns Hopkins University Studies in Historical and Political Science,* Series XXI, Nos. 8–10, Baltimore, 1903; and his *Maryland under the Commonwealth* in the same series, Series XXIX,

No. 1, Baltimore, 1911; Herbert L. Osgood, *The American Colonies in the Seventeenth-Century*, 3 vols., New York, 1903–1907, Vol. II, Part Third, Chapter II, "The Land System of the Later Proprietary Provinces," and Vol. III, Part Fourth, Chapters IV, V; Matthew Page Andrews, *History of Maryland, Province and State*, Garden City, 1929, Chapters III, IV; and for curious documents about Claiborne, John Leeds Bozman, *A Sketch of the History of Maryland during the First Three Years After Its Settlement*, Baltimore, 1811, pp. 278f.

8. "Narrative of Bacon's Rebellion," *The Virginia Magazine of History and Biography*, 4(2): 122 (October 1896).

9. Philip Alexander Bruce, *Institutional History of Virginia in the Seventeenth-Century*, 2 vols., New York, 1910, Vol. I, p. 459. Only about half of forty of Bacon's followers who petitioned for pardon were able to sign their names. There is an excellent brief account of the rebellion in the biographical sketch of Bacon in the *Dictionary of American Biography*. Some leading documents are reprinted in Vol. I of the Force *Tracts*. There is an enormous literature on this topic.

10. See Osgood, *American Colonies*, Vol. III, Chapter XV, and references.

11. Edwin P. Tanner, *The Province of New Jersey, 1664–1738, Columbia University Studies in History, Economics and Public Law*, No. 30, New York, 1908, p. 79 and *passim*. The uproar was usually over land-titles and rents. There were notable difficulties in 1670–1673 and again in 1699–1701. Insurgents in Monmouth County appeared in military array with drums and colors, courts in Elizabeth, Newark, Piscataway, and Middletown were broken up, proprietary officials were insulted or beaten, and prisoners taken from jail by force.

12. Albert Harkness, Jr., "Americanism and Jenkins' Ear," *MVHR*, 37(1): 61–90 (June 1950).

13. I follow the account of fracases over the *Polly* and the *St. John* given in Edmund S. Morgan and Helen M. Morgan, *The Stamp Act Crisis: Prologue to Revolution*, Chapel Hill (N.C.), 1953, pp. 42f. On mob action in Rhode Island see Chapter VI of David S. Lovejoy, *Rhode Island Politics and the American Revolution, 1760–1776*, Providence, 1958.

14. See Morgan, *Stamp Act Crisis* and Arthur Meier Schlesinger, "Political Mobs and the American Revolution, 1765–1776," *Proceedings of the American Philosophical Society*, 99(4): 244–50 (August 30, 1955).

15. Mob action is mentioned or described on pp. 22–23, 23–24, 26, 29, 30, 120, 122–23, and 131 of Richard Francis Upton, *Revolutionary New Hampshire*, Hanover, 1936.

16. Philip Davidson, *Propaganda and the American Revolution, 1763–1783*, Chapel Hill (N.C.), 1941, pp. 4–5, 7, 9, 22–23, 94. But there is much more of this sort of thing. See pp. 5, 12, 15, 112–13, 122, 126, 130, 140, 141, 144, 148, 149, 150, 151, etc.

17. Jeremy Belknap, *History of New Hampshire*, 3 vols., 2d ed., Boston, 1813, Vol. II, pp. 360–64.

18. Vernon Louis Parrington, ed., *The Connecticut Wits*, New York,

1926, pp. 428–30. *The Anarchiad* appeared at intervals in *The New Haven Gazette* and *The Connecticut Magazine* from October 26, 1786, to October 13, 1787. I follow Parrington in thinking that the number I quote was by Humphreys and Lemuel Hopkins. But Joel Barlow and John Trumbull also contributed to the satire.

19. See Clement Eaton, "Mob Violence in the Old South," *MVHR*, 29(3): 351–70 (December 1942). On violence in the Southern Great Plains see C. C. Rister, "Outlaws and Vigilantes on the Southern Great Plains, 1865–1885," *MVHR*, 19(4): 537–54 (March 1933).

20. See Laura A. White, "The United States in the 1850's as Seen by British Consuls," *MVHR*, 19(4): 509–36 (March 1933), especially pp. 512, 522–24.

21. See Myron F. Brightfield, "America and the Americans, 1840–1860, as Depicted in English Novels of the Period," *American Literature*, 31(3): 309–24 (November 1959). The coffee-colored clothing and the rest appears in Charles Lever, *One of Them* (1861 ?). For a gentler picture of the cocksure American read Anthony Trollope's *The American Senator* (1877) in the admirable edition published by Random House, New York, 1940.

22. Henry Caner, *Joyfulness and Consideration; or, the Duties of Prosperity and Adversity. A Sermon Preached at King's-Chapel, in Boston . . .*, Boston, 1761, pp. 6, 20.

23. In Lindsay Swift, "The Massachusetts Election Sermons," *Publications of the Colonial Society of Massachusetts*, I, *Transactions, 1892–1894*, p. 424.

24. W. J. Bate, ed., *Edmund Burke: Selected Works*, New York, 1960, "Speech on American Taxation," p. 46.

25. *Royal American Magazine*, January 1774.

26. The first phrases are of course from the Declaration of Independence. The others are from Philip S. Foner, ed., *The Complete Writings of Thomas Paine*, 2 vols., New York, 1945, "Common Sense," Vol. I, pp. 10, 13, 29. See also Vol. II, pp. 79, 217, 219, 518.

27. Quoted in Samuel Eliot Morison and Henry Steele Commager, *The Growth of the American Republic*, 2 vols., New York, 1937, Vol. I, p. 22, but the source is not given. See note 28.

28. See the admirable essay by Michael Kraus, "America and the Utopian Ideal in the Eighteenth-Century," *MVHR*, 22(4): 487–504 (March 1936). Turgot's letter to Dr. Price is quoted in Morison and Commager, *Growth of the American Republic*, Vol. I, p. 205.

29. Thus in the discussion of Nedham in his *Defence of the Constitutions of the United States, Works*, Vols. IV–VI, Adams writes that "whenever the constitution becomes democratical, such austerities disappear entirely"; "a simple democracy . . . as dangerous as a simple aristocracy"; "the word democracy signifies nothing more nor less than a nation without any government at all" (pp. 22, 39, 211), and asserts that the American constitutions are designed to check the evils of American democratical elements.

30. See the opening number of *The Federalist* in any good edition, also numbers eight and ten (by Madison). The tenth asserts: "The valuable improvements made by the American constitutions on the popular models, both ancient and modern, cannot certainly be too much admired," that improvement lying in the control of "factions" by representative republican forms. I have used the edition edited by Benjamin F. Wright, Cambridge (Mass.), 1961.

31. Foner, *Complete Writings of Thomas Paine*, Vol. I, pp. 251, 322–23 (*The Rights of Man*); Vol. II, pp. 290 ("Address to the People of Pennsylvania"); 518 ("A Republican Manifesto").

32. Boyd, *Papers of Thomas Jefferson*, Vol. VIII, pp. 409–10 (Letter to Walker Maury); pp. 568–69 (Letter to Charles Bellini, September 30, 1785); pp. 636, 637 (Letter to John Banister, Jr., October 17, 1785).

33. Timothy Dwight, *Greenfield Hill* in Parrington, *The Connecticut Wits*, pp. 190, 192, 204.

34. Ralph Waldo Emerson, *English Traits*, new and rev. ed., Boston, 1884, pp. 289, 296.

35. I here follow two excellent articles by Chester E. Eisinger, "The Freehold Concept in Eighteenth-Century American Literature," *William and Mary Quarterly Magazine*, 3d series, 4(1): 42–59 (January 1947); and "Land and Loyalty: Literary Expressions of Agrarian Nationalism in the Seventeenth- and Eighteenth-Centuries," *American Literature*, 21(2): 160–78 (May 1949). The rustic heroes of Mrs. Mowatt's *Fashion* and Westcott's *David Harum* are as characteristic as Daniel Boone or David Crockett in another context.

36. Parrington, *Connecticut Wits*, pp. 187–88.

37. The two standard works on the earlier immigration to America are Marcus Lee Hansen, *The Atlantic Migration, 1607–1860*, Cambridge (Mass.), 1940, and his *The Immigrant in American History*, Cambridge (Mass.), 1940. Note especially the list of immigrants' manuals discussed in Chapter II of the latter volume.

38. The Harvard College Library copy of this pamphlet has been lost. I quote from an excerpt in Michael Kraus, "America and the Utopian Ideal in the Eighteenth-Century," a study to which I am much indebted.

39. J. Hector St. John de Crèvecœur, *Letters from an American Farmer*, new ed., London, 1783, pp. 49, 86–87.

40. *Thoughts on Emigration, to which are Added, Miscellaneous Observations Relating to the United States of America, and a Short Account of the State of Kentucky*. No place of publication is given, only the date "October, 1792." I assume this is an English publication. The quoted matter is on pp. 17 and 24.

41. Thomas Cooper, *Some Information Respecting America*, London, 1794, pp. 52–53.

42. Matthew Carey, *Miscellaneous Essays*, Philadelphia, 1830, pp. 129, 130, 136–37. A "second edition" of the pamphlet appeared in 1826, but I can find no trace of a first. Carey is alarmed by low wages and the "degraded rate" of female labor in the United States, but cheerfully ob-

serves: "There is probably not a single person in Philadelphia or New York, beyond the condition of a mere pauper, who cannot afford to eat flesh meat at least once a day" (p. 146–47, and note on p. 147).

43. For a succinct account of later emigration propaganda see Merle Curti and Kendall Birr, "The Immigrant and the American Image in Europe, 1860–1914," *MVHR*, 37(2): 203–30 (September 1950); and on a related theme Merle Curti, "The Reputation of America Overseas, 1776–1860," *The American Quarterly*, I(1): 58–82 (spring 1949).

44. Charles Sprague, *An Oration delivered on Monday, Fourth of July, 1825, in . . . the City of Boston*, Boston, 1825, p. 15.

45. See Joseph L. Blau, *Cornerstones of Religious Freedom in America*, Boston, 1950, pp. 128–29.

46. *The Poetical Works of Thomas Moore . . . ,* six vols. in three, Boston, n.d., Vol. I, pp. 76–77 ("To the Lord Viscount Forbes"), 95–96 ("To the Honourable W. R. Spencer"). In this edition the "Poems Relating to America" are grouped together.

47. Brissot de Warville, *New Travels in the United States of America*, Vol. I, pp. 1, 2, 10, 13–15, 54, 73, 144; Vol. II, pp. 10–11.

48. Le Chevalier Félix de Beaujour, *Sketch of the United States of North America, at the Commencement of the Nineteenth-Century, from 1800 to 1810*, translated by William Walton, London, 1814, pp. viii–xi, 64–65, 74, 106–107, 120, 127, 133–34, 144, 145–46, 154–55, 164–65, 273. Walton supplies the materials on pp. viii–xi.

49. Among excellent studies to be consulted are Henry T. Tuckerman, *America and Her Commentators*, New York, 1864; John Graham Brooks, *As Others See Us,* New York, 1908; Jane Louise Mesick, *The English Traveller in America, 1785–1835*, New York, 1922; Allan Nevins, ed., *American Social History as Recorded by British Travellers*, New York, 1931; and Max Berger, *The British Traveller in America, 1836–1860*, New York, 1943.

50. Thomas Brothers, *The United States of North America As They Are; Not As They Are Generally Described. Being a Cure for Radicalism*, London, 1840. Brothers describes himself on the title page as having been a "resident of the United States fifteen years." Why emigrate? "The poverty and misery" of the American laboring population "are as great as, indeed, greater than in the densely-populated European nations" (p. iv).

51. Isaac Weld, Jr., *Travels Through the States of North America and the Provinces of Upper and Lower Canada, during the Years 1795, 1796, and 1797*, London, 1799, p. 464.

52. Captain Basil Hall, *Travels in North America in the Years 1827, and 1828*, 3 vols., Edinburgh, 1829; Frances Trollope, *Domestic Manners of the Americans*, 2 vols., London, 1832, but the reader is advised to consult the excellent edition edited by Donald Smalley, New York, 1949; Captain Marryat, *A Diary in America, with Remarks on its Institutions*, 3 vols., London, 1839; Charles Dickens, *American Notes Printed for Private Circulation*, 2 vols., London, 1842.

53. Basil Hall, *Travels*, Vol. II, pp. 278, 302.

54. Marryat, *Diary*, Vol. I, pp. 22, 29.

55. Richard Parkinson, *A Tour in America in 1798, 1799, and 1800*, London, 1805, pp. 30–31.

56. Alex. Mackay, *The Western World; or, Travels in the United States in 1846–1847*, 2 vols., Philadelphia, 1849 (from the second London edition).

57. Marquis de Chastellux, *Travels in North America*, Vol. II, p. 347. On French travelers see Frank Monaghan, *French Travellers in the United States, 1765–1932; a Bibliography*, New York, 1933.

58. C. F. Volney, *A View of the Soil and Climate of the United States of America*, translated by C. B. Brown, Philadelphia, 1804, pp. vi–vii, xv. And see in connection with Volney and Tocqueville, Seymour Drescher, "American and French Romanticism during the July Monarchy," *The American Quarterly* 11(1): 3–20 (spring 1959) and Carl Wittke, "The America Theme in Continental European Literatures," *MVHR*, 28(1): 3–26 (June 1941).

59. But on the need of a new philosophic interpretation of the American way, one to be based somehow on eighteenth-century principles in a twentieth-century world, see Adrienne Koch, *Power, Morals, and the Founding Fathers*, Ithaca (N.Y.), 1961.

Chapter IX: Republican Culture

1. On this see Estwick Evans, *A Pedestrious Tour, or Four Thousand Miles, Through the Western States and Territories, during the winter and spring of 1818*, Concord (N.H.), 1819, most easily available in Reuben G. Thwaites, *Early Western Travels*, Cleveland, 1904, vol. 8.

2. Claude Halstead Van Tyne, *The Loyalists in the American Revolution*, New York, 1902; Alexander Clarence Flick, *Loyalism in New York During the American Revolution, Columbia Studies in History, Economics, and Public Law*, 14, No. 1, New York, 1901. See also Wilbur C. Abbott, *New York in the American Revolution*, New York, 1929, especially on the activities of Isaac Sears and others, and the sport of "Tory-riding."

3. Thomas Jefferson Wertenbaker, *Father Knickerbocker Rebels: New York City During the Revolution*, New York, 1948, p. 81.

4. David John Mays, *Edmund Pendleton, 1721–1803: A Biography*, 2 vols., Cambridge (Mass.), 1952, Vol. II, pp. 75, 101–102.

5. E. Alfred Jones, *The Loyalists of Massachusetts: Their Memorials, Petitions, and Claims*, London, 1930, *passim*.

6. Evarts Boutell Greene, *The Revolutionary Generation, 1763–1790* (*History of American Life*, IV), New York, 1943, p. 220.

7. Flick, *Loyalism*, pp. 32–35; Van Tyne, *Loyalists*, pp. 5, 25–26. On both the political and cultural importance of the great families in New York see Carl Lotus Becker, *The History of Political Parties in the Province of New York, 1760–1776, Bulletin of the University of Wisconsin* No. 286, History Series, Vol. 2, No. 1, Madison, 1909, pp. 1–14.

8. Van Tyne, *Loyalists,* pp. 247, 248. E. Alfred Jones, *Loyalists of Massachusetts, passim.*

9. Ellis Paxon Oberholtzer, *Philadelphia: A History of the City and its People, A Record of 225 Years,* 3 vols., Philadelphia [1912], I: 270–81.

10. Wertenbaker, *Father Knickerbocker Rebels,* pp. 63–73. The British stayed longer, but the Americans did what they could. In August 1776 the Provincial Convention authorized Washington to use as hospitals the Apthorpe, Oliver De Lancey, and Robert Bayard houses at Bloomingdale; the William Bayard house at Greenwich; the John Watts house near Kip's Bay; the William McAdams house "near the old glass house," and the Peter Stuyvesant house (p. 80). When the Tories flocked in, they found it "a most dirty, desolate, and wretched place."

11. See Lyman H. Weeks, *A History of Paper-Manufacturing in the United States, 1690–1916,* New York, 1916; and Eugenie Andruss Leonard, "Paper as a Critical Commodity during the American Revolution," *Pennsylvania Magazine of History and Biography,* 74(4): 488–99 (October 1950); *Familiar Letters of John Adams and his Wife Abigail Adams, During the Revolution,* Boston, 1875, p. 153. Non-importation agreements naturally increased the drain on colonial paper.

12. E. Wilder Spaulding, *New York in the Critical Period, 1783–1789,* New York, 1932, pp. 263, 273. See also Harry B. Yoshpe, *The Disposition of Loyalist Estates in the Southern District of the State of New York,* New York, 1939.

13. Tench Coxe, *A View of the United States of America, in a Series of Papers, written at various times, between the years 1787 and 1794,* Philadelphia, 1794, pp. 26–27.

14. Foner, *Writings of Thomas Paine,* Vol. I ("Common Sense"), pp. 10, 15, 27; ("The Rights of Man"), pp. 256, 289, 292, 296–97, 323, 341. Cf. the passage on "monarchy is all a bubble," Vol. II, p. 374.

15. Any of the standard editions of Jefferson will produce these passages and others like them. My quotations can be conveniently found in Adrienne Koch and William Peden, eds., *The Life and Selected Writings of Thomas Jefferson,* New York, 1944, pp. 65, 97, 412, 149, 110, 372, 382, 708–10. I give the pages in the order of my citations.

16. Adams, *Works,* Vol. III, pp. 308, 316.

17. Harold C. Syrett and Jacob E. Cooke, eds., *The Papers of Alexander Hamilton,* New York, 1961——. Seven volumes have appeared. My first quotation is from Vol. IV, p. 92, but see also Vol. II, p. 663 and Vol. III, pp. 495 and 553. My second is from *The Federalist,* No. 11 (November 24, 1787, in Vol. IV, pp. 345–46, but see also *The Federalist,* Nos. 15, 24, 34, and 59). "It ought never to be forgotten, that a firm Union of this country, under an efficient government, will probably be an encreasing object of jealousy to more than one nation of Europe; and that enterprises to subvert it will sometimes originate in the intrigues of foreign powers, and will seldom fail to be patronised and abetted by some of them" (Vol. IV, p. 544).

18. *The Federalist,* p. 335.

19. Fitzpatrick, *Writings of Washington,* Vol. XXXV, pp. 233–34.

20. The "Anglican" Church was disestablished in Virginia in 1785, but as late as 1810 suit was brought in Massachusetts by a Universalist Society in Falmouth praying that the taxes they paid should support their own minister and not a Congregationalist one. See my *The Pursuit of Happiness,* pp. 32–35.

21. I am aware that revisionist historians have virtually abolished the old notion of the Jacksonian revolution as representing the triumph of Western agrarianism. But a study of the pronouncements collected in Joseph L. Blau, *Social Theories of Jacksonian Democracy,* New York, 1954, reveals a continuing appeal to "the sovereignty of the people." Nor should it be forgotten that Jacksonianism came along during the decade of the worship of humanity in Europe. Heine was active in the thirties, George Sand was in her wrongs-of-womanhood period, Michelet began his *Histoire de France* in 1833, and Mrs. Browning brought out "Cowper's Grave" in 1838—

O men, this man in brotherhood your weary paths beguiling,
Groaned inly while he taught you peace, and died while ye were smiling!

22. Crèvecœur, *Letters from an American Farmer,* pp. 21, 26, 46, 47, 48, 49–50, 53, 57, 59, 63–66, 67, 76; and see the several chapters on Nantucket.

23. Coxe, *A View of the United States,* pp. 49, 50. Coxe agrees that "America has not many charms for the dissipated and voluptuous part of mankind, but very many indeed for the rational sober minded and discreet" (pp. 441, 442).

24. Evans, *A Pedestrious Tour,* pp. 121, 133, 269.

25. Harry R. Warfel, ed., *Letters of Noah Webster,* New York, 1953, pp. 4, 266, 294–95; M. M. Mathews, *The Beginnings of American English: Essays and Comments,* Chicago, 1931, pp. 31–43; Harry R. Warfel, *Noah Webster: Schoolmaster to America,* New York, 1936, pp. 53, 126, 191, 289. The matter from the *Royal American Magazine* is dated *"America,* 1774," and is found in 2: 6–7 (January 1774). The incredible vogue and influence of Webster can be guessed from Emily Ellsworth Ford Skeel, *A Bibliography of the Writings of Noah Webster,* ed. Edwin H. Carpenter, Jr., New York, 1958. An early, yet judicious, survey of the linguistic controversy is that by Charles A. Bristed, "The English Language in America," *Cambridge Essays Contributed by Members of the University, 1855,* London, 1855, pp. 57–78.

26. See George L. Haskins, "Law and Colonial Society," *American Quarterly,* 9(3): 354–64 (fall 1957). On the general colonial situation see the admirable discussion (Chapter 32, "The Unspecialized Lawyer") in Daniel J. Boorstin, *The Americans: Colonial Experience,* New York, 1958; and Richard B. Morris's standard *Studies in the History of American Law with special reference to the Seventeenth- and Eighteenth-Centuries,* New York, 1930. Morris makes the important observation that after 1750 a kind of conservative reaction in law appears as an effort to keep the empire in better order.

27. James Wilson, *Works,* 3 vols., Philadelphia, 1804, Vol. I ("Lectures

on Law"), pp. 9, 416–17. Wilson thoroughly disapproves of Blackstone's doctrine that law is a command laid by a superior on an inferior which the inferior is bound to obey, and in the second chapter of this volume spiritedly defends the contract theory, including custom and customary law as forms of contractual assent.

28. For example, Edward S. Corwin, in "The 'Higher Law' Background of American Constitutional Law," *Harvard Law Review*, 42(2): 149–85 (December 1928) and 42(3): 364–409 (January 1929), asking why legislative sovereignty did not establish itself in the constitutional generation, replies that "higher law" made possible the attribution in the Constitution of a new validity for law as a statute emanating from the sovereign people. This in turn had to be backed up by the characteristically American practice of judicial review.

29. Whig lawyers in New England, says Richard B. Morris, "acted with plausible consistency in erecting a code of political liberalism upon the legal foundations of social reaction to which they were devoutly attached. In reality they were fighting for the common law and the common law remained inviolate." "Legalism versus Revolutionary Doctrine in New England," *New England Quarterly*, 4(2): 195–215 (April 1931).

30. James Woodress, *A Yankee's Odyssey: The Life of Joel Barlow*, Philadelphia, 1958, pp. 80–82.

31. Claude Milton Newlin, *The Life and Writings of Hugh Henry Brackenridge*, Princeton, 1932, pp. 283–86; Frank Luther Mott, *A History of American Magazines, 1741–1830*, New York, 1930 (later published by Harvard University Press), p. 155; William T. Utter, "Ohio and the English Common Law," *MVHR*, 16(3): 321–33 (December 1929). *The American Law Journal* of Philadelphia ran from 1808 to 1817, and the *American Jurist and Law Magazine* from 1829 to 1843. And see on the whole problem Alfred Z. Reed, *Training for the Public Profession of the Law*, Bulletin 15, Carnegie Foundation for the Advancement of Teaching, New York, 1921.

32. G. Adolf Koch, *Republican Religion*, New York, 1933, is standard. One should also consult Eugene Perry Link, *Democratic-Republican Societies, 1790–1800*, New York, 1942, and on the later history of theological radicalism Albert Post, *Popular Studies in History, Economics and Public Law*, No. 497, New York, 1943. On the more immediate religious reaction and the lasting stamp it impressed on American religious life a convenient introduction is Martha L. Edwards, "Religious Forces in the United States, 1815–1830," *MVHR*, 5(4): 434–49 (March 1919).

33. See Peter Guilday, *The Life and Times of John England*, 2 vols., New York, 1927. England was one of the most colorful figures in nineteenth-century American Catholicism.

34. See William G. McLoughlin's edition of Charles Grandison Finney, *Lectures on Revivals of Religion* (1835) in the John Harvard Library series, Cambridge (Mass.), 1960, and Professor McLoughlin's other studies in American revivalism, *Billy Sunday was His Real Name*, 1955; *Modern Revivalism: Charles Grandison Finney to Billy Graham*, 1959; and *Billy Graham: Revivalist in a Secular Age*, 1960.

35. One of the most illuminating introductory studies of the peculiarities

of American religious life is Willard L. Sperry, *Religion in America,* New York, 1946.

36. The standard histories are Paul Monroe, *Founding of the American Public School System: A History of Education in the United States from the Early Settlements to the Close of the Civil War,* 2 vols., New York, 1940; and Ellwood P. Cubberley, *Public Education in the United States,* rev. and enl. ed., Boston, 1934. There are later editions. But all theorizing about the origins of American education must be modified in the light of Bernard Bailyn's brilliant analysis, *Education in the Forming of Society; Needs and Opportunities for Study,* Chapel Hill (N.C.), 1960.

37. See Walter Herbert Small, *Early New England Schools,* Boston, 1914. Mr. Small's doubts about the uniform enforcement of the law are confirmed by an unpublished doctoral dissertation at Harvard, "Massachusetts Bay Colony: The Role of Government in Education" by Geraldine Murphy.

38. See my article, "Horace Mann's Crusade" in Daniel Aaron, ed., *America in Crisis,* New York, 1952, pp. 91–107.

39. Charles F. Thwing, *A History of Higher Education in America,* New York, 1906, p. 165.

40. Colyer Meriwether, *Our Colonial Curriculum, 1607–1776,* Washington, 1907, pp. 283–86.

41. Merle Curti, "Human Nature in American Thought: The Age of Reason and Morality, 1750–1860," *Political Science Quarterly,* 68(3): 354–75 (September 1953). One should also consult the sequel, "Human Nature in American Thought: Retreat from Reason in the Age of Science" in the same magazine, 4: 492–510 (December 1953).

42. On Jefferson consult Roy J. Honeywell, *The Educational Work of Thomas Jefferson,* Cambridge (Mass.), 1931. On the general problem the standard work is Allen Oscar Hansen, *Liberalism and American Education in the Eighteenth-Century,* New York, 1926. Leading contemporary titles are: Benjamin Rush, *Thoughts upon the Mode of Education proper in a Republic* (1786); Robert Coram, *Plan for the General Establishment of Schools in the United States* (1791); James Sullivan, *Observations upon the Government of the United States of America* (1791); Nathaniel Chipman, *Principles of Government* (1793); Samuel H. Smith, *Remarks on Education Illustrating the Close Connection between Virtue and Wisdom: to which is annexed a System of Liberal Education* (1798); and Samuel Knox, *Essay on the Best System of Liberal Education Adapted to the Genius of the Government of the United States* (1799). I do not discuss the influence from France, though Jefferson was interested in the ideas of Du Pont de Nemours, and Lafitte du Courteil, *Proposal to Demonstrate the Necessity of a National Institution in the United States of America for the Education of Children of Both Sexes* (1797), has a considerable interest, for Lafitte du Courteil insists that ancient republics had a unity superior to that of the United States—hence the necessity of a "national institution." See Hansen, pp. 170–73.

43. Hansen, *Liberalism and American Education,* pp. 50f.; Dagobert

D. Runes, *Selected Writings of Benjamin Rush*, New York, 1947, pp. 90–91; Benjamin Rush, *Essays Literary, Moral and Philosophical*, 2d ed., Philadelphia, 1806, p. 9.

44. Four excellent studies are Russel Blaine Nye, *The Cultural Life of the New Nation, 1770–1830*, New York, 1960; Benjamin T. Spencer's turgid but informed *The Quest for Nationality: An American Literary Campaign*, Syracuse, 1957; Oskar Hagen, *The Birth of the American Tradition in Art*, New York, 1940 (which, however, deals principally with the colonial and revolutionary periods); and Harry Hayden Clark, "The Influence of Science on American Ideas, from 1775 to 1809," *Transactions of the Wisconsin Academy of Sciences, Arts and Letters*, 35: 305–49 (1943). For those anxious to obtain further information about science in America during the earlier years of the republic I recommend the useful bibliography in Nye, pp. 297–300.

45. I here follow Oliver W. Larkin, *Art and Life in America*, New York, 1949, the only competent work of its kind. The matter concerning the Pennsylvania Academy of Fine Arts is on p. 114. On the quarrel over the Pennsylvania Academy see James Thomas Flexner, "The Scope of Painting in the 1790's," *Pennsylvania Magazine of History and Biography*, 74(1): 74–89 (January 1950).

46. John Burchard and Albert Bush-Brown, *The Architecture of America: A Social and Cultural History*, Boston, 1961, is a competent, though oddly proportioned, guide. On the balloon frame see Siegfried Giedion, *Space, Time and Architecture*, 4th ed. enl., Cambridge (Mass.), 1962.

47. I quote from Channing's text as given by Richard Beale Davis in *The Key Reporter*, 26 (3), p. 4 (spring 1961).

48. William Charvat, *Origins of American Critical Thought*, Philadelphia, 1936. Still authoritative is W. B. Cairns, *On the Development of American Literature from 1815 to 1833*, Bulletin of the University of Wisconsin: Philology and Literature Series, Vol. I, No. 1, Madison (Wis.), 1898.

49. See Donald A. Ringe, "Bryant's Use of the American Past," *Papers of the Michigan Academy of Science, Arts and Letters*, 41 (1955 meeting), 1956, pp. 323–31.

50. Richard Flower, *Letters from Lexington and the Illinois, containing a Brief Account of the English Settlements in the Latter Territory, etc.*, London, 1819, in Thwaites, *Early Western Travels*, Vol. X, p. 92.

Chapter X: American Landscape

1. There seem to be very few analyses of the American landscape *qua* landscape, despite the importance of the subject. Most of the books, like Ellen Churchill Semple's influential *American History and Its Geographic Conditions*, Boston, 1903, deal with physiographic conditions. Among the exceptional few, however, three are outstanding: Dorothy Anne Dondore, *The Prairie and the Making of Middle America; Four Centuries of Description*, Cedar Rapids (Ia.), 1926; N. Bryllion Fagin, *William Bartram: Interpreter of the American Landscape*, Baltimore,

1933; and Henry Nash Smith, *Virgin Land*, Cambridge (Mass.), 1950. Most of the comment on the Hudson River School, and, for that matter, most of the comment on American landscape painting seems to me anecdotal.

2. See Chester E. Eisinger, "The Freehold Concept in Eighteenth-Century American Letters," *William and Mary Quarterly*, 3d series, 4: 42–59 (January 1947), and his "Land and Loyalty: Expressions of Agrarian Nationalism in the Seventeenth- and Eighteenth-Centuries," *American Literature*, 21(2): 160–78 (May 1949). I have referred to these in another connection.

3. In Chapter I.

4. William Bradford, *History of Plymouth Plantation 1620–1647*, 2 vols., Boston, The Massachusetts Historical Society, 1912, Vol. I, p. 164.

5. *Poems on Several Occasions. By a Gentleman from Virginia*, Williamsburg, 1736, pp. 5–6. Most conveniently accessible in the Facsimile Text Society reprint, New York, 1930.

6. Thomas Godfrey, *Juvenile Poems*, Philadelphia, 1765, pp. 20, 21. The volume is said to display "romantic" tendencies, but it is hard to distinguish them.

7. Moses Coit Tyler, *A History of American Literature, 1607–1765*, 2 vols., New York, 1878, Vol. II, p. 195.

8. Mather Byles, *The Flourish of the Annual Spring, Improved in a Sermon Preached at the Thursday Lecture in Boston, May 3, 1739*, 2d ed., Boston, 1769, p. 20.

9. *The Discoveries of John Lederer in three several Marches from Virginia, to the West of Carolina, and other parts of the Continent: Begun in March 1669, and Ended in September 1670*, London, 1672; ed. William P. Cumming, *The Discoveries of John Lederer*, Charlottesville (Va.), 1958, pp. 18–19.

10. The description of the confluence of the two rivers is in Query IV, that of the Natural Bridge in Query V of the *Notes on Virginia*, which can be found as a whole in any collection of Jefferson's major writings. I have followed the text in Koch and Peden, *Life and Selected Writings*, pp. 192–93.

11. The Houghton Library copy at Harvard has no title page, and some of the plates are wrongly numbered.

12. Louis L. Noble, *The Course of Empire, Voyage of Life and Other Pictures by Thomas Cole, N. A., with Selections from the Letters and Miscellaneous Writings*, etc., New York, 1853, pp. 58–59, 62. This odd but illuminating volume is to be reprinted in the John Harvard Library; it throws more light upon the psychology of the Hudson River painter than does any other. Cole was a mediocre versifier and essayist, but he arrived at some interesting "laws" of painting; e.g., "The very trees were wild and savage in their forms and expression. This I have found a kind of law, the law of congruity in nature. Where the region is one of savage character, the trees in their predominant traits correspond: in places where the aspects of nature are more gentle, there the expression of the woods is soft and pleasing, and the general outline of the trees

graceful and beautiful" (1828), p. 98. On American landscape painting in general, and the Hudson River School in particular see Frederick A. Sweet, *The Hudson River School and the Early American Landscape Tradition* (catalogue), Chicago and New York, 1945; Clara Endicott Sears, *Highlights Among the Hudson River Artists*, Boston, 1947; H. M. Huebner and V. Pearce Delgado, *Die Maler der Romantik im Amerika*, Bonn, 1953; and Wolfgang Born, *American Landscape Painting*, New Haven, 1948.

13. Parke Godwin, *A Biography of William Cullen Bryant*, 2 vols., New York, 1883, Vol. II, p. 33.

14. The long quotation is from Hitchcock's *The Religion of Geology and Its Connected Sciences*, Boston, 1851, pp. 183–85; the statement about the purposes of government is from his "The Inseparable Trio" in *Religious Truth, Illustrated from Science, in Addresses and Sermons on Special Occasions*, Boston, 1857, p. 332. "The Inseparable Trio" was an Election Sermon delivered January 2, 1850, in Old South Church. Still excellent on the interests of naturalists, painters, and literary men in the White Mountains is Frederick W. Kilbourne, *Chronicles of the White Mountains*, Boston, 1916.

15. Thaddeus Mason Harris, *The Journal of a Tour into the Territory Northwest of the Alleghany Mountains, Made in the Spring of the Year 1803*, Boston, 1805, reprinted in Thwaites, *Early Western Travels*, Vol. III, pp. 322–23.

16. From a poem, "Western Emigration," but I have either lost or never knew the book or magazine from which it comes.

17. Average response is represented by Estwick Evans, author of *A Pedestrious Tour*, pp. 174, 175, in which he lists the "lofty and rude banks of this part of the river, the deafning [*sic*] clamour of the falls, and the huge clouds of vapour which arose from them" as inspiring him with an "indiscribable emotion." "How impressive is the grand in nature! It withdraws the human mind from the trifling concerns of time, and points it to its primeval dignity, and lofty destinies."

18. Francis Hobert Herrick, *Delineations of American Scenery and Character by John James Audubon*, New York, 1926, collects the principal sketches. These, though they contain a charming essay on the Ohio and the canonical admonition: "should you not have seen them, and are fond of contemplating the most magnificent of the Creator's works, go to Niagara, reader" (p. 78), are more often anecdotes of adventure than delineations of American scenery. Exceptions are "The Earthquake," "The Hurricane," "A Flood," and "The Force of the Waters."

19. I follow the text of Bryant's *Poems*, New York, 1832. It is interesting that the first of the *Smithsonian Contributions to Knowledge* (Vol. I, 1848) by E. G. Squier and E. H. Davis is *Ancient Monuments of the Mississippi Valley: Comprising the Results of Extensive Original Surveys and Explorations*. But the preface is dated from Chillicothe, Ohio, June 1847. The "concluding observations" are to the effect that the "ancient population was exceedingly dense," and in an address before

the Historical Society of Ohio, Squier exclaimed: "Of what immense age then must be the works so often referred to, covered as they are by at least the second growth, after the primitive forest state was regained?" (pp. 302, 306).

20. Francis Parkman, *Works*, 20 vols., Boston, 1897–1898, Vol. XVIII ("The Conspiracy of Pontiac," iii), pp. 121–23; Vol. VI ("La Salle and the Discovery of the Great West," ii), p. 52. Mark Twain greatly admired the paragraph on La Salle.

21. Ibid., Vol. XVIII, pp. 119–20.

22. Thomas Nuttall, *A Journal of Travels into the Arkansa [sic] Territory, During the Year 1819* . . . , Philadelphia, 1821, in Thwaites, *Early Western Travels,* Vol. XIII, pp. 80–81, 93, 205.

23. Edwin James, *Account of an Expedition from Pittsburgh to the Rocky Mountains, in the Years 1819, 1820* . . . *under the Command of Maj. S. H. Long,* Philadelphia, 1823, in Thwaites, *Early Western Travels,* Vols. XIV–XVII. The passage on the Rocky Mountains is in Vol. XIV, p. 264. The James account should be checked against Harlin M. Fuller and LeRoy R. Hafen, eds., *The Journal of Captain John R. Bell, Official Journalist for the Stephen H. Long Expedition to the Rocky Mountains, 1820,* Glendale (Calif.), 1957 (The Far West and the Rockies Historical Series, Vol. VI).

24. Josiah Gregg, *Commerce of the Prairies,* Max. L. Moorhead, ed., Norman (Okla.), 1954, p. 362. The book was first published in 1844. The material from James is in Thwaites, *Early Western Travels,* Vol. XVII, p. 148, and Vol. XVI, pp. 43, 129.

25. There is happily an increasing library of reproductions, special studies, and illustrated exhibition catalogues. Among these latter Perry T. Rathbone, *Mississippi Panorama*, rev. ed., 1950, and his *Westward the Way,* 1954, both dealing with exhibits at the City Art Museum, St. Louis, are notable. Popular but good is Harold McCracken, *Portrait of the Old West, with a Biographical Check List of Western Artists,* New York, 1952. Both text and illustration in Bernard de Voto, *Across the Wide Missouri,* Boston, 1947, are relevant. I have found two special studies of great value: Lloyd Haberly, *Pursuit of the Horizon: A Life of George Catlin,* New York, 1948; and *The West of Alfred Jacob Miller,* Norman (Okla.), 1951, the introduction to which is by Marvin C. Ross. Of the Pacific Railroad Survey studies I shall speak in a moment.

26. Henry Blackman Sell and Victor Weybright, *Buffalo Bill and the Wild West,* New York, 1955, *passim.*

27. The only thorough study I have seen is George Leslie Albright, *Official Explorations for Pacific Railroads, 1853–1855, University of California Publications in History,* Vol. XI, 1921. But the first chapter of Robert Taft's *Artists and Illustrators of the Old West* deals wonderfully well with the pictorial side of the surveys. One of the artists, Richard H. Kern, was killed by Indians in Utah in 1853. Most of the originals of the lithographs seem to have disappeared. I add that the bibliography of this set (which sometimes appears as 13 vols.) is as complex and inconsistent as is customary in government publications.

On this subject see the footnote in Albright, p. 44, and the even more detailed accurate listing in Taft, pp. 254–55. Taft's whole discussion of the reports (pp. 254–69) is the best in print.

28. See the two enormous bibliographies, "Travellers and Observers, 1763–1846" and "Travellers and Explorers, 1846–1900" in *Cambridge History of American Literature,* New York, 1950, Vol. I, pp. 468–90, and Vol. IV, pp. 681–728; Harlow Lindley, "Western Travel, 1800–1820," *MVHR,* 6(2): 167–91 (September 1919), and Edmund William Gilbert, *The Exploration of Western America, 1800–1850: Historical Geography,* Cambridge, 1933.

29. I quote from the abridged account, Allan Nevins, ed., *Narratives of Exploration and Adventure by John Charles Frémont,* New York, 1956, p. 164.

30. From Merrill J. Mattes, "Behind the Legend of Colter's Hell: The Early Exploration of Yellowstone National Park," *MVHR,* 36(2): 251–82 (September 1949). The matter I have summarized is on p. 267, but see also the naïve account on p. 266.

31. Washington Irving, *Astoria,* author's revised edition (Kinderhook edition of Irving's *Works*), pp. 219–20. Stanley Williams unkindly describes *Astoria* as "another potboiler." I can only commend to the reader the account of the winter expedition out of Caldron Linn and point out that Bernard De Voto, a professional judge, takes *Astoria* seriously.

32. From the description of an ascent of Long's Peak, Colorado, in Isabella L. Bird, *A Lady's Life in the Rocky Mountains,* London, 1879, pp. 108, 114.

33. George Catlin, *Letters and Notes on the Manners, Customs, and Condition of the North American Indians,* 2 vols., New York, 1841, Vol. I, p. 19.

34. Mark Twain, *Roughing It* (1872), Chapter 38.

35. Quoted by William Culp Darrah, *Powell of the Colorado,* Princeton, 1951, p. 314.

36. There is a considerable literature on the passing of the open-range cattle industry. A good general book is Ernest Staples Osgood, *The Day of the Cattleman,* Minneapolis, 1929. On phases of its decline I find the following articles from the *MVHR* illuminating: Edward Everett Dale, "The Ranchman's Last Frontier," 10(1): 34–36 (June 1923); Robert S. Fletcher, "The End of the Open Range in Eastern Montana," 16(2): 188–211 (September 1929); Harold E. Briggs, "The Development and Decline of Open Range Ranching in the Northwest," 20(4): 521–36 (March 1934); Edward Everett Dale, "The Cow Country in Transition," 24(1): 3–20 (June 1937); Paul Wallace Gates, "Cattle Kings in the Prairies," 35(3): 379–412 (December 1948).

37. From L. B. France, *Mountain Trails and Parks in Colorado,* Denver, 1886, quoted in Levette Jay Davidson and Prudence Bostwick, *The Literature of the Rocky Mountain West, 1803–1903,* Caldwell (Idaho), 1939, p. 357. I have not been able to see the original volume. In connection with abandoned mining towns nothing is more melancholy than the illustrations in Muriel Vincent Sibell Wolle, *The Bonanza Trail:*

Ghost Towns and Mining Camps of the West, Bloomington (Ind.), 1953.

38. "Joaquin Murietta," *The Complete Poetical Works of Joaquin Miller*, San Francisco, 1897, p. 38.

39. It is not argued that all Western scenery, particularly California scenery, left an impression of nescience upon sensitive beholders. Contrast Clarence King's *Mountaineering in the Sierra Nevada* (1871), largely stoic in tone, with the joyous theism of John Muir in his *Mountains of California* (2 vols., 1894) and *Our National Parks* (1901). Thomas Hornsby Ferril is quoted as saying: "It comes as a shock to an imaginative person to realize for the first time that landscape as such has no particular meaning and he may reject for years—costly years in the life of an artist—the human experience which gives it meaning." Meridan H. Bennett, "The Scenic West: Silent Mirage," *Colorado Quarterly*, 7(1): 15–25 (summer 1959), p. 17.

40. See the stimulating article by Sidney E. Mead, "The American People: Their Space, Time, and Religion," *The Journal of Religion*, 34(4): 244–55 (October 1954). The author expresses his indebtedness to a discussion by Ray Billington of Walter Prescott Webb's *The Great Plains*.

Afterword

1. See in this connection the admirable article by John William Ward, "Who Was Benjamin Franklin?" *The American Scholar*, 32(4): 541–53 (autumn 1963); and on the evolution of the American money-getter into the Florentine merchant prince, see my article, "The Renaissance and American Origins," in *Ideas in America*, Cambridge (Mass.), 1944, pp. 140–51.

2. In "The Drift to Liberalism in the American Eighteenth Century" in *Authority and the Individual* (Harvard Tercentenary Publications), Cambridge (Mass.), 1937, pp. 319–48, I tried to demonstrate that in America the Enlightenment served as the liberating force and that attempts to align American romanticism with European romanticism arise from a misunderstanding of the operation of the Enlightenment in the American eighteenth century.

INDEX

Thanks are due to Glendon T. Odell for his patience and care in helping to prepare this index.

H. M. J.

450